Critical Acclaim for Runn

MW00710220

*"RUNNING WINDOWS contains the most thorough details
on the various topics....the text is clear and concise."*

PC Magazine

*"This book presents the most thorough coverage of working
with Microsoft Windows...written in a clear and concise manner....
This book opens up Windows for all levels of users."*

Bay Area Computer Currents

*"With all the fat computer software books on the market, it can
be tough to distinguish the truly worthwhile volumes [on Windows]
from the mere rewrites of software manuals. RUNNING WINDOWS
is one of the former."*

PC Computing

"Comfortable user's guide to Windows.... Detailed yet a delight to read."

Computer Book Review

*"...the definitive book on Microsoft Windows...an excellent text
for those who want to learn this new operating system."*

Online Today

*"RUNNING WINDOWS is well written; it has lots of screen
shots to help the reader through exercises."*

PC Computing

*"[RUNNING WINDOWS] is a mandatory guide to Microsoft's
operating environment."*

Computer Book Review

Running

Windows™
3.1

THIRD EDITION

Running
Windows™
3.1

Craig Stinson

THIRD EDITION

The Authorized Edition

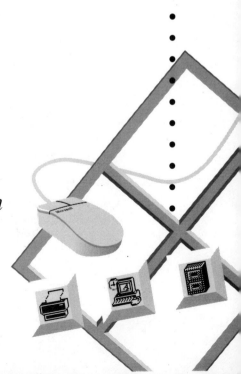

PUBLISHED BY
Microsoft Press
A Division of Microsoft Corporation
One Microsoft Way
Redmond, Washington 98052-6399

Library of Congress Cataloging-in-Publication Data
Stinson, Craig, 1943–
    Running Windows 3.1 / Craig Stinson, -- 3rd ed.
      p. cm.
    Includes index.
    ISBN 1-55615-373-2
    1. Microsoft Windows (Computer program) I. Title.
    QA76.76.W56S75   1992
    005.4'3 -- dc20   92-3972
                                               CIP
Printed and bound in the United States of America.

 2 3 4 5 6 7 8 9 AGAG 7 6 5 4 3 2

Distributed to the book trade in Canada by Macmillan of Canada, a division
of Canada Publishing Corporation.

Distributed to the book trade outside the United States and Canada by Penguin Books Ltd.

Penguin Books Ltd., Harmondsworth, Middlesex, England
Penguin Books Australia Ltd., Ringwood, Victoria, Australia
Penguin Books N.Z. Ltd., 182–190 Wairau Road, Auckland 10, New Zealand

British Cataloging-in-Publication Data available.

1-2-3, Ami, and Lotus are registered trademarks of Lotus Development Corporation.
Apple, Macintosh, and TrueType are registered trademarks of Apple Computer, Inc.
AT and IBM are registered trademarks of International Business Machines Corporation.
Microsoft, MS-DOS, and PowerPoint are registered trademarks and Visual Basic and
Windows are trademarks of Microsoft Corporation. OS/2 is a registered trademark
licensed to Microsoft Corporation. Paintbrush is a trademark of ZSoft Corporation. All
other trademarks and service marks are the property of their respective owners.

The publisher gratefully acknowledges use of the artwork on pages 366–69, 387, and
393–99 from Archive Arts. Reprinted with permission of the copyright owner, Archive
Arts, copyright 1989.

Acquisitions Editor: Marjorie Schlaikjer
Project Editor: Peggy McCauley
Manuscript and Technical Editors: Siechert & Wood Professional Documentation

Contents

Acknowledgments

Once again I would like to express intense and heartfelt thanks to Carl Siechert and Chris Wood, of Siechert & Wood Professional Documentation, for their vigilance and support as technical editors of *Running Windows*. Such errors as may remain are my responsibility exclusively. But, believe me, there are fewer of them, thanks to Siechert & Wood.

Thanks, too, to the indefatigable band at Microsoft Press: Marjorie Schlaikjer, Sally Brunsman, Peggy McCauley, Mary DeJong, and David Rygmyr. One could not ask for a more professional editorial team.

And thanks to my wife and son, for endless unconditional support, and to my editors at *PC Magazine*, *PC/Computing*, and *Computer Shopper*, for their patience during the course of this book's development.

Introduction

Microsoft Windows is a software system that works hand in hand with MS-DOS to create what is commonly called a *graphical operating environment,* or *graphical user interface.* Working with your computer in this environment offers many advantages over working with it in normal MS-DOS.

Windows replaces the MS-DOS command line, so that you no longer have to deal with difficult-to-remember MS-DOS commands. Instead of typing at the MS-DOS A or C prompt to start programs, for example, you can start them by selecting easily recognizable graphic symbols, called *icons.* And instead of having to look up command syntax in an MS-DOS manual when you want to copy files or check the amount of free space on a disk, you can perform these functions with Windows' *drop-down menus* and *dialog boxes.* These menus and dialog boxes free you from concern about command syntax.

Windows lets you run more than one program at a time and move easily and quickly between programs. You don't have to quit your word processor, for example, when you want to consult your calendar.

Windows lets you perform more than one task at a time. You can print one document while you create another, for example. Or you can download information from a remote computer through your modem while you set up a spreadsheet model to tabulate and format the downloaded data.

Windows provides a standard mechanism for copying or moving information from one program to another. This mechanism, called the *Clipboard,* means that information created in one context is instantly reusable in another; you don't need to reenter information or work with clumsy data-transfer utilities.

Windows also includes a facility called *object linking and embedding* (OLE) that allows certain programs to exchange information automatically. Programs that support OLE can be linked together so that changes within one are instantly reflected in the other.

Windows makes more efficient use of all your computer's memory than does standard MS-DOS. All programs written for version 3 (or later) of Windows can take advantage of memory beyond 640 KB, without requiring special hardware or driver files.

Windows encourages consistency among applications, making it easier for you to use a variety of complementary programs in your work. Applications written specifically for the Windows environment have a great deal in common, because they all use standard Windows drop-down menu and dialog box formats. Thus, when you learn to use *one* Windows program, you're well on your way toward knowing how to use *any* Windows program.

In short, Windows is a system that makes your computer easier to use, allowing you to be more productive and get the maximum value from your hardware and software investment.

WINDOWS APPLICATIONS AND NON-WINDOWS APPLICATIONS

Fortunately, when you adopt Windows you don't have to give up any of the programs you're already accustomed to. Windows lets you run standard MS-DOS applications as well as applications created specifically for Windows. As you'll see, some advantages exist to using programs designed from the beginning with Windows in mind, but you're by no means limited to such programs.

PROGRAMS THAT COME WITH WINDOWS

To help you get started with Windows, your Windows package includes a suite of small-scale Windows applications. Among them are Clock, a timepiece with digital and analog display options; Calculator, a graphical recreation of a desktop calculator; Cardfile, an electronic Rolodex; Calendar, a scheduling program with an alarm; and Notepad, a simple text editor that can serve as an ever-ready scratch pad. These and other "desktop accessories" are described in Chapter 7.

Your package also includes three larger applications: a word processor (Write), a communications program (Terminal), and a drawing program (Paintbrush). These are sophisticated programs that might meet your needs for quite a while. Write, Terminal, and Paintbrush are described in Chapters 14, 15, and 16, respectively.

WHAT WINDOWS LOOKS LIKE

Windows transforms your computer screen into an electronic desktop. The programs you use are displayed within rectangular frames called *windows*. Just as you might have a notebook, a calendar, a cardfile, and perhaps a paper spreadsheet all lying on your desk at the same time, so can you keep several windows on your Windows desktop at once. The following illustration shows how your screen might look with two programs—a word processor and a calendar—running.

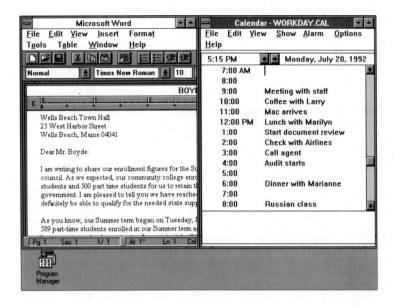

On your conventional desktop, you might have objects lying haphazardly on top of one another, neatly stacked, or arranged so that all are in full view. Windows gives you the same freedom to manipulate the objects on your electronic desktop. When you run two or more programs, you can have their windows overlap, as shown in the following illustration.

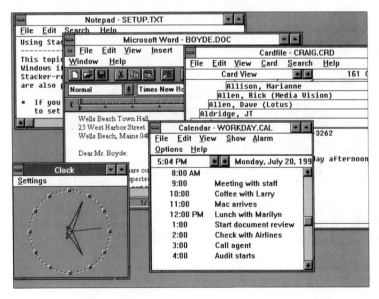

Or you can have the windows *cascade.*

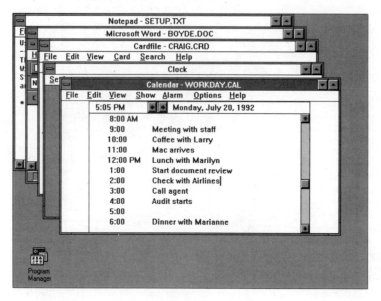

Or you can *tile* the windows.

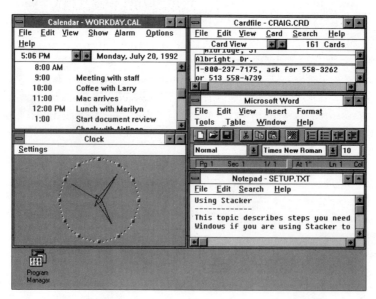

But Windows also has some options not available on standard desktops. For instance, when you want to focus all your attention on a particular program, you can issue a simple command to *maximize* it. When maximized, a program fills the entire screen, like this:

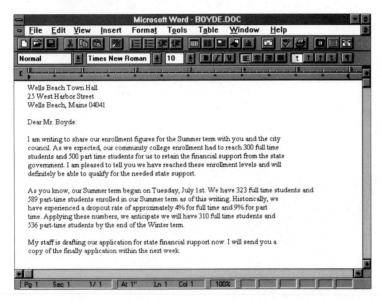

The other programs on your desktop are still there, and you can still switch to another program with a mere keystroke or two.

When you want to keep a program available, but you know you're not going to be using it for a while, you can *minimize* it. A minimized program is represented by an icon at the bottom of the desktop. In the illustration shown at the top of the following page, four Windows applications—Program Manager, Calendar, Clock, and Cardfile—are minimized.

However you arrange your windows—whether maximized, minimized, cascaded, tiled, or simply lying atop one another—you can always switch easily and quickly between programs.

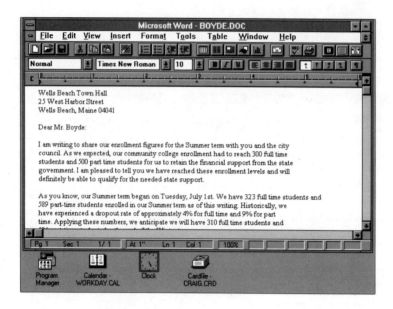

WHAT'S NEW IN VERSION 3.1?

Users of Windows 3.0 will recognize many major improvements in version 3.1. These improvements make the Windows environment faster, more robust, and more versatile than ever before.

Object Linking and Embedding

Windows 3.1 includes full support for *object linking and embedding* (OLE), an improved mechanism for integrating documents created in multiple applications. OLE, described in Chapter 8 of this book, allows you to create automatic links between documents, so that changes in a "server" document are immediately reflected in a "client" document. It also allows you to embed data created in one application, such as a spreadsheet program, in a document managed by another, such as a word processor. Simple commands, which can be invoked with either mouse or keyboard, allow you to edit the embedded data in its source application without leaving the client program.

Windows 3.1 also provides more robust support for *dynamic data exchange* (DDE), the first-generation mechanism for data exchange between Windows applications. As more and more Windows programs include support for OLE, you will probably have less need for DDE. But, of course, DDE-linked documents created under earlier versions of Windows will continue to function normally under Windows 3.1.

TrueType Font Technology

Windows 3.1 includes a built-in scalable font technology called TrueType. With TrueType, you can generate high-quality fonts in any point size on any supported screen and printer. Windows 3.1 continues to support alternative font-scaling systems, such as Adobe Type Manager, but the inclusion of TrueType means that you no longer need to purchase additional font software to generate high-quality documents.

The TrueType technology built into Windows 3.1 is identical to the font-scaling technology used on Apple Macintosh computers. Using cross-platform applications such as Microsoft Word, therefore, you can generate documents that look identical, whether printed from Windows or a Macintosh.

Windows 3.1 is shipped with five families of TrueType fonts: Arial (similar to Helvetica), Courier New, Symbol, Times New Roman, and Wingdings. Because most major font vendors have promised support for TrueType, a wide variety of compatible fonts will be available from third parties.

An Improved File Manager

The File Manager shell, one of the weakest links in Windows 3.0, has been completely redesigned for Windows 3.1. The new version is much faster, is easier to learn, allows you to work with directory trees and file listings in side-by-side windows, and includes a variety of "drag-and-drop" enhancements. (File Manager is described in detail in Chapter 6.) With the Windows 3.1 File Manager, you can finally send your favorite MS-DOS shell program to its well-deserved rest.

An Improved Program Manager

Program Manager, the other shell program included with Windows 3.1, has also been significantly improved. You can now name a program group Startup, and at the beginning of each Windows session, Program Manager automatically launches any programs contained in that group. You can also assign keyboard shortcuts to any Program Manager program-item icon (including Program Manager itself), for easier switching between programs. The new version also automatically wraps icon labels onto multiple lines, obviating the need to increase icon spacing to avoid title overlap.

Most significant, perhaps, Program Manager 3.1 uses far fewer system resources than did its predecessor. Many users will find that this improvement alone allows them to run far more programs at once than they could under Windows 3.0.

Improved Printing

The Windows 3.1 Print Manager has been improved in small, but valuable ways. First, you can use Print Manager as a drag-drop target. Drag a document icon from a File Manager window and drop it onto the Print Manager icon (or onto an open Print Manager window), and your document will be printed by its parent application. Second, Print Manager now waits until a document's spool file is complete before sending output to your printer. This change allows you to get back to work in your application sooner.

In addition to these improvements in Print Manager, Windows 3.1 incorporates a "universal printer driver." This is a generic printer driver that hardware vendors can quickly fashion into printer-specific drivers. The universal printer driver means that users have less to learn (because the configuration dialog boxes for most printer drivers look nearly alike) and that vendors will get updated drivers to market in a more timely fashion.

Greater Robustness

As a result of various under-the-hood changes in Windows 3.1, unrecoverable application errors (UAEs) should occur less frequently than in early versions. When such errors do occur, moreover, they are usually signalled by messages that include the name of the module that caused the error. This makes it easier for software vendors' technical support staff to troubleshoot problems.

Windows 3.1 also incorporates a feature called *local reboot* that, in most cases, allows you to terminate an application that causes a UAE without having to restart Windows itself. When you press Ctrl-Alt-Del, Windows gives you the choice of closing down only the current application or rebooting the entire system.

Windows 3.1 is also shipped with a diagnostic utility program called Dr. Watson (described in Chapter 19). Dr. Watson performs autopsies on UAE-causing applications, providing useful details about the state of your system at the time of your program's demise.

Better Support for Non-Windows Applications

Windows 3.1, in its 386 enhanced mode, offers improved support for non-Windows MS-DOS applications. If you've installed a supported mouse driver before beginning a Windows session, you can use the mouse with an MS-DOS application, even when that program is running in a window. Whether or not you use a mouse, you can select from a variety of font alternatives when displaying a non-Windows program in a window. You can also now create a windowed display of an MS-DOS program that runs in a standard VGA graphics mode.

Better Support for Portable Computers

Windows 3.1 includes several color schemes optimized for use on LCD displays. It also offers a feature called Mouse Trails that can make it easier to follow a mouse pointer on an LCD screen. With Mouse Trails on, Windows leaves a trail of pointer images as you move your pointer across the screen. (The Mouse Trails feature is described in Chapter 9.)

If hard disk space is limited on your laptop or notebook computer, you may also want to take advantage of a new feature in the Windows 3.1 Setup program. This feature, described in Appendix A, makes it easy to remove components of your Windows system that you don't absolutely need—such things as game programs, accessory programs, wallpaper files, help files, and "read me" files.

Better Network Support

Unlike earlier versions, Windows 3.1 remembers network settings from session to session, allowing users to reconnect to remote server directories by choosing them from a menu. Windows 3.1 also provides easier network setup and improved error reporting for the benefit of network administrators.

Multimedia Support

Windows 3.1 includes support for most popular audio boards, as well as a Sound Recorder program, a Media Player, and a MIDI Mapper. With a supported sound board, a simple microphone, and external speakers or headphones, you can use the Sound Recorder application to create audible annotations and embed them in programs that support OLE. With a supported MIDI synthesizer, you can also edit, create, and play MIDI music files.

If you have a sound board and external speakers, you can also use the Sounds section of Control Panel to map certain system events to particular sound (WAV) files. For example, you can set Windows up so that it greets you with a chime or a "ta-da" at the beginning of the day, strums a chord on closing, and replaces its strident beep with a more musical utterance.

With some additional hardware, you can turn your Windows 3.1 PC into a full-fledged multimedia personal computer. For example, by adding a CD-ROM drive to your system, you can take advantage of the growing number of CD-ROM-based multimedia applications available for the Windows environment. You can also use the supplied Media Player to play audio compact disks through your computer's external speakers.

HARDWARE AND SOFTWARE REQUIRED FOR WINDOWS 3

Windows 3.1 requires a minimum of 1 MB of memory (RAM) and a computer with an 80286, 80386, or 80486 microprocessor. (Practically speaking, you should have at least 2 MB of memory to run Windows 3.1.) In addition, you need MS-DOS 3.1 or later and a video display supported by Windows 3. You'll find a list of computers, video displays, printers, and other devices supported by Windows in your Windows package.

A mouse or other pointing device is extremely helpful but not strictly required. In most Windows applications, you can choose commands with either a pointing device or the keyboard, and this book will show you both methods. But manipulating objects such as windows and graphic images is almost always easier with a pointing device. If you don't have a mouse now, however, you can start using Windows with keyboard only; you can always add a pointing device later.

WINDOWS 3.1 OPERATING MODES

Windows 3.1 has two operating modes, called *standard mode* and *386 enhanced mode*. When you type *win* to start Windows, the software automatically chooses the operating mode that is appropriate for your hardware.

Note that the *real mode* that was available in earlier versions of Windows has been eliminated in Windows 3.1. That means that Windows no longer runs on 8088- and 8086-based computers, and that applications designed for Windows 2 (and not updated) might not work reliably under Windows 3.1.

Standard Mode

Windows automatically runs in standard mode on computers with at least 1 MB of memory that use the Intel 80286 microprocessor. In standard mode, your Windows applications can use memory in excess of 640 KB. You can run non-Windows applications as well as Windows applications, but non-Windows applications must use the full screen. In addition, non-Windows applications can run in the *foreground* only; that is, when you switch from a non-Windows application to another application (either a Windows application or another non-Windows application), the program you switched away from is suspended until you switch back to it.

386 Enhanced Mode

Windows automatically runs in 386 enhanced mode on computers that use the Intel 80386, Intel 80386SX, or Intel 80486 microprocessor and that have at least 2 MB of memory. The memory must include 640 KB of conventional memory plus at least 1 MB of *extended* memory. Windows' 386 enhanced mode provides two advantages over standard mode:

- In 386 enhanced mode, Windows can use free space on your hard disk as an extension of internal (RAM) memory. When your internal memory becomes full, Windows writes data that you're temporarily not using to the hard disk; when you need that data again, Windows retrieves it and moves other data out to disk.

- In 386 enhanced mode, you have more control over the way non-Windows applications run. You can display non-Windows programs in full-screen fashion or in a window, and you can choose to have a non-Windows application continue running, even when you've switched to a different program.

You can find out which operating mode Windows is using by choosing the About command, on the Help menu, in Program Manager, File Manager, or most of the Windows desktop accessory programs. This command also tells you how much memory is currently available to Windows.

ABOUT THIS BOOK

This book is organized in six parts.

Part I introduces you to the Windows interface. You'll learn how to start and end a session in Windows, how to manipulate the rectangular frames in which Windows programs reside, and how to choose commands and fill out dialog boxes. Part I also discusses the use of the Clipboard for transferring information between programs and the basic procedures for printing Windows documents.

Part II provides details about using the two Windows shell programs, Program Manager and File Manager.

Part III includes four chapters to help you hone your skills in Windows. Chapter 7 describes the use of the desktop accessory programs that come with Windows—Clock, Calculator, Notepad, Calendar, Cardfile, Character Map, and Sound Recorder. Chapter 8 provides more details about how information is transferred between programs via the Windows Clipboard. Chapter 9 describes the use of Control Panel for adjusting screen colors, changing keyboard and mouse sensitivity, setting the date and time, and so on. And Chapter 10 shows you how to automate routine tasks by recording and playing back macros.

Part IV includes three chapters devoted to printing. You'll learn how to install and set up printer drivers, how to add new fonts to your system, and how to manage a print queue with Print Manager.

Part V is about using major applications with Windows. Chapters 14 through 16 are devoted to Write, Terminal, and Paintbrush, the three large programs that come with Windows. Chapter 17 provides thumbnail sketches of major Windows applications, Chapter 18 describes the use of non-Windows applications, and Chapter 19 provides some information about optimizing performance of both Windows and non-Windows applications.

Part VI contains some important reference information. Appendix A describes the use of the Setup program for performing various maintenance chores—installing new drivers, creating program items, and removing files that you might not need. Appendix B explains different types of memory—what they are and how to use them. Appendix C describes some valuable online and printed resource materials. The Glossary defines and explains terms you'll encounter in this book and while using Windows.

Mouse Terminology

You'll encounter the following mouse terminology in this book:

Mouse pointer: The mouse pointer is the symbol that moves around on screen as you move the mouse. Usually, the mouse pointer is a single-headed arrow, but it can change to a different symbol—a double-headed arrow or a cross, for example—in certain contexts.

Click: To click an object (such as an icon or a menu command) is to position the mouse pointer on that object, and then press and release the active mouse button once. Normally, the active mouse button is the left button; you can switch it to the right with the Control Panel program, described in Chapter 9.

Double-click: To double-click an object is to position the mouse pointer on that object and press the active mouse button twice in relatively quick succession. Be sure not to move the mouse between the first and second clicks. You can adjust the speed with which you execute a double-click via the Control Panel program, described in Chapter 9. At the normal setting, you don't have to be a concert pianist or world-class finger wrestler to carry out the two clicks in time; in fact, if you try to do it too quickly, you'll probably move the mouse inadvertently, which will nullify the double-click.

Drag: To drag an object means to position the mouse pointer on the object, and then successively press and hold the active mouse button, move the mouse to a new position, and release the mouse button.

Keyboard Terminology

In this book, when you see a key combination written with a hyphen, like this:

Alt-F5

it means, "hold down the key on the left side of the hyphen, and then press the key on the right side." So, for example, to press Alt-F5 means to hold down the Alt key and press the F5 key.

When you see two key names separated by a comma, like this:

Alt, S

it means, "press and release the first key, and then press the second."

Other Terminology

In this book, the terms *program* and *application* are synonyms.

All references to the Intel 80386 microprocessor apply equally to the 80386SX and 80486 microprocessors as well.

GETTING TO KNOW WINDOWS

The first four chapters of this book cover the basic skills you need to use Windows.

In Chapter 1, you'll learn how to start and end a Windows session, how to run an application from Program Manager, and how to organize application windows on your screen.

Chapter 2 introduces the Windows system of drop-down menus and dialog boxes.

Documents—files that you create using Windows applications—are the subject of Chapter 3. You'll learn how to manipulate document windows, how to open and save files, how to enter and edit text and graphics, and how to move information from one place to another with the Windows Clipboard.

Part I concludes with a short chapter about the Windows Help facility.

1

Working with Windows

This chapter introduces Windows and windows—the graphical environment it-self and the rectangular frames that are its main working units. Using hands-on exercises, you'll learn how to start Windows from the MS-DOS prompt, how to start applications, how to organize the various windows that grace (or clutter) your electronic desktop, and how to leave Windows and return to the MS-DOS prompt.

STARTING WINDOWS FROM MS-DOS

To start Windows, simply type *win* at the MS-DOS prompt, and press Enter. In a moment, the Windows logo appears, replaced a moment later by one of the Windows *shells*—Program Manager or File Manager.

A shell is a master program that starts and ends each of your sessions in Windows. It's also the command post from which you start the various programs and accessories that you use to get your work done. Windows gives you a choice of shells, because different people have different styles of working.

In Program Manager, the more visually oriented of the Windows shells, programs are represented by *icons* (graphic symbols), and you can start an application simply by double-clicking the mouse on the program's icon. You can also change settings so that when you start a program, a particular document is loaded into memory at the same time.

In File Manager, you see program names instead of icons. File Manager has the advantages of letting you see more program names at once and letting you sort those names; it also includes valuable tools for organizing files on your hard disk. File Manager is a comprehensive replacement for the MS-DOS Executive, the shell that was used in Windows versions 1 and 2. Its performance and organization have been improved dramatically in Windows 3.1; if you looked at File Manager in Windows 3.0 and promptly put it away for good, you might want to take a second look in version 3.1.

INTRODUCING PROGRAM MANAGER

Chapters 5 and 6 describe the Windows shells in detail, and Chapter 9 tells you how to set Windows up to start with the shell of your choice. This chapter assumes that your copy of Windows is using Program Manager as its shell. That's a reasonable assumption, because Windows is always set to use Program Manager when it has just been installed.

Your first Windows screen, then, looks something like this:

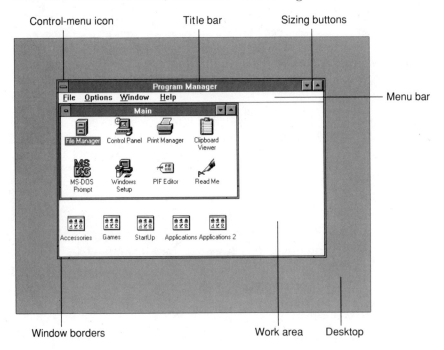

A window labeled Program Manager partially fills your screen.

NOTE: *If Program Manager fills your entire screen, press Alt, Spacebar, R. Also press Alt, Spacebar, R if, instead of an open Program Manager window, you see an icon labeled Program Manager at the bottom of your screen.*

The contents of your Program Manager window may not match the illustration above, but, for now, that doesn't matter. We'll come back to what's inside the Program Manager later in this chapter. First, let's look at the external properties of this window.

THE ANATOMY OF A WINDOW

Although Program Manager is a special kind of Windows application (because it's used to start other programs), the window in which it appears looks and behaves exactly like that of any other Windows application. It has the following important landmarks:

Window borders: The four edges that define the perimeter of the window are called *borders*.

Title bar: Directly below the top border of the window is a region that includes the window's name. That part of the window is called the *title bar*.

Control-menu icon: Just to the left of the title bar is a little box with a big dash inside. That's the *Control-menu icon*. As you'll see in Chapter 2, that icon can be "opened up" to reveal a set of commands.

Sizing buttons: In the upper right corner of the window is a pair of arrows—one pointing down, the other pointing up. These are called *sizing buttons*. They're used to *minimize* and *maximize* the window, respectively. (We'll see them in action in a moment.)

Menu bar: Directly below the title bar is the *menu bar*. The menu bar provides access to most of an application's commands (see Chapter 2). The contents of the menu bar vary from application to application, but nearly all Windows applications have menu bars directly below their title bars.

Work area: The inside of a window is called the *work area*, or *workspace*.

THE WINDOWS DESKTOP

The area outside your Program Manager window is your *desktop*. Think of this area as the electronic equivalent of an ordinary desktop. You can stack as many objects on this surface as the memory in your computer will allow. You can keep it neat and tidy, or you can turn it into an unsightly heap. Fortunately, Windows makes it easy to maintain order on your electronic desktop.

MAXIMIZING, MINIMIZING, AND RESTORING

Whenever you first start a program, Windows chooses a size and position for the program's window. That size and position depend on what else you have on your desktop and probably won't be the same each time you start the program. In most cases, the window will fill something less than your entire screen.

When you want to focus all your attention on a particular program, you'll probably want to devote as much screen space as possible to that application. You can do that by *maximizing* the application's window. Here are two ways to *maximize* a window:

- If you have a mouse, click the window's maximize button—the upward-pointing arrow at the upper right corner of the window.

- If you don't have a mouse or you prefer to use the keyboard, press Alt, Spacebar, X.

Try either method now. Your Program Manager window expands to fill the entire screen.

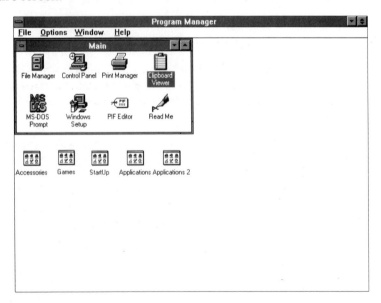

KEYBOARD TIP: When you press Alt, Spacebar, you're opening Program Manager's *Control menu*. From the menu, pressing the underlined letter of the desired action completes the command. The Control menu is discussed fully in Chapter 2.

If you had any other programs on your desktop, they would be obscured by the maximized Program Manager window. (But you could still switch between programs.)

Notice one other change that has occurred: The button at the upper right corner of the window is no longer a simple arrow pointing up; it has become a double-headed arrow pointing up and down. In Windows terminology, the maximize button has been replaced by a *restore button*.

That suggests our next experiment: If you have a mouse, click the restore button. If you don't, press Alt, Spacebar, R. The Program Manager window is *restored* to its former size and position, and the restore button is replaced by the maximize button.

 MOUSE TIP: Instead of aiming for the maximize button, you can also maximize a window by double-clicking its title bar. Similarly, you can restore a maximized application by double-clicking its title bar.

Now let's try minimizing. With the mouse, click the downward arrow just to the right of Program Manager's title bar. With the keyboard, press Alt, Spacebar, N. Your Program Manager window becomes an icon at the lower edge of your desktop, as shown in the illustration at the top of the following page.

The downward arrow is called the *minimize button,* and the act of minimizing reduces a window to an icon. Windows puts icons for minimized applications at the bottom of your screen, starting at the left edge.

Minimizing an application gets it out of your way, so you can concentrate on something else, but leaves it available on your desktop. It's like putting a physical object in your top desk drawer, except that you don't have to rummage in the drawer to see what's there. Each Windows application you use has its own distinctive icon, so you can see at a glance what minimized applications you have on your desktop. (And just in case you forget what a program's icon looks like, Windows prints the program's name under the icon.)

Now let's return Program Manager once more to its original size and position. With the mouse, double-click the Program Manager icon. With the keyboard, press Alt, Spacebar, R. You've just *restored* Program Manager again.

 MOUSE TIP: If a menu pops up out of the icon when you double-click it, it's probably because you moved the mouse slightly between the two halves of your double-click. Double-clicking takes a little practice. You can restore the window from this menu by clicking on the word *Restore.*

Notice that the term *restore* means to return a window to its previous size and position from either a maximized state or a minimized state. The keyboard command—Alt, Spacebar, R—is the same in both cases. The mouse procedure is a little different, but only because a minimized window doesn't have room for sizing buttons.

MOVING AND SIZING WINDOWS

In addition to being able to maximize, minimize, and restore windows, you can also move them around on your desktop and expand or contract their borders.

To move a window with the mouse, drag its title bar. That is, put the mouse pointer anywhere on the title bar, press and hold the left mouse button, move the mouse in the direction you want the window to move, and then release the left mouse button. The window simply follows your mouse.

To move a window with the keyboard, start by pressing Alt, Spacebar, M. Then use any of the four direction keys to move your window. When you get the window where you want it, press Enter.

To cancel a move, press Esc before releasing the mouse button or pressing Enter. The window will remain where it was before you began the move.

 WINDOWS TIP: You can move a minimized window the same way you move an open one. That is, you can drag its icon around with the mouse or you can press Alt, Spacebar, M and use direction keys to relocate the icon. It can be helpful to move icons if you have several minimized applications on your desktop at the same time and their labels overlap one another.

To change the size of a window, you move one or more of the window's borders inward or outward. Moving a border inward contracts the window, and moving it outward expands the window.

To change the size of a window with the mouse, simply position the pointer on the border you want to adjust. The mouse pointer changes from a single-headed arrow to a double-headed one. Press and hold the left button, move the border as you please, and then release the button.

You can move two adjacent borders at once by positioning the mouse pointer in the corner between those borders.

To change a window's size with the keyboard, start by pressing Alt, Spacebar, S. A four-headed pointer will appear in the center of the window. Use one of the direction keys to move that pointer to the border whose position you want to adjust. Then use direction keys to adjust the border. When you're happy with the border's position, press Enter.

To cancel a sizing operation, press Esc before releasing the mouse button or pressing Enter.

APPLICATION WINDOWS AND DOCUMENT WINDOWS

By now, you've undoubtedly noticed that the Program Manager window itself contains windows and icons. In the first illustration in this chapter, for example, Program Manager is shown holding one open window (titled *Main*) and five minimized windows.

Those internal windows are known as *document windows*. The outer window—Program Manager—is an example of an *application window*. (In some other publications, you may see document and application windows called *child* and *parent windows*, respectively.)

Application windows hold programs, such as Program Manager. Document windows are used by some programs to encapsulate information used by those programs. For example, if you write a letter in a word processing application, that letter might be displayed in a document window.

Program Manager uses document windows to hold *program groups*. Each program group contains icons for starting applications. The document window named Main has icons for starting certain essential Windows "utilities," such as Print Manager, Clipboard Viewer, Windows Setup, and Control Panel. Another document window, named Games, holds icons for Solitaire and Minesweeper, the two game programs that come with Windows. Chapter 5 shows you how to set up your own program groups and rearrange the ones that Windows provides for you.

MANIPULATING DOCUMENT WINDOWS

Document windows have a lot in common with applications windows—and a few differences.

Like application windows, document windows can be maximized. To maximize a document window with the mouse, click its maximize button or double-click its title bar. To maximize a document window with the keyboard, press Alt, Hyphen, X.

To restore a maximized document window with the mouse, click its restore button. To restore a maximized document window with the keyboard, press Alt, Hyphen, R.

Whether a document window can be minimized as well as maximized depends on the program that created the document window. In earlier versions of Windows, document windows could never be minimized. Therefore, in applications that were originally created for Windows 1 or Windows 2, you might find document windows that can be maximized but not minimized.

If a document window can be minimized, you'll find a minimize button in its upper right corner. Click that button, or press Alt, Hyphen, N, to turn the document window into an icon. Double-click the icon, or press Alt, Hyphen, R, to restore the icon to an open document window.

Document windows can be moved and sized in the same way as application windows can, but they must stay within the confines of their application windows. The mouse procedures for moving and sizing are exactly like those for moving and sizing application windows. The keyboard procedures begin with Alt, Hyphen, M (for moving) and Alt, Hyphen, S (for sizing).

For more information about working with document windows, see Chapter 3, "Working with Documents."

STARTING A PROGRAM FROM PROGRAM MANAGER

So far in this chapter, we've been working with a single application window—Program Manager. Now let's see what happens when we get more than one application window on the desktop. To open a second window, we'll start a program from Program Manager.

The general procedure for starting a program from Program Manager is as follows:

1. Open the program-group window containing the icon for the program you want to run.

2. Double-click the icon. Or use the direction keys to highlight the icon, and then press Enter.

Chapter 5 has all the details about using Program Manager.

For now, we want to start the program Minesweeper, and the icon for that program is stored in the Games program group. So, we'll proceed as follows:

1. If Program Manager is currently minimized or maximized, restore it.

2. Click the word *Window* on Program Manager's menu bar, or press Alt, W.

    Program Manager's Window menu unfolds, looking something like the illustration shown at the top of the following page.

3. Click the mouse on the word *Games*. Or press the number next
to the word *Games*. (In the illustration, that number is 5, but it
might be different on your system.)

   The Games program group appears.

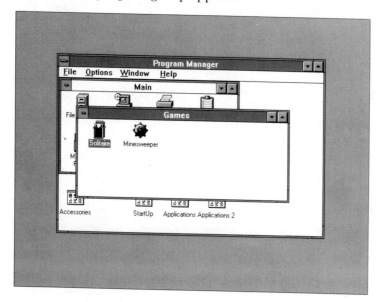

   Your Games program group probably contains two icons, one
   for Solitaire and one for Minesweeper.

4. With the mouse, double-click the Minesweeper icon. With the
   keyboard, press M to highlight the word *Minesweeper*, and then
   press Enter.

   A new window, containing the game Minesweeper, appears. Minesweeper
is a challenging game of intuition and strategy. You can get complete instructions
for playing the game by exploring the program's help messages. (For details
about using the Windows help system, see Chapter 4.)

FOREGROUND AND BACKGROUND

At this point, you have two applications on your desktop—Minesweeper and Program Manager. (Depending on how your system has been set up, you might have additional programs running. We can ignore them for the purposes of this discussion.) Your screen looks something like this:

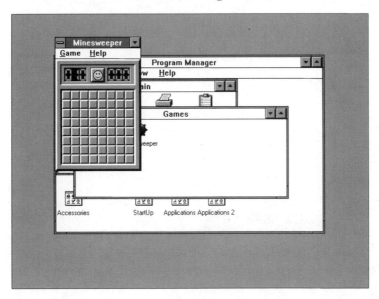

(Depending on how one of Program Manager's options is set, your Program Manager window might be minimized.)

Whenever you have two or more applications on your desktop at once, whether the windows are open or minimized, one application is treated differently from all the others. That application is called the *foreground application*. The foreground application is the one that Windows assumes you are currently using. The window in which it resides is known as the *foreground window*, the *current window*, or the *active window*.

If two or more applications are lying in open windows on your desktop, as Minesweeper and Program Manager are in the illustration above, Windows always makes certain the active window lies on top. That's one way you can tell which window is active. (Another way you can tell is by looking at the title bars, as we'll see a little later in this chapter.)

Because Windows is a *multitasking* system, several programs on your desktop can run concurrently, but the foreground application usually gets the largest share of your computer's processing time. All other programs are said to run *in the background.* Programs usually run more slowly in the background, because they get a smaller share of your computer's attention, but they run nevertheless.

Thus, for example, if you are working with a spreadsheet program and need to recalculate a large worksheet, you can begin the recalculation and then switch to a different program, putting the spreadsheet into the background. While you work in the foreground application, the spreadsheet program continues to re-calculate your worksheet. But the process takes somewhat longer than it would if you left the spreadsheet in the foreground.

CHANGING THE FOREGROUND APPLICATION

In most cases, when you start a new program, that program automatically be-comes the foreground application. But you can switch at any time to a different open application, bringing *it* to the foreground. This action is usually called *switching windows,* or *switching programs.* You might also see it referred to as *acti-vating* a different program or window.

Windows gives you quite a few ways to switch programs. In many cases, the simplest method is to point to the window you want to activate, and then click the mouse button. But that works only if you can see the window you want to switch to (as you can in the preceding illustration). What if the window you're switching away from is maximized, or if you have so many windows on your desktop that you can't see the program you want to switch to?

One way to switch under those circumstances is to press Alt-Tab. Another is to press Alt-Esc. (Still another method is to use Task List, which we'll come to in a moment.)

Alt-Tab and Alt-Esc differ slightly in their effects. To see exactly how they differ, we need to get at least one more program open. So:

1. If you have a mouse, click anywhere within the Program Manager window. Otherwise, press Alt-Tab.

   Program Manager becomes the active window. Notice that it now lies on top of Minesweeper.

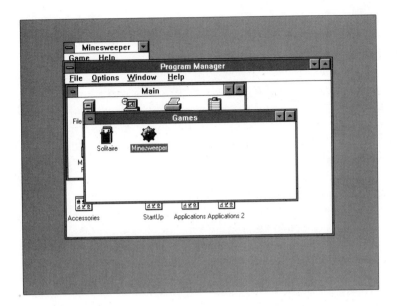

2. Double-click the icon for Solitaire. Or press S to highlight the Solitaire icon, and then press Enter.

A game of Solitaire emerges, becoming the foreground application.

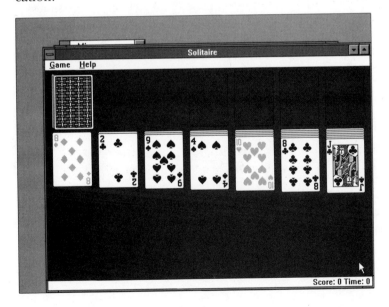

Now that you have three windows on your desktop, try pressing Alt-Esc a few times. Notice that each time you use this key combination, Windows brings a different program to the foreground. You can cycle through all the programs on your desktop with Alt-Esc.

Now try holding down the Alt key and pressing Tab a few times. Keep your finger on the Alt key for at least three or four Tabs; then release the Alt key. Notice that with each Alt-Tab, Windows displays the name and icon for a different application, but it doesn't display that application's window until you release the Alt key. This behavior of the Alt-Tab combination allows you to cycle through open windows a little more quickly than you could with Alt-Esc, because Windows doesn't have to waste time redrawing window contents. (This behavior of the Alt-Tab combination, called "Fast Alt-Tab Switching," is new with Windows 3.1. If you're used to the way earlier versions of Windows responded to Alt-Tab, you can use the Control Panel program to turn Fast Alt-Tab Switching off. See Chapter 9 for details.)

 WINDOWS TIP: Alt-Tab has one other important advantage over Alt-Esc. When you switch from one program to another with Alt-Tab, Windows remembers the program you switched from. Another press of Alt-Tab then returns you to the first application. So when you want to toggle back and forth between two of several programs on your desktop, you'll find Alt-Tab more convenient than Alt-Esc. On the other hand, Alt-Esc (but not Alt-Tab) allows you to switch to a minimized program without restoring it. You might find this convenient at times.

SWITCHING PROGRAMS WITH TASK LIST

Another way to switch from one program to another is to summon a handy Windows utility called Task List. You can do this in either of two ways:

- Press Ctrl-Esc.

- Double-click the mouse anywhere on the desktop, other than within a window.

Try either of these methods now. Task List pops up in a little window that looks like this:

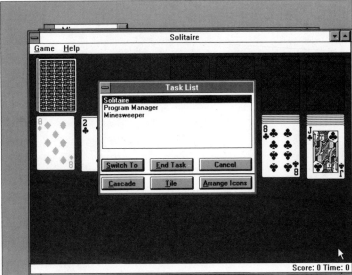

In the top half of the Task List window, you'll find a list of all programs open on your desktop. In the bottom half of the window are six *command buttons*.

To switch applications with the mouse, click the name of the application you want to switch to. Then click the Switch To button. Or, more simply, double-click the name of the application you want to switch to.

To switch applications with the keyboard, use the direction keys to highlight the name of the application you want to switch to. Then press Alt-S.

Task List goes away as soon as you use it. If you want to make it go away without switching programs, click the Cancel button or press Esc.

ARRANGING WINDOWS WITH TASK LIST

Task List is more than a program switcher. To see what else it can do, get it back on your screen again by pressing Ctrl-Esc or double-clicking on the desktop. Now click the Tile button or press Alt-T. Task List puts all your open windows side by side, so that each is as large as it can be without encroaching on its neighbor.

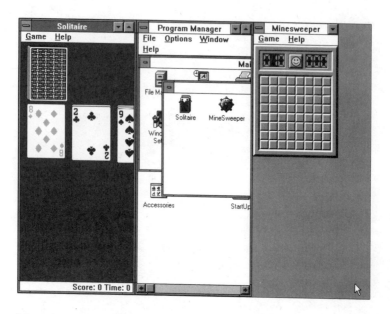

Now that you have three windows lying open and side by side, you can easily verify that Windows uses title bars to distinguish the foreground application from all background applications. Try clicking the mouse in each window in turn, and notice what happens to the title bars. (If you don't have a mouse, simply press Alt-Esc a couple of times.) The title bar of the active window is always displayed in a color or texture that's different from all other title bars. Exactly how it's displayed depends on what color scheme you're using (color schemes are discussed in Chapter 9), but it's different, in any case. In this book's illustrations, the foreground program's title bar is always shown in dark gray; title bars of inactive programs are white.

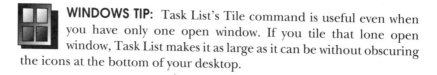

WINDOWS TIP: Task List's Tile command is useful even when you have only one open window. If you tile that lone open window, Task List makes it as large as it can be without obscuring the icons at the bottom of your desktop.

Now summon Task List again, and click the Cascade button (or press Alt-C). This time Task List stacks your open windows like a hand of cards.

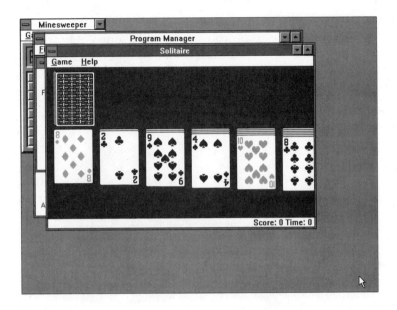

USING TASK LIST TO ORGANIZE ICONS

You can also use Task List to neaten up a set of icons. Try this exercise:

1. Minimize each of your open windows.

2. Move some or all of your icons to different parts of the screen.

3. Call up Task List. Click the Arrange Icons button, or press Alt-A.

CLOSING APPLICATION WINDOWS

As you've probably noticed, Task List also includes a button called End Task. This button provides one way to close an application window and remove it from your desktop. Try that now with Minesweeper:

1. Press Ctrl-Esc, or double-click on the desktop to invoke Task List.

2. In the Task List window, highlight Minesweeper, either by clicking the name with the mouse or by using the direction keys.

3. Click the End Task button, or press Alt-E.

Minesweeper is terminated, and its window (or icon) is removed from the desktop.

Because you can close a window with Task List without first making that window active, Task List is an especially convenient way to quit applications when you have many windows on your desktop. When the program you want to quit is already the active window, however, you'll find either of the following methods a little quicker:

- Double-click the Control-menu icon of the window you want to close.

- Press Alt-F4.

Try quitting Solitaire now by pressing Alt-F4. Be sure to make Solitaire the active window first.

 WINDOWS TIP: Most Windows programs have at least one additional command for quitting. Usually, that command is found on the File menu (see Chapter 2). But the methods just described will work in any case.

WINDOWS TIP: Most Windows applications check to be sure you don't have unsaved work in memory before they allow you to quit. If you work on a document in, say, a Windows word processor, and you quit the word processor without saving the latest version of your document to disk, you get a warning message from the application. This message usually offers you the choice of saving the document and then quitting, quitting without saving, or not quitting.

QUITTING WINDOWS AND RETURNING TO THE MS-DOS PROMPT

To quit Windows itself and return to MS-DOS, all you have to do is close the application window for your *default shell*. Your default shell is the shell program that runs when you first start your Windows session. In the examples in this chapter, Program Manager is the default shell. (To learn how to make a different program your default shell, see Chapter 9.)

Try quitting Windows now, by closing your Program Manager window. You can use Alt-F4 to do this, or you can double-click the Control-menu icon.

Program Manager displays the following *information window* to let you know that you're about to depart from Windows.

If you had issued the quitting procedure by mistake, you could click the Cancel button or press Esc to remain in Windows. To confirm that you really do want to leave, click the OK button or press Enter.

2
Using Menus and Dialog Boxes

One of the big advantages of working with Windows applications is that they all use the same basic methods for command entry. In virtually all Windows programs, commands are chosen from *drop-down menus*—sets of options that emerge from a menu bar at the top of the application window. When a program needs additional information from you before it can carry out your command, it presents a *dialog box*—a smaller window with places for you to fill in blanks or choose between preset options.

This chapter explains the workings of drop-down menus and dialog boxes. Because these devices behave in a consistent and predictable way in all Windows applications, when you've learned the material in this chapter, you'll be well on your way toward knowing how to use any Windows program.

THE CONTROL MENU AND THE MENU BAR

The two main elements of a Windows application's menu system are the *Control menu* and the *menu bar*. The Control menu emerges from the Control-menu icon, the large dash at the left side of the title bar. The menu bar is the row of command words directly below the title bar.

The Control menu (also sometimes called the *System* menu) provides a set of generic commands common to all applications. With a few exceptions, each program's Control menu includes the same commands.

The menu bar includes commands specific to the window's application. Each word on the menu bar can be opened into a set of related commands. For example, an application's File menu includes commands for opening and saving document files, the Edit menu has commands for changing the contents of a document, and so on.

CHOOSING COMMANDS WITH THE MOUSE

To access the menu system with the mouse, simply click on the desired word in the menu bar. To open the File menu, for example, click the word *File.* To open the Control menu, click the Control-menu icon.

To choose a command from a drop-down menu, simply click the mouse again on the command you want. For example, to choose the Delete command on Program Manager's File menu, do the following:

1. Click the word *File* on Program Manager's menu bar.

2. Click the word *Delete* on the File menu.

You can blend these two steps into a single action by putting the mouse pointer on the word *File*, holding down the mouse button, sliding the mouse pointer down to the word *Delete*, and releasing the mouse button.

To get out of the menu system without choosing a command, click the mouse (or release the mouse button) anywhere outside the drop-down menu.

CHOOSING COMMANDS WITH THE KEYBOARD

To choose any command with the keyboard, begin by pressing the Alt key. When you do that, Windows highlights the first command on the menu bar, like this:

At this point, you can move around the menu bar by pressing the Left and Right direction keys. Pressing the Right direction key in the illustration above, for example, highlights the word *Options.* Pressing it again moves the highlight to the word *Window,* and so on. If you press the Right direction key with the highlight on Help, the highlight moves to the Control-menu icon. From there it moves to the document window's Control-menu icon (see "Document Control Menus," in this chapter), then back to File, and so on around.

 KEYBOARD TIP: Another key you can use to access the menu system of any Windows application is F10. Certain applications may provide other access keys as well; in Microsoft Excel, for example, you can reach the menu system by pressing the slash key (/).

Pressing either the Up or Down direction key opens the drop-down menu associated with the highlighted menu-bar word. In the preceding illustration, for example, you could press the Down key to open the File menu.

A more direct way to open a particular drop-down menu is to press the underlined letter of the menu you want. For example, to open the Options menu in Program Manager, do the following:

1. Press Alt to access the menu system.

2. Press O, the underlined letter for the Options menu.

To open the Control menu, press Alt followed by Spacebar. (Think of the Control-menu icon as a picture of a Spacebar, and you'll never have trouble remembering this key combination.)

After you've opened a drop-down menu, you can choose a command in either of the following ways:

■ Use the Up and Down direction keys to highlight the command you want, and then press Enter.

■ Press the underlined letter of the command you want.

To get out of the menu system without choosing a command, press Alt or F10 again. Or press Esc. (In some applications, you might need to press Esc twice—once to get out of a drop-down menu and a second time to leave the menu bar itself.)

Keyboard Shortcuts

Some menu commands have *keyboard shortcuts* assigned to them. These are single keystrokes or simple keystroke combinations that execute a command directly. For example, as the following illustration shows, Shift-F5 and Shift-F4 are keyboard shortcuts for the Cascade and Tile commands on Program Manager's Window menu.

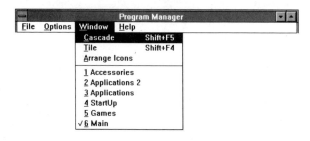

Keyboard shortcuts, when available, are usually the quickest way to choose a command, because you don't have to open a drop-down menu to use them. (And Windows doesn't have to redraw the screen to display the menu.)

WHAT'S ON THE CONTROL MENU

As mentioned, the Control menu is a standard item on all Windows applications. Typically, it looks like this:

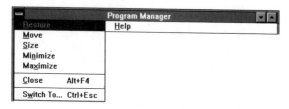

The Control menu provides commands for maximizing, minimizing, restoring, sizing, moving, and closing a window. It also includes a command (Switch To) that invokes Task List. As you learned in Chapter 1, you can carry out these procedures by direct mouse action, but invoking Task List by double-clicking on the desktop is awkward if the active window is maximized.

Non-Windows applications also have Control menus when they're running in a window (in 386 enhanced mode) or when they're minimized on the desktop.

Accessing the Control Menu on a Minimized Application

You can access a minimized application's Control menu in either of two ways:

- Click the application's icon once with the mouse.

- Use Alt-Esc to select the application's icon, and then press Alt, Spacebar.

The Control menu pops up from the icon, as shown in the following illustration of a minimized Program Manager.

Document Control Menus

Document windows do not have menu bars, but they do have abbreviated Control menus. You can access the Control menu of a document window by clicking the mouse on the little bar in the upper left corner of the window (the document Control-menu icon) or by pressing Alt, Hyphen.

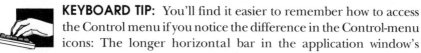 **KEYBOARD TIP:** You'll find it easier to remember how to access the Control menu if you notice the difference in the Control-menu icons: The longer horizontal bar in the application window's Control-menu icon suggests a Spacebar, whereas the document Control-menu icon's shorter bar looks more like a hyphen.

MENU CONVENTIONS

Like the pictorial traffic signs increasingly used throughout the world, certain symbols and conventions have universal significance in the menus of Windows applications. On the following pages is a brief survey.

Grayed-out Commands

A command that appears in gray or dim characters is one that's inappropriate in the current context. The following menu, from Write (the mini-word processor included in your Windows package) presents several examples.

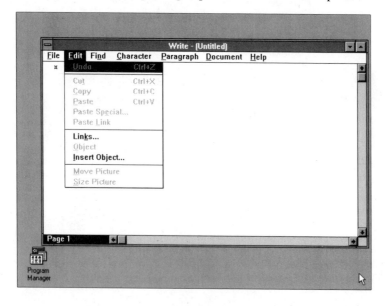

Write's Edit menu has commands to undo a previous action; to cut, copy, and paste; to manage links and objects from other applications; and to move and size a graphic image imported into a Write document. But, in this example, Write has just been started and no document has been opened. No editing action is possible yet, so most commands on the Edit menu are temporarily grayed out.

Check Marks

A check mark next to a menu command indicates that a feature is currently in effect. For example, in the illustration shown at the top of the following page, you can tell at a glance that Program Manager's Minimize On Use option has been selected.

Commands that use check marks typically act like on-off switches, or *toggles*. You choose the command once to turn a feature on, and you choose the same command a second time to turn the feature off again. The check mark tells you which state the toggle is in.

Menus That Change

In some applications, menus change their text to reflect current conditions. For example, the Undo and Repeat commands on Microsoft Excel's Edit menu actually spell out what they're currently able to undo and repeat.

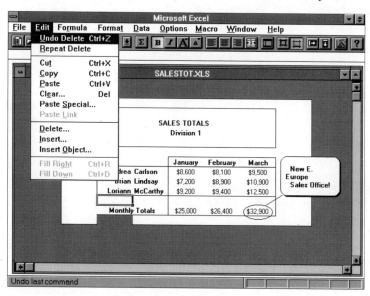

In this example, the last editing action was a deletion, so the Undo and Repeat commands say Undo Delete and Repeat Delete.

Short and Long Menus

Some applications let you choose an abbreviated form of the menu system if you find the complete command repertoire distracting. The command to select the short menu system is typically called Short Menus. When you choose this command, some of the more advanced options disappear from the menus, and the

Short Menus command itself changes to say Full Menus. Choosing Full Menus reinstates the whole command set.

User-Modifiable Menus

Some Windows applications let you add your own commands to the menus. For example, in Microsoft Word for Windows, you can write macros (small programs that carry out command sequences) and add their names to Word's drop-down menus. Commands installed in this fashion behave exactly like any built-in menu command.

Cascading Menus

A symbol like the arrowhead to the right of the Edit command in the following menu usually indicates the presence of a secondary menu.

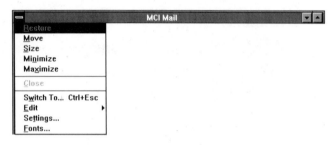

Selecting that command will bring up a *cascading* secondary menu, like this:

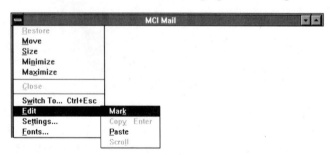

The Control menu used by non-Windows applications running in 386 enhanced mode employs cascading menus.

Commands That Bring Up Dialog Boxes

The ellipsis (...) is a punctuation symbol signifying an incomplete command. In a Windows menu, an ellipsis following a command name means the command brings up a *dialog box*. A dialog box is a device used by Windows to get more information from you.

THE INS AND OUTS OF DIALOG BOXES

Dialog boxes come in all sizes and shapes. Some are simple:

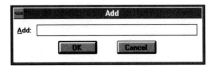

Others are quite complex.

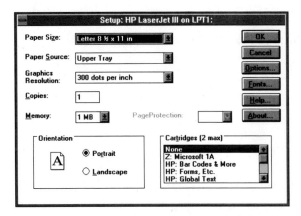

But nearly all dialog boxes have the following components:

■ One or more places for you to enter information or choose options

■ One or more *command buttons*

For example, the simple dialog box shown above (the Add dialog box from the Cardfile desktop accessory) has a place for you to enter some text (the box marked Add) and two command buttons—one marked OK and one marked Cancel. The complex example above (the dialog box used for setting up a Hewlett-Packard LaserJet III printer) has eight places for you to enter information and six command buttons. The command buttons are the rectangular objects, starting with OK and Cancel, along the upper right edge of the dialog box.

You can move between elements of a dialog box most easily with a mouse, but pressing the Tab key also moves you to the next element. Pressing Shift-Tab moves you back to the previous element.

Most dialog boxes have a command button that you click after you've filled out the dialog box to your satisfaction and another button that you click if you want to back out of the dialog box without making an entry. In many cases (as in the two examples shown above), these buttons are marked OK and Cancel, respectively. But you might also see verbs such as "Save" or "Accept" for the OK button and "Escape" for the Cancel button.

In some applications, you might find dialog boxes where the Cancel button has been omitted (probably to conserve space or memory). In such dialog boxes, you can generally press either Esc or Alt-F4 to back out without making an entry.

Other Dialog Box Elements

In the section of a dialog box where you enter information or choose options, you'll encounter the following kinds of elements:

- Text boxes

- List boxes

- Drop-down list boxes

- Option buttons

- Check boxes

Text boxes are a place for you to type something. The big rectangle next to the words Find What in the following illustration is an example of a text box.

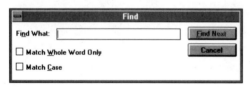

Note that the term *text* here doesn't mean words only, as opposed to numbers. In some text boxes, you will be expected to enter numbers—or perhaps both words and numbers.

Occasionally you may find a text box that already has text in it. Such text is called a *default entry*, or *default value*. A default entry is an entry proposed by your application program. If you're satisfied with that entry, you can simply leave the text box alone to accept it.

To fill out a text box, first click the mouse in the box. You'll then see a flashing vertical line, which is called an *insertion point*. If the text box is empty, the insertion point appears at the left side of the box. If the box already contains text, the insertion point is located at the spot where you clicked the mouse. The insertion point then marks the spot where the characters you type appear.

A *list box* presents a set of options in the form of a list, like this:

Typically, the options in a list box are mutually exclusive, but they may not always be so. In the printer cartridge list shown above, for example, you can select zero, one, or two cartridges.

If the list contains more items than can be displayed at once in the list box, you will find a *scroll bar* at the right side of the list box. (The example above includes a scroll bar.) You can move through the list one item at a time by clicking on the arrows at the top and bottom of the scroll bar. (Chapter 3 has more information about scroll bars.) You can also move through a list box by pressing the Up and Down direction keys, PgUp, or PgDn.

 KEYBOARD TIP: Another way to move quickly through a list box is to press the first letter of the item you want to move to. Pressing F, for example, takes you directly to the first item beginning with F. If you're already on an item starting with F, pressing F takes you to the next item beginning with that letter—and so on. This technique works in all Windows list boxes and works with numbers as well as letters. It's usually the most efficient way to navigate in a large list.

To select an item in a list box with the mouse, simply click on the item you want. To select with the keyboard, use direction keys or any other method to move the highlight to the item you want.

In list boxes where you're allowed to select more than one item, the technique for making a multiple selection varies somewhat from application to application. Consult the documentation for the program you're using if you're not sure how to proceed.

A *drop-down list box* is an ordinary list box displayed in a more compact space. The following illustration shows four drop-down list boxes.

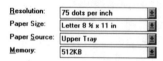

You can recognize a drop-down list box by the underlined arrow on the right. Click the mouse on that arrow (or press Alt-Down), and an ordinary-looking list box unfolds:

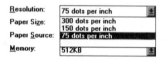

When the drop-down list box has opened up, it behaves exactly like a normal list box.

 KEYBOARD TIP: You can use the first-letter method of navigating through a drop-down list box without first opening the list box.

Option buttons (sometimes called *radio buttons*) present a set of mutually exclusive options. The following pair of option buttons lets you choose between portrait and landscape orientation when printing on a LaserJet Series II.

The distinguishing feature of a set of option buttons is the circle next to each option name. One option in each group—the currently selected option— has a darkened circle. Option buttons get their nickname because they work like station-selector buttons on a car radio.

To select an option button, simply click the item you want to select. Usually, you don't have to click in the circle itself; clicking anywhere on the associated text also works.

To select an option button with the keyboard, look for an underlined letter in the text associated with the option you want. Then hold down the Alt key and press that letter. To select Portrait orientation in the preceding illustration, for example, press Alt-P.

If the option you want doesn't have an underlined letter, press the Tab key until one of the options in the group is encircled by a dotted line. Then press the direction keys until the item you want has the darkened circle.

Option buttons always come in groups of two or more and have circles beside them. *Check-box* items may come either in groups or one at a time and are marked by squares instead of circles. The following example includes two check-box items.

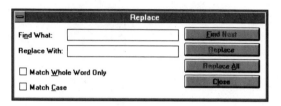

A check box is a ballot with two choices—yes and no. An X in the box means you accept the option indicated by the associated text. An empty box means you reject that option.

To select (put an X in) a check box, click the mouse on the box or the associated text. To remove the X, click again.

To select a check box with the keyboard (or deselect one that's currently selected), look for an underlined letter in the associated text. Hold down the Alt key and press that underlined letter. If the text has no underlined character, press Tab until the option is encircled. Then press the Spacebar.

Some check boxes have *three* states—checked, unchecked, and gray. Usually, this means that a certain condition applies to some of a selection, but not all of it. For example, in the following illustration, some of the selected cells in a Microsoft Excel worksheet have been formatted italic. The rest of the cells are in normal type. In the Format Font dialog box, therefore, the Italic check box is gray.

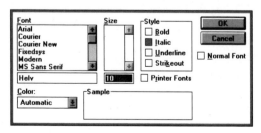

If a Dialog Box Gets in the Way

Many, though not all, dialog boxes appear in windows with title bars and Control menus. Like ordinary application and document windows, such dialog boxes can be moved. You usually can't change their size, however. Moving a dialog box is sometimes useful; you may need to see what lies beneath it.

If the dialog box has a Control menu, you can use it as an alternative way to back out of the box without making an entry. Simply double-click the Control-menu icon. Or press Alt, Spacebar and choose the Close command from the Control menu.

3
Working with Documents

A *document* in Windows is a file you create with a Windows application. A picture drawn in Paintbrush is a document, for example; so is a memo written in Notepad, a budget report formulated in Wingz, or a project file created in Visual Basic.

Many Windows applications display documents in separate document windows. Document windows allow you to work with more than one document at a time in the same application.

Here is a picture of the application Microsoft Word for Windows with two document windows, named NEWS.DOC and ARTICLE.DOC:

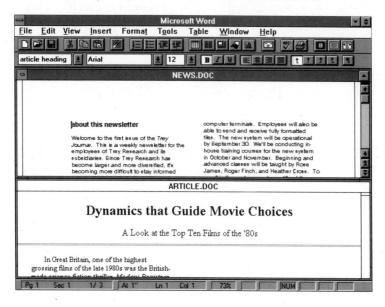

Some programs can't handle more than one document at a time. These programs do not use document windows. The desktop accessory Notepad is an example.

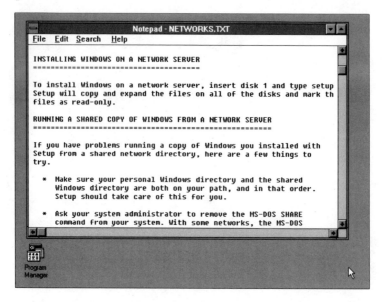

In this illustration, Notepad displays a document called NETWORKS.TXT. The text of this document appears in Notepad's own application window, and the title of the document is displayed alongside the word *Notepad* in the window's title bar.

In this chapter we'll start by exploring the characteristics of document windows. Then we'll look at some basic procedures for working with text and graphics in Windows documents.

MANIPULATING DOCUMENT WINDOWS

As you'll recall from Chapter 1, document windows can be sized and moved, maximized and restored, exactly as application windows can. In some programs, they can also be reduced to icons.

The mouse procedures for maximizing, sizing, and moving a document window are exactly like those for an application window. To change a document window's size or position with the keyboard, you can use commands on the document window's Control menu. To open that menu, press Alt, Hyphen.

KEYBOARD TIP: Another key combination you can use to open a document Control menu is Alt, Minus. (Use the minus sign on your numeric keypad.)

A typical document Control menu looks like this:

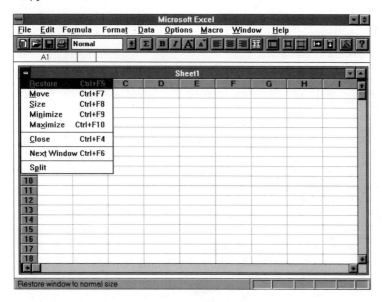

Notice that this menu is full of keyboard shortcuts. Unfortunately, not all document Control menus are so generously endowed.

Restoring a Maximized Document Window

When a document window is maximized, it merges with the application window to which it belongs, like this:

The two windows now share a common set of borders. The title bars are merged, and two symbols from the document window—the document Control-menu icon and the document window's restore button—now appear at the left and right ends, respectively, of the application window's menu bar.

When you want to restore the document window, be sure to click on the document window's restore button, rather than on one of the application window's sizing buttons.

Some maximized document windows don't have restore buttons. The following is an example.

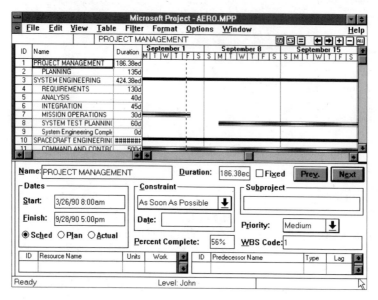

To restore a document window like this, you have to open the document Control menu (or use a keyboard shortcut, if one is available). Simply click the little dash to the left of the menu bar or press Alt, Hyphen. Then choose the Restore command.

Switching Between Document Windows

When you have several document windows open at once in an application, one window is said to be *active* or *current*. The active document window is analogous to the foreground application window (see Chapter 1). It's the window in which the program assumes you're currently working.

In the following illustration, the document window titled SALESTOT.XLS is active.

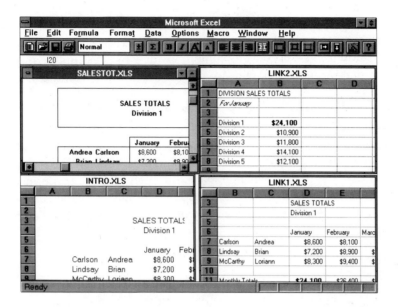

Notice that the active window's title bar is displayed in a distinctive color or pattern, exactly as the title bar for the foreground application window is. Notice, too, that Windows removes the Control-menu icon and sizing buttons from the inactive document windows.

Using the mouse, you can make a different document window active by clicking in that document window. In the illustration above, for example, you can switch to LINK2.XLS by clicking anywhere within that window's borders.

To switch document windows with the keyboard, press Ctrl-F6. This key combination works with document windows the way Alt-Esc works with application windows: It cycles through each open document window in turn.

Many applications that use document windows also have a Window command on their menu bars. Typically the Window drop-down menu looks something like this:

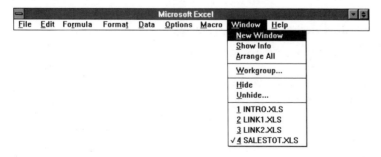

One part of the menu, usually the bottom part, lists all open document windows by name, with a check mark next to the document window that's now active. You can switch to a different document window by pressing the number associated with that window or by clicking the window's name with the mouse.

Stacking, Cascading, Arranging, and Tiling Document Windows

Applications that have Window menus sometimes include commands for cascading and tiling document windows. As you'll recall, *cascading* windows means setting them in a stack, like a fanned hand of cards. *Tiling* windows means setting them side by side so they fill the available space without overlapping one another.

In some programs, cascading is called *stacking*, and tiling is called *arranging*. For example, in the preceding illustration (from Microsoft Excel), the Arrange All command tiles the open document windows.

Closing a Document Window

You can close a document window either with the File menu's Close command (if your application has such a command) or with the Close command on the document Control menu. Ctrl-F4 is a keyboard shortcut for the document Control menu's Close command. If you haven't saved the document, your program will ask if you want to do so.

So much for working with document windows. Now let's look at some general procedures for working with the documents themselves, whether they appear in document windows or application windows.

USING SCROLL BARS

If a document is too long to be displayed completely within the confines of a window, Windows adds a *vertical scroll bar* to the right side of the window. If the document is too wide to be displayed entirely, Windows adds a *horizontal scroll bar*. If it's both too deep and too wide, Windows adds both kinds of scroll bar. The illustration on the following page shows a window with vertical and horizontal scroll bars.

Scroll bars provide an easy way to navigate through a document with the mouse. They also indicate your current position relative to the length or width of the document.

Notice the square boxes in the scroll bars shown in the following illustration. In the vertical scroll bar, the box is about a third of the way down the length of the bar. That means that the text you're looking at is about a third of the way into the document. Similarly, the position of the box in the horizontal scroll bar tells you that you're looking at the left edge of the document.

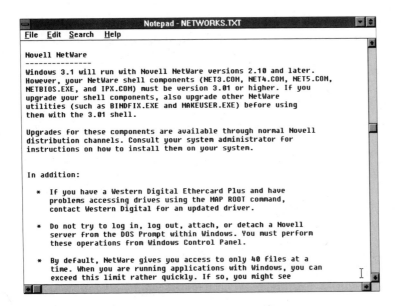

You have several ways to scroll with a scroll bar:

■ To move up or down a line at a time, simply click the arrow at either end of the vertical scroll bar. To move side to side a character at a time, click the arrow at either end of the horizontal scroll bar.

■ To move several lines at once (or several characters), click an arrow and hold the mouse button down. When you arrive where you want to be, release the mouse button.

■ To move by a larger increment (by approximately one windowful), click the mouse in the scroll bar itself. To move up, click above the box in the vertical scroll bar; to move down, click below the box. To move left, click to the left of the box in the horizontal scroll bar; to move right, click to the right of the box.

■ To move to a specific location, drag the box. To move directly to the last lines in the document, for example, drag the box to the bottom of the vertical scroll bar.

MOUSE TIP: Windows also uses scroll bars in dialog boxes. They work exactly the same way there as they do in windows that display documents.

SCROLLING WITH THE KEYBOARD

In most applications, you can scroll the contents of a document a line at a time by pressing the Up and Down direction keys when you reach the edge of the window. To scroll by larger increments, use PgUp and PgDn. In most applications that work with text, you can jump directly to the end of the document by pressing Ctrl-End or to the beginning of the document by pressing Ctrl-Home.

CREATING, OPENING, AND SAVING FILES

Nearly all Windows applications use a similar set of procedures for creating a new file, loading an existing file from disk into memory, and saving a file to disk. We'll look at those procedures now, using Notepad as an example.

The File Menu

Because file operations are such a basic and indispensable part of working with applications, nearly every Windows program puts its File menu on the left side of the menu bar where it's easy to find. Notepad's File menu looks like this:

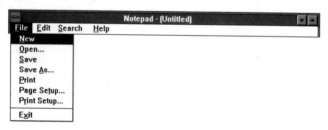

Notepad's File menu is typical of many Windows programs. It has three basic command groups: a set of commands for moving files between disk and memory (New, Open, Save, and Save As), a group of commands for printing (Print, Page Setup, and Print Setup), and an Exit command.

Creating a New File

The New command, in Notepad and many other Windows applications, allows you to create a brand new document. In programs that use document windows,

New generally opens a new, blank document window. In programs (such as Notepad) that don't use document windows, New erases any document currently in memory and presents you with an empty window in which to create a new document. If you haven't saved the document currently in memory, your program will warn you—and give you an opportunity to save—before removing the current document.

Loading an Existing File from Disk into Memory

To load an existing file from disk into memory, use the File menu's Open command. Your program will present a dialog box something like this:

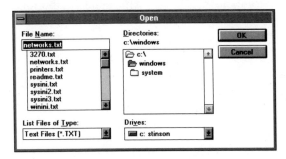

In addition to the usual command buttons, this dialog box has a File Name text box and four list boxes. Let's take a quick tour.

The File Name text box is a place where you can type the name of the file you want to load—if you happen to know its name and don't mind typing. If you prefer, you can select the name of your file from the accompanying list box.

In most programs, the File Name text box starts out by displaying a *wildcard specification*—an asterisk followed by a period, followed by a three-letter filename extension. In the illustration above, Notepad's dialog box displays the specification *.TXT, because the *default filename extension* for Notepad (the extension the program uses if you don't tell it to do otherwise) is TXT. If your program's dialog box includes a list box labeled *List Files of Type* (or something similar), you might be able to use this list box to change the wildcard specification. Opening the file-type list box in Notepad, for example, reveals the following choices:

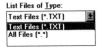

If you wanted to open a file with an extension other than TXT, you could click the All Files entry. The dialog box would then list all files in the current directory. The options available in the file-type list box vary from program to program. Some programs, such as Notepad, offer you a choice of the program's "native" file type (TXT, in this case) or files of any extension. Other programs, such as Paintbrush, have several native file types and so offer a larger assortment of file-type choices.

 WINDOWS TIP: Some programs allow you to enter two or more wildcard specifications, separated by semicolons, in the File Name text box. For example, if you type *.TXT;*.INI in Notepad's File Name text box, the accompanying file list includes files with either extension. If the program you're working with does not support this option, it simply ignores the second and subsequent wildcard specifications.

When the file you want to open is listed in the files list box, you can open it in any of the following ways:

- Double-click the filename.

- Click once on the filename. Then, with the filename highlighted, click the OK button.

- Press the Tab key until you see a dotted line around the first name in the file list, like this:

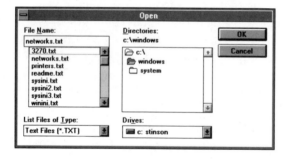

Use the Up and Down direction keys to highlight the name of the file you want. Then press Enter.

KEYBOARD TIP: To open the first file in the file list, press Tab until the dotted line appears around that filename. Press the Spacebar to highlight the name, and then press Enter.

If the file you want to open is not stored in the current directory, you can use the Directories list box to change directories. In the illustration above, for example, the current directory is C:\WINDOWS, and the dialog box lists all TXT files in that directory. To open a file in the SYSTEM directory, a subdirectory of C:\WINDOWS, you could double-click the SYSTEM entry in the Directories list box. The file list would then present the names of all TXT files in C:\WINDOWS\SYSTEM. To open a file in the root directory, you would double-click on the entry at the top of the Directories list, C:\.

If the file you want to open is not stored on the current disk drive, use the Drives list at the bottom of the dialog box. You'll find all your local drives listed here (complete with volume labels, if any), along with all connected network drives. After switching drives, you can pick the appropriate directory from the Directories list and the file from the File Name list.

NOTE: *The style of File Open dialog box illustrated above was introduced with Windows 3.1 and will probably be used by more and more Windows programs as time passes. Programs written for earlier versions of Windows typically use a more compact form of dialog box in which your system's disk drives and directories are presented together in a single list. In this older style of dialog box, the names of your disk drives appear at the bottom of the list, enclosed within brackets. The parent directory of the current directory is signified by two periods within a pair of brackets.*

Saving a File for the First Time

To save a file that you've just created—a file that's never been saved on disk before—use the File menu's Save or Save As command. It doesn't matter which you choose; either way, you get a dialog box similar to the illustration shown on the following page.

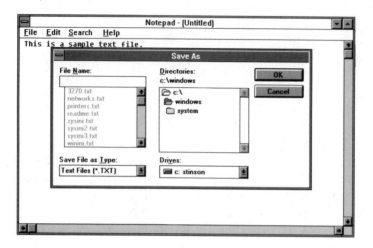

This dialog box looks like the File Open dialog box, except that the file-names in the list box on the left are all grayed out. This is Windows' way of telling you what filenames are already in use. Type the name under which you want to save your new file, and click OK or press Enter. (If you type the name of an existing file, Windows presents a warning message and asks you to confirm that you want to overwrite the existing file.)

 MOUSE TIP: If you *do* want to replace an existing file with the document in memory, click the file's name to put the name in the File Name text box.

After you've saved a file, most Windows applications display the name of your file in the title bar of the file's document window (if the program uses document windows) or in the title bar of the application itself. Until the file has been saved that first time, programs typically display the word *(untitled)* in their title bars.

Resaving a File

After you save a file at least once, you can save it again simply by choosing the file menu's Save command. You won't see a dialog box when you do this, because Windows already knows the name of the file.

Saving a File Under a New Name

To save a file on disk under a new name, use the File menu's Save As command. You'll see the current name highlighted in the Save As dialog box.

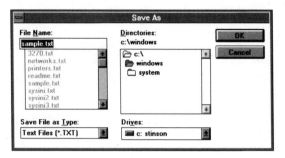

Simply type the new name for your file, and press Enter (or click the OK button).

 WINDOWS TIP: When you use the Save As command to give a file a new name, the version of the file that you saved most recently under the old name remains on disk.

COPYING, MOVING, AND RENAMING FILES

The most effective way to copy, move, or rename documents is to use the File Manager program. File Manager is described in Chapter 6.

ENTERING AND EDITING TEXT IN WINDOWS DOCUMENTS

Unless you happen to be concerned only with visual images, you will probably spend much of your time in Windows entering and editing text. This is true whether your primary application is word processing, financial planning, database management, project management, communications, or something else altogether. Even though Windows is a graphical environment and uses your computer's graphics display modes, the information you work with consists primarily of letters and numbers—in other words, text.

Fortunately, a basic set of concepts and procedures applies to text work in most Windows applications.

The Insertion Point

The flashing vertical line that you see whenever you work with text in a Windows program is called the *insertion point.* It's analogous to the cursor in a non-Windows word processing program. The insertion point indicates where the next character you type will appear.

There's one difference between the insertion point and the cursor in most non-Windows programs: The insertion point is always positioned *between* two characters, *before* the first character in a block, or *after* the last character in a block. It never appears directly under a character. That's because characters are always *inserted* at the insertion point; they don't overstrike existing text.

In the following illustration, for example, the insertion point is located between the *i* and the *n* in the word *tiny.*

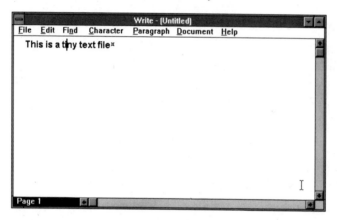

To replace existing text with new characters that you type, Windows uses a different concept, called *selection.* We'll see more about selection in a moment.

The I-Beam

When you work with text, Windows changes your mouse pointer from an arrow to something that looks like a lanky capital *I.* The pointer is then usually called an *I-beam.* In the illustration above, you can see the I-beam near the lower right corner of the window.

The I-beam provides a way to relocate the insertion point. In the tiny text file above, for example, if you want to move the insertion point to the beginning of the line, simply use the mouse to position the I-beam before the capital *T,* and then click. (You can also use the keyboard to move the insertion point, as we'll see in a moment.)

When you're typing text, you may sometimes find the I-beam distracting. If that happens, simply use the mouse to move the I-beam out of your way. It doesn't matter where you put it.

The Selection

To *select* something in Windows means to highlight it—with the keyboard or mouse. In the illustration below, for example, the word *tiny* has been selected.

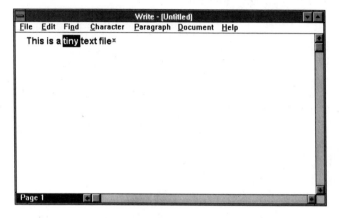

The object that you select is called the *selection*.

You might select a block of text for any of several reasons:

- To apply a formatting change to the entire block at once (In the illustration above, for example, if you choose Write's Underline command after selecting the word *tiny*, the entire word is underlined.)

- To *copy, cut,* or *delete* the entire block at once

- To replace the entire block at once

Notice that there's no insertion point in the illustration above. The insertion point disappears when you make a selection, because the next character you type *replaces* the entire selection.

Positioning the Insertion Point

As mentioned, the easiest way to move the insertion point is with the mouse. Simply put the I-beam wherever you want the insertion point, and then click.

You can also use the keyboard. The following keystroke combinations apply to all Windows applications that work with text.

- The Right and Left direction keys move the insertion point forward and backward a character at a time. Ctrl-Right and Ctrl-Left move forward and back a word at a time.

- End moves the insertion point to the end of the line. Home moves it to the beginning of the line.

- The Up and Down direction keys move the insertion point up and down a line at a time.

- PgUp and PgDn move up and down a windowful at a time.

- Ctrl-End moves to the end of the document. Ctrl-Home moves to the beginning of the document.

Some applications use additional keystroke combinations for moving the insertion point. In Microsoft Word for Windows, for example, pressing Ctrl-Down takes you to the first word in the next paragraph, and Ctrl-Up takes you to the beginning of the previous paragraph.

Selecting Text

To select text with the mouse, put the I-beam at one end of the block you want to select. Then hold the mouse button down, move to the other end, and release the mouse button. In other words, simply drag the mouse across the text you want to select. You can select a word by double-clicking anywhere in it.

To select text with the keyboard, first put the insertion point at one end of the block you want to select. Then hold down the Shift key and *extend* the selection to the other end of the block. The same keystrokes you use to move the insertion point extend the selection.

For example, to select three characters within a word, you put the insertion point before the first character, and then hold the Shift key down while pressing the Right direction key three times. To select an entire word, put the insertion point to the left of the word, hold down the Shift key, and press Ctrl-Right. To select from the insertion point position to the end of the line, hold down the Shift key and press End—and so on.

Some programs implement additional keyboard and mouse procedures for selecting text. In Write, for example, if you position the mouse pointer to the left of a line of text and then click, the entire line is selected. If you put the mouse pointer to the left of a line, hold down the Ctrl key and then click, Write selects the entire document.

Erasing Characters

To erase a few characters of text, put the insertion point where you want to make the deletion. Then use the Backspace or Del key to make your corrections. Backspace deletes characters to the left of the insertion point; Del removes characters to the right of the insertion point.

Erasing Blocks of Text

To erase a block of text, first select the block. Then do one of the following:

- Press Del or Backspace.
- Choose the Edit menu's Delete or Clear command (if your application's menu has such a command).
- Choose the Edit menu's Cut command.

Pressing Del or Backspace simply removes the selected text. Choosing Delete or Clear from the Edit menu does exactly the same thing. Choosing the Cut command, however, does something quite different. It removes the text from your document but stores it in an area of memory called the Clipboard. After the selection has been stored on the Clipboard, you can *paste* it somewhere else—either within the same or another document (even in a document created by a different application).

NOTE: *The Clipboard, which is fully explained in Chapter 8, can store only one selection at a time. When you choose Cut, the current contents of the Clipboard is replaced by the new selection.*

Undoing a Deletion

Many applications include an Undo command on their Edit menus. This command gives you an opportunity to change your mind about a deletion. The Undo command usually can reverse only your most recent edit, however. So, for example, if you delete a line of text, and then apply a formatting command to a different block of text, you won't be able to use the Undo command to reverse your deletion; at this point the Undo command is poised to undo the formatting change, not the deletion.

Copying and Moving Text

The Clipboard makes it easy to copy or move text from one place to another. Follow these steps.

1. Select the text you want to move or copy.

2. To move, choose the Edit menu's Cut command. To copy, choose the Edit menu's Copy command.

3. Move the insertion point to the place where you want to move or copy your text.

4. Choose the Edit menu's Paste command.

This simple procedure can be used to move or copy text from one place to another in the same document, from one document to another created by the same application, or from one application to an entirely different application.

For more information about using the Clipboard, see Chapter 8.

WORKING WITH GRAPHICS

A few generalizations can be made about entering and editing material in graphics documents.

First, most graphics programs provide a set of *tools* for adding objects to an image or editing existing objects. Typically, the tool set is presented as an icon *toolbox* alongside or below the program's work area. In the following illustration, which shows the desktop accessory Paintbrush with a blank canvas, the toolbox is the set of icons to the left of the canvas.

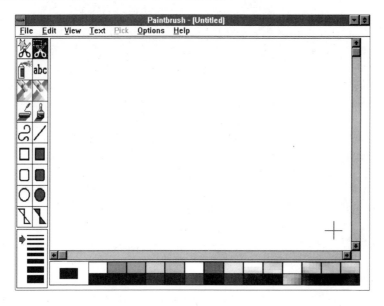

The icon with the diagonal line, about halfway down the toolbox, is a *line tool* and allows you to add straight lines to the drawing. The rectangles, rounded rectangles, and circles below the line tool allow you to create various kinds of shapes, and so on. You choose a tool from the toolbox by clicking on its icon or using the keyboard's Tab and direction keys.

Notice the big cross in the lower right corner of the work area. That's the graphics equivalent of a text window's I-beam. You move the cross with the mouse to tell the program where you want to position a new object or modify an existing one. (Graphics programs commonly use other pointer shapes in addition to the cross. The shape of the pointer typically varies with the kind of graphics tool you're using.)

Graphics programs, like text programs, employ the concept of the selection. In Paintbrush, for example, you can select a rectangular portion of an image by using the *pick* tool—the scissors with the rectangle in the upper right corner of the toolbox. In the following illustration, a chessman has been selected (it's enclosed in the dotted rectangle), and that portion of the image can now be cut or copied to the Windows Clipboard.

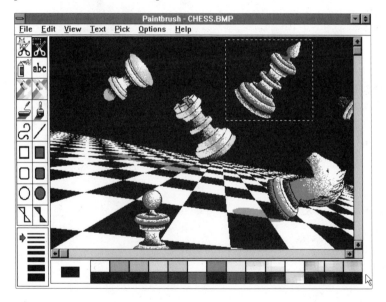

A graphics image cut or copied to the Clipboard can be pasted into another graphics image (or into a different part of the same image) or into a text document, provided the text application is able to accept images. The desktop accessory Write is an example of a text program that can handle graphics pasted from the Clipboard.

When a portion of an image has been selected, it can be manipulated in various ways, just as selected text can be formatted all at once in a text document. Here, for example, the selected chessman has been turned on its head.

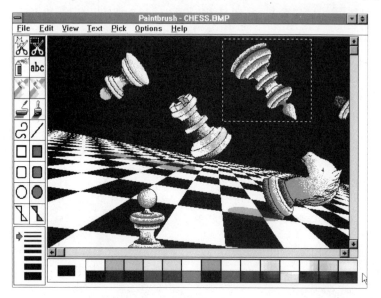

PRINTING WINDOWS DOCUMENTS

As mentioned earlier in this chapter, most Windows applications include printing commands on their File menus. If your printer is correctly set up, you can print a document simply by choosing the File menu's Print command and filling out the ensuing dialog box (if any).

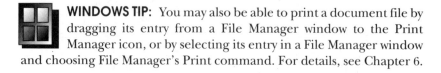

WINDOWS TIP: You may also be able to print a document file by dragging its entry from a File Manager window to the Print Manager icon, or by selecting its entry in a File Manager window and choosing File Manager's Print command. For details, see Chapter 6.

Most programs also have a command on the File menu for setting page dimensions and margins, as well as a command that lets you change the setup of your printer or choose between printers if you have more than one installed.

For details about printing in Windows, see Part IV of this book.

4

Getting Help

Most Windows applications include a Help menu as the rightmost command on the menu bar. Any time you're unsure how a feature or command works, you can pull down the Help menu and find useful information.

One of the major improvements introduced with version 3 of Windows was a special help facility that application developers could use if they chose. Because most of the newer Windows programs do use this facility, finding help in one program is essentially the same process as finding help in any other.

The Windows help facility is a hypertext system, which means that it lets you jump easily from one topic to another while keeping track of the path you follow. The system includes a Search command to help you find exactly the topic you're looking for, a Bookmark command with which you can flag topics of particular interest, an Annotate feature that lets you add your own comments to the built-in help text, a Copy command that lets you replicate important help messages in Notepad or your word processor, and a Print command to convey screen text onto paper.

In this chapter, we'll take a quick tour of the Windows 3.1 help system, using the help text for Program Manager as an example.

THE HELP MENU

When you pull down Program Manager's Help menu, you see the following.

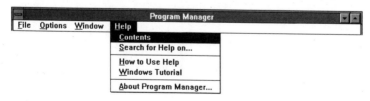

Notice that the menu is in three sections. The top section provides information specifically about Program Manager. The center section includes information about the help system itself, as well as an interactive tutorial on the Windows environment. The bottom section consists of a single command, called About, that provides version and copyright information about the current application. In this example, the command reads About Program Manager. In some programs, this command also displays other useful information, such as the amount of available memory and disk space you have and whether or not your system includes a math coprocessor.

In most of the shells, utilities, and accessories shipped with Windows 3.1, the About command also tells you what operating mode you're working in (standard or 386 enhanced), the name of the software's registered user, the amount of memory available, and the percentage of system resources available. The latter two bits of information can be particularly valuable for troubleshooting purposes. Any time you suspect you're running low on memory, you can switch to Program Manager, File Manager, or one of the Windows accessories, and choose the About command. If your suspicion turns out to be correct, you can free up memory by closing a few applications.

Accessing the Help Facility

The remainder of the commands on the Help menu summon various sections of your application's help text. When you're first getting to know an application, a good place to start exploring the help text is with the index or table of contents. If you choose Contents on Program Manager's Help menu, the following window appears.

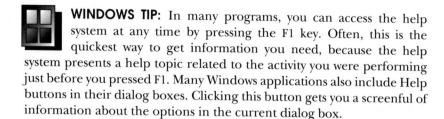 **WINDOWS TIP:** In many programs, you can access the help system at any time by pressing the F1 key. Often, this is the quickest way to get information you need, because the help system presents a help topic related to the activity you were performing just before you pressed F1. Many Windows applications also include Help buttons in their dialog boxes. Clicking this button gets you a screenful of information about the options in the current dialog box.

WINDOWS TIP: If you are using Windows on a multimedia PC, you may find an icon labeled HyperGuide in your Main program group. HyperGuide is a somewhat more elaborate and interactive version of the Windows help system. The help-text files, stored on your Windows with Multimedia CD-ROM disk, cover all the shells, games, accessories, and utility programs included in your Windows package.

Notice that Help appears in a full-fledged application window, complete with its own menu bar. You can maximize it and minimize it the same way you can any other Windows application.

WINDOWS TIP: While you're learning a new application, you might want to keep its help text available on your desktop. You can use Alt-Tab to switch quickly back and forth between the program and its help window. Alternatively, by selecting the Always On Top command, on the Help window's own Help menu, you can ensure that the help text remains visible no matter what you do within your application.

The help window belongs to an application called WINHELP.EXE. The text inside the window is a document file with the extension HLP. If you want to switch to a different program's help text, you can do so by using WINHELP's File Open command and choosing another HLP file.

Notice that some of the text in the help window appears in a contrasting color and underlined. These are *keywords.* If you position the mouse pointer on or beside one of these keywords, the pointer changes from an arrow to a hand. To see at a glance what keywords are available in the current help window, hold down the Ctrl key and Tab key.

Keywords provide access to additional information. If you click the mouse while the hand is pointing to *Organize Applications and Documents*, for example, you get the following window.

From this window you can click on another key phrase to get specific information about any listed topic. In the illustration above, for example, a click of the mouse button on *Creating and Deleting Groups* will bring up a screenful of text about adding and removing program groups in Program Manager.

 KEYBOARD TIP: If you don't have a mouse, you can use the Tab key to skip from keyword to keyword. To get information about a topic, select its keyword, and then press Enter.

KEYWORDS WITH DOTTED UNDERSCORES

Keywords underscored by a dotted line are defined terms, as opposed to major topics. Clicking a defined term pops up a definition window without changing the underlying screen. When you have finished reading the definition, you can remove the definition window by clicking the mouse again.

KEYBOARD TIP: To pop up a definition window with the keyboard, press Tab to select the underscored term. Then press Enter. To remove the definition window, press Enter again.

Some programs' help files include a Glossary button. Clicking this button gets you a listing of all defined terms in the help text.

FINDING PARTICULAR TOPICS
WITH THE SEARCH COMMAND

Scanning through a help document's index is one way to find particular topics in which you're interested. You can redisplay the index at any time by clicking the Contents button (or by reinvoking the Help Contents command in your application).

Another way to find a particular topic is to click the Search button or press Alt-S. When you do this, you see a display similar to the following illustration.

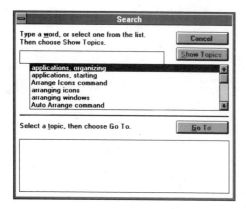

The upper window in this dialog box lists the concepts and commands described by all the various topics in the current help document. When you select a concept and click the Show Topics button, the bottom window reveals the names of all topics that discuss the selected concept. In Program Manager's help document, for example, if you select *starting applications* and click the Show Topics button (or press Enter), five topics appear in the lower window.

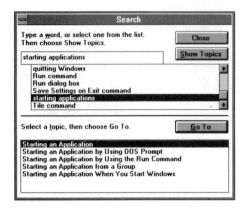

To read one of these topics, select its name in the lower box, and click the Go To button (or press Enter).

 KEYBOARD TIP: A quick way to move directly to a concept in the Search command's upper window is simply to begin typing in the text box. As you type, Windows searches through the list and displays those concepts beginning with the letters you have typed.

RETRACING STEPS WITH THE BACK AND HISTORY BUTTONS

A hazard of using some hypertext-style information systems is that you can lose your way while exploring the web of interrelated topics. You may want to reread the screen you looked at moments ago, but not remember how to get back to it.

Fortunately, the Windows help system keeps track of every move you make. You can retrace your steps at any time, simply by clicking the Back command button or pressing Alt-B.

You can also use the History button to revisit a topic you read earlier without tracing through all the intervening steps. Clicking History (or pressing Alt-T) presents a list of the topics you've displayed in the current Windows session.

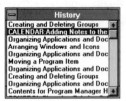

Both the Back command and the History command can take you from the current help document to a document you've read earlier in the current Windows session. As you can see in the illustration above, topics from applications other than the current application are prefixed by a program name. To return to a topic you read earlier, double-click its name. Or select it and press Enter.

USING THE BROWSE COMMAND BUTTONS

Some help documents implement a pair of arrow buttons, one pointing left, the other pointing right. These buttons provide "browse" services for the current document, moving you between logically related topics. When you're first learning a new Windows application, check to see if its help document includes these browse buttons. They offer an excellent path to learn about your new program's features.

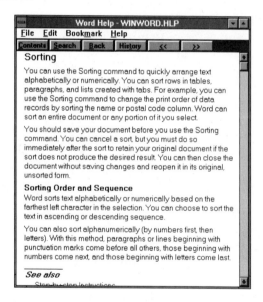

SETTING BOOKMARKS

The Back and History commands are useful for revisiting topics you've read during the current working session, but they won't help you relocate some information you found useful three days ago. If you want to have certain topics at your fingertips at all times, you might want to flag them with a bookmark. To do this, first display the topic. Then pull down the Bookmark menu, and choose Define. You'll see a dialog box like the following illustration.

The top part of this dialog box displays the name of the topic you're looking at. The bottom part lists any bookmarks you've previously defined in the current help document.

To define the bookmark, click the OK button or press Enter. If you want, you can change the name of the bookmark before clicking OK.

After you define a bookmark, the name of that bookmark appears on the Bookmark menu, with a number next to it—like this:

To find your way back to the flagged topic, simply pull down the Bookmark menu, and choose the appropriate item.

PRINTING HELP TOPICS

The Print Topic command, on the File menu, does just that—prints all of the current help topic on the default printer. To print to a different installed printer, first choose the File menu's Print Setup command, and then select the printer you want to use from the list that appears.

COPYING INFORMATION FROM THE HELP SYSTEM

To copy some information from a help document into another Windows application, first display the information you want to copy. Then choose the Edit menu's Copy command. You'll see a dialog box like the following.

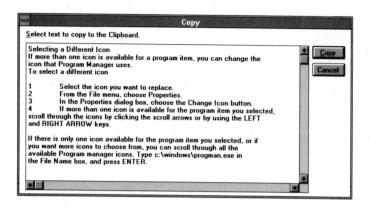

The dialog box displays and highlights the entire text of the current help topic. To copy the entire topic, simply click the Copy button. To copy a portion of the topic, select the part you want to copy, and then click the Copy button.

The Copy button transfers a copy of the selected text to the Windows Clipboard. To move the information into another application, simply use that application's Paste command. (For more about copying and pasting information in Windows, see Chapter 8.)

USING THE ANNOTATE COMMAND TO ADD YOUR OWN HELP MESSAGES

The Edit menu's Annotate command allows you to add your own text to a help document. To annotate a help topic, first display that topic. Then pull down the Edit menu and choose Annotate. The dialog box that appears has a large area in which you can type your comments. Here's how it might look with an annotation for the Change Properties topic:

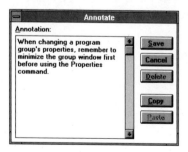

After you fill out the Annotation dialog box and click Save or press Alt-S, a paper-clip icon appears to the left of the annotated topic.

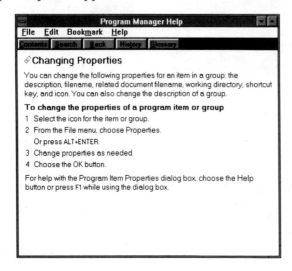

To reread your annotation, click the paper clip—or tab to it and press Enter.

GETTING HELP ON HELP

Because the help facility is an application in its own right, it has its own help document. You can get help about using Help in either of two ways:

- Within any application that uses the help facility—Program Manager, for example—pull down the Help menu and choose How To Use Help.

- Within the help facility itself, pull down the Help menu and choose How To Use Help. (Pressing F1 is a keyboard shortcut for this method.)

Either way you access it, the help facility appears with a document called WINHELP.HLP.

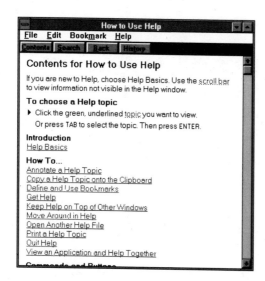

By far the best way to learn what the help facility can do and how it works is to wander through all the nooks and crannies of WINHELP.HLP. That way, you'll be using the system and reading about it at the same time.

PART II

THE WINDOWS SHELLS

Every working session in Windows 3.1 begins and ends in one of Windows' shell programs—Program Manager or File Manager. Your shell program begins automatically when you run Windows. When you quit the shell, your Windows session ends.

But the shell programs do more than start and end a Windows session. They help you organize programs and files, and they provide a way to start the applications you use in Windows.

Because different users have different needs and preferences, Windows 3.1 gives you your choice of shells. When you first install Windows, your shell is Program Manager. But you can switch shells at any time if you prefer to use File Manager.

The next two chapters show you how to use Program Manager and File Manager, so you can select the shell that's right for you.

5

Managing Programs with Program Manager

Program Manager is the default shell supplied with Windows 3.1. That means each working session in Windows starts in Program Manager—unless you take deliberate steps to change matters. And when you're ready to quit Windows at the end of a day, you do so by quitting Program Manager.

In addition to starting and ending your Windows sessions, Program Manager serves two vital purposes: It gives you a simple way to start applications, and it makes it easy for you to organize your programs and documents into logical working groups.

PROGRAM GROUPS AND PROGRAM ITEMS

Program Manager's application window contains one or more document windows called *program groups*. Each program group contains icons called *program items*. (See the following illustration.) You start a program from Program Manager by selecting its program-item icon and pressing Enter or, more simply, by double-clicking the program-item icon. You can select a program-item icon either by using the direction keys or by clicking on it with the mouse.

 KEYBOARD TIP: You can also select a program-item icon by pressing the first letter of its name. This navigation method works the same way in a program-group window as it does in any Windows list box.

Program groups

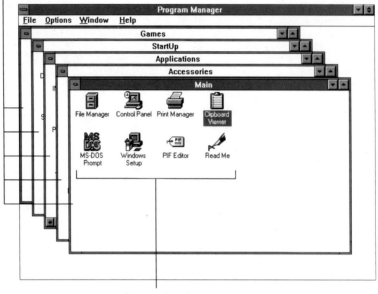

Program items

A program item can be *associated* with one or more specific document files, so that the program automatically loads the specified document(s) into memory when you start the program. For example, if you frequently use the spreadsheet application Microsoft Excel with two worksheets named EAST.XLS and WEST.XLS, you could create a program item to start Microsoft Excel with both worksheets already in place. Or if you have a half dozen worksheets you use more often than any others, you might create separate program items for the combination of Microsoft Excel and each of those worksheets.

Program Manager is extremely malleable; you can set it up in whatever manner best serves your working style, and you can easily modify your setup as your needs change. Program Manager lets you organize your applications and documents in logical groups. These groups have nothing to do with the directory structure on your hard disk. (To reorganize your files as they're stored on your hard disk, use File Manager.)

WINDOWS TIP: Any program items you store in a program group named Startup are automatically launched at the beginning of each Windows session. See "Using the Startup Program Group," later in this chapter.

PROGRAM GROUPS CREATED WHEN YOU INSTALL WINDOWS

When you installed Windows, the Windows Setup program created at least four program groups for you. It put icons for certain essential Windows programs—including Control Panel, File Manager, Print Manager, Clipboard Viewer, and Setup itself—in a program group called Main. For the two Windows games, Minesweeper and Solitaire, Setup created a group called Games. And it lumped together the remaining tools supplied with Windows—Notepad, Write, Terminal, Calculator, and so on—in a group called Accessories. Setup also creates a group called Startup, which is used for programs that you want to start automatically each time you start Windows (see "Using the Startup Program Group," below).

As the last step in the installation process, Setup offered to search your hard disk for other applications it might recognize—programs that did not come with your Windows package. For those it found, Setup created another program group, called Applications. So, for example, if you had Lotus 1-2-3 Release 2.3, Micrografx Designer, and WordPerfect on your hard disk when you ran Setup, you probably now have icons for those programs in your Applications group.

Using the Startup Program Group

A program group with the name Startup gets special treatment by Program Manager. Any program items in this group are automatically launched at the beginning of every Windows session. Items for which you've checked the Run Minimized box are launched as icons (see "Starting a Program Item as an Icon," later in this chapter); the others are launched as open windows.

Earlier versions of Windows let you run programs automatically at the start of a session by modifying the WIN.INI file (see Chapter 9). You can still do this in Windows 3.1. (Windows launches the programs listed on the *load=* and *run=* lines of WIN.INI first, and then launches the program items in your Startup group.) But using the Startup group is a lot simpler than modifying WIN.INI.

 WINDOWS TIP: To make it easy to switch to Program Manager at any time, put a copy of your Program Manager launch icon in your Startup group and assign it a keyboard shortcut. (See "Assigning a Shortcut Key," later in this chapter.)

 WINDOWS TIP: To start a Windows session *without* launching the programs in your Startup group, hold down the Shift key while the Windows startup logo is on your screen.

WORKING WITH GROUP WINDOWS AND ICONS

Program-group windows are ordinary document windows in all respects but one. They can be maximized, moved, sized, restored, and minimized. (The exception is that you can't close them. If you double-click the Control menu for a program group, Program Manager minimizes the group window.) When program groups are minimized, their icons all look alike, except for the identifying text beneath them.

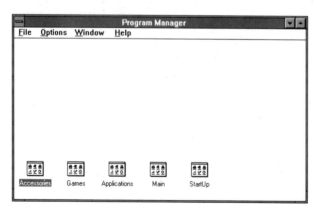

Minimizing program groups that you're not using lets you focus on the one(s) you are.

Using the Window Menu

The Window menu, shown in the following illustration, has commands for each of your program groups, so you can activate any group window by choosing the appropriate command.

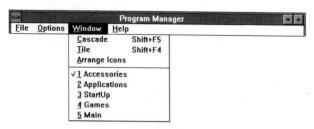

You can also use the Window menu to cascade or tile all or some of your program-group windows. The Cascade and Tile commands affect open windows only, so you could minimize the groups you don't currently need and tile the rest, like this:

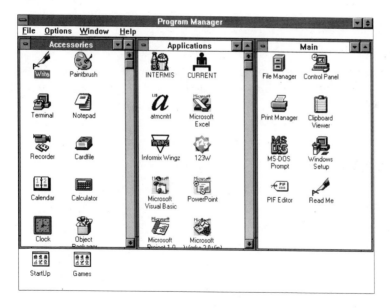

Choosing the Tile command with only one program group open makes that group as large as it can be without covering the other groups' icons.

Arranging Program Items

With the mouse, you can drag program-item icons from one place to another within a program group. Thus, for example, if you use particular programs more often than others, you can put their icons in the upper left corner of a window. If you have several icons for the same program (each associated with a different document file), you can put them all together—and so on.

Getting icons lined up neatly with the mouse can be a trial, though, so Program Manager's Options menu includes a command called Auto Arrange. If this command is selected (that is, if a check mark appears beside it), Windows will automatically keep your icons in orderly rows any time you rearrange them. If you elect not to use the Auto Arrange command, you can still tidy up the current program group at any time by using the Arrange Icons command on the Window menu.

The Arrange Icons command is also useful for straightening up the icons that represent closed program groups. If your program-group icons get out of line, simply select any one of them, pull down the Window menu, and choose Arrange Icons.

CHANGING YOUR PROGRAM GROUPS

You're not limited to using the program groups created by the Setup program. You can add new groups, rename groups, or delete groups to suit your needs.

Creating New Program Groups

The steps to create a new program group are as follows:

1. Choose the New command from the File menu.

2. In the New Program Object dialog box, choose Program Group and click OK.

    The following dialog box appears.

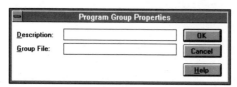

3. In the Description text box, type a name for the new group.

4. In the Group File text box, type a legal filename. Don't include an extension; Program Manager automatically uses GRP.

Step 4 is optional. The Group File text box records the name of an MS-DOS file in which Program Manager stores information about the contents of your program group. If you leave the Group File box blank, Program Manager fills that out for you, using the first eight characters of what you put in the Description box, plus the extension GRP.

5. Click OK.

 WINDOWS TIP: When you first install Windows, Program Manager is organized by application type. Accessories furnished with Windows are in one group, other applications in another, and so on. Other organizational schemes are possible and might serve your needs better. For example, you can create program groups for each broad category of your work. If you're primarily a spreadsheet user, you can have a group called Budgeting, another called Forecasting, and so on. If you're a self-employed professional, you can create a separate group for each of your clients. The possibilities are endless.

Renaming Program Groups

To rename a program group, follow these steps:

1. Minimize the program-group window you want to rename.

2. Click once on the group's icon.
   The Control menu for the program-group window pops up. You can ignore it.

3. Choose the File menu's Properties command.
   The Program Group Properties dialog box appears.

4. Enter a new name in the Description text box, and click OK.

 KEYBOARD TIP: To rename a program group with the keyboard, first minimize the program group's window. Then press Ctrl-Tab or Ctrl-F6 until the group's icon is highlighted. Then choose the File menu's Properties command, and fill out the dialog box.

Deleting Program Groups

To delete a program group:

1. Minimize the program-group window you want to delete.

2. Click the mouse on the group's icon.

3. Choose the Delete command from the File menu.
   Windows presents a confirmation prompt.

4. Click OK to confirm the deletion.

Be careful when deleting program groups. When you delete the group, you delete all the program items inside as well. You won't delete any files on disk (other than the GRP file that contained the program group information) when you delete a program group, but if you take out the wrong group by mistake, you have to rebuild it from scratch.

CUSTOMIZING PROGRAM ITEMS FOR YOUR APPLICATIONS

It's easy to modify program groups and program items as your needs and preferences change. You can rearrange the furniture at any time with a few simple mouse actions.

Moving Program Items Between Program Groups

The easiest way to move program items is by dragging with the mouse. Alternatively, you can use the File menu's Move command.

As an example, suppose you use the Windows Terminal program often, but you seldom use Write, Notepad, or any of the other desktop accessories that came with your Windows package. In this circumstance, you might prefer to move the Terminal icon from your Accessories group (which you rarely use) to your Applications group.

To move Terminal with the mouse, you could proceed as follows:

1. Set up Program Manager so that your Accessories and Applications windows are both open. (One easy way to do this would be to minimize all your other program groups and then use the Tile command.)

2. Put the mouse pointer on the Terminal icon.

3. Hold the mouse button down and drag Terminal to the Applications group.

4. Release the mouse button.

If you prefer working with the keyboard, you can perform the move as follows:

1. Make Accessories the active program group.

2. Press T to select the Terminal icon.

3. Press Alt, F, M to choose the File menu's Move command.
   Program Manager presents the following dialog box.

4. Press Alt-Down to open the drop-down list box, and then use the Down direction key to select Applications.

5. Press Enter.

 WINDOWS TIP: If your Windows system files are stored on a network server, your network administrator might have made your program groups "read only." In this case, you will see an error message if you try to move, copy, create, or delete program items.

Copying Program Items

Copying a program item is as easy as moving it. With the mouse, simply hold down the Ctrl key while you drag the item from one window to another. With the keyboard, select the item you want to move. Then use the File menu's Copy command. This command works exactly like the Move command, described in the preceding paragraphs.

 WINDOWS TIP: You can copy a program item within a program group as well as between program groups. You might want to create several copies of an application's item within the same window, and then modify some of them to associate different document files with the application. See "Changing a Program Item's Properties," later in this chapter.

Creating New Program Items

To add a new program item, begin by activating the group window in which you want the new item to reside. Then pull down the File menu, and choose New. Program Manager presents the following dialog box.

The default option is Program Item, so all you need to do is click OK, or press Enter. You see the following dialog box.

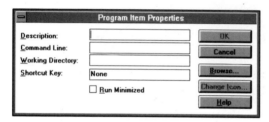

The information you supply in this dialog box constitutes your program item's *properties*. Only one property is mandatory—the Command Line. If you leave the other areas of the dialog box blank, you can always come back later and fill them out—or change them. (See "Changing a Program Item's Properties," later in this chapter.)

Describing Your Program Item

In the Description text box, type whatever you want to appear beneath your new program-item icon. In Windows 3.0, it was advisable to keep the description short so that your icon labels would not overlap one another. But Windows 3.1 wraps long descriptions onto two or three lines if necessary, so you no longer need to be so terse.

You can enter from 0 through 40 characters in the Description text box. If you leave the box blank, Program Manager will supply a description for you.

Specifying the Command Line

The Command Line text box is where you tell Program Manager what you want it to do when you launch your new program item. You must supply something in this part of the dialog box; the OK button will be grayed until you do.

To launch a program by itself, without a particular document file, simply enter the name of that program's executable file. For example, suppose you want to create an item that launches the Wizzy Word Processor from WizzyWare, Inc. If the executable file for this program is named WZ.EXE and you've stored it in your Windows directory, you would type *wz.exe* in the Command Line text box.

If the executable file is not stored in your Windows directory but is stored in a directory included in your MS-DOS PATH environment variable, you can omit the path in the Command Line text box. It's a good idea to type the complete path, however. That way, Windows will always be able to start your program, even if you subsequently change the contents of the PATH variable.

If you don't happen to know what directory your program's executable file is stored in, if you aren't sure how to spell its name, or you just don't feel like typing, you can call on the Browse button for help. Click Browse, and Program Manager presents a dialog box like this:

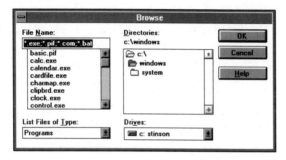

This dialog box looks and works just like the File Open dialog box described in Chapter 3. When you select a filename and click OK, you'll be returned to the Program Item Properties dialog box with your command line in place.

Specifying a Working Directory

The Working Directory text box gives you the opportunity to make a particular directory current when Windows starts your program. You might want to fill out this line if you expect to use documents stored in a particular directory. For example, you could create a program item tailored to working with Microsoft Excel files stored in your C:\PERSONAL directory by entering *c:\personal* in the Working Directory text box.

Assigning a Shortcut Key

A shortcut key lets you switch easily to the program or document launched by your new program item. For example, if you assign Ctrl-Alt-W and Ctrl-Alt-S as shortcuts for your word processor and spreadsheet, respectively, you can switch between those programs quickly and easily, just by pressing the appropriate key combinations.

A shortcut key also makes it a little easier to launch your program item. As long as Program Manager itself is the active window and at least one of your program groups is open (it can be any group; it doesn't have to be the one that contains the item you want to launch), you can launch a program item by pressing its shortcut key. So if you use a lot of program groups and have trouble remembering which one contains which programs, try assigning shortcut keys and memorizing them instead!

Program Manager allows you to assign the following combinations as keyboard shortcuts: Ctrl-Alt-*Key*, Ctrl-Shift-*Key*, Shift-Alt-*Key*, or Ctrl-Shift-Alt-*Key*, where *Key* can be anything other than Esc, Backspace, Enter, Tab, Del, Shift, Alt, or Ctrl. To assign a keyboard shortcut, simply move the insertion point to the Shortcut Key text box, and press the key combination you want.

When you close the Program Item Properties dialog box, Program Manager checks to be sure you haven't assigned your new item a shortcut key that's already in use. If you have, you'll see a warning message, and you'll have an opportunity to choose a different shortcut. "Overbooking" your shortcut keys is legal but inadvisable.

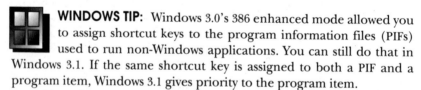

WINDOWS TIP: Windows 3.0's 386 enhanced mode allowed you to assign shortcut keys to the program information files (PIFs) used to run non-Windows applications. You can still do that in Windows 3.1. If the same shortcut key is assigned to both a PIF and a program item, Windows 3.1 gives priority to the program item.

To avoid unintentional duplication of shortcut keys, it's good strategy to avoid assigning shortcut keys to PIFs in Windows 3.1. Instead, create a program item for each PIF and assign a shortcut key to the program item.

WINDOWS TIP: To assign a shortcut key to Program Manager itself, create a program item for Program Manager in your Startup program group. Then assign it a shortcut key the same way you would any other program item.

Starting a Program Item as an Icon

If you want your program item to be launched as a minimized window, put a check in the Run Minimized box. This option is particularly handy for program items launched via the Startup program group.

Creating Program Items with File Manager

If you have a mouse, you can create new program items by opening File Manager and dragging filenames from one of File Manager's windows into a Program Manager program group. For details, see Chapter 6.

Using the Setup Program to Create Program Items

When you first installed Windows, the Setup program created program items for the Windows and non-Windows applications that it recognized on your hard disk (if you selected the Set Up Applications option). If you chose to bypass this step or if you've added new programs to your system since you installed Windows, you might want to rerun Setup and let it search your hard disk again.

You can rerun Setup whenever you please. Simply double-click its icon in the Main program group. For details about using Setup to create program items, see Appendix A.

Creating Program Items to Launch Documents

Windows maintains a list of *associations* between document filename types and the applications in which the documents are created. It knows, for example, that files with the extensions WRI and TRM belong to Write and Terminal, respectively. Any filename whose extension is included on the associations list can be launched directly from a program item.

For example, let's say you use Terminal once or twice a day to log onto MCI Mail, a public electronic mail service. You've created a Terminal document, called MCIMAIL.TRM, that specifies the MCI Mail telephone number, the communications settings you use to dial this service, your password, and so on. (See Chapter 15 for details about using Terminal.)

Because you regularly use the same application (Terminal) with the same document (MCIMAIL.TRM), you can make your life a little easier by connecting the two in a single program item. It's easy to do:

1. Activate the Accessories program group (or whichever program group you want your MCI Mail item to reside in).

2. Open the File menu, choose New, choose Program Item, and press Enter.

3. In the Description text box, type the text you want to appear under the MCI Mail icon.

4. In the Command Line text box, type *mcimail.trm*.

5. Fill out the remainder of the dialog box as appropriate, and then click OK.

Program Manager adds your MCI Mail program item to the Accessories program group.

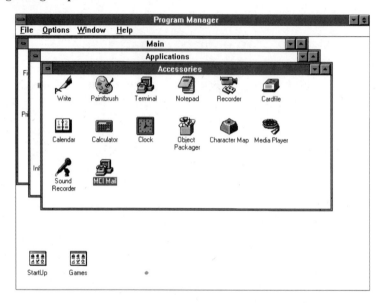

If you're not sure whether an association exists for the type of document you want to launch, go ahead and create the program item on the assumption that it does. If you're mistaken, you'll get a polite error message. Click OK to return to the Program Item Properties dialog box. Then amend the Command Line entry to include the name of your program as well as the document file you want to launch.

For example, suppose you attempt to create a program item for REPORT.WZ, a document created by your Wizzy Word Processor. If the extension WZ hasn't been associated with WZ.EXE, Program Manager responds with an error message. Click OK to acknowledge the message, and then change the Command Line text box to read

wz.exe report.wz

To add to or change the associations list, you can use File Manager's Associate command. See Chapter 6 for details.

 WINDOWS TIP: If your Windows application can work with two or more documents at once, you can create program items that launch multiple documents. To do this, specify the name of the executable file (even if an association exists for the type of document you want to launch), followed by the name of each document. Separate the names with space characters. For example, to load Microsoft Excel with the worksheets EAST.XLS and WEST.XLS, you could create a program item with the following command line:

c:\excel\excel.exe east.xls west.xls

Changing a Program Item's Properties

The File menu's Properties command lets you change the properties associated with a program item. You might want to do this for any of several reasons: because you've moved a program's executable file to a new directory, because you want an item to launch a different document file, because you want to change the descriptive text that appears under the item's icon, or because you want to change the icon itself. Whatever your reason, choosing the Properties command takes you back to the same dialog box you filled out when you created the item, allowing you to make the appropriate modifications.

 WINDOWS TIP: You can also get to the Properties dialog box by selecting an icon, holding down the Alt key, and pressing Enter. Or you can hold down the Alt key and double-click the item.

Changing a Program Item's Icon

Ordinarily, when you create a new program item, Program Manager uses the same icon that the application itself uses when minimized. But if the program happens to use other icons for other purposes, you can select one of those other icons for your program item instead. For example, the time-management program Ascend uses the following symbol as its main icon—the one that appears at the bottom of the screen when you minimize Ascend.

But it also uses numerous other icons as shortcuts for various commands within Ascend. You could select any one of the program's many icons to represent Ascend in your program group.

To change the icon assigned to a program item, invoke the Properties dialog box, as described above. Then click the Change Icon button. You'll see a dialog box similar to the following.

Select the icon you want to use (use the scroll bar to bring additional icons into view if necessary), and then click OK twice—once to return to the Properties dialog box, a second time to return to Program Manager.

Using External Icons

The dialog box that appears when you click Change Icon includes a File Name text box. The default entry in this box is the name of the program whose item you're modifying. By entering a different filename here, you can appropriate an icon from another program. For example, if you happen to like the calculator icon used by the Norton Desktop better than the one that Windows supplies for its Calculator desktop accessory, you could select the Calculator item, press Alt-Enter to invoke the Change Properties dialog box, and then click Change Icon. In the File Name text box, then, you could type *\ndw\sicalc.exe* (the name of the Norton Desktop calculator's executable file) and click OK. Program Manager would respond by displaying SICALC's icon. Two more OK clicks, then, and you'd have Norton's icon for your Windows calculator.

 WINDOWS TIP: In your Windows directory, you'll find a file called MORICONS.DLL that includes dozens of useful icons. PROGMAN.EXE (Program Manager's executable file) also contains many useful icons for a variety of applications. Some of these icons are particularly suitable as alternatives to the default MS-DOS icon that Windows assigns to non-Windows applications. To sample the contents of these icon files, use the Properties command, click the Change Icon button, specify MORICONS.DLL or PROGMAN.EXE on the File Name line, and then scroll through the list of icons that appears.

You can also link a program item to an icon that is not part of an executable file—for example, to an icon that you create yourself with an icon-editor program. Many public bulletin boards and online information services (such as the WINNEW and WINADV forums on the CompuServe Information Service) have public-domain or shareware icons available for downloading. Such icons may be stored in stand-alone files (common extensions are ICN and ICO) or in icon-library files. Simply specify the name of the file containing the icons in the Change Icon dialog box, and then choose an icon from the scrollable display.

Deleting Program Items

Because program items take up a fair amount of space in your program-group windows (and also consume system resources), it's a good idea to delete them when they're no longer needed. To delete a program item:

1. Activate the program group containing the item you want to delete.

2. Select the item by clicking on it or highlight it with the direction keys.

3. Press Del, or pull down the File menu and choose Delete.

4. Click Yes to respond to the confirmation prompt.

WORKING WITH NON-WINDOWS APPLICATIONS

You can start a non-Windows application (a program not created specifically to run in the Windows environment) from Program Manager the same way you start a Windows application—by double-clicking its program-item icon. Non-Windows applications do not use memory the same way Windows applications do, however, so you need to know about some special considerations when running such programs. For details, see Chapter 18.

Creating a Program Item for a Non-Windows Application

The Command Line text box of the Properties dialog box for a non-Windows program item can specify either the program's executable file (which may have the extension EXE, COM, or BAT) or a *program information file* (PIF) set up for that program. A PIF is a special file that tells Windows such things as how much memory the program needs, whether the program uses expanded memory, whether it runs in text mode or graphics mode, and so on. Some programs come supplied with their own PIFs, or you can create PIFs with the help of a Windows utility called PIF Editor. (PIFs and PIF Editor are described in Chapter 18.) PIFs have the extension PIF.

If you create a program item that specifies the program's executable file, Windows runs that program as though you had created a PIF for it with default settings. Most non-Windows applications run fine this way, although they might not use your system's memory in the most efficient way possible. Windows might give them more memory than they need, reducing the amount available for other programs.

Probably the simplest way to add a program item for a non-Windows application is to rerun the Setup program and let Setup create the item for you (see "Using the Setup Program to Create Program Items," earlier in this chapter). Setup maintains a list of popular non-Windows programs. If yours is on that list, Setup creates a PIF for you and sets up the program item to start your program from the PIF instead of the executable file.

If Setup doesn't install your non-Windows program, try creating a program item that specifies the program's executable file. If the program doesn't run the way you expect it to from that program item (or from one that Setup creates), skip ahead to Chapter 18 for information about creating and editing PIFs.

 WINDOWS TIP: Program Manager assigns all non-Windows programs a default icon using a familiar five-letter acronym. You can use the Change Icon command to differentiate your MS-DOS program items. See "Using External Icons," earlier in this chapter.

Associating a Document with a Non-Windows Application

If your non-Windows application can accept the name of a document (data) file as a command-line parameter, then you can associate a program item for it with a document, as you can with a Windows application.

The simplest way to associate a document file with an existing non-Windows program item is as follows:

1. Copy the program item as it stands without the associated file-name.

2. Select the copied program item.

3. Press Alt-Enter to invoke the Program Item Properties dialog box.

4. With the mouse, click in the Command Line text box, to the right of whatever now appears there. (With the keyboard, press Tab. Then press the End key to place the insertion point to the right of the text on the Command Line.)

5. Type a space, followed by the name of your document file. Then click OK or press Enter.

 WINDOWS TIP: Some non-Windows applications accept other kinds of command-line parameters, in addition to names of document files. For example, the parameter /L causes Microsoft Word 5.0 or 5.5 to load the last file you were working with. You can include such parameters with your program items, in the same way as you can include document filenames.

Running the MS-DOS Prompt from Program Manager

One of the program items in your Main program group (as set up by the Setup program) is labeled MS-DOS Prompt. If you double-click this icon, Windows clears the screen and presents the same prompt you would see if you quit Windows and returned to MS-DOS.

After invoking the MS-DOS prompt this way, you can run most non-Windows applications the same way you would if you were not using Windows. You can run MS-DOS utilities, such as DIR and TYPE, as well as full-blown applications such as 1-2-3 or WordPerfect. And you can switch at any time between your non-Windows application and whatever Windows programs you're running, simply by pressing Alt-Tab.

WARNING: *It is not safe to run CHKDSK with the /F parameter while Windows is running. If you need to use CHKDSK /F, quit Windows first.*

If you run a non-Windows application this way, you need to do two things to shut that program down and return permanently to Windows:

1. Use your non-Windows application's normal quit command.

2. At the MS-DOS prompt, type *exit* and press Enter.

Note that because Windows is still running, if you try to return to Windows by typing *win*, you will receive an error message from Windows.

STARTING PROGRAMS WITH THE RUN COMMAND

Program items are the most convenient way to start programs that you use frequently. When you want to run a program only once—as, for example, when you want to run the installation program for a new software package—you'll probably find it simpler to use the File menu's Run command. When you choose this command, Program Manager presents the following dialog box.

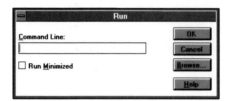

Enter the name of your program in the Command Line text box. Check the Run Minimized box if you want the program to start as an icon instead of an open window (you might want to do this if your program doesn't require input from you or if you're not planning to work with the program immediately). Then click the OK button.

If your program is not stored in the current directory or in a directory included in your MS-DOS PATH environment variable, be sure to include the full path specification in the dialog box.

 WINDOWS TIP: To be sure that Windows runs the appropriate executable file, it's best to include the file's extension in the Command Line text box. If you omit the extension, Windows searches for files with the extensions listed on the *programs=* line of your WIN.INI file (the WIN.INI file is discussed in Chapter 9), following the order in which those extensions are listed. The default extension set is COM, EXE, BAT, and PIF.

Finding Files with the Browse Button

If you need some help filling out the Command Line text box, click the Browse button. You'll see the dialog box pictured on page 81. When you select a filename in the Browse dialog box and click OK, Windows takes you back to the Run dialog box, with the selected name in place. All you need to do then is hit the OK button one more time to run your program.

THE MINIMIZE ON USE COMMAND

After you've used Program Manager to start a program, it's nice to have Program Manager out of the way (unless you immediately need to launch another program). If you select the Minimize On Use command, on the Options menu, Program Manager automatically reduces itself to an icon each time you launch a program.

QUITTING PROGRAM MANAGER

Quitting Program Manager (by closing its window) is like quitting any other Windows application, with one exception. If Program Manager is your default shell (the program that first appears when you start Windows), quitting Program Manager terminates your session in Windows.

Program Manager's Options menu includes a Save Settings On Exit command. If you have selected this option (if a check mark appears beside it), Program Manager records the positions of each of your group windows and will restore your group layout at the start of your next session. Program Manager also saves the size and position of its own window, including whether it is minimized or maximized. Note that this setting concerns only the layout of your group windows. Any changes you have made to the content of those windows are preserved regardless of whether you choose Save Settings On Exit.

WINDOWS TIP: If you use the Save Settings On Exit feature and you exit Windows while Program Manager is minimized (by selecting the Close command from the minimized icon's Control menu), Program Manager will be minimized the next time you start Windows. If you want to ensure that Windows always starts with the Program Manager window restored, create a program item for Program Manager in the Startup group.

WINDOWS TIP: You can save Program Manager's window size and position settings without quitting Windows. To do so, hold down the Shift key while you select the Exit command from Program Manager's File menu. This method allows you to set the windows the way you want them, save the information to disk, and not worry about subsequent changes being inadvertently saved when you quit Windows (be sure to deselect the Save Settings On Exit option).

Program Manager will close any open Windows applications when you issue the Exit command, but it won't close any non-Windows programs. (One exception: If you run Windows in 386 enhanced mode, a non-Windows application whose PIF has the Allow Close When Active option selected may be terminated by Program Manager; see Chapter 18.) If you have forgotten to close a non-Windows application when you quit Program Manager, you see an *alert box* like this:

Click OK to acknowledge the box, and then quit your non-Windows program.

6

Managing Files, Directories, and Disks with File Manager

Like Program Manager, File Manager is a Windows shell program. That means you can use it as a launchpad for starting other programs and documents. If you make File Manager your *default shell* (see the instructions in Chapter 9), your Windows sessions will begin and end with File Manager.

File Manager is a great deal more than a program starter, however. As its name implies, it's designed to help you work with the organization of files on your hard disk, file servers, and floppy disks. Here are some of the "housekeeping" chores you can do with File Manager:

- Copy, move, delete, or rename files

- Search for files on local or remote hard disks

- Assign files to be "read only," so they can't easily be deleted or changed

- Print files directly, without starting the application in which they were created

- Create, delete, or rename directories

- Copy entire directories

- Format system and data disks

- Copy floppy disks

- Assign volume labels to hard disks or floppy disks
- Connect to or disconnect from a network file server

 WINDOWS TIP: One of File Manager's main purposes is to help you manage files and directories on your hard disk. If you're brand new to MS-DOS as well as to Windows, you might want to get some background for using File Manager by reading the sections of your MS-DOS manual that discuss files and directories.

STARTING FILE MANAGER

To start File Manager from Program Manager, follow these steps:

1. Activate the Main program group by clicking on the Main window, by choosing the Main command on the Window menu, or by pressing Ctrl-Tab until Main is the active window.

2. Double-click the File Manager icon.

Alternatively, you can use the Run command on Program Manager's File menu. Specify WINFILE.EXE in the Command Line text box.

FILE MANAGER'S WINDOWS

The first time you run File Manager, you'll see a display similar to the one in the illustration on the following page. (File Manager lets you customize its display in many ways, so on subsequent runs, it might look quite different from this illustration.)

Inside File Manager's application window you see a document window named C:\WINDOWS*.* (or whatever the current directory is on your system). This document window behaves like others you've seen so far, with one exception: It's divided into two *panes*. The left pane shows the directory structure for the current disk, while the right pane shows the contents of the current directory. In this book, we'll call the left pane the *tree pane* and the right pane the *directory pane*. The directory pane shows the contents of the directory whose name is selected in the tree pane.

At the top of the document window, you see icons for each drive on your system. At the bottom of the application window, you see a status bar, which reports information about items selected in the current document window.

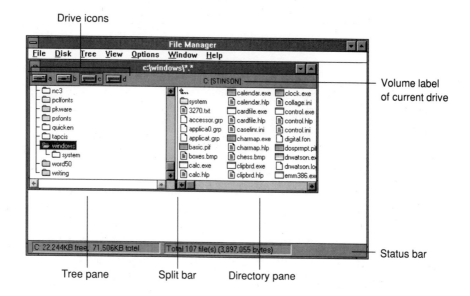

Drive icons

Volume label of current drive

Status bar

Tree pane   Split bar   Directory pane

You can change the contents of File Manager's windows in all sorts of ways. For example, you can eliminate the division into two panes, so that you see only the tree structure for a disk or only the files contained in a particular directory. You can also open more windows so that you see two—or several—directories at once. We'll look at all these options in the course of this chapter.

Icons Used by File Manager

The illustration above shows a system with four drives: two floppies (A and B) and two local hard disks (C and D). As you can see, the drive icons at the top of the window distinguish these types of drives. If your system includes a RAM disk, one or more network drives, or a CD-ROM drive, you will find distinguishing drive symbols for these as well.

In File Manager's tree panes, directories are symbolized by two kinds of folder icons, a closed folder and an open folder. The open folder (WINDOWS in the tree pane of the illustration above) simply denotes the currently selected directory; it says nothing about whether or not the current directory has subdirectories.

A folder icon in a directory window also indicates a directory, but here it always means a subdirectory of the current directory. For example, the directory pane in the illustration above shows one folder icon, for a directory named SYSTEM. This is a subdirectory of the current directory, WINDOWS.

At the top of a directory pane, you might see an upward-pointing arrow with two dots next to it. This is your "go-back" icon; it represents the current directory's parent directory.

File Manager uses the following symbols to distinguish file types:

The rectangle with the stripe across the top indicates an executable, or program, file. These are files with the extensions BAT, COM, EXE, or PIF.

The dog-eared page symbol with horizontal lines across it represents a document file. A document file, you may recall, is a data file that has been associated with an application. You can launch a document by double-clicking its icon. In the figure on page 95, for example, the files with extensions TXT, BMP, HLP, and INI are documents. The TXT files and INI files are associated with Notepad, the BMP files are associated with Paintbrush, and the HLP files are associated with the Windows help facility. So, for example, double-clicking the filename 3270.TXT opens a copy of Notepad with 3270.TXT ready for reading and editing; double-clicking BOXES.BMP opens Paintbrush and loads the bitmap file named Boxes—and so on.

Looking at a File Manager directory window won't tell you what programs your documents are associated with. But the Associate command, described later in this chapter, supplies that information. It also allows you to change associations or create new ones.

The dog-eared page symbol *without* horizontal lines represents an unassociated data file. Examples in the illustration on page 95 include the files with extensions GRP and FON. The GRP files contain data about your Program Manager groups, and the FON files contain font information. In both cases, the data contained by the file cannot be viewed or edited directly, so these files are not associated with a particular application.

A page symbol with an exclamation point inside represents a file that has either the hidden attribute, the system attribute, or both. These attributes are generally assigned to files that are critical to functioning of your system. Because deleting or altering such files is likely to have disastrous consequences, File Manager doesn't ordinarily include them in its directory displays. You can override this default by choosing the View menu's By File Type command, described later in this chapter.

Changing the Directory Display

Seeing the directory structure of your hard disk at a glance may be edifying, but the tree pane's real purpose is to make it easy to change the contents of the directory pane. Select a new directory in the tree, and File Manager immediately displays that directory's files and subdirectories in the directory pane.

You can also change the contents of the directory pane without going to the tree pane. Double-click a subdirectory name to switch to that subdirectory. Or select the subdirectory name with the keyboard, and press Enter. To display the parent directory, double-click the upward arrow icon at the top of the directory pane—or select it and press Enter.

Navigating in the Tree Pane

You can move about the tree pane quickly with the mouse, either by clicking on the directory you're interested in or by scrolling with the scroll bars and then clicking. But often you'll find it even quicker to use the keyboard. Directories that share the same level in the tree are always listed alphabetically, and you can move between them the same way you move in any other Windows list, by pressing the first letter of the directory name you want to move to.

The first time you use File Manager, the tree pane shows the current disk's structure to two levels of detail. That is, you'll see the root directory and all of the root's immediate subdirectories. To "open" a directory so that its own subdirectories are visible, you can either double-click that directory or move to it with the keyboard and then press Enter. (Repeat this process to close the directory and hide the names of its subdirectories.)

File Manager's Tree menu also has a set of commands to help you manage the level of detail shown in the tree pane.

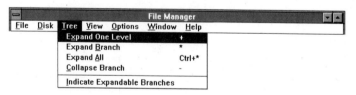

Use Expand One Level or press the plus key to reveal the immediate subdirectories of the current directory. Use Expand Branch or press the asterisk key to reveal *all* subdirectories of the current directory. Use Collapse Branch or press the minus key to hide subdirectories of the current directory. And, if you want to see your directory tree in all its detailed glory, press Ctrl-asterisk or choose Expand All. Be aware that if your disk is large, you may need to wait a few moments for File Manager to build its full tree display.

WINDOWS TIP: If you choose the Expand All command and get tired of waiting for File Manager to create its full tree display, press the Esc key or click one of the drive icons. File Manager interrupts its directory scan and displays as much of the tree as it has built to that point. The warning message "Incomplete Tree Displayed" appears at the bottom of the directory pane in place of the text that normally indicates the free and total disk space available.

The last option on the Tree menu, Indicate Expandable Branches, puts File Manager into a mode that mimics the File Manager of Windows 3.0. Plus and minus signs mark the icons beside directory names that can be expanded or collapsed. You might find this information useful, but File Manager will perform a little more slowly.

The direction keys work in ways that should be pretty self-evident. The Right and Left keys, for example, take you down and up a level in the directory hierarchy, respectively. Backspace does the same duty as Left. The Up and Down keys move between adjacent names. To move between nonadjacent names at the same level (skipping over intervening subdirectories), press Ctrl-Up or Ctrl-Down.

 KEYBOARD TIP: To get from anywhere in the tree to the root directory one level at a time, press Left or Backspace repeatedly. To get directly to the root, press Home.

Changing the Drive Display

To change the current File Manager window so that it shows the tree and contents of a different drive, click once on the appropriate drive icon. (You can also double-click, but that opens a new window, leaving the current one on screen.) If you're without a mouse, you can hold down the Ctrl key and press the drive letter you want to switch to. For example, to display the tree and contents of drive D, press Ctrl-D.

Another way to change the drive display is to choose the Disk menu's Select Drive command.

WINDOWS TIP: Because the Select Drive command's dialog box lists the volume labels associated with each available disk drive, you might find it the easiest way to switch to a network drive—particularly if you don't remember which of several drive letters has been assigned to which server.

Changing the Size of File Manager's Panes

The first time you run File Manager, the program divides the screen real estate roughly equally between the tree pane and the directory pane. If your tree pane is displaying only two hierarchical levels (the root directory and the first-level subdirectories) though, that equal division doesn't make a lot of sense. You'd probably rather have a narrower tree pane and a wider directory pane. Fortunately, you can redistribute the screen space at any time.

To adjust pane size with the mouse, put the pointer over the *split bar*—the narrow vertical bar to the right of the tree pane's vertical scroll bar (see the first illustration in this chapter). When the mouse is positioned correctly, the pointer changes to a two-headed arrow. Now drag the split bar to the left to widen the directory pane or to the right to widen the tree pane.

To adjust pane size with the keyboard, choose the View menu's Split command. A dark vertical bar will appear within your document window.

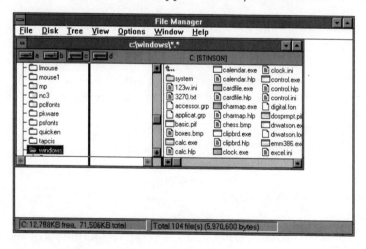

Use the Left and Right direction keys to reposition this split bar, and then press Enter.

Displaying Only One Pane at a Time

By dragging the split bar all the way to the left or right side of your document window, you can get rid of either pane altogether. That way, you can concentrate entirely on the file contents of a directory or the directory structure of a disk. You can also use commands on the top section of the View menu to eliminate one pane or the other.

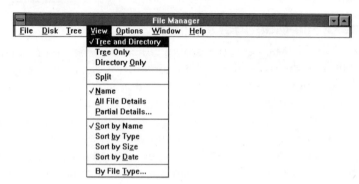

To restore the two-pane setup, revisit the View menu and choose the Tree And Directory command.

Updating Directory Windows

When you use File Manager with floppy disks, be aware that your tree and directory panes are not automatically updated when you switch disks. For example, suppose you are looking at the tree and directory panes for the floppy disk in drive A. If you put a new disk in drive A, neither pane will be correct. File Manager will still display information regarding the disk that *was* in drive A.

To update a window after changing a floppy disk, select the window and press F5. (Or use the Window menu's Refresh command.)

Depending on the capabilities of your network, you might also need to use the Refresh command to update the information displayed for a directory on a network file server.

Opening New Document Windows

When you're working with two directories or drives at once—for example, when you're copying files between a hard disk and a floppy—you'll find it convenient to display each directory or drive in its own document window. File Manager lets you open as many document windows as you please, and it has commands to organize them neatly on your screen.

To open a new window, choose the Window menu's New Window command. Initially, the contents of the new window will be the same as the one you were just working with; use the procedures described earlier in this chapter to change the new window's contents.

If you want to open a new window for a different drive—for example, if you're working with drive C and you want to open a window for drive D—you can take advantage of a mouse shortcut: Simply double-click the appropriate drive icon.

To remove a document window, double-click its Control-menu icon. Or select it and press Ctrl-F4. Note that you cannot remove *all* of File Manager's windows. The program insists on keeping at least one open at all times. You can, however, minimize any or all windows.

Organizing Your Windows

File Manager's directory windows can be moved and sized, tiled and cascaded, exactly as Program Manager's group windows can. You'll find that a tiled display of two File Manager windows often makes it easier to copy or move files between disk or directories.

You can tile directory windows in either of two ways—horizontally or vertically. To split the screen space vertically, press Shift-F4. Your screen will look something like this:

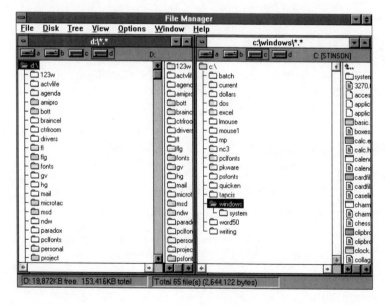

To display tiled windows in an over-and-under style, pull down the Window menu and choose Tile. The result will look like this:

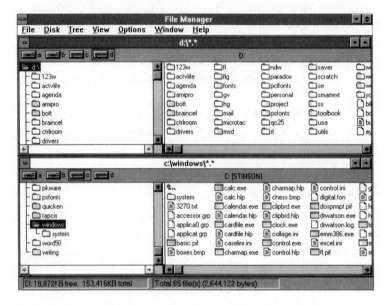

You can switch back and forth between these two modes of tiling at any time.

 WINDOWS TIP: When you tile windows, File Manager avoids covering any minimized document windows. To get the maximum screen space for your directories, therefore, close any windows you're not working with, rather than minimize them.

STARTING PROGRAMS FROM FILE MANAGER

To start a program from File Manager, open a window for the directory in which the program's executable file resides. Then do one of the following:

- Double-click the name of the executable file.

- Use the keyboard or mouse to select the name of the executable file. Then press Enter.

- Pull down the File menu, and choose Run. Then fill out the dialog box with the name of your program's executable file.

WINDOWS TIP: Using the File Run command is more work than double-clicking a filename. But it has the advantage of allowing you to specify a command-line parameter along with the name of your program.

Using Drag-and-Drop to Launch a Document File

You can start a Windows program with a particular document in place by dragging the document's icon onto the program's icon. For example, to open Notepad and edit your AUTOEXEC.BAT file, you can do the following:

1. Display two File Manager windows, one for your root directory and one for your Windows directory.

2. In your root-directory window, click the AUTOEXEC.BAT icon to select it. Drag it to your Windows-directory window and drop it on the icon for NOTEPAD.EXE.

When you bring your AUTOEXEC.BAT icon into position above the NOTE-PAD.EXE icon, File Manager draws a rectangle around the NOTEPAD.EXE icon. That tells you that you've reached the "drop zone" and it's okay to let go of the icon. At that point, depending on how you've set File Manager's confirmation options (see "Confirmation Options," later in this chapter), you might see the following prompt.

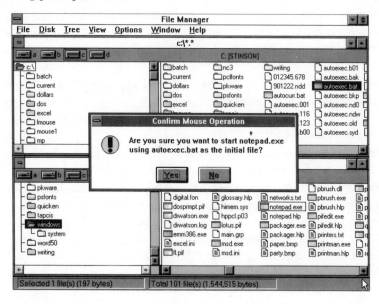

Click OK, and Notepad will appear with AUTOEXEC.BAT.

Note that if you drop a document icon onto a directory or drive icon, File Manager thinks you want to move or copy your file, rather than launch it. In this case, you might see a different confirmation prompt.

 MOUSE TIP: You can also launch a document by dragging its icon onto a running application. If Notepad is already running, for example, you can drag a text-file icon and drop it onto Notepad's title bar or into Notepad's window. If Notepad is minimized, you can drop the file icon onto Notepad's icon.

The drag-and-drop approach to launching files is particularly useful with document types that you open only occasionally. For files that you use regularly with a particular application, it's more efficient to create an association (if you don't already have one). If the document file has been associated with an application, you can launch it by simply double-clicking its entry in a File Manager window.

ASSOCIATING DOCUMENTS WITH PROGRAMS

Associations between document files and program files are recorded in a table called the *registration database*. This table, stored in a file named REG.DAT in your Windows directory, is created for you when you install Windows and automatically includes associations for Cardfile, Paintbrush, Write, Terminal, Notepad, Calendar, and Recorder. Thus, you don't need to worry about creating associations for the Windows desktop accessories.

The installation programs for many Windows applications also automatically update the registration database. If you install Microsoft Excel, for example, you will not need to take any additional steps to create associations for the files that Microsoft Excel uses.

You might, however, need to create associations for older Windows applications that were designed without awareness of the registration database. You might also occasionally want to change or delete an existing association. For example, suppose you have two programs that create files with the extension DOC. A given extension can be associated with only one program. If you find your DOCs hooked up to Program B, when you'd rather have them linked to Program A, then you'll need to modify the registration database.

WARNING: *REG.DAT is a binary file. Attempting to modify this file directly with a text editor may damage it irreparably. Instead, use File Manager's Associate command or REGEDIT.EXE (described later in this chapter).*

To create, modify, or delete an association, first select any file with the extension you want to associate. Then pull down the File menu, choose Associate, and fill out the dialog box.

For example, let's assume you used to do your spreadsheet work in Lotus 1-2-3 Release 2.2, and you've recently converted to Microsoft Excel. Your hard disk has hundreds of files with the extension WK1, and because Microsoft Excel can read these files without a translation step, you'd like to associate the WK1 extension with EXCEL.EXE. Here's how you would do this:

1. Open a File Manager directory window for one of your 1-2-3 data directories.

2. Select any file with the extension WK1.

3. Choose the Associate command on the File menu.

    The following dialog box appears, showing that WK1 files are currently associated with (None):

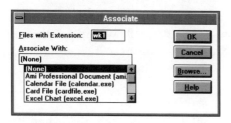

4. Press Tab once to highlight the word *(None)* in the Associate With text box.

5. Type *excel.exe* and click OK.

If your EXCEL.EXE file is not stored in the Windows directory or another directory in your MS-DOS path, you will need to provide the full path specification. For example, if EXCEL.EXE is stored in a directory named D:\SS\EXCEL, you would type *d:\ss\excel\excel.exe* in the Associate With text box. And if you're not sure where your EXCEL.EXE file is stored, you can find it by clicking the Browse button.

> **WINDOWS TIP:** You can save yourself time and trouble by being sure that any programs you associate documents with are stored in your MS-DOS path. That way, if you decide some day to move your program to a new directory (which is also in your MS-DOS path), you won't need to update the registration database.

After you've associated your WK1 files with EXCEL.EXE, double-clicking any WK1 filename starts a copy of Microsoft Excel and automatically loads the selected worksheet.

Changing or deleting an association is as easy as creating one. Select a file with the extension in question, use the Associate command, and then change or remove whatever appears in the Associate With text box. For example, suppose you still have your 1-2-3 program files on disk. Lotus 1-2-3 uses files with the extension XLT as "filters" for translating data from one format to another. Microsoft Excel uses the same extension to designate a worksheet template. If you've installed Microsoft Excel, your XLT files are automatically associated with EXCEL.EXE. If you find yourself occasionally double-clicking one of 1-2-3's XLT files and getting an error message (because the 1-2-3 file is not a valid Microsoft Excel template), you might prefer to disassociate this file type from Microsoft Excel. You can do that by selecting any XLT file, using the Associate command, and deleting the contents of the Associate With text box.

Program Names and File Types

If you choose the Associate command and scroll through the list at the bottom of the dialog box, you'll find that most of the entries there are not simple program names, such as NOTEPAD.EXE. Rather, they're descriptions of document types, such as Ami Pro Document, Calendar File, Excel Chart, and so on. The reason you see file descriptions in this list is that the registration database provides other services besides launch associations. In Windows 3.1, REG.DAT may record either or both of the following:

- Information that allows you to print a document by dragging its icon onto the Print Manager icon (see "Printing from File Manager," later in this chapter)

- Information about an application's support for object linking and embedding

Future versions of Windows may use the registration database for other purposes as well.

 WINDOWS TIP: You can see and change other details stored in the registration database by running a program in your Windows directory called REGEDIT.EXE. You can run it by double-clicking its name in a File Manager directory window, or by using either File Manager or Program Manager's File Run command. For the most complete view of the registration database, use the File Run command and type *regedit.exe /v*. (Note: REGEDIT.EXE is provided for the benefit of software developers and advanced users. If you don't fall into either category, you don't need to be concerned with it.)

The Registration Database and WIN.INI

If you've upgraded Windows 2.x or 3.0 with Windows 3.1, your WIN.INI file probably includes a section called [Extensions] that specifies associations between document files and program files. (The WIN.INI file is described in Chapter 9.) The registration database, which is new with Windows 3.1, is designed to supersede the [Extensions] section of WIN.INI. If a particular file extension happens to appear in both places, Windows 3.1 ignores the WIN.INI setting.

PRINTING DOCUMENTS FROM FILE MANAGER

Most data files that have been associated with applications can be printed directly from File Manager. You can do this in either of two ways:

- By dragging filenames from a File Manager window to the Print Manager icon (or the open Print Manager window)

- By selecting one or more files in a File Manager window and choosing the File menu's Print command

Either way, File Manager opens the document's associated program and uses the program's printing command to print the document.

USING DRAG-AND-DROP TO EMBED PACKAGED OBJECTS

A *packaged object* is an iconic representation of a data object, such as a graphic image or a sound annotation. The data so encapsulated must originate in a program that supports Object Linking and Embedding (OLE) as a server application, and it must be embedded in a program that supports OLE as a client application. You'll find a full description of these features in Chapter 8.

File Manager provides a drag-and-drop shortcut procedure for embedding packaged objects. If you drag the icon for a file created by an OLE server and drop it in an OLE client's application window, Windows embeds the file as a packaged object. For example, if you wanted to embed the graphic image CHINTZ.BMP in a Write document, you could do the following:

1. Display Write and File Manager in tiled windows.

2. Scroll the File Manager window so that the icon for CHINTZ.BMP is visible.

3. Drag the icon for CHINTZ.BMP and drop it into the Write window.

Note that the Write window must be open for this to work. If you drop the BMP file into a minimized Write icon, Write thinks you want to import CHINTZ.BMP as a text file.

WORKING WITH FILES AND DIRECTORIES

In addition to starting programs and associating files with programs, File Manager lets you perform all kinds of housekeeping operations on files. You can move and copy files from one directory to another by dragging their icons with the mouse. And you can delete files by highlighting filenames and pressing the Del key.

You can also use commands on the File menu to move, copy, and delete files. Additional commands on that menu let you rename files, print files, and change files' attributes.

You can perform these chores on individual files or on groups of files, as you choose.

Confirmation Options

Before experimenting with the procedures for manipulating files, you might want to acquaint yourself with the Confirmation command on the Options menu. That command brings up the following dialog box.

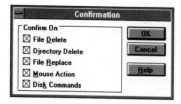

It's a good idea to keep all options in this dialog box checked at all times. That way, File Manager warns you if you're about to do anything that might accidentally delete or overwrite data that you need. While you're learning to use File Manager's various drag-and-drop options, it's a particularly good idea to leave the Mouse Action confirmation setting checked.

Selecting Files with Mouse or Keyboard

Most of the file operations described on the next several pages require that you first select one or more filenames, and then choose a command. Selecting one filename is straightforward: Simply click the mouse on the filename entry in a directory window—or use the keyboard to move the highlight to the filename. Selecting more than one filename at once is also easy, and File Manager gives you several ways to do it.

To select a contiguous group of filenames with the mouse, do this:

1. Click the first filename in the group.

2. Hold down the Shift key.

3. Click the last filename in the group.

To deselect the group, click the mouse anywhere else in the directory pane, without pressing the Shift key.

To select a contiguous group of filenames with the keyboard, do the following steps:

1. Move the highlight to the first filename in the group.

2. Hold down the Shift key.

3. Move the highlight to the last filename in the group.

To deselect the group, use the cursor keys to move the highlight somewhere else. You can also deselect the group by pressing Ctrl-backslash.

To select a noncontiguous group of filenames with the mouse:

1. Click the mouse on the first filename.

2. Hold down the Ctrl key while you click each additional filename you want to select.

To deselect the group, click the mouse anywhere else in the directory pane, without pressing the Ctrl key.

To select a noncontiguous group of filenames with the keyboard:

1. Move the highlight to the first filename you want to select.

2. Press Shift-F8.

3. Use the direction keys to move the dotted rectangle to the next item you want to select.

4. Press the Spacebar to select that item.

5. Repeat steps 3 and 4 until you have selected all items.

To deselect the group, press Shift-F8 again, and then use the cursor keys to move the highlight somewhere else. You can also deselect the group by pressing Ctrl-backslash.

To select all files in a directory window, press Ctrl-slash.

Selecting Files with the Select Files Command

You can also use the Select Files command, on the File menu, to select all files that meet a wildcard specification. When you choose this command, File Manager presents the following dialog box.

Clicking Select *adds* all files meeting the wildcard specification to the current selection. Clicking Deselect does the opposite—removes the specified group of files from the current selection.

Be aware that the Select Files command does not replace the current selection with the wildcard group. Thus, for example, if the current selection is a file named MYFILE.BAK, and you want to select all files with the extension BMP, you might want to do the following:

1. Choose the Select Files command.

2. With the wildcard specification set to *.*, click the Deselect button.

3. In the File(s) text box, type *.BMP*.

4. Click the Select button.

5. Click the Close button.

Step 2 clears the current selection. If you omit this, your selection will consist of all BMP files *plus* MYFILE.BAK.

 WINDOWS TIP: The Status Bar at the bottom of File Manager's window shows the size of the current selection—both the number of files and the number of bytes. When you're copying a lot of files from one disk to another, glance at this information to be sure your selection isn't too large to fit on the target disk.

Moving and Copying Files by Dragging Icons

Although File Manager includes menu commands for moving and copying files, you might want to ignore them if you have a mouse. The simplest way to move and copy is simply to drag icons from one place to another. You can drag and drop one file at a time or in bunches, and you can drag from one directory to another on the same disk or between disks.

Here are some principles to remember when dragging File Manager icons:

- To move files, drag without holding down the Ctrl key.

- To copy files, hold down the Ctrl key as you drag.

- You can't use the mouse to move files from one drive to another. (File Manager interprets a drag between drives as a copy request, whether or not you hold down the Ctrl key.) To move a file from one disk to another, either use the File menu's Move command or first copy the file and then delete it from the source drive.

- The icon that File Manager displays while you drag is "document-shaped" (looks like a page with a dog-eared corner), regardless of the kind of file(s) you're dragging.

- If your drag-and-drop operation is going to perform a copy, File Manager displays a plus sign in the drag icon. If it's going to perform a move, the plus sign is not displayed.

- When moving or copying, it's safest to drop files onto directory icons. If you drop them onto an executable file's icon, File

111

Manager will think you want to run the executable. (See "Using Drag-and-Drop to Launch a Document File," earlier in this chapter.)

■ When you drop file icons onto a drive icon, File Manager copies the files into the current directory of the target drive. If you're not sure what that current directory is, it's a good idea to open a directory window and drop your files there—instead of dropping them onto the drive icon.

■ If you leave the Mouse Action confirmation setting on, File Manager will always tell you what you're about to do—so you needn't worry about misplacing files.

Now let's look at a few examples. First, suppose your Windows directory looks like this:

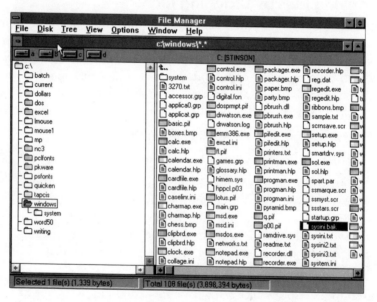

And you want to move the file SYSINI.BAK to the SYSTEM subdirectory of C:\WINDOWS. You can do this by dragging SYSINI.BAK either to the SYSTEM icon in the tree pane or to the SYSTEM icon near the top of the directory pane. In either case, you will see the following prompt.

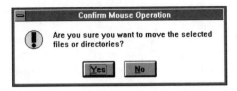

Click Yes to forge ahead or No to retreat.

Now suppose you want to copy all files with the extension INI to the root directory of your C drive. The surest way to proceed is to use the Select Files command to build a selection consisting of all files that meet the wildcard specification *.INI. (See "Selecting Files with the Select Files Command," earlier in this chapter.) Next hold down the Ctrl key while you grab any one of the selected files with the mouse. Continue to hold down the Ctrl key, drag the selection to the upward-arrow icon at the top of your directory pane, release the mouse button and Ctrl key, and then reply to the confirmation prompt.

Because the current directory in this case is immediately subordinate to the root directory, there's an icon for the root in the directory pane. Dropping your selection there saves you the trouble of scrolling the root directory into view in the tree pane. If you were two levels below the root, however, you'd have to drag from the directory pane to the tree pane. (In this case, you might find it easier to use the File menu's Move command.)

Note that you cannot copy the selection to the root directory by dropping it onto the C-drive icon at the top of the document window. If you do that, File Manager will think you want to copy your files into the current directory of drive C, which also happens to be the source directory for your selection. Copying files into the same directory without giving those files new names generates an error message.

Finally, suppose you want to copy all of your BMP files to the root directory of a floppy disk in drive A. First, select *.BMP, following the Select Files procedure described earlier. Then make sure a disk is in drive A and drag your selection to the A-drive icon. You don't need to hold down Ctrl in this case (although you may), because File Manager treats all transfers between disks as copies, not moves. When you see the confirmation prompt, verify that the current directory on A is the root (it will be, unless you've recently been working in a subdirectory on that disk), and then click Yes.

WINDOWS TIP: You can format a floppy disk and transfer files to it in a single operation. File Manager checks the disk before trying to copy files, and if it's not formatted, you'll get a prompt asking if you want to format. After finishing the format, it copies the selected files.

If the Target Disk Is Full

File Manager's Copy command is more accommodating than MS-DOS's. If you try to copy two megabytes' worth of files onto a 1.44-megabyte floppy disk, File Manager will copy as many as it can. Then it displays the following message.

Simply insert a fresh disk and click OK.

If the File Already Exists on the Target Disk

If you try to move or copy a file into a directory where a file of the same name already exists, File Manager will present a prompt similar to the following.

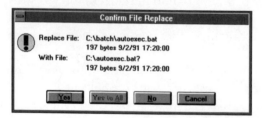

Click Yes to proceed or Cancel to bail out. If you are copying or moving a multiple selection, you can also click Yes To All—in which case you won't see this prompt again. Or you can click Yes or No for each file that already exists on the target drive or directory.

Note that this prompt does not appear if you deselect the File Replace option in the Confirmation dialog box. (See "Confirmation Options," earlier in this chapter.)

Copying and Moving Entire Directories

You can copy and move entire directories in either of two ways—by selecting and dragging all files in a directory pane or by dragging a directory icon. If you select and drag all the files in a directory, File Manager simply moves or copies the files. If you drag a directory icon, File Manager creates a new subdirectory in the target directory.

For example, suppose you want to store a backup copy of each file in C:\EXCEL\BUDGET in the root directory of the floppy in drive B. To do that, you could select everything in the directory pane for the BUDGET directory, and then drag to the B-drive icon. Now suppose instead that you want to create a directory named BUDGET on drive B and back up your budgeting files into that new directory. The simplest way to do this is to drag the directory icon for C:\EXCEL\BUDGET from a tree pane to the B-drive icon. File Manager responds by creating the directory B:\BUDGET and then copying all of C:\EXCEL\BUDGET's contents to this new directory.

Moving and Copying with Menu Commands

If you use Windows without a mouse, or if you simply prefer working with the keyboard, you can take advantage of two convenient keyboard shortcuts for performing moves and copies. The F7 and F8 keys invoke the File menu's Move and Copy commands, respectively. With either command, you'll see a dialog box similar to the following.

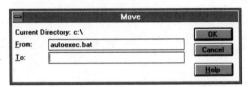

File Manager fills the top box with the current selection. Your job is to fill out the bottom box and click OK. (The Copy command's dialog box also includes a Copy To Clipboard option that can be used for creating packaged objects. For details, see Chapter 8.)

If the current selection is a multiple selection, the Move or Copy dialog box lists each selected file, with spaces between the filenames. You can edit particular filenames out of this list (or add new names) if you wish.

WINDOWS TIP: You can rename a file at the same time as you copy or move it. Simply use the File menu's Copy or Move command, and supply a new name in the To text box.

Deleting Files and Directories

To delete one or more files or directories, simply select what you want to delete, and then press the Del key (or choose the File menu's Delete command). Unless you have turned off the File Delete and Directory Delete options (in the Confirmation dialog box), you'll be asked to confirm your intentions.

Unlike MS-DOS, File Manager allows you to axe a directory that is not empty. When you do that, though, you'll get two or more confirmation prompts—one for the directory and another for each of the directory's files. You can bypass most of the latter prompts by clicking the Yes To All button.

> **WARNING:** *Be careful with deletions if you turn confirmation prompts off! In particular, be aware that if you have deselected the File Delete and Directory Delete options in the Confirmation dialog box and you delete a directory, everything in that directory*—including all subdirectories and all files stored in all subdirectories—*will automatically be expunged from your hard disk. If you're not comfortable with that level of automation, leave the Confirmation check boxes checked.*

Renaming Files and Directories

To rename one file or directory, select its icon, choose the File menu's Rename command, and then complete the dialog box.

Creating New Directories

The File menu's Create Directory command creates a new subdirectory in whatever directory is now selected. The easiest way to use this command is to start by selecting the new parent in the tree pane. For example, to create a new directory directly subordinate to the root directory, activate the tree pane and press Backspace until you're at the root. Then choose the File menu's Create Directory command and fill out the dialog box.

Searching for Files

The File menu includes a handy Search command that can help you locate files that have gone astray. You can search for a particular file or all files that match a wildcard specification, and you can search an entire disk, a particular branch of the directory tree, or a particular directory.

The Search command is useful in the following situations:

■ When you know you have a file somewhere on your hard disk, but you can't remember where

■ When you think you have several versions of the same file scattered in different directories, and you need to figure out which is the most recent version

When you choose the File menu's Search command, File Manager presents the following dialog box.

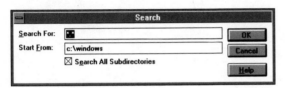

File Manager will search for all files meeting the specification in the top text box, beginning at the directory-tree branch specified in the lower text box. If you leave the check box selected, all subdirectories of the directory named in the lower text box will be included in the search.

The Search command presents its results in a special window titled Search Results. Each file found is listed there with its complete directory path. Here's an example of what you might see if you asked to search for all files on your C drive that have the extension SYS.

If you need more information about the found files—for example, their sizes and save dates, you can take advantage of commands on the View menu. These commands are described later in this chapter. (See "Customizing the Contents of Directory Panes.")

Note that the status bar tells you how many files were found.

You can use the filename entries in the Search Results window the same way you can use filenames in a directory pane. For example, you can double-click a program name to start that program; select a group of files to be copied, moved, or renamed; and so on.

Changing Files' Attributes

Attributes are markers that the MS-DOS directory system (upon which Windows is based) employs to identify certain characteristics of files. In the current version of MS-DOS, files may have any combination of the following attributes (or none of them):

A   Archive
H   Hidden
R   Read only
S   System

The *archive* attribute indicates that a file has been modified since it was last backed up. Each time you create a new file or change an old one, MS-DOS assigns the archive attribute to that file. Commercial backup programs (and MS-DOS's own BACKUP command) typically remove the archive attribute when they back up a file. If you change the file again after backing it up, the file again gets the archive attribute so your backup program can recognize it as needing to be backed up again—and so on.

A few programs use the *hidden* and *system* attributes (either but typically both) to mark important files that must not be modified or deleted. MS-DOS, for example, assigns both attributes to the files MSDOS.SYS and IO.SYS, because if you delete or alter either file, the operating system would no longer operate. Hidden and system files do not appear in directory listings produced by the MS-DOS DIR command, nor are they included in wildcard specifications such as *.*.

You can load a file with the *read-only* attribute into a program, but you can't save it unless you first rename it. Programs that are designed for use on local area networks commonly employ the read-only attribute as a way of letting several people access the same file at once. With such programs, the first user to open a file typically gets both read and save privileges, but subsequent users must access files in read-only fashion. As soon as the file has been opened by the first user, the program assigns it the read-only attribute.

In many contexts, the read-only attribute not only prevents a file from being altered, it also keeps it from being deleted. For example, the MS-DOS

ERASE and DEL commands refuse to delete files that are marked read only. (File Manager lets you delete read-only files, but only if you answer Yes in a confirmation dialog box.)

To change the attributes associated with one or more files, select the appropriate filename(s) and choose the File menu's Properties command (or press Alt-Enter). Select the check boxes for each attribute you want to assign, and then click OK.

WORKING WITH DISKS

Commands on File Manager's Disk menu allow you to format, copy, and assign volume labels to disks.

Formatting Floppy Disks

To format a floppy disk, choose the Disk menu's Format Disk command, and fill out the following dialog box.

First choose the drive you want to format—if your system has more than one floppy disk drive. When you have chosen the drive, the Capacity drop-down list box will show all the formatting options available for the specified drive. In the illustration above, for example, drive A is a 1.44-MB $3\frac{1}{2}$-inch drive, so the Capacity list box offers choices of 720 KB and 1.44 MB.

> **NOTE:** *The Capacity options are determined by your disk drive, not the disk you put in the drive. If you choose a high-density formatting option for a double-density floppy disk, you will see an error message shortly after File Manager begins formatting. At that point, you'll have the option of replacing the disk with a high-density disk or switching to a double-density format.*

The check boxes in this dialog box allow you to make a *system disk* and perform a *quick format*. A system disk is one that can be used to start up a computer in MS-DOS. If you choose a quick format, File Manager formats the disk but doesn't bother checking for bad sectors.

NOTE: *File Manager doesn't let you format a hard disk or format the disk shown in the current document window.*

Finally, you can assign a volume label to your floppy disk by filling out the Label text box. (If you decline this opportunity, you can always assign a label later, using the Label Disk command.)

Copying System Files to an Already-Formatted Floppy Disk

The disk menu's Make System Disk command lets you add the MS-DOS system files to a floppy disk that has already been formatted. Choose this command, and answer the prompt about which disk drive to use. If your floppy disk can't accommodate the MS-DOS system files, File Manager issues a message to that effect.

The Make System Disk command is equivalent to MS-DOS's SYS command.

Duplicating a Floppy Disk

The Disk menu's Copy Disk command allows you to make a duplicate of a floppy disk. Source and destination disks must be of the same format (for example, both $3\frac{1}{2}$ inch or both $5\frac{1}{4}$ inch). This command is equivalent to MS-DOS's DISK-COPY command.

Adding a Volume Label to a Hard Disk or Floppy Disk

The Disk menu's Label Disk command lets you assign a volume label to a hard disk or floppy disk. A *volume label* is a name you assign to a hard disk or floppy disk. Volume labels help you keep track of what kind of information each of your disks contains. File Manager displays the volume label at the top of a disk's directory pane.

ESTABLISHING AND BREAKING NETWORK CONNECTIONS

If you use Windows on a network, you can access any other remote disk drive connected to the network. To do this, you might need first to *attach* the remote drive, using the Disk menu's Network Connections command. (This command does not appear on the Disk menu if you are not connected to a network.) After you have connected to a remote drive, File Manager remembers and attempts to reestablish the connection at the beginning of each working session—unless you explicitly disconnect your system from the remote drive.

When you choose the Network Connections command, you see a dialog box similar to the one on the following page.

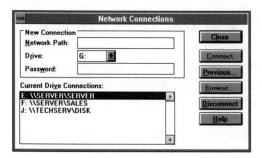

If you are connecting to a remote drive for the first time, start by filling out the Network Path text box. (Depending on the capabilities of your network, you might be able to use the Browse button to find the correct path.) Next, select a drive letter from the drop-down list. This list begins with the next available drive letter and extends to Z. Finally, enter a password if one is required, and then click the Connect button.

NOTE: *The Network Connections box always allows you to connect to any drive letter through Z, but if the LASTDRIVE statement in your CONFIG.SYS file doesn't enable the drive letter you choose, Windows issues a network error. To solve the problem, add the line LASTDRIVE=Z to your CONFIG.SYS file.*

Disconnecting a Network Drive

To disconnect a network drive, choose the Disk menu's Network Connections command again and select the drive in the ensuing dialog box. Then click the Disconnect command button. You'll see a confirmation prompt; click OK to proceed.

Note that your network drive must not be the current drive when you disconnect it.

Reestablishing a Previous Network Connection

File Manager keeps track of the network drives you use. When you want to reconnect to a remote drive you've previously disconnected, revisit the Network Connections dialog box, and click the Previous command button. You can then select the drive from a list of previous connections.

CUSTOMIZING THE CONTENTS OF DIRECTORY PANES

A directory pane normally lists all of a directory's subdirectories and files except those that have either the hidden or system attribute. Subdirectories appear at the top of the list, followed by filenames, and both parts of the list are alphabetized. Normally, you see only the names of the files and subdirectories, not their sizes, dates, times, or attributes.

But you can customize File Manager's display in a number of ways. With commands on the View menu, you can:

- Change the information included in the list

- Change the order of the list

- Filter the list, so that only particular kinds of files appear

With a command on the Options menu, you can also change the font that File Manager uses to list your files.

 WINDOWS TIP: File Manager's customizing options affect only the current document window. If you want to change the appearance of all windows, close all but one. The changes you make to that window will then be inherited by any windows you subsequently open.

Changing the Information Included in the File Listing

Each entry in a directory pane ordinarily includes only an icon and a name. This arrangement allows you to see the largest possible number of files and subdirectories without having to scroll. For some directory windows, though, you might want a little more information. To see all the details about the files in a directory pane, activate it and choose the View menu's All File Details command.

Your listing will look like the illustration at the top of the following page.

In addition to the icon and filename, the detailed directory listing shows the size of each file, the date and time it was last modified, and the presence of any attributes.

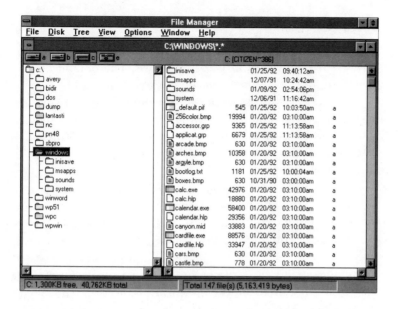

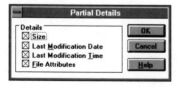

WINDOWS TIP: If you want detailed information about a particular file but don't need it for the whole directory, it's simplest to select the file and press Alt-Enter. That invokes the Properties dialog box, which displays the file's size, date and time of most recent save, and attributes (if any).

In addition to the names-only and full-details displays, File Manager offers several in-between options. To see your choices, pull down the View menu again, and choose the Partial Details command. File Manager responds with the following dialog box.

You can select any combination of the four check boxes.

Changing the Sorting Order

The four Sort By commands near the bottom of the View menu let you change the order in which items appear in directory windows. The default order is by name. At times you might find it more convenient to group files by type—that is, by their extensions. For example, suppose you're looking at a spreadsheet directory that contains a large number of program and worksheet files mixed together. If the document files all have the same extension (as they do with most spreadsheet programs), you might find it easier to locate particular files if you sort the directory by type.

Sorting by size is convenient when you copy files from a hard disk to a floppy disk. The first thing you might want to know under these circumstances is whether any of your files are too large to fit on the floppy. If you sort by size, the largest files appear first in the list. (You might also want to include the file-size information in the listing.)

If you back up files manually at the end of each day, using File Manager's Copy command, you might want to choose the Sort By Date command. That way, the files you worked with most recently appear at the top of your directory window and you can tell at a glance which ones you need to back up.

Filtering the Listing

Looking for a specific file in a directory containing many files can be difficult and time-consuming, especially when you're not sure about the file's name. To make the task simpler, you can "filter" the pane so that it displays only particular kinds of files.

To do this, pull down the View menu, and choose By File Type. File Manager presents the following set of choices.

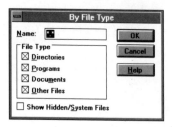

To use this dialog box, start by setting the check boxes to include the types of files you're interested in. If you want to see only program files, for example, deselect everything but Programs. Then, if you need to refine the filter, you can change the wildcard specification in the text box. For example, if you want to see only program files that begin with the letter *S*, you can type *S*.** in the text box.

Note that if you deselect all five check boxes, File Manager reselects all of them! (The program assumes you want to see *something*.)

Changing File Manager's Font

The Font command, on File Manager's Options menu, lets you change the typeface and style used in File Manager's current window. You might find this command useful if you want to see more filenames without scrolling (choose a smaller point size)—or if you just get bored with the default font.

USING FILE MANAGER TO CREATE PROGRAM ITEMS

If you have a mouse, you can use File Manager to create program items in Program Manager. Here's how:

1. Be sure that both Program Manager and File Manager are open and visible on your desktop.

2. In File Manager, open a directory pane for the directory containing the program you want to add to Program Manager.

3. In Program Manager, be sure the program group to which you want to add the program item is open and visible.

4. Drag the icon for your program's executable file from File Manager into Program Manager.

That's all there is to it. Program Manager displays a new icon for the selected program. You can double-click that icon at any time to start your program.

 MOUSE TIP: If you drag an icon for an associated document file from File Manager into Program Manager, you get a new program item that launches the document's associated application and loads the document.

QUITTING FILE MANAGER

To quit File Manager, double-click the Control-menu icon, press Alt-F4, or pull down the File menu and choose Exit. If you have set File Manager up as your default shell, you'll get a prompt informing you that you're about to return to the world of MS-DOS.

If the Options menu's Save Settings On Exit command is checked (its default state), File Manager will remember the current settings of all commands on the View and Options menu. It will also remember the names, sizes, and positions of any open document windows. All these choices will be restored the next time you start File Manager.

PART III

USING WINDOWS TOOLS

The next four chapters introduce a number of tools that will help make your work in Windows more productive.

Chapter 7 describes seven desktop accessories—Clock, Calculator, Notepad, Calendar, Cardfile, Character Map, and Sound Recorder. These simple programs will serve as valuable adjuncts to your larger Windows applications.

Chapter 8 details the ins and outs of moving data from one application to another, using the Windows Clipboard, DDE, and OLE. In this chapter, you'll also be introduced to Clipboard Viewer, the application that lets you view and save the contents of the Clipboard.

Chapter 9 provides a tour of Control Panel, your primary tool for customizing Windows to your needs and tastes.

And Chapter 10 introduces Recorder, the Windows program that lets you automate frequently used command sequences by creating and playing back macros.

7

Using the Windows Desktop Accessories

In this chapter, we'll look at seven desktop accessories: Clock, Calculator, Notepad, Calendar, Cardfile, Character Map, and Sound Recorder.

Clock is just what its name implies—an electronic timepiece. You can run it either as an analog (traditional) or a digital clock. And even when it's minimized, you can tell at a glance what time it is.

Calculator is an electronic calculator with a full set of scientific functions. Calculations made by Calculator can be transferred easily into any Windows program by way of the Windows Clipboard.

Notepad is a simple text editor with a handy time-stamping feature. You can use it as a scratch pad while you work in other applications. Files created by Notepad can be read by virtually any Windows or non-Windows word processing program.

Calendar is a modest appointment-book program. You can use it to record upcoming meetings and other agenda items, and—if you choose—Calendar will present an alarm to remind you shortly before those events occur.

Cardfile is Windows' implementation of a Rolodex file. But unlike any standard physical Rolodex, Cardfile automatically sorts your cards, merges cards from different files, and even dials the phone for you (provided your computer is equipped with a modem).

Character Map's main purpose is to help you enter special characters, such as accented letters or mathematical symbols, in your text documents. With Character Map, you can look at the complete character set for each font installed on your system and copy special characters to your document by pointing and clicking with the mouse.

Sound Recorder allows you to record, play, and edit sound files in waveform (WAV) format. Because Sound Recorder supports object linking and embedding

(OLE) as a server application, you can also use it to embed sound annotations in programs, such as Microsoft Excel, that support OLE as client applications.

To use Sound Recorder, your computer needs to be equipped with audio hardware, and you must have installed an appropriate sound driver. The procedure for installing a sound driver is described in Chapter 9. Chapter 8 includes information about object linking and embedding. You may want to read ahead to this material in Chapters 8 and 9, and then return to the discussion of Sound Recorder near the end of this chapter.

Your Accessories group probably also includes Media Player, a simple playback utility that can be used with waveform or MIDI sound files, animations, audio compact disks, video disks, and any other kind of media for which you have the appropriate hardware and drivers.

The Windows Setup program installs icons for all of these accessories in a program group called Accessories. Unless you have made changes to this arrangement, you can start any of these accessories by opening Program Manager's Accessories window and double-clicking the appropriate icon. (Or you can use Program Manager's Window command to select the Accessories window, use the direction keys or first-letter navigation to highlight the appropriate icon, and then press Enter.)

If you find that you use any of these accessories every day, you'll probably want to move their Program Manager icons into your Startup program group. That way, the accessories you need will always be at hand, only an Alt-Tab or two away from whatever you're doing.

CLOCK

Clock is the simplest of the Windows accessories. It does nothing but report the date and time. (Clock doesn't have an alarm feature, but you can use the Calendar accessory as an alarm clock. Calendar is described later in this chapter.) Because Windows can run more than one application at a time, Clock continues to operate when minimized. In fact, you can still read the time when Clock has been reduced to an icon. This makes Clock a handy item to have around; it doesn't take up much space, it doesn't use much memory, and you can glance at it whenever you need to know the time.

Version 3.1 of Clock also includes a handy Always On Top command on its Control menu. If you choose this command, Clock will always be visible, whether minimized or open, even when you're working in a maximized application. In the following illustration, for example, the foreground program (Current) is maximized, but Clock can still be seen in a small window near the upper right corner of the screen.

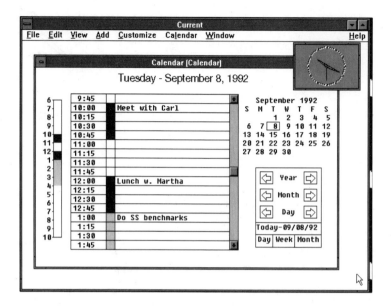

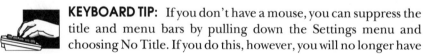

If you like to keep Clock visible at all times, you might also want to simplify its display by removing the title and menu bars. You can do that by double-clicking anywhere within the Clock window. (The title bar and menu bar have been removed in the illustration above.) Double-click a second time to restore the title bar and menu bar.

KEYBOARD TIP: If you don't have a mouse, you can suppress the title and menu bars by pulling down the Settings menu and choosing No Title. If you do this, however, you will no longer have access to the Settings menu. To restore the "normal" display with the keyboard, you can do the following: Close Clock by pressing Alt-F4. Open Notepad and open the file CLOCK.INI. Look for the line beginning *Options=*, followed by six numbers separated by commas. Make the fourth number a 0, resave the file under the name CLOCK.INI, and then restart Clock.

Clock's Settings menu includes commands to switch between Digital and Analog display modes, and to turn on or off the second hand and the display of the current date. If you use Clock in its digital mode, you can also change the font by choosing the Settings menu's Set Font command. Any screen font available on your system can be used for the digital display. You'll get the best results, however, by sticking with TrueType or other scalable fonts. (For a complete discussion of fonts in Windows, see Chapter 13.)

 WINDOWS TIP: Clock gets its time from your computer's internal clock. If you need to reset the clock, you can do so with Control Panel. See Chapter 9.

CALCULATOR

Calculator has two operating modes. You can use it as a standard arithmetic calculator with memory buttons, in which case it looks like this:

Or you can us it as a scientific calculator, in which case it looks like this:

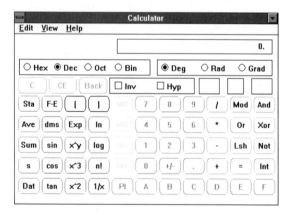

To switch from one mode to the other, use the View menu.

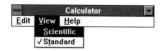

Calculator retains any displayed value and any value in its memory register when you switch from one mode to the other.

In both standard and scientific modes, Calculator can operate on numbers ranging from -10^{308} through 10^{308}, including numbers as small as 10^{-323}. Results or entries outside that range produce an error message. (To recover from an error, click the C or CE button, or press Esc.)

Entering Numbers and Symbols into Calculator

You can enter numbers and symbols either by clicking them with the mouse or by typing them at the keyboard. For example, to have Calculator compute the sum of two and two, you could:

1. Click 2.

2. Click the plus sign (in the lower right corner of the standard-mode window).

3. Click 2.

4. Click the equal sign (right next to the plus sign).

Or you could type

2+2=

Try experimenting with both methods to see what works best for you.

If you're adept at typing numbers, you'll probably find it quicker to enter numbers at the keyboard. To get the result of a calculation, you can press either the Enter key or =. You'll find the mouse convenient for entering such things as sqrt and 1/x. The calculator buttons all have keyboard equivalents (they're listed in Tables 7-1 and 7-2), but you can select them directly with the mouse.

Cutting and Pasting with Calculator

Calculator can exchange numbers with other applications by way of the Windows Clipboard. If you choose the Copy command (on the Edit menu) in Calculator, whatever number Calculator is currently displaying is transferred to the Clipboard. If you choose the Edit menu's Paste command while in Calculator, the current contents of the Clipboard are transferred into Calculator character by character, as if you typed the characters at the keyboard.

Using the Standard Calculator

Here's a quick tour of the standard arithmetic calculator. It functions almost exactly like an inexpensive pocket calculator, except that you don't have to fumble around looking for it on your desk.

Clearing and Correcting

If you make a mistake while entering a number, press Backspace or click the Back button. This will erase the last digit from the display; you can continue erasing a character at a time until you correct the error.

To clear the last entry in a sequence of numbers and arithmetic symbols, press Del or click CE (clear entry). For example, if you're adding up a list of numbers and you make a mistake, simply click the CE button and reenter the last number; you don't have to start over.

To clear the current calculation entirely and return the display to 0, press Esc or click C.

Numbers and Operators

The heart of Calculator's standard window is the ten-key pad. To the right and below the pad are all the basic arithmetic operators. Note that for division, you use the slash button (/), and for multiplication, you use the asterisk (*).

The sqrt button produces the square root of whatever number is in the display. To get the square root of 796.5, for example, enter *796.5* and click sqrt. You don't have to click the = button.

The % button lets you figure percentages. Let's say you wanted to figure the 8.75% sales tax on a $56.50 purchase. You would do the following:

1. Enter *56.5* (with or without the trailing 0; it doesn't matter).

2. Click the multiplication button (*).

3. Enter *8.75*.

4. Click the percentage operator (%).
   Your sales tax will be 4.94375, or $4.94.

The 1/x button produces the reciprocal of whatever number Calculator is currently displaying. Entering *10*, and then clicking 1/x, for example, will give you 0.1.

The +/– button changes the sign of the number currently on display. The typical use for this button is to enter a negative number in the middle of an arithmetic operation. For example, to multiply 52 times –23, you would:

1. Enter *52.*

2. Click the multiplication button.

3. Enter *23.*

4. Click the +/– button.

5. Click =.

You'll get the result –1196. Note that if you enter *52,* then click the multiplication button, then click the minus sign, and then enter *23* followed by =, you get a different result. Calculator treats the minus sign as a replacement for the multiplication operator and simply subtracts 23 from 52.

Repeating Calculations

After you've clicked the = button to finish a calculation, you can make Calculator repeat the last element of the calculation by clicking = (or pressing Enter) again. For example, if you enter

1034.5+23471/4=

Calculator displays 6126.375. Click = again, and Calculator divides that result by 4, giving 1531.59375. Subsequent hits on the = button produce further division by 4.

Using Calculator's Memory Features

In both standard and scientific modes, Calculator has four memory buttons, marked MC, MR, MS, and M+. These provide a storage bin from which you can use a value repeatedly.

For example, suppose you want to divide each of a dozen numbers by the same factor—say, .01375. To spare yourself the drudgery of entering that factor in a dozen separate calculations, you could do this:

1. Enter *.01375.*

2. Click the MS (store in memory) button.
   Calculator stores the current value (.01375) in its memory register and displays an *M* in a box near the upper right corner of the window.

3. Enter the first of your dozen numbers.

4. Click the / button.

5. Click the MR (recall from memory) button.

6. Click =.

7. Repeat steps 3 through 6 for each remaining number.

Here's what each memory button does:

- MS *stores* the currently displayed value in the memory register, replacing any value that might have been there before.

- M+ *adds* the value currently displayed to the value in the memory register.

- MR *recalls* the value currently in memory and enters it into the current calculation. The value remains in memory.

- MC *clears* the memory register. The *M* displayed near the upper right corner of the Calculator window disappears.

Keyboard Equivalents for the Standard Calculator's Buttons

Table 7-1 lists the keyboard equivalents for each of the standard calculator's buttons.

Button	Keyboard Equivalent	Button	Keyboard Equivalent
+	+	Back	Backspace or Left
−	−	C	Esc
*	*	CE	Del
/	/	M+	Ctrl-P
+/−	F9	MC	Ctrl-C
.	. or ,	MR	Ctrl-R
%	%	MS	Ctrl-M
=	= or Enter	sqrt	@
1/x	R		

Table 7-1.
Keyboard equivalents for the standard calculator buttons.

Using the Scientific Calculator

Calculator's scientific mode provides all the features of the standard calculator, plus the following:

- Additional arithmetic operations

- Exponential and logarithmic operations

- Calculations in the binary, octal, and hexadecimal numbering systems

- Bitwise operations

- Trigonometric calculations

- The ability to open a statistics window, enter a sequence of numbers in that window, and calculate the numbers' sum, average, and standard deviation

Order of Evaluation in the Scientific Calculator

In Calculator's standard mode, calculations are always performed in the order in which they're entered. If you type *4+5*6=*, for example, Calculator displays 54, the result of adding 4 to 5 and multiplying the sum by 6.

This is not the case in Calculator's scientific mode. Here, the order in which an expression is evaluated depends on the operations involved. Multiplication and division, for example, are always performed before addition or subtraction. In the scientific calculator, therefore, the expression 4+5*6 returns 34, the result of adding 4 to the product of 5 and 6.

Fortunately, it is not necessary to memorize Calculator's rules about operator precedence. You can simply watch Calculator's display as you enter your calculation. Whenever you type an operator (for example, +, *, or /), Calculator checks to see if the operator you just typed has higher precedence than the previous operator you entered. If it does not have higher precedence, Calculator evaluates the last operation and displays an intermediate result. If it does have higher precedence, no intermediate result is displayed.

For example, suppose you type the following in Calculator's scientific mode:

4*5+

After you type the plus sign, Calculator, recognizing that addition has lower precedence than multiplication, evaluates 4*5 and displays the intermediate result—20. If, on the other hand, you type

4+5*

Calculator sees that your last operation, multiplication, has *higher* precedence than the previous one, addition. So it *does not* display an intermediate result. Instead it waits for your next number or numbers. If you follow the asterisk with

6=

Calculator goes ahead and multiplies 5*6. Then it adds 4 to the result.

What if you need to override Calculator's normal order of operations? You can do that in either of two ways. In the case of 4+5*6, for example, you can simply click the = button after entering the 5. That forces Calculator to carry out the addition and display the intermediate result—9. Now you can complete the calculation by entering *6=.

Alternatively, you can enter parentheses before and after the operation you want Calculator to perform first. Expressions within parentheses are always evaluated immediately, regardless of what follows the closing parenthesis.

With that discussion of precedence out of the way, let's now take a tour of the scientific calculator's capabilities.

Additional Arithmetic Operations

The Mod button is a *modulus* operator. It returns the remainder of a division. For example, 65 mod 7 is 2 (because 7 goes into 65 9 times, leaving a remainder of 2). To perform this calculation, you enter *65*, click the Mod button, enter *7*, and then click the = button.

The n! button returns the *factorial* of the currently displayed number. For example, if you enter *6* and then click the n! button, Calculator returns 720 ($6 \times 5 \times 4 \times 3 \times 2 \times 1$).

The ((left parenthesis) and) (right parenthesis) buttons allow you to nest calculations within calculations, in effect changing the order in which expressions are evaluated. You can nest up to 25 levels.

The Int button (short for *integer*) strips the fractional component from the currently displayed number. For example, if you click Int when 456.789 is displayed, the display changes to 456. To strip the integer portion of a number, first click the Inv (inverse function) box, and then click Int. The Int button works only when Calculator is using the decimal numbering system.

The Exp (exponent) button lets you enter numbers in scientific notation. For example, to enter 6.4×10^{-14} (which is displayed as 6.4e−014), you would enter *6.4*, click Exp, enter *14*, and then click +/−. The Exp button works only when Calculator is using the decimal numbering system.

Exponential and Logarithmic Operations

The x^y button lets you raise a number to any power. For example, to find the seventh power of 2, enter *2*, click x^y, enter *7*, and then click the = button.

The x^3 button returns the cube of the currently displayed number.

The x^2 button returns the square of the currently displayed number.

The log button returns the base-10 logarithm of the currently displayed number.

The ln button returns the natural (base *e*) logarithm of the currently displayed number.

The Inv check box, located next to the Back button, provides the *inverse function* of the above operations. First click Inv, and then the function you want to use. After you use an inverse function, the Inv box is automatically turned off.

When the Inv box is checked, x^y returns the yth root. For example, to find the seventh root of a number, enter the number, click Inv, click x^y, and then click 7.

Similarly, the inverse of x^3 and x^2 return the cube root and square root, respectively, of a number. And the inverse of log and ln return 10 and *e*, respectively, raised to the power of a number.

F-E toggles the display (in decimal numbering) between normal and scientific (exponential) notation.

Using Binary, Octal, and Hexadecimal Numbering

The Hex, Dec, Oct, and Bin option buttons let you switch numbering systems. If Calculator is displaying a number when you switch, it converts that number to the system you switch to. So, for example, if you want to know the octal equivalent of 123456 decimal, you can simply enter that number (be sure you're in decimal mode when you do), and then click the Oct button.

You can enter only those digits that are appropriate for the current numbering system. If you're in binary, for example, Calculator accepts only 0 and 1. If you're in hexadecimal, you can use the A through F buttons, as well as the numerals 0 through 9.

When you're in binary, octal, or hexadecimal numbering, you can use the option-button group at the right side of the Calculator window to change the size of the value currently displayed. If this group is set at Dword, Calculator displays the full value of the current number. If you switch to Word, Calculator displays only the least significant sixteen bits. If you choose Byte, you see only the least significant eight bits.

Bitwise Operations

The And, Or, Xor, and Not buttons perform logical bitwise operations on numbers in any numbering system. The Lsh button shifts numbers left one bit, and Inv followed by Lsh shifts one bit to the right.

Trigonometric Functions

The sin, cos, and tan buttons return sine, cosine, and tangent, respectively. Preceded by a click on the Inv box, they return arcsine, arccosine, and arctangent.

For hyperbolic functions, first click the Hyp box, then the button for the function you want.

When you're in the decimal numbering system, the option-button group on the right side of Calculator's window governs the way Calculator expects to see angles expressed. The default setting is Deg (degrees), but you can switch to Rad (radians) or Grad (grads).

To switch the displayed number from normal decimal format to degree-minute-second format, click dms. In degree-minute-second format, the degrees are to the left of the decimal point. The minutes are the first two digits to the right of the decimal, and the seconds are to the right of the minutes. To switch back, click Inv, and then click dms.

Pressing the PI button enters the constant pi. A shortcut for entering 2π is to click Inv, and then click PI.

Opening a Statistics Window

To calculate sums, averages, and standard deviations of groups of numbers, first click the Sta button. That opens a separate window, in which you can enter as many numbers as your computer's memory allows. The statistics window looks like this:

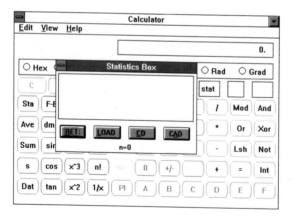

The first thing you'll want to do after opening this window is move it to another part of the screen so that it doesn't overlap the main Calculator window. You'll be moving back and forth between the two windows, so it's helpful to be able to see both at once.

If you have a mouse, you move between the two windows simply by clicking the one you want. If you're working with keyboard only, press Alt-R (RET) to move from the statistics window to the main window. Press Ctrl-S to move from the main window back to the statistics window.

To enter numbers into the statistics window, do the following:

1. Activate the main Calculator window.

2. Enter the number.

3. Click the Dat button or press Ins.

When you have entered all the numbers you need to work with, you can perform the following calculations. The result will be displayed in the main Calculator window.

Sum: Click the Sum button.

Sum of squares: Click Inv, Sum.

Mean: Click Ave.

Mean of squares: Click Inv, Ave.

Sample standard deviation: Click s. Calculator uses $n-1$ for the population parameter.

Population standard deviation: Click Inv, s. Calculator uses n for the population parameter.

The four buttons in the statistics window do the following:

■ RET activates the main Calculator window.

■ LOAD makes the main Calculator window display the number that's currently selected in the statistics window. This makes it easy to perform arithmetic operations on particular values in the statistics window.

■ CD deletes the currently selected number from the statistics window.

■ CAD deletes all numbers from the statistics window.

Keyboard Equivalents for the Scientific Calculator's Buttons

Table 7-2 on the following page lists the keyboard equivalents for each button in Calculator's scientific mode.

Button	Keyboard Equivalent	Button	Keyboard Equivalent
(	(	log	L
)	)	Lsh	<
And	&	Mod	%
Ave	Ctrl-A	n!	!
Bin	F8	Not	~
Byte	F4	Oct	F7
cos	O	Or	|
Dat	Ins	PI	P
Dec	F6	Rad	F3
Deg	F2	s	Ctrl-D
dms	M	sin	S
Dword	F2	Sta	Ctrl-S
Exp	X	Sum	Ctrl-T
F-E	V	tan	T
Grad	F4	Word	F3
Hex	F5	x^y	U
Hyp	H	x^2	@
Int	;	x^3	#
Inv	I	Xor	^
ln	N		

Table 7-2.
Keyboard equivalents for the scientific calculator buttons.

NOTEPAD

Notepad is an editor that reads and writes plain text files—files that contain words and numbers but no formatting information. Although it works with only one font and has very little formatting capability, Notepad is a more effective tool for certain tasks than a full-featured word processor. It's quicker on screen than programs that display text in a variety of styles and sizes, and it's extremely easy to learn.

The fact that Notepad creates plain text files is also a virtue under some circumstances. For example, you'll find Notepad ideal for creating files that you can upload via modem to a bulletin board, a public e-mail service, or another personal computer. It's also good for creating and modifying batch files (such as an AUTOEXEC.BAT file) that you run at the MS-DOS command line, and for working with the Windows initialization files, WIN.INI and SYSTEM.INI.

 WINDOWS TIP: Unlike many other Windows applications, Notepad permits you to open multiple copies of itself. Thus, for example, you can keep one copy of Notepad around for logging phone conversations, another for tracking to-do-list items, a third for miscellaneous ruminations—or whatever. If you like to work with the same number of Notepad files each day, consider putting multiple copies of the Notepad launch icon in your Startup program group.

Opening and Saving Files

Notepad uses the standard Windows File Open, File Save, and File Save As dialog boxes, as described in Chapter 3. If you save a file without specifying a file extension, Notepad uses the extension TXT. (If you want to save a file with no extension at all, add a period at the end of the filename.)

Notepad's File-Size Limit

Notepad's limit is about 50,000 characters. If you exceed that amount, you'll get an insufficient-memory error message, regardless of how much memory your system has. If you need to work with more than 50,000 characters at once and you don't want to switch to Write or another word processor, break your file into two or more smaller files.

Turning Word Wrap On or Off

Unlike all word processing programs, Notepad does not automatically perform *word wrap.* That is, when you reach the right side of the window, Notepad does not automatically move the insertion point to the beginning of the next line.

The fact that Notepad doesn't automatically wrap words makes it convenient for entering program source code, but it's less convenient for ordinary notes and memos. To keep your lines from extending beyond the right side of Notepad's window, pull down the Edit menu and choose Word Wrap. To turn word wrap off again, repeat the Word Wrap command.

NOTE: *Notepad does not save the Word Wrap setting between sessions. Therefore, if you want to use Word Wrap, you must select it each time you start Notepad.*

Word Wrap is a display and printing option. It does not affect the Notepad file in any way. If you change the width of Notepad's window while Word Wrap is on, the lines will be adjusted to fit the new window width. Without word wrap, some information might not show in the window.

Using Notepad's Time-and-Date Stamp

Notepad has a feature that automatically places a time-and-date stamp in a document every time it is opened. If you frequently use Notepad to jot down notes on conversations, ideas, or just changes in schedules, you can have the time printed above your notes. You can also use it to keep a time log of your activities and determine the amount of time you spend at specific tasks. If the first line in a Notepad file consists of the characters *.LOG* (a period followed by the word *LOG*), then each time the file is opened, Notepad adds the current time and date to the end of the file. So, to keep a time log, you would do the following:

1. Start Notepad.

2. In the empty Notepad window that appears, type

   .LOG

3. Choose the File menu's Save command and give your file a name. Notepad is now ready to record the time and date each time the file is opened.

4. Use the File menu's Open command to reopen the file you just saved.

   Your file reappears. Below the word *.LOG*, you see the current time and date.

5. Below the time-and-date stamp, type a description of the task you're about to start.

6. Use the File menu's Save command, and then close Notepad.

7. When you finish your task, start Notepad again and open your file.

Once again, Notepad adds the current time and date to the end of the file. You can now subtract the first time from the second to determine the amount of time you spent on this task. You can go on using this log file to time additional tasks, or you can start a new one for each task.

WINDOWS TIP: Another way to log time usage with Notepad is to use the Edit menu's Time/Date command. Choose this command—or press its keyboard shortcut, F5—and Notepad types the time and date at the current location of the insertion point.

WINDOWS TIP: You can use Calculator's scientific mode to add or subtract times expressed as hours and minutes. Use the inverse dms function to convert a time to decimal, do your calculation, and then use the dms function to convert the result back to hours and minutes.

Using the Undo Command

The Edit menu's Undo command reverses your last editing action in Notepad. For example, if you delete a paragraph and then realize you meant to delete a different paragraph instead, you don't have to retype the one you accidentally deleted. Simply choose Undo (or press Ctrl-Z).

Using the Clipboard with Notepad

You can copy or cut any amount of Notepad text to the Clipboard, and then paste it into a different Notepad file or a different application. You can also use the Clipboard to paste unformatted text that originated in a different application into Notepad.

To place a block of Notepad text on the Clipboard, start by selecting the block. Simply drag the mouse over the text you want to select. To select with the keyboard, position the insertion point at the beginning of the block, hold down the Shift key, and move the insertion point to the end of the block. To select all the text in a Notepad file, use the Edit menu's Select All command.

After you have selected your text, use the appropriate Edit menu command. Copy puts the selection on the Clipboard without removing it from your file; Cut puts it on the Clipboard and deletes it from the file.

To insert text from the Clipboard into a Notepad file, position the insertion point where you want the text to go. Choose Paste from the Edit menu, and the Clipboard text will be inserted into the file before the remainder of the file's text.

If you want to replace a block of Notepad text with text stored on the Clipboard, start by selecting the text you want to replace. Then choose Paste.

Searching for Text in Notepad

The Search menu has two commands, Find and Find Next. When you choose Find, Notepad presents this dialog box:

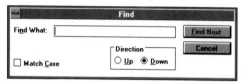

Type what you're looking for in the Find What text box. Choose Up or Down in the Direction box, depending on whether you want to search toward the beginning or the end of the file, starting from the insertion point. Click the Find Next button to begin the search.

The Find command normally ignores case; that is, it considers *NEXT*, *next*, and *NeXT* to be equivalent. If you want it to limit its search so that it finds only text that matches your string exactly—including capitalization—check the Match Case box.

Notepad's Find command does not accept wildcard characters. The asterisk and question mark are treated as ordinary text characters.

After you have used the Find command, you can use Find Next to search for the next occurrence of the same text. F3 is a keyboard shortcut for Find Next.

Notepad's Printing Commands

To print a Notepad file, choose the File menu's Print command. If you have Word Wrap turned on, Notepad will do its best to make the printout's line breaks match those of the display window. If you want your lines longer or shorter, adjust the window accordingly.

To change to a different printer, choose the File menu's Print Setup command. The dialog box that appears, shown in the illustration at the top of the following page, lists all installed printers and offers a few other useful options as well. (For more information about printing options in Windows, see Chapter 11.)

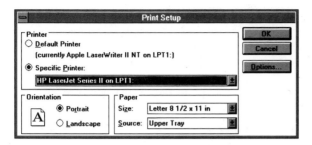

Select the printer you want to use, and then click OK.

To change the default margins, header, or footer, choose the File menu's Page Setup command. You'll see the following dialog box.

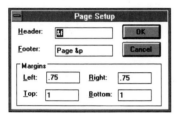

The margin values are expressed in inches.

The header and footer boxes can use a combination of text and special codes recognized by Notepad (and the other accessory programs). Four of these codes are replaced by text when your file is printed. The codes and their replacements are as follows:

&d the current date

&t the current time

&f the name of your file

&p page number

You can use the following three codes to tell Notepad how to position the header and footer:

&l flush with the left margin

&c centered between the left and right margins

&r flush with the right margin

The header and footer codes can be used singly or in combination. So, for example, to create a header with today's date flush left and the name of your file flush right, you could type the following in the header line:

&l&d&r&f

Headers and footers are centered by default.

> **WINDOWS TIP:** If your Notepad window is maximized and you're printing with default margins in portrait orientation, Notepad might try to print more characters per line than your printer will accommodate. The result will be a very ragged printout with alternating long and short lines. You can avoid this problem in either of two ways: by choosing the Print Setup command and selecting landscape orientation, or by choosing the Page Setup command and decreasing the left and right margins. Unfortunately, the orientation and margin settings are not saved with a file's contents when you use the File Save command. Therefore, you might need to make these adjustments each time you print a file.

Using Drag-and-Drop with Notepad and File Manager

If you have File Manager and Notepad running at the same time, you can take advantage of a convenient drag-and-drop feature for opening files in Notepad. Simply drag a file icon from a File Manager window and drop it onto a Notepad window (or icon). Notepad opens your file, exactly as it would if you used the File Open command. This feature makes Notepad into a convenient file-viewer utility for plain-text files.

CALENDAR

Calendar is a simple scheduling program. You can use it to enter two kinds of information: time-specific appointments and notes that apply to an entire day. If you want, Calendar will remind you (audibly or visually) at a designated time prior to selected appointments.

Calendar offers two views of your schedule. You can look at a day view.

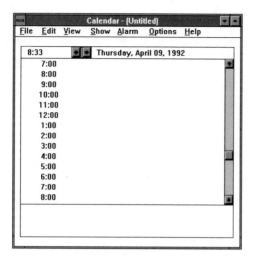

Or, for the "big picture," there's a month view.

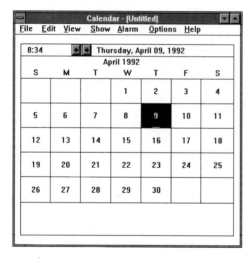

You can switch from one view to the other using commands on the View menu, shown in the following illustration.

The bottom portion of the window in both views is a scratch pad reserved for notes. You can enter up to three lines of notes for any day, and those notes are visible in both day view and month view.

WINDOWS TIP: Another way to switch to month view is to press F9. To return to day view, you can press F8. You can also switch views by double-clicking the date near the top of the Calendar window. To return to day view for a particular day, double-click that day in month view, or select it with the keyboard and press Enter.

Navigating in Day View

To move between the scratch pad area and the appointment times, press the Tab key (or click the mouse).

To move between days, you can do either of the following:

- Click the left and right arrows next to the date, near the top of the day-view window.

- Press Ctrl-PgDn to move forward a day or Ctrl-PgUp to move back a day.

To move to a particular day, do the following:

1. Pull down the Show menu.

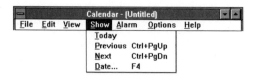

2. Choose the Date command.

3. In the dialog box, type the date you want to move to, and press Enter.

150

WINDOWS TIP: Calendar's Date command requires you to enter the year as well as the month and day you want to move to. But you can leave out the "19" if the date you're looking for is in the twentieth century. And you can use either slashes or hyphens to separate month, day, and year.

To return to today's appointments, choose the Show menu's Today command.

Navigating in Month View

In month view, you can use your keyboard direction keys to move from day to day or week to week. Today's date is flagged with > < symbols. Notice that if you're on the last day of the month and you press the Right direction key, Calendar takes you to the first day of the next month.

With the mouse, of course, you can move to any day in the current month simply by clicking the appropriate numeral in the calendar.

To move from one month to the next, click the left and right arrows near the top of the window. With the keyboard, press Ctrl-PgUp to display the previous month or Ctrl-PgDn to show the next month.

In month view, as in day view, you can move to the scratch pad area by clicking the mouse there or pressing Tab.

Customizing the Time Slots

Calendar's day view ordinarily supplies appointment slots for each hour of the day, from midnight to midnight. If you often schedule meetings on the half hour or quarter hour, you might want to change the default time-slot interval. You can do that by pulling down the Options menu and choosing Day Settings. Calendar responds by presenting a dialog box with three elements.

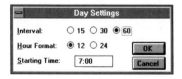

On the Interval line, click the option button for the time interval (in minutes) you want to use.

As you can see, the Day Settings command also allows you to change the style of clock Calendar uses. If you select 24 on the Hour Format line, Calendar uses a European, or military-style, clock. With this option, 1 P.M. is represented as 13:00, 4:30 P.M. as 16:30, and so on.

The remaining element of this dialog box might be a little misleading. The Starting Time value indicates only the first time displayed for each day. If this is set at 7:00 A.M., for example, the time slot you see at the top of the window whenever you move Calendar to a new day is always 7:00 A.M. But you can scroll upward to earlier hours—all the way to midnight—no matter how the Starting Time is set.

Adding a Particular Time Slot

If a 60-minute time-slot interval is normally fine for you, but you occasionally need to add an entry for an oddball time, such as 2:25 P.M., you might want to leave the default interval alone, and add special time slots only as needed. The Options menu's Special Time command lets you do that.

For example, to add a slot for 2:25 P.M. on July 16, first move to July 16 in day view. Pull down the Options menu, choose Special Time, type *2:25*, click the PM button, and click Insert. Calendar adds the special time slot—but only to the selected day (July 16).

Entering Appointments

To enter an appointment, display the day view for the appropriate day, click the mouse on the appointment's time slot, and type. If you're working without a mouse, use the Up and Down direction keys to position the insertion point on the time slot you want, and then type.

Entering Notes

You can enter notes in the scratch pad area in either month view or day view. Simply select the day you want to apply the note to, click in the scratch pad area (or Tab to it), and type.

Marking Days in Month View

You can use up to five symbols, singly or in combination, to call attention to particular days in month view. You can mark days in either month view or day view; follow the steps on the next page.

1. Select the day you want to mark.

2. Choose the Options menu's Mark command (or press F6, its keyboard shortcut).

   Calendar presents a dialog box with five check boxes.

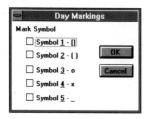

3. Select whichever symbol(s) you want to use, and click OK.

The selected day is marked with the chosen symbol whenever you display month view. You might want to experiment a bit to come up with an effective marking code.

Setting an Alarm

The Windows Clock accessory does not have an alarm command, but Calendar does. You can have Calendar alert you at any time of any day, whether or not you have an appointment entered at that time. You don't have to have Calendar visible for this feature to work, but you must have it somewhere on your desktop.

To set an alarm, follow these steps:

1. In day view, move to the day you want the alarm to go off.

2. Put the insertion point at the time slot for the time you want to hear the alarm.

3. Pull down the Alarm menu, and choose Set (or simply press that command's keyboard shortcut, F5).

A bell symbol appears next to the selected time, as shown in the illustration at the top of the following page.

WINDOWS TIP: You can set as many alarms as you like. To remove an alarm, select the time slot and press F5 again. The bell symbol will disappear.

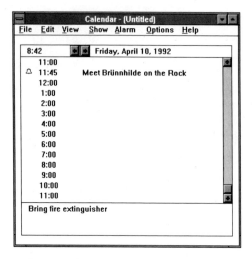

You can make the alarm go off a few minutes ahead of a time-slot time if you want. To do this, use the Alarm menu's Controls command.

For example, if you want to be reminded ten minutes before a 4:00 P.M. appointment, you would do the following:

1. Select the 4:00 time slot and press F5 (or choose the Alarm menu's Set command).

2. Pull down the Alarm menu and choose Controls.
   You see the following dialog box.

3. Type *10* in the Early Ring box, and click OK.

Whatever option you select in this dialog box will apply to all alarm settings—not only the one you have selected.

Notice that the Controls dialog box also gives you the choice of having your alarm audible or not. Calendar uses the Default Beep sound for its audible alarm; if you have a sound board installed, you can change the sound associated with Default Beep (see Chapter 9 for details). If you work in close quarters with other people, you might prefer to turn the sound off and let Calendar alert you visually. With or without the sound option on, the Calendar alarm gets your attention in the following ways.

- If Calendar is minimized, the icon flashes.

- If Calendar is open and the active window, a dialog box appears.

- If Calendar is open but not the active window, Calendar's title bar flashes.

- If you're working in a non-Windows application that uses the full screen, you'll see or hear the alarm as soon as you return to any Windows application.

If Calendar is not active when the alarm goes off, Calendar continues to flash until you acknowledge it. To do that, activate the Calendar window, and then click OK in the dialog box.

Saving and Loading Calendar Files

Calendar stores your scheduling information in a file with the extension CAL. You can create and use as many of these files as you please, so it's easy to use Calendar to manage the schedules of others as well as yourself.

The Calendar program in Windows 3.1 can read files created under the Windows 2 and Windows 3.0 versions of Calendar.

You can use File Manager's drag-and-drop capabilities to open and print Calendar files; see Chapter 6 for more information.

Purging Appointments

If you find your Calendar files getting too large for comfort (for example, if they're taking too long to load or you're running short of disk space), you can use the Edit menu's Remove command to purge complete days of past appointments. The Remove command presents the following dialog box.

Fill out the From and To dates, and click OK.

Printing

To print a range of appointments, choose the File menu's Print command. Calendar presents the dialog box shown at the top of the following page.

Fill out the From and To boxes, and click OK. Calendar prints one copy of your appointments, using the current default printer and the current margin, header, and footer settings. The printout is simple but serviceable; each appointment appears on a separate line, and any scratch pad notes appear at the bottom of each day's listings.

To switch to a different printer, use the Printer Setup command. To change the margins, the header, or the footer, use Page Setup. These commands work the same way in Calendar as they do in Notepad.

CARDFILE

Cardfile is an electronic index card system. You can use it to store the kind of information you might have in a Rolodex, to maintain research notes for a project, to log telephone calls, and for many other similar tasks.

Cardfile has several features you won't find in your conventional Rolodex system. You can store colorful pictures as well as text on your cards, you can have Cardfile dial your phone for you (if you have a modem), and you can merge cards from separate Cardfile files.

Cardfile's Display

A Cardfile card consists of a one-line index and an area for notes.

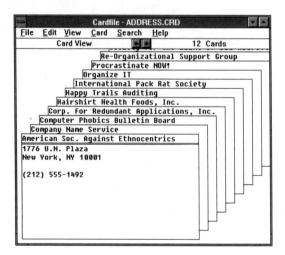

Cardfile automatically sorts your cards according to what's on the index lines, so if you're using the program to store information about people, you'll want to enter their last names first.

 WINDOWS TIP: You can have more than one card with the same index line. When you add a card that has the same index line as an existing card, Cardfile inserts the new card in front of the existing card.

In addition to the card view shown here, Cardfile also offers a list view. In list view, you see only the index lines.

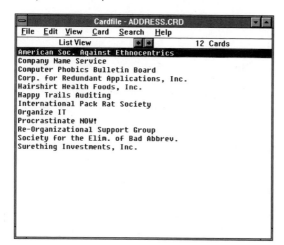

To switch from one view to the other, use the commands on the View menu.

When you first open Cardfile, the program gives you one blank card. You can simply start typing information in the note area, or you can begin by filling out the index line.

To fill out the index line, double-click the mouse there or press F6. Cardfile presents a dialog box.

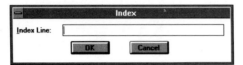

Type whatever you want to appear on the index line, and then click OK or press Enter to get back to the note area.

Cardfile's note area can hold up to eleven lines of text. When you fill the card, simply start a new card.

 WINDOWS TIP: You can write notes in Notepad or another Windows application, and then transfer them into Cardfile cards with the help of the Clipboard. If your Clipboard text would overflow Cardfile's eleven-line limit, however, Cardfile beeps and refuses the transfer.

Starting a New Card

To enter a new card into your file, choose the Card menu's Add command—or press F7, its keyboard shortcut. Then type in the new index line, and click OK. Your new card will always appear at the front of the stack, and will remain there until you select a different card. When you do that, your new card will be placed in its proper alphabetic position within the existing card stack.

Duplicating Cards

Should you ever need to create two or more cards that are identical except for minor details, you can take advantage of the Card menu's Duplicate command. Select the card you want to duplicate (see the information about navigating in Cardfile, below), and then choose Duplicate from the Card menu. Then you can select the duplicate card and make whatever changes are needed.

Changing a Card's Index Line

If you need to change the index line of a duplicate card (or any other card), simply select that card, and choose the Edit menu's Index command. Or press F6, the keyboard shortcut for the Index command. Or you can use the mouse shortcut: Double-click the index line. With any of these techniques, Cardfile presents a dialog box in which you can edit the index line.

Another way to change an index line is to switch to list view. Then double-click the card whose index you want to change. Cardfile presents the same dialog box you would get by pressing F6.

Navigating in Cardfile

You can use any of a number of ways to move from card to card. If you have a mouse and you can see the index line of the card you want to move to, simply click that index line. If you can't see the card you want or you don't have a mouse, here are some other methods:

- Click the left or right arrow below the menu bar to move forward or back through the card stack.

- Press PgUp to move forward in the stack or PgDn to move back.

- Press Ctrl with any alphabetic or numeric key to move to the next card in the stack that begins with that letter or number. You can continue pressing the same Ctrl-key combination to cycle through all the cards beginning with a particular letter.

- Switch to list view (so you can see the index lines for more cards than you can see in card view), select the card you want, and then switch back to card view.

- Choose the Search menu's Go To command (or press F4, its keyboard shortcut).

Go To is a search command that looks only at index lines, disregarding the note area of your cards. When you press F4, you see the following dialog box.

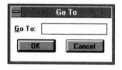

Fill out any part of the index line (even the middle of a word, if you like), and Cardfile will take you to the first matching card.

Whatever method you use to select a card, Cardfile "cuts the deck" to bring the selected card to the front. For example, suppose your file consists of cards for Campbell, Jones, Miller, Smith, and Wilson. If you select Miller, the Miller card comes to the front. Behind Miller are Smith and Wilson (as before), and behind Wilson come the cards at the front of the alphabet—Campbell and Jones.

Searching for Cardfile Text

The Go To command is fine when you're looking for a card with a particular (known) index line. But what if you want to find some text that's out there somewhere on a card—and you have no idea which card? For that need, Cardfile supplies the Find command.

The Find command is located on the Search menu. Fill out the dialog box, click OK, and Cardfile takes you to the first card containing the text you specify. To find another card that matches your search text, simply press F3 (or choose the Search menu's Find Next command).

Unlike the Go To command, which looks only in the index lines, the Find command limits its search to the cards' note area.

Editing Cards

To change the contents of a card, first bring it to the front of the deck. Position the insertion point where you want to make changes, and then use the same editing procedures you would use in Notepad.

Cardfile's Edit menu has the usual Copy, Cut, and Paste commands. These commands make it easy to duplicate information on several cards or move information from one card to another.

The Edit menu also has two commands to assist you in case you make changes you regret. The Undo command reverses your last edit, and the Restore command reverses all changes made to the current card since you brought it to the front of the deck.

Note that after you have moved a new card to the front of the deck, any changes you made to the card that was in front before cannot be reversed with the Restore command.

Using Pictures

You can put pictures as well as text on Cardfile's cards. You might want to use this feature to do such things as add scanned photographs to a personnel file or clarify research notes with charts created in a Windows spreadsheet program.

Any graphic information that can be stored on the Windows Clipboard can be pasted onto a Cardfile card. The procedure is as follows:

1. Use a graphics program (such as Paintbrush) to create or import an image.

2. Use the graphics program's Cut or Copy command to transfer the image to the Clipboard.

3. Bring the card you want to use to the front of your Cardfile deck.

4. Choose the Edit menu's Picture command.

5. Choose the Edit menu's Paste command.

    Your image appears in the upper left corner of the card's note area. The aspect ratio (ratio of width to height) of the original is preserved.

6. Drag the image with the mouse or use the direction keys to position the image where you want it on the card.

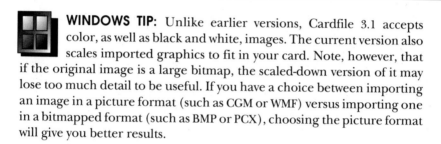

WINDOWS TIP: Unlike earlier versions, Cardfile 3.1 accepts color, as well as black and white, images. The current version also scales imported graphics to fit in your card. Note, however, that if the original image is a large bitmap, the scaled-down version of it may lose too much detail to be useful. If you have a choice between importing an image in a picture format (such as CGM or WMF) versus importing one in a bitmapped format (such as BMP or PCX), choosing the picture format will give you better results.

Graphics and text can be mixed on the same card. To annotate an image, for example, choose the Edit menu's Text command and begin typing. You can use the Spacebar or the Tab key to move your text away from the graphic. Or you can switch back to Cardfile's graphics mode and use the mouse or keyboard to reposition the image away from the text.

Linking and Embedding

Cardfile 3.1 supports *object linking and embedding* (OLE) as a *client application*. (OLE is explained in Chapter 8.) If you paste an object that was created in a program that supports OLE as a server application, you can establish a permanent connection to the source, enabling you either to edit the object more easily or to have it updated automatically if it changes in the source application.

    In the next several paragraphs, we'll look at the procedures for embedding and linking objects, using Paintbrush as an example of a server application. The procedures described here apply to any OLE server, however. If you have a multimedia-capable system, for example, you can also link or embed sound objects from a program that can act as a server for such objects.

Using Paste to Embed a Graphic

If you copy an image from an OLE server application—such as the Windows Paintbrush program—onto the Windows Clipboard, then use Cardfile's Paste command to replicate the image in a Cardfile card, Windows treats the image as an *embedded object*. This means that when you double-click the image in your Cardfile card, Windows brings the server application to the desktop with your image in place. There you can make any changes you need. After you edit the image, you can use an update command in the server program to send the modified image back to Cardfile.

For example, suppose you want to create a cardfile of maps to friends' houses. You can create such maps in Paintbrush. After creating a map, you use Paintbrush's Copy command to put the map on the Clipboard. Then you switch to Cardfile, create a new card, and use the Picture command on the Edit menu to tell Cardfile you want the current card to display an image instead of text.

Next, you pull down the Edit menu again and choose Paste. After the image arrives in Cardfile, you can verify that it is an embedded object (as opposed to a *static* image) by pulling down the Edit menu once more. This time, you find that the penultimate command on the menu, a grayed-out "Object" only moments before, has changed to indicate the source of the graphic.

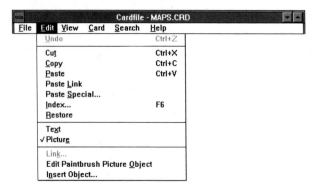

Now suppose you decide to change a few details on the map. If you either double-click the image in Cardfile or choose the Edit Paintbrush Picture Object command on Cardfile's Edit menu, Windows brings a copy of Paintbrush to the desktop (a new copy if Paintbrush happens to be on the desktop already) and loads your original map image.

NOTE: *Before you can edit an embedded object, Cardfile must be in Picture mode. To put it in Picture mode, pull down the Edit menu and choose Picture. Cardfile always defaults to Text mode, even if it was in Picture mode when you last quit the program.*

After you make your changes, you pull down Paintbrush's File menu.

Because you're using Paintbrush to edit an embedded object, the File menu differs in two respects from the normal Paintbrush File menu. In place of the Save command, you see an Update command. And the Exit command now says "Exit & Return to" followed by the name of your Cardfile document.

As you edit your image in Paintbrush, you can pass along the changes to the Cardfile document by choosing the Update command. And when you have finished, you can close Paintbrush (and update the Cardfile document) by choosing the Exit command. If you don't want the changes you've made to appear in your Cardfile document, use the Control menu's Close command (or double-click the Control-menu icon) instead of the File menu's Exit command.

Embedding an Object with the Insert Object Command

The simplest way to embed an object in a Cardfile document is to copy that object from the OLE server application to the Clipboard, and then use Cardfile's Paste command. The Insert Object command, at the bottom of Cardfile's Edit menu, provides an alternative route. When you choose this command, you see a dialog box listing all object types recognized on your system. Select an object type, click OK, and Windows invokes the appropriate server application. There you can create the document you want to embed.

Linking an Object with Paste Link

Another way to establish a connection between an image in Cardfile and its source is to use Cardfile's Paste Link command. Using Paste Link instead of Paste creates an "automatic" or "hot" link to the source application, so that whenever the object is changed in the source program, the changes are immediately reflected in Cardfile. If you prefer, you can change the link to a "manual" or "cold" link. In this case, changes in the source application are not reflected in Cardfile until you explicitly ask for them to be.

After you Paste Link an image into Cardfile, you will find the Link command, near the bottom of Cardfile's Edit menu, available. Choosing Link brings up a Link dialog box. (As a shortcut to the Link dialog box, you can hold down the Alt key and double-click the object.)

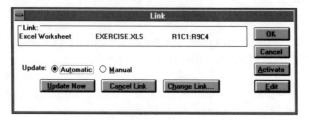

The top part of this dialog box provides information about the source of the linked object. Here, for example, you can see that the linked object is the range R1C1:R9C4 in the Microsoft Excel worksheet EXERCISE.XLS.

Changing a Hot Link to a Cold Link—and Vice Versa

The Link dialog box gives you a way to change the "temperature" of a link from hot to cold or vice versa. Choose Automatic for a hot link or Manual for a cold link. If you make the link manual, changes to the linked object in the source document will not be reflected in Cardfile until you click the Update Now button.

Editing a Linked Object

Just as you can edit an embedded object by double-clicking it, so can you edit a linked object. Double-clicking a linked object, however, invokes a normal copy of the source application, not one with a modified title bar and File menu. If your link is automatic, changes you make in the source application are immediately passed to Cardfile. If the link is manual, the changes don't take effect until you use the Update Now button in Cardfile's Link dialog box.

> **NOTE:** *Before you can edit a linked object or modify the link in any way, Cardfile must be in Picture mode. To put it in Picture mode, pull down the Edit menu and choose Picture. Cardfile always defaults to Text mode, even if it was in Picture mode when you last quit the program.*

KEYBOARD TIP: If you don't have a mouse, you can invoke a linked object's source application by selecting the object in Cardfile, and then pressing Alt, E, O. Alternatively, if you happen to be in the Link dialog box, you can press Alt-E.

Breaking the Link

If you decide you no longer want a linked object to respond to changes in the source document, you can convert it to a *static* object. To do this, select the object in your Cardfile document. Then invoke the Link dialog box (by holding down Alt while double-clicking, or by choosing the Edit menu's Link command). In the dialog box, click the Cancel Link button.

Changing a Link

If you move or rename the document to which a Cardfile object is linked, you will need to let Cardfile know about the change. You can do that by invoking the Link dialog box and clicking the Change Link button. When you do, you'll get a familiar-looking dialog:

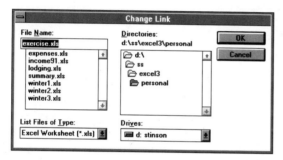

This is simply the standard Windows File Open dialog box with a Change Link title bar. Find the current location or name for your source file, click OK, and your link will remain up to date.

Controlling the Format of a Graphic Object with Paste Special

By default, when you paste or paste-link a graphic object into Cardfile, you get the most information-rich format available. For example, if the object on the Clipboard came from an OLE server application and you choose Paste, you get an embedded (rather than a static) object. If the image on the Clipboard is a drawing made in Paintbrush and you choose Paste Link, the image is displayed in your Cardfile document in *picture* format rather than *bitmap* format. (These terms are discussed in Chapter 8.)

Cardfile's Paste Special command (available only in Cardfile's Picture mode) gives you an opportunity to override the default. When you choose this command, a dialog box appears listing all the formats accessible to Cardfile for whatever data is currently on the Clipboard. Here, for example, is how this dialog box would appear if the object on the Clipboard is a range of cells copied from an Excel worksheet:

To paste or paste link a particular format into Cardfile, choose that format from the list and click the appropriate command button.

Using Cardfile to Dial the Phone

If you have a Hayes-compatible modem, you can use the Card menu's Autodial command to dial any phone number listed on the card at the front of your file.

Before you use this feature the first time, follow these steps to set up the modem's speed, its dialing method, the communications port you'll be using, and any access code you may require:

1. Choose the Card menu's Autodial command (you can press F5, its keyboard shortcut, if you prefer).

2. On the dialog box that appears, click Setup or press Alt-S. Cardfile presents this dialog box:

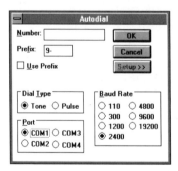

3. In the Dial Type box, select Tone if your telephone uses tone dialing or Pulse if it does not.

4. In the Port box, select the communications port to which your modem is connected.

5. In the Baud Rate box, select the speed (baud rate) at which you want to use your modem.

6. If you need to dial a prefix to get an outside line (or for some other purpose), enter that prefix in the Prefix box.

7. If you will always be using the dialing prefix, check the Use Prefix box. Otherwise, leave it blank for now.

8. Click the OK button.

To dial a number, bring the card containing the phone number to the front of the stack. Then press F5 or choose the Card menu's Autodial command. Cardfile will display in a dialog box the number it proposes to dial.

Select the Use Prefix box if you want the prefix dialed, check the number to be sure it's correct, and then click the OK button. Cardfile will dial the number and display a message instructing you to pick up the telephone.

If the card you're dialing from contains more than one telephone number, Cardfile will propose to dial the first one it finds—or the first one Cardfile thinks is a telephone number. If you want to dial a different number, you can type that number in the dialog box. Alternatively, you can select the number itself on the card before using the Autodial command.

 WINDOWS TIP: To ensure that Cardfile's Autodial command automatically chooses the correct number, you might want to type in the phone number above the address, which might contain numbers confusing to Cardfile.

Saving, Loading, and Merging Cardfile Files

Cardfile's New, Open, Save, and Save As commands work the same way as in the other desktop accessories. Cardfile's files have the extension CRD.

> **WINDOWS TIP:** Because of its support for OLE, Cardfile 3.1 uses a slightly different file format from earlier versions. To load a card file created in Windows 2 or Windows 3.0, choose the Open command. Then open the file-type list box and choose 3.0 Card File (*.CRD).

Cardfile's File menu also has a Merge command that lets you combine a CRD file stored on disk with one currently in memory. Cardfile simply blends the two files together into a single alphabet. The combined file retains the name of the file you're currently working with.

Printing Cardfile Information

You can print Cardfile information in three ways:

- To print a single card, move that card to the front of the file and choose the File menu's Print command.

- To print all cards in a file, first be sure you're in card view (not list view). Then use the File menu's Print All command.

- To print a summary consisting of only the index lines for each card in your file, put Cardfile in list view. Then choose the File menu's Print All command.

As in Notepad and Calendar, you can switch to a different installed printer by choosing the Printer Setup command. And you can change Cardfile's margins, header, or footer by using Page Setup. These commands work the same way in Cardfile as they do in Notepad.

CHARACTER MAP

Character Map is a simple utility program that simplifies the use of accented letters and symbols in your tex t documents. Character Map's initial display looks like the following illustration.

In the top left corner of the window is a drop-down list in which you choose any font available on your system (for more about fonts, see Chapter 13). Below the font list is a table displaying all the characters available in the chosen font. You can't change the size of the Character Map window (other than to minimize it), but you can get an enlarged view of any character simply by selecting it with the mouse or the keyboard. Here is how Character Map looks when the copyright symbol in the TrueType font Arial is selected:

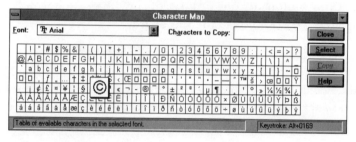

The panel in the lower right corner of the Character Map window tells you how you can produce any character directly, with the keyboard. For example, in the illustration above, the panel reads "Keystroke: Alt+0169." This means that if you are working on a document in a word processor and need a copyright symbol in the Arial font, you do the following:

1. Use the word processor's formatting commands to specify Arial as your font.

2. Hold down the Alt key.

3. Type *0169* on the numeric keypad.

4. Release the Alt key.

Note that you must type the numbers 0169 on the numeric keypad; the number keys at the top of your keyboard won't work.

If you don't want to type Alt-key sequences, you can generate special characters with the help of Character Map's Select and Copy commands. For example, you could enter a copyright symbol in your document by doing the following:

1. Be sure the Characters To Copy box (in the upper right corner of the Character Map window) is blank. If it is not blank, clear it by selecting whatever is currently there and pressing the Del key.

2. Use the mouse or keyboard to select the copyright symbol in the main part of the Character Map window.

3. Click the Select button (or press Alt-S).

4. Click the Copy button (or press Alt-C) to copy the contents of the Characters To Copy box to the Clipboard.

5. Activate your word processor and use its Paste command.

You can use this method to copy more than one character at a time. Each time you click the Select button, Character Map adds the current character to the end of the character sequence in the Characters To Copy box.

 MOUSE TIP: Double-clicking a character in the main part of the Character Map window is equivalent to selecting the character and then clicking the Select button.

Fonts and Character Sets

Most of your Windows fonts share a common character layout known as the eight-bit American National Standards Institute (ANSI) character set. This is simply a table in which each character in the font is mapped to a particular number from 0 through 255. In memory and on disk, the characters in your documents are recorded by their ANSI character-set numbers, and because most of your fonts use the same mapping scheme, switching a block of text from one font to another usually produces a change in the typeface, style, or size, but not a change in the characters themselves.

You should be aware, however, that the ANSI character set used by most Windows fonts is not the same as the IBM PC, or extended ASCII, character set used by most MS-DOS applications. The "normal" alphabetic and numeric characters—the letters *A* through *Z* in uppercase and lowercase, the numerals 0 through 9, and the common punctuation symbols—are mapped to the same character values in both the ANSI and extended ASCII character sets. But the two systems diverge widely for accented letters and other special symbols. Therefore, an Alt-key sequence that produces a particular symbol in your favorite MS-DOS application will probably have quite a different effect in a Windows program.

When you copy text to the Clipboard from most Windows applications, the text is stored on the Clipboard in at least two formats, called *Text* and *OEM Text*. (See Chapter 8 for more details about data formats and the Clipboard.) The inclusion of the OEM Text format, in most cases, allows you to copy symbols from a Windows application to the Clipboard, and then paste those symbols (unchanged) into an MS-DOS application.

For example, if you copy the letter *u* with a circumflex accent (û) from Word for Windows to the Clipboard, and then paste this character into an MS-DOS application, you will still get a *û* in your MS-DOS program, despite the fact that this character is mapped to the value 251 in the ANSI character set and the value 150 in the extended ASCII set. Windows takes care of the translation for you. A similar conversion process takes place automatically when you copy text to the Clipboard from an MS-DOS program.

Unfortunately, the extended ASCII character set includes characters not available in the ANSI set, and vice versa. The block-graphics characters in the extended ASCII character set, for example, are not available in the ANSI set (because Windows is a graphical environment, that's usually no great loss). If you attempt to copy such incompatible characters from one environment to the other, you will get something—but not what you started out with.

> **WINDOWS TIP:** If you use Character Map to compare the character sets of your various Windows fonts, you will find some differences in the fourth row of the Character Map table. In most non-TrueType fonts, the values in this portion of the character set are undefined. (Character Map uses either a solid vertical bar or an open square to indicate an undefined character value.) In most TrueType fonts, many values in the fourth row have been assigned to useful symbols, such as true quote marks, em and en dashes, and an ellipsis. You may want to use these TrueType characters occasionally, even if the document you're creating is based primarily on non-TrueType fonts.

The Symbol Font

In addition to the Wingdings "dingbat" font, your Windows system includes one TrueType font that does not use the ANSI character set. That font, called Symbol, includes the Greek alphabet, the four standard card-suit symbols, plus a variety of other mathematical, logical, chemical, and business symbols. The following illustration shows what's available in the Symbol font.

Some of the characters in the bottom row of this character set are meant to be combined with one another in an over-and-under fashion. The tenth and twelfth characters from the right in the bottom row, for example, can be assembled to produce a large integral symbol.

SOUND RECORDER

Sound Recorder is a utility that lets you record, edit, and play sound files in waveform format. You can also use it to provide sound annotations for documents created in programs that support object linking and embedding as client applications (see Chapter 8 for details about object linking and embedding). Before you can use Sound Recorder, your computer must include audio hardware, and you must have installed a driver appropriate for that hardware. For details about installing sound drivers, see Chapter 9.

Sound Recorder's display looks somewhat like a tape recorder with a built-in oscilloscope.

You can operate the buttons by clicking on them with the mouse, or you can tab to them with the keyboard and press Enter when the button you want to use is highlighted.

The two-headed arrow buttons in the lower left corner are rewind and fast-forward controls, respectively. The single-headed arrow is the play button, the square is the stop button, and the microphone icon at the right is the record button.

Your Windows software includes a few sample sound files, all of which have the extension WAV. To listen to these files, simply use Sound Recorder's Open command (on the File menu), and then click the play button. As the sound is played, the scroll box moves from left to right across the scroll bar, and the oscilloscope display gives you a visual representation of the sound.

To record a new sound file, use the File menu's New command. Then click the record button and begin speaking into your microphone. Unlike most tape recorders, Sound Recorder doesn't require you to press two buttons at once to begin recording. As soon as you click the microphone button, Sound Recorder is in record mode. You can record up to a minute's worth of sound. When you finish, use the File menu's Save command and supply a filename.

You can embed a sound file in any application that supports object linking and embedding as a client program. To do so, follow these steps:

1. Open or record the file you want to embed.

2. Use Sound Recorder's Copy command to put the sound data on the Clipboard.

3. Activate the application into which you want to embed the sound (the client application).

4. Put the cursor where you want the sound file to be embedded. Then use the client program's Paste command.

In your client document, the embedded sound file is displayed as a small microphone icon. To play the sound, simply double-click this icon.

Editing Sound Files

Sound Recorder's Edit menu has four editing commands, in addition to the Copy command.

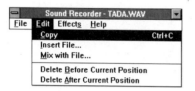

The Insert File and Mix With File commands allow you to combine two or more sound files. To use either command, first use the scroll arrows to position the scroll box at the point in the current file where you want the incoming file to appear. The Position indicator to the left of the oscilloscope display will help you find the appropriate spot.

The Insert File command adds a sound file at the current location and moves the remainder of the file forward. The Mix With File command superimposes the incoming sound file on whatever sound data is already at the current location.

The last two commands on the Edit menu simply delete data from the current location to the beginning or end of the file.

You can also edit a sound file with commands on the Effects menu.

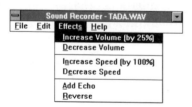

Note that these commands actually change the sound data that makes up your file, not simply the playback mode. So, for example, if you increase the speed of a file and then use the Save command, the file plays at the increased speed each time you open it.

Note that regardless of how you edit a sound file, its total playback length is limited to 60 seconds.

8

Integrating Applications: the Clipboard, DDE, and OLE

Windows 3.1 offers three means of sharing information between applications: the Clipboard, Dynamic Data Exchange (DDE), and Object Linking and Embedding (OLE). These three services stand at distinct levels of automation.

The Clipboard is a passive transfer mechanism. You use a Copy or Cut command to store a chunk of text, a graphical image, or some other kind of data on the Clipboard, and then you use a Paste command to grab that data and put it somewhere. The Clipboard simply holds the information on its way from one place to another. Windows also includes a program called Clipboard Viewer that lets you see the contents of the Clipboard and save them to a disk file. You don't need to use Clipboard Viewer to take advantage of the Clipboard. But the viewer will show you what the Clipboard is storing—and in what formats—at any given moment, and you may sometimes find that information useful.

Dynamic Data Exchange (DDE) is a protocol (a set of conventions) that lets applications share information automatically. With a DDE link in place, you can do such things as have information transferred in real time from a stock market service to a Microsoft Excel worksheet; each time the service updates the stock data, your Windows communications program can feed it directly into your Microsoft Excel file.

DDE works only with applications that explicitly support it. In the days of Windows 2, only Microsoft Excel and few other programs met that qualification.

Since the arrival of Windows 3.0, most new versions of major Windows applications have supported DDE.

As its name suggests, Object Linking and Embedding (OLE) provides two kinds of integrating services: linking and embedding. Both can be applied to a variety of data types—a block of text, a graphics image, a voice annotation, a piece of music, or even a recorded video. Windows uses the generic term *object* to describe the data that you link or embed.

The linking component of OLE can be thought of as a superior version of—and the eventual replacement for—DDE. The embedding component allows you to store elements of one document inside another—a Paintbrush picture in a Write report, for example. When an object is embedded in a document (as opposed to being merely pasted in from the Clipboard), the object "remembers" where it came from. If you need to change it, you can simply double-click the object to launch the source application. After editing the object, then, you can use another simple procedure to send the changes back to the document in which the object is embedded.

Like DDE, OLE works only with programs that support it. Version 3.1 of Windows includes several such programs: Cardfile, Write, Paintbrush, Object Packager, and Sound Recorder.

In this chapter we'll look at all three modes of information sharing in Windows: the Clipboard, DDE, and OLE. Along the way, we'll also tour the Clipboard Viewer program and a new utility called Object Packager, which allows you to embed an iconic representation of an object (a *package*) in an OLE-supporting document.

USING THE CLIPBOARD WITH WINDOWS APPLICATIONS

The procedures for using the Clipboard are essentially the same in all Windows applications. The basic steps are as follows:

1. Select the information you want to move or copy.

2. Choose the application's Cut command if you want to move the information, or the Copy command if you want to copy it.

3. Switch to the application that you're going to copy or move the information to.

4. Position the insertion point or cursor at the place where you want the information to go.

5. Choose the receiving application's Paste command.

So, for example, if you want to copy the range A1:G10 from a Microsoft Excel spreadsheet into a note you are writing in Notepad, you start by activating Microsoft Excel and selecting cells A1:G10. Then you choose the Copy command, on Microsoft Excel's Edit menu.

At this point, Windows puts a copy of your Microsoft Excel information in the area of memory known as the Clipboard.

Next you make Notepad the current window, position the insertion point at the part of your note where you want the table to appear, and choose the Paste command from Notepad's Edit menu.

After a copy operation, such as the one just described, the Clipboard's contents remain unchanged. This means that after you have put something on the Clipboard, you can paste it as many times as you like—into several different places within the same document or into several different documents. Generally speaking, the Clipboard retains its contents until you replace them with something else or unless you explicitly delete them with Clipboard Viewer. (Like all generalizations, this one has a few exceptions. Microsoft Excel, for example, erases the Clipboard after you have pasted data and then performed other commands.)

The Copy, Cut, and Paste Commands

Almost all Windows applications that work with user data have an Edit menu with Copy, Cut, and Paste commands. The three commands behave in a predictable and consistent way in almost all programs. Copy puts selected information on the Clipboard without removing it from the source document. Cut puts the information on the Clipboard and at the same time deletes it from the source document. Paste puts a copy of the Clipboard's contents into the destination document without emptying the Clipboard. (Once again, Microsoft Excel is an exception. When you use Microsoft Excel's Cut command, the selected information remains in place on your worksheet until you use Paste. If you change your mind and don't paste, Microsoft Excel leaves your cut data in place on the worksheet.)

Many programs also have Delete or Clear commands on their Edit menus. These commands differ from Cut in that they simply remove data from the current application without putting a copy of that data on the Clipboard.

Copying a Full Screen or Window

Windows has commands for copying a windowful or an entire screenful of information to the Clipboard all at once. These commands are particularly useful when you're transferring information from a non-Windows application (see "Using the Clipboard with Non-Windows Applications," later in this chapter). But you might also find them useful when your source program is a Windows application.

For example, if you are working in IBM Current and want to show someone in a letter exactly what a particular Current Gantt chart looks like, you can display the chart in one of Current's document windows, and then transfer the entire window—frame, title bar, scroll bars, and all—to the Clipboard. Then you can paste the Clipboard's contents into a letter created in Write.

To transfer a snapshot of the current window to the Clipboard, you simply press Alt-PrtSc. (On some keyboards, the PrtSc key is labeled Print Screen.)

To transfer a snapshot of the current screen into the Clipboard, you press PrtSc (without Alt).

 KEYBOARD TIP: With some older keyboards, where PrtSc shares the asterisk key, you must press Shift-PrtSc to transfer a snapshot of the entire screen.

Note that these commands transfer a graphic *image* (a bitmap) of the current window or screen to the Clipboard. What you see on screen when you take the snapshot is exactly what goes onto the Clipboard and exactly what you can subsequently paste into another program. Any information beyond the confines of the current screen or window is not transferred.

The illustration on the following page shows what Clipboard Viewer would look like if you used Alt-PrtSc to take a picture of a window in IBM Current.

The Control menu at the upper left of this picture, the title bar that says "Clipboard Viewer," the Maximize and Restore buttons at the upper right of the picture, and the scroll bars at the bottom and right are all part of Clipboard Viewer. Everything else is an image copied from Current.

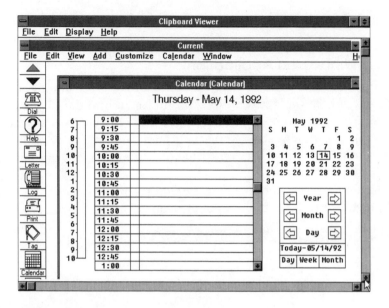

USING THE CLIPBOARD WITH NON-WINDOWS APPLICATIONS

You can use the Clipboard to transfer information in and out of applications that weren't designed specifically for Windows, although a few restrictions apply. These restrictions are as follows:

- You can *copy* information from a non-Windows application to the Clipboard, but you can't *cut* information from a non-Windows application to the Clipboard.

- If you're running Windows in standard mode, your non-Windows applications use the entire screen (you can't run them in a window). In this situation, you must copy the entire screen to the Clipboard at once.

- If you're running Windows in standard mode, you can copy only text screens; you can't copy information from programs that run in graphics mode.

In 386 enhanced mode, you can run non-Windows applications either in a window or in full-screen mode. When you're running in a window, you can copy selected portions of the window to the Clipboard, the same way you can in a Windows application.

For more information about running applications not designed specifically for Windows, see Chapter 18.

Copying from a Windowed Application

If you're using Windows in 386 enhanced mode and you're running a non-Windows program in a window, you can copy information to the Clipboard in nearly the same way you would copy information from a Windows application. As the following illustrations show, your application will appear much like an ordinary Windows program, with a Control menu, a title bar, sizing buttons, and scroll bars.

If you have a mouse, start by opening the Control menu and choosing Edit. A small Edit menu cascades to the right of the Control menu.

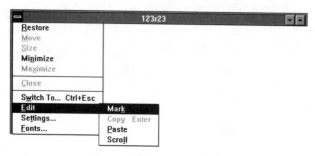

Choose the Mark command on this cascading Edit menu. At this point, the title bar for your program starts with the word *Mark*.

Now put the pointer at one corner of the area you want to copy, hold the button down and drag the pointer to the opposite corner, and then release the button. Your program's title bar now says "Select," instead of "Mark," and the window looks something like this:

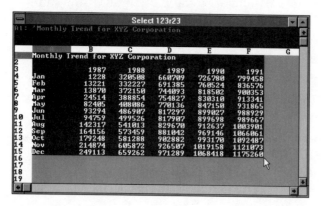

Pull down the Control menu once more, choose Edit again, and choose Copy from the cascading menu. Your selection will now be replicated on the Clipboard, and you can paste it into another program, the same way you would paste data from a Windows application.

 MOUSE TIP: As a shortcut for the Edit Copy command on your non-Windows application's Control menu, you can simply click the right mouse button to copy the selected information to the Clipboard.

 KEYBOARD TIP: The Control menu's Edit Copy command also has a keyboard shortcut: Simply press Enter to copy the selected area to the Clipboard.

 MOUSE TIP: If you find it irksome to have to choose the Mark command before selecting data in a windowed MS-DOS application, you can change your SYSTEM.INI file to make that step unnecessary. To do this, add the line

MouseInDOSBox=0

to the [NonWindowsApp] section of SYSTEM.INI (for details about the SYSTEM.INI file, see Chapter 9). The tradeoff for making this change is that your non-Windows program can no longer recognize mouse actions when it's running in a window.

To copy from a non-Windows application without using a mouse, you need to use a keyboard procedure to select the area you want to copy. Here's what to do:

1. Display your non-Windows application in the active window.

2. Press Alt-Spacebar to pull down the Control menu.

3. Press E to choose the Edit command.

4. Choose Mark on the Edit menu.

   At this point, a blinking selection cursor appears in the upper left corner of your non-Windows application.

5. Use the direction keys to move the selection cursor to the upper left corner of the area you want to copy.

6. Hold down the Shift key, and move the selection cursor to the other corner of the area you want to copy.

7. Release the Shift key. Press Enter, the keyboard shortcut for the Control menu's Edit Copy command.

WINDOWS TIP: If Windows beeps when you try to enter information in your non-Windows application, check to see if the word *Mark* or *Select* appears in the application's title bar. If either word is there, press Esc, and everything will be normal again.

Copying from an Application Running in the Full Screen

To copy information from a non-Windows application that uses the full screen, simply press PrtSc. Windows takes a snapshot of the entire screen and puts the result on the Clipboard.

If the program you're copying from is in character mode, the screen snapshot you create by pressing PrtSc will consist entirely of text characters, and you can paste the result into any program that accepts text. (Most non-Windows applications run in character mode.) After you have pasted the Clipboard's contents into your destination document, you'll be able to remove any parts of the transferred data that you don't really need.

If the program that you copy from runs in graphics mode, the screen snapshot will produce a graphic image (a bitmap), which you'll be able to paste only into other programs that accept graphics. Remember, you can capture graphics screens only if you are running in 386 enhanced mode.

WINDOWS TIP: Some non-Windows programs, such as the MS-DOS versions of Microsoft Word and Quattro Pro, can run in either character mode or graphics mode. If you're unable to copy information from one of these programs, try switching display modes.

If you're running Windows in 386 enhanced mode and you're using a non-Windows application in full-screen fashion, you might want to display the application in a window before copying from it to the Clipboard. That way you'll be able to copy a selection to the Clipboard, instead of copying the entire screen. In 386 enhanced mode, you can switch a non-Windows application from full-screen to windowed display—and back—by pressing Alt-Enter.

Pasting from the Clipboard to a Windowed MS-DOS Application

If you're running Windows in 386 enhanced mode, you can paste from the Clipboard into a non-Windows application in much the same way you would paste into a Windows application. The steps are as follows:

1. Put the information you want to paste on the Clipboard, using whatever method is appropriate.

2. Use Alt-Tab, Alt-Esc, Task List, or any other technique to make your target non-Windows application the current application.

3. If your non-Windows application is using the full screen, press Alt-Enter to switch it to windowed display.

4. Use the keyboard to position the insertion point or cursor at the place where you want to paste the information.

5. Open the non-Windows application's Control menu, and choose Edit.

6. From the Edit menu, choose Paste.

Your non-Windows application must be able to receive the type of information stored in the Clipboard. If the information in the Clipboard is incompatible with the destination application, you'll see an error message when you use the Paste command.

Pasting from the Clipboard to a Full-Screen MS-DOS Application

If you're running Windows in standard mode, you can't display non-Windows applications in a window; you must run them in full-screen fashion. You can still paste data from the Clipboard to such programs, though. Here's how:

1. Put the information you want to paste on the Clipboard, using whatever method is appropriate.

2. Use Alt-Tab, Alt-Esc, Task List, or any other technique to make your target non-Windows program the current application.

3. Position the cursor at the place where you want to paste the information.

4. Use Alt-Tab or Alt-Esc to switch back to any Windows application—Program Manager, File Manager, or any other Windows program.

5. If the current application is maximized, restore it so it doesn't cover the bottom part of the screen.

   At this point, you should see an icon for your non-Windows application.

6. Click once on your destination program's icon to open its Control menu. If you're using the keyboard, press Alt-Esc as many times as necessary to highlight the destination program's icon; then press Alt-Spacebar to open its Control menu.

7. Choose the Paste command from your destination application's Control menu.

   Windows redisplays your destination application in the full screen and begins copying data from the Clipboard into the program.

 WINDOWS TIP: If you're running Windows in 386 enhanced mode, you'll probably find it easiest to switch your destination non-Windows application from full-screen display to windowed display before pasting information into it. You can switch display modes at any time by pressing Alt-Enter.

CLIPBOARD VIEWER

Now let's turn our attention to CLIPBRD.EXE, the Windows program that lets you see what's on the Clipboard before you paste it. You'll find a program-item icon for Clipboard Viewer in your Main program group, if you haven't altered the arrangement of program groups and items that the Windows Setup program initially created for you.

NOTE: *If you upgraded from Windows 3.0 to Windows 3.1, your Clipboard Viewer program item might be titled simply "Clipboard."*

With text on the Clipboard, Clipboard Viewer looks a little like a Notepad window.

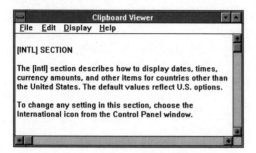

As you can see, it has the usual Windows application paraphernalia—a title bar, a Control menu, sizing buttons, scroll bars, a menu bar, and a work area. The work area is misnamed in this case, though; the only "work" you can do there is to read what's on the Clipboard.

Clipboard Viewer does offer a few services in addition to displaying the Clipboard's contents, however. To see what else it can do, let's check out the program's menus.

The File Menu

Commands on the File menu let you save and reuse the contents of the Clipboard.

Use the Save As command to store whatever the Clipboard currently contains in a disk file. Clipboard Viewer assigns your disk file the extension CLP. Use the Open command to replace the current contents of the Clipboard with an existing CLP file.

WINDOWS TIP: The file created by Clipboard Viewer's Save As command preserves all of the information currently on the Clipboard. Because the Clipboard often stores the same text block or graphic in multiple data formats, CLP files tend to be rather large. If you're tempted to use the Save As command to preserve boiler-plate text, you can usually save disk space by pasting the data into Notepad and saving a TXT file instead of a CLP file. Similarly, if you want to create a library of graphic images, you will probably find it more efficient to save them with a graphics program than with Clipboard Viewer.

The Edit Menu

The Edit menu has a single command, Delete, which empties the Clipboard. Information on the Clipboard can sometimes use a lot of memory, reducing the amount available for other programs. If you find yourself running low on memory, one quick way to alleviate the problem (in addition to closing down applications you're not currently using) may be to delete whatever's on the Clipboard. If you don't have Clipboard Viewer open, you'll need to open it first, of course. But the viewer uses a negligible amount of memory; unless you're truly running on empty, you should be able to launch Clipboard Viewer, use its Delete command, and then close the viewer—thereby freeing up space for your distressed program.

The Display Menu

The Display menu's commands let you see what formats the Clipboard is storing your data in.

When you cut or copy information from an application to the Clipboard, the application—if it's well-behaved—transfers the information in as many formats as it can. Paintbrush, for example, normally supplies an image to the Clipboard in both *bitmap* and *picture* formats. Microsoft Word for Windows copies a block of text in three textual formats, called *text*, *OEM text*, and *rich text format*. Microsoft Excel puts worksheet data on the Clipboard in a large assortment of formats, including some designed to allow the data to be exported to other spreadsheet programs. (See Table 8-1 on page 188.)

This multiple-format arrangement allows the pasting application to receive the data in whatever format best suits it. The fact that a block of cells from a Microsoft Excel worksheet arrives on the Clipboard in both graphics and textual formats means that you can paste it into Notepad, a program that accepts only text, as well as into programs that accept only graphic material.

Depending on what kind of information you've put on the Clipboard, Clipboard Viewer's Display menu can look rather simple, like this:

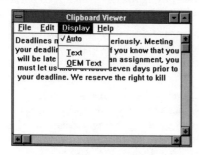

Or it can be impressively complex:

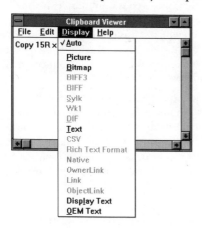

Table 8-1 lists a few of the terms you might encounter on Clipboard Viewer's Display menu.

You can change the appearance of Clipboard Viewer's window by selecting any of the Display-menu names that appear in dark type. (Grayed-out names represent formats that the Clipboard is currently using but that Clipboard Viewer is incapable of displaying.) To return the viewer to its default display, choose Auto, at the top of the Display menu.

It's important to recognize that changing the format displayed in Clipboard Viewer's window has no bearing on the format that will be pasted into a receiving application. If you use the receiving program's Paste command, the program requests a particular format from the Clipboard, regardless of what happens to

Display-menu Term	Description
Text	Unformatted character information (without style attributes, such as boldface and italics), using the ANSI standard character set (the one used by all Windows programs).
OEM Text	Unformatted character information, using the "extended ASCII" character set (the character set used by non-Windows programs). If you paste text data into a non-Windows program, Windows supplies it in OEM-text format.
Rich Text Format	A text format that uses embedded codes to store styling information, such as boldface and italics. Microsoft Excel, Microsoft Word for Windows, and a growing number of other programs support the rich text format.
Bitmap	A graphic format in which each pixel in an image is represented by one or more data bits. Unlike a picture or metafile, bitmapped data is specific for a given output device. If you display a bitmap on a device with different resolution or color capability than the one on which it was created, you're not likely to be pleased with the result. Also, while bitmapped images can be resized or reshaped, this process generally introduces gross distortions.
Picture	A graphic format in which image elements are stored as a sequence of commands. An image in picture format can be reproduced without gross distortion at different sizes or shapes, as well as on different kinds of output devices. But a bitmapped image may display more quickly, because it doesn't have to be recreated from programmatic instructions. A picture format is also sometimes called a metafile (although the terms are not precisely equivalent).
DIB	A device-independent bitmap. This is a newer bitmap format (introduced with OS/2 1.1) that eliminates some (not all) of the device-specificity of the standard bitmap format by including information about the color palette and resolution of the originating device.
BIFF, BIFF3, CSV, DIF, Sylk, Wk1	Formats used for the exchange of spreadsheet or database information.
Link, OwnerLink, ObjectLink	Formats used to establish DDE or OLE links between documents.

Table 8-1.
Some common Clipboard formats.

be displayed in the viewer. Some applications include a Paste Special command, however, in addition to the ordinary Paste command. This command in many cases lets *you* choose which of several formats you want to paste. Clipboard Viewer's Display menu, in that case, might help you make the choice by showing you what formats are there and what they look like.

CONNECTING DOCUMENTS WITH DDE

Information transferred by way of the Clipboard is completely static. After you've pasted a table of worksheet cells from 1-2-3 for Windows into Word for Windows, for example, that table never changes—unless you edit it in Word or change it and recopy it from 1-2-3 for Windows.

Dynamic Data Exchange (DDE) was conceived as a dynamic paste mechanism, one that would update the pasted data automatically as information in the source document changed. In practice, it has proved to be somewhat difficult to use reliably and considerably less friendly than its designers probably hoped. You can expect to see it supplanted eventually by OLE. But that process will take some time, and the programs you use every day may not yet support OLE. So it's useful to have a basic understanding of the establishment, care, and feeding of DDE links.

DDE Terminology

A DDE connection is usually described as a *conversation* between two parties, a *client application* and a *server application.* The client program is the one that receives the information, and the server is the one that supplies it. For example, if you connect a Microsoft Excel spreadsheet with a Word for Windows report in such a way that changes to the spreadsheet are reflected automatically in the report, then Word for Windows is the client and Microsoft Excel is the server.

A DDE conversation always concerns a particular *topic* and a particular *item.* The topic and item spell out the nature of the information that the client is requesting from the server. For example, if the Word for Windows document is to receive data automatically from a range named IBM in a Microsoft Excel worksheet named STOCKS.XLS, then STOCKS.XLS is the topic and IBM is the item.

A DDE link may be *automatic* or *manual.* An automatic link is refreshed whenever the source data changes, provided both the client and server applications are running. A manual link is refreshed only when you issue a command in the client application. (You may see *hot link* and *cold link,* or *active link* and *inactive link,* used as approximate synonyms for *automatic link* and *manual link.*)

Setting Up a DDE Link

With most programs, the simplest way to set up a DDE link is to copy a block of data from the server application to the Clipboard, activate the client application, move the insertion point to the location in the receiving document where you want the information to go, and then use a Paste Link command. Some applications present a confirmation dialog box when you do this.

In programs that use Paste Link to establish DDE conections, the client program's Paste Link command is grayed out if the data in the Clipboard did not originate with a program capable of acting as a DDE server. You might also find the Paste Link command gray if the data in the server application has not yet been saved to disk. With most DDE server programs, you must save your data in a disk file before you can paste-link it into a DDE client.

Using Paste Link is the easiest way to establish a DDE link, but it's not the only way. Some programs that act as DDE clients have commands that allow you to set up a DDE connection without first putting the source data on the Clipboard. Many DDE-supporting applications also have macro languages that you can use to establish DDE links. This is true of Microsoft Excel, Word for Windows, 1-2-3 for Windows, Ami Pro, Dynacomm, and many other advanced Windows applications. The macro-language syntax varies, of course, from program to program, so to establish DDE links this way you need to consult the documentation for the application you'll be using.

Some spreadsheet programs allow you to build DDE links with spreadsheet formulas. The following Microsoft Excel formula, for example, establishes a link with a Word for Windows document:

```
{=WinWord|'C:\WINWORD\RUNWIN\CHAP08\CHAP08.DOC'!DDE_LINK}
```

Fortunately, Microsoft Excel builds this formula for you automatically when you use its Paste Link command. But you can enter such formulas directly if you wish, and you can use standard formula-editing procedures to modify the link. (Note: The formula above is an array formula; if you enter it directly or edit it, you do not type the opening and closing braces. Instead, you terminate the entry by pressing Ctrl-Shift-Enter; Microsoft Excel then adds the braces for you.)

Some Limitations of DDE

DDE has some significant limitations: You need to learn the idiosyncrasies of individual applications to use it. You need to take care not to move or rename whatever's on the server end of the linkage. And the link established by DDE is essentially one-way; it provides no cookie trail back to the data in the server application.

The first problem is a little less daunting now than it was in earlier versions of Windows, thanks to the growing number of applications that offer Copy and Paste Link procedures, as described in the preceding paragraphs. Losing a link (or worse, having the link return invalid data) because the data source has been moved or renamed remains a hazard, however. One way you can minimize the hazard is by trying to used named entities as your data sources. For example, if you're linking from a Microsoft Excel worksheet, name the source data range. That way, if you move the data to another location on the worksheet, the link will remain valid.

If the server-application file that contains your linked data is moved or renamed, the link produces an error message in the client application. In many cases, you can "repair" the link by using a Change Links command. (Typically, you'll find this on the program's Edit menu. You might need to choose a Links command first, and then click an Edit Links or Change Links button in the ensuing dialog box. Here, as elsewhere with DDE, procedures vary from program to program.) Obviously, it's best never to tamper with the name or location of any file that acts as a DDE server, but in the real world such advice may be hard to heed.

As for the one-way nature of DDE links, that is one of the chief advantages of establishing linkage with OLE, instead of DDE.

MAKING CONNECTIONS WITH OLE

Object linking and embedding, as the name suggests, is two services wrapped up under a single acronym. Both are carried out with simple Edit-menu procedures. To link with OLE, copy data from an OLE-supporting program to the Clipboard. Then use the Paste Link command in another OLE-supporting program. To embed, follow the same procedure but use Paste instead of Paste Link.

Both programs must, of course, support OLE. Moreover, the program that supplies the data must support OLE as a *server application*, and the one that receives the data must support OLE as a *client application*.

Some programs may support OLE in only one mode or the other. Paint-brush, for example, can act only as an OLE server. Write and Cardfile can act only as OLE clients. Other programs you use may support OLE in both modes; to be sure, you need to consult your programs' documentation.

From the user's perspective, linking with OLE offers one large advantage over linking with DDE—namely, the ability to launch the server program directly from the client document. You do not have to remember where your data came from. (There are other improvements under the hood, as well.) The hazards of DDE linking still apply, however. If you rename or relocate a server document, you will need to repair or abandon any links in client documents. Most OLE client applications include commands to assist you with this.

Linking versus Embedding

Here is a summary of the differences between linking and embedding:

- When you link, the linked data is stored only in the server document. Although you see the linked data in the client document, the client document records only pointers to the server document.

- When you embed, a copy of the embedded data is stored in the client document.

- When you link, any changes made to the linked data in the server document are reflected in the client document—either immediately (if you've established an automatic link) or on request (if the link is manual).

- When you embed, changes in the server document have no effect on the client document.

- Linked data must have been saved at least once in a disk file.

- When you double-click a linked *object* (a data item paste-linked from an OLE server) in a client application, Windows launches a normal copy of the server application, loads the file containing the object, and selects the linked data. Changes you make in the server are then reflected in the client immediately or on request, according to the mode of the link.

- When you double-click an embedded object, Windows launches a special copy of the server application (one with a modified title bar and File menu), loads the file containing the object, and selects the linked data. Changes you make in the server are not reflected in the client until you use the server's Update command; you'll generally find that command on the File menu. Alternatively, you can update the client document by quitting the server and answering an update prompt affirmatively.

- A linked object in one OLE client document may be linked to other OLE client documents.

You should use linking in preference to embedding when your source data is likely to change over time and you need to have it updated automatically in your client document. You should also prefer linking over embedding when you use the same data in many client documents; you can ensure consistency in this case by linking each client document to a single server.

Embedding's chief advantages over linking are permanence and portability. Because the embedded data actually resides in the client application, you don't have to worry about renaming or moving the data's source. Obviously, you'll want to choose embedding over linking if you're going to send your client document to an off-site colleague who doesn't have access to your files.

Editing embedded data is just as easy as embedding linked data. Simply double-click the embedded object, make your changes in the server program, and use Update to send the changes back to the client document.

For examples of linking and embedding procedures in Cardfile and Write, see Chapters 7 and 14, respectively.

EMBEDDING PACKAGES

Windows 3.1 includes a facility called *packaging* that lets you do the following:

- Embed an iconic representation of a data object in an OLE client document (the object can be any block of data—text, graphic, sound, or video—that originates in an OLE server application)

- Embed an iconic representation of an entire file in an OLE client document (the file may be a data file or an executable and does not have to originate in an OLE server application)

- Embed a Windows command line, attached to an icon, in an OLE client document

In all three cases, the embedded object is called a *package* or *package object*. In all three cases, the package is *embedded* in the client document. But the *contents of the package* may be either an embedded object or a linked object. If the package contains embedded data, then embedding the package stores an encapsulated copy of the data object in the client document. If the package contains linked data, embedding the package stores pointers to the package's source. (See "Linking versus Embedding," earlier in this chapter.)

Regardless of what the package contains, what you see after embedding the package is an icon. The illustration on the following page, for example, shows how a Write document with an embedded package might look.

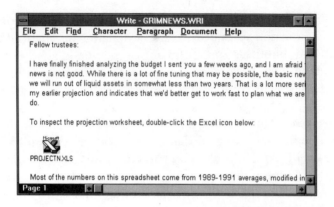

After you have embedded a package you can *play* it by double-clicking it or choosing a menu command. Playing a packaged data object (a portion of a file) provides a convenient way to inspect or edit that object. Playing a packaged file is equivalent to choosing File Manager or Program Manager's File Run command and typing the name of the file. The same is true of playing a packaged command line; for example, if you encapsulate the command line TODOLIST.TXT, then playing the package invokes Notepad with a copy of your to-do list in place (assuming that TXT files are associated with NOTEPAD.EXE).

To assist you in embedding packages, Windows 3.1 includes a utility program called Object Packager. You'll find a program-item icon for it in your Accessories group, if you still have the Windows default arrangement of Program Manager groups. In addition to helping you create packages, Object Packager also lets you change the icons and text associated with those packages.

Why Use Packages?

At this point you might be wondering why you would want to bother embedding a package when you could instead embed or link a data object directly. One reason is compactness. In the previous figure, the embedded package represents a large range of cells in a Microsoft Excel worksheet. While this worksheet presumably supports the argument you're making in your Write document, a full visual representation of the worksheet would be distracting. By encapsulating supporting data in packages, you can create a kind of footnoting system. Interested readers can summon supporting materials, while others can skip over the icons without losing the continuity of the main text.

A second reason for using packages is that they're not limited to data that originates in OLE server programs. If you encapsulate an entire file in a package, as opposed to a block of data, that file can come from any program.

Embedding a Packaged Object or File

The general procedure for embedding a packaged file or data object is as follows (the procedure for packaging a command line is described later in this chapter; see "Embedding a Packaged Command Line"):

1. Place the data or file you want to package on the Clipboard.

2. Use Object Packager to create your package.

3. Use Object Packager to make any desired changes to the package's icon or label.

4. Use Object Packager's Copy Package command to copy the package to the Clipboard.

5. Use the client application's Paste command to embed the package.

If you're packaging an entire file and you're content to use the default text and icon for your package, you can bypass Object Packager. We'll come back to this point in a moment (see "Packaging Files—the Direct Route," below).

Putting the Data on the Clipboard

If you're going to package an entire file, start by selecting that file in a File Manager directory window. (See Chapter 6 for details about using File Manager.) Then use the Copy command on File Manager's File menu (or press F8, its keyboard shortcut). You'll see a dialog box like the following.

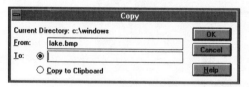

Choose the Copy To Clipboard option, and click OK.

If the data you want to package constitutes only a portion of a file, simply select that data in the customary way, and then use the Edit Copy command to put the data on the Clipboard. Remember, however, that in this case the data must originate in an OLE server application.

Creating the Package

After the data you want to encapsulate is stored on the Clipboard, the next step is to run Object Packager. (If Object Packager is already running, activate it and choose its File New command.) Object Packager presents two work spaces—an

Appearance window on the left and a Content window on the right. To create your new package, first activate the Content window (click the mouse there or press Tab until you see the word *Content* highlighted). Then choose either the Paste or the Paste Link command from Object Packager's Edit menu.

If you choose Paste, your package will contain a copy of the data or file on the Clipboard. Object Packager's display will look something like this (in this example, the encapsulated data is a Paintbrush file):

If you choose Paste Link, your package will contain only a link to the source data, not the data itself. Object Packager's display will then look something like this:

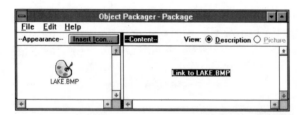

If you're not sure whether you want the package to contain embedded data or a link, see "Linking versus Embedding," earlier in this chapter.

Using Object Packager to Customize Your Package

By default, Object Packager uses a standard application icon to represent your packaged data. And, as you can see in the preceding two illustrations, it describes that data with either the name of a file or a standard object description. But you can change either the icon or the descriptive text if you want.

To change the descriptive text associated with a package, activate the Appearance window and choose the Edit menu's Label command. Type your new text in the dialog box, and click OK.

To change the icon associated with a package, click the Insert Icon button. Object Packager presents the standard Windows change-icon dialog box—the same one you see if you use Program Manager's Properties command and choose

Change Icon. For details about this dialog box, see "Changing a Program Item's Icon," in Chapter 5.

Copying the Package to the Clipboard

After your package is all wrapped up and ready to go, it's time to put it on the loading dock—which, as usual, is the Windows Clipboard. The only trick to remember in this step is to use the Copy Package command, not the Copy command. (If Object Packager's Content window is active when you pull down the Edit menu, Copy will be grayed out and you'll only be able to choose Copy Package.)

Embedding the Package

The final step is to activate your client application and choose the Paste command. (If your client program is Cardfile, be sure to put Cardfile in Picture mode first. Cardfile does not accept any kind of embedded data in Text mode.)

After you've pasted in your package, your client document should display the same icon and text you saw in Object Packager's Appearance window. You can now play or edit your embedded package. (See "Playing and Editing Embedded Packages," later in this chapter.)

Embedding a Packaged Command Line

To embed a command line encapsulated as a package, follow these steps:

1. Start Object Packager. (If Object Packager is already running, activate it and choose the New command.)

2. Choose the Edit menu's Command Line command.

3. In the dialog box, type the command line you want to encapsulate.

   This can be any legal Windows command line—the name of an executable file, the name of a document file, or whatever. When you embed this command line and play it from your client application, Windows behaves exactly as though you had used Program Manager's File Run command and typed this command string.

4. Make any changes desired to the package's appearance and descriptive text. (See "Using Object Packager to Customize Your Package," above.)

   You'll probably want to click the Insert Icon button and choose an icon for your packaged command line.

5. Choose Object Packager's Copy Package command.

6. Activate your client application, move the insertion point to the appropriate location, and choose the client application's Paste command.

Here is a Cardfile card with a command line embedded as a package.

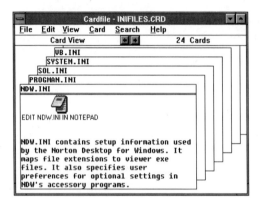

The command line, which is not visible, reads simply *NDW.INI*. Double-clicking the icon, or the line of descriptive text beneath, runs Notepad with the NDW.INI file.

Note that, while it would be possible to package the entire file NDW.INI and embed that in Cardfile, there would be no advantage to doing so (and it would add unnecessary bulk to the Cardfile file). If all we want is to be able to get to the INI file quickly, an embedded command line is more efficient.

Playing and Editing Embedded Packages

Playing an embedded package invokes the source application for the packaged data, allowing you to read the data—or hear it or watch it, as the case may be. *Editing* the package invokes Object Packager, allowing you to change the package's appearance or descriptive text.

More specifically, this is what happens when you play a package:

- If the package contains embedded data that originated in an OLE server application, Windows invokes a modified copy of the server program, with the data in place. You can then edit your data and send changes back to the client document by choosing the server program's Update command.

- If the package contains an embedded file that did not originate in an OLE server program, Windows invokes a normal copy of the source application (the program in which the file was created) with a *temporary copy* of your packaged file. (The application's title bar will bear a filename beginning with a tilde character.) If you edit the file and use the application's Save command, Windows updates the contents of the package but does not change the original disk file.

- If the package contains a linked file, Windows invokes the source application, with the packaged file in place.

To play a package, you can either double-click it in the client application or select it and use the client application's Play command. To edit the package, select it and use the client application's Edit command. In most OLE client programs, you can get to the Play and Edit commands by first choosing a command called Package Object. Cardfile, for example, produces the following cascading menu when you choose Package Object.

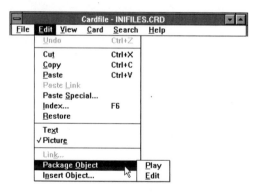

Packaging Files—the Direct Route

If you plan to package an entire file (not a data object), you can bypass Object Packager with the following shortcuts:

- If you want your package to contain an embedded file, you can drag the filename from a File Manager window and drop it into your client application. Or you can use File Manager's Copy command, choose the Copy To Clipboard option, and then use your client program's Paste command.

- If you want your package to contain a linked file, you can select the filename in File Manager, copy the file to the Clipboard, and then use your client program's Paste Link command.

Note that dragging the file from File Manager to your client program *always* creates a package containing an embedded file.

9

Customizing Windows with Control Panel and the INI Files

This chapter introduces Control Panel, the Windows utility that lets you tailor your system to suit your needs and tastes. You can use Control Panel to change the appearance of your electronic desktop, adjust the sensitivity of your mouse or the repeat rate of your keyboard, set your computer's clock and calendar, install printer drivers, configure serial ports, change the size or type of swap file used by Windows in 386 enhanced mode, and do other similar tasks.

In this chapter, we'll look in detail at most of Control Panel's options. Two of the options not covered here—Printers and Fonts—are sufficiently complex to warrant chapters of their own. (The Printers section of Control Panel is discussed in Chapter 11, and the Fonts sections is discussed in Chapter 13.) The 386 Enhanced section of Control Panel is discussed in two other chapters. Options having to do with the way Windows runs non-Windows applications in 386 enhanced mode are discussed in Chapter 18. Virtual Memory options—the settings that determine the type and location of your Windows swap file—are discussed in Chapter 19.

Most changes that you make to your system using Control Panel are recorded in a file called WIN.INI (the name is short for *Windows Initialization*). For example, if you change the colors of your desktop, Control Panel writes some information under the [colors] heading of the WIN.INI file.

If you've used an earlier version of Windows, you may know that it is possible to customize your system by modifying the contents of WIN.INI yourself, with the help of Notepad or another text editor. You can still do that in Windows 3.1, but there's less incentive to do it now. Most of the customizing changes that Windows 1 and Windows 2 users had to do by direct modification of WIN.INI can now be done either through Control Panel or through one of the Windows shells—Program Manager or File Manager. Nevertheless, there are still a few things you may want to do by adding information to WIN.INI. So this chapter concludes with an overview of this important initialization file.

STARTING CONTROL PANEL

To start Control Panel, double-click its icon in the Main program group of Program Manager. To start it from File Manager, double-click the name CONTROL.EXE in the directory window of the directory containing your Windows files.

Control Panel offers a window full of icons.

NOTE: *Your own Control Panel might not look exactly like this one. For example, if you're connected to a network, you'll see a Network icon in addition to the icons shown here. If you're not using the Windows multimedia extensions or an audio board, your Control Panel probably does not include the MIDI Mapper icon—and so on.*

Each icon can be used to launch one section of the program. If you work without a mouse, you can use the direction keys to move among icons, or you can ignore the icons and choose equivalent commands from the Settings menu.

CHANGING DESKTOP COLORS OR PATTERNS

When you first install Windows, it uses a color scheme called Windows Default. It's a fine color scheme, but you're not stuck with it; you can choose from a number of alternative schemes. And if you don't like any of the color schemes offered, you can concoct your own. You can assign a color (or a pattern, if you're working with a monochrome display) to each of 21 different screen elements, and then name and save the arrangement you create. You can design as many custom color schemes as you want, adding each to the menu of color schemes that Windows supplies. As mood or necessity dictates, you can switch from one scheme to another by choosing from a simple drop-down list.

To see how easy this all is, double-click Control Panel's Color icon, or choose Color from the Settings menu. Windows presents the following dialog box.

The illustration shows the Windows Default color scheme as you would see it in VGA resolution. (Of course, like all the illustrations in this book, this one is merely a black-and-white representation of a color display.) If you're using a different display resolution, your screen will look different. But the basic elements will be the same.

 WINDOWS TIP: Windows 3.1 includes three color schemes that are particularly useful for LCD displays, one scheme designed to conserve power on plasma displays, and a number of other color schemes that were not offered in Windows 3.0.

Choosing from the List of Color Schemes

Next, to see what the built-in color schemes are called and what they look like, click the downward arrow near the upper right corner of the dialog box. The drop-down list unfolds, revealing the first five color-scheme options, as shown in the illustration at the top of the following page.

Now use the Down direction key to step through the list box. As you high-light the name of each color scheme, Windows displays a sample of that scheme in the bottom part of the dialog box. You can apply any color scheme to your Windows environment by highlighting its name and clicking the OK button in the lower left corner of the window.

Creating Your Own Color Scheme

If you'd rather create your own color scheme, click the Color Palette button. Windows expands the dialog box.

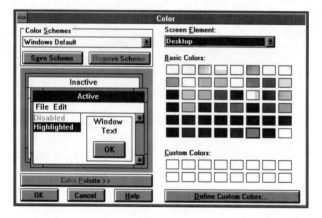

Now on the right side of the dialog box is another drop-down list, called Screen Element. And directly below that you see a set of color options. As the illustration above shows, with a color system, you may see as many as 48 colors. With a monochrome or CGA display, you get 16 monochromatic patterns, ranging in density from pure black to pure white.

Now click the downward arrow to open the Screen Element drop-down list box. This list shows the names of the 21 screen elements to which you can assign colors.

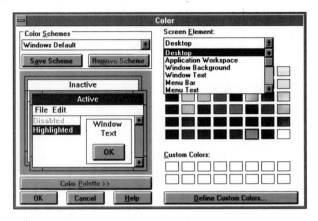

Each screen element in this list is represented in the sample desktop on the left side of the dialog box. If you have a mouse, the simplest way to change colors is to click on one of the screen elements in the sample desktop. When you do this, the name of the screen element you click is selected in the drop-down list on the right side of the dialog box. With the appropriate screen element selected, click on the color you want to assign. Then check the sample desktop to see if you're satisfied with the new color assignment.

For example, suppose you want to change the active title bar so that it shows yellow text on a solid red background. You would click in the title bar labeled Active (anywhere except directly on the word *Active*), and then click on the first sample in the second row of the Basic Colors palette. That assigns the solid red color to the active title bar. Next you would click on the word *Active* and then click on the second color in the third row.

 MOUSE TIP: Successive clicks on the OK button in the sample desktop cycle the screen-element selection from Button Face through Button Shadow, Button Text, and Button Highlight. Similarly, clicking on the word *Highlighted* in the sample desktop toggles the selection between Highlight and Highlighted Text. To see which element you've selected, check the drop-down list on the right side of the dialog box.

If you don't have a mouse, here's how you can change screen colors:

1. If the Screen Element list box isn't highlighted, press Alt-E to highlight it.

2. Use the direction keys to highlight the name of the screen element you want to change.

3. Press Tab to get to the color palette.

4. Use the direction keys to move from color to color in the palette.

5. When you get to a color you want to assign, press the Spacebar to select it.

6. Press Shift-Tab to move back to the list box.

7. Repeat steps 2 through 6 until you've assigned all the colors you want to assign.

8. Press Enter to return to Control Panel, or follow the instructions below for naming and saving your new color scheme.

Feel free to experiment with color combinations. The definitions for the built-in color schemes are stored in a file named CONTROL.INI (a private initialization file; see "Modifying the INI Files Directly," later in this chapter). Unless you deliberately modify the contents of this file, the built-in color schemes always look the same, no matter what changes you make in Control Panel. If in your experimenting with color you turn your Windows desktop into something gruesome, you can always restore order by reinstating one of the built-in color schemes.

 WINDOWS TIP: If you make a lot of color changes at a single session in Control Panel, you might reduce your *system resources* to the point where you experience anomalous performance or receive low-memory messages from Windows. If that happens, simply close and reopen Control Panel. (System resources are discussed in Chapter 19.)

WINDOWS TIP: It's possible to make your menus invisible; all you have to do is set Menu Text and Menu Bar to the same color. If you happen to make this mistake, here's one way to recover: If Control Panel is still running, press Alt-Tab until it becomes the current application. (If Control Panel isn't running, press Alt-Tab until Program Manager is the active application. Then press Alt, F, R to choose the Run command. Type *control* and press Enter to get to Control Panel.) Then press Alt, S, C to choose the Colors command on the Settings menu. When the Colors dialog box appears, reinstate one of the built-in color schemes.

A Few Limitations

Here are some additional points to note about setting colors in Control Panel:

- Some applications set their own colors, overriding the choices you make in Color Panel. Solitaire, for example, uses a "Las Vegas" green background, no matter what selection you make for the Application Workspace screen element.

- You cannot assign a new color to the text that Windows uses to label minimized icons. Windows uses either black or white for this text, depending on the color of your desktop.

- Some of Control Panel's colors—for example, the sixth and seventh options in the second row—are *dithered* (blended from two or more solid colors). If you assign a dithered color to any text element, Windows substitutes a solid color of its choice.

 WINDOWS TIP: If you switch from a 256-color display driver to a 16-color driver—or vice versa—you might find that some of your color choices look quite different. This is particularly likely to happen when dithered colors are assigned to text elements. A color scheme that looks fine in one resolution might not look good in another. The simplest way to deal with this phenomenon is to name your color schemes and switch when you change resolutions.

Saving a Color Scheme

Unlike many of the other customizing decisions you can make in WIN.INI, color changes take effect immediately; you do not have to restart Windows. Your new colors will stay in effect for the rest of your working session and all future sessions—until you change colors again.

When you assign new colors and press Enter or click OK, Windows records your selections as an unnamed color scheme (the information is registered in the [colors] section of WIN.INI). Do not be concerned if the Color Schemes list box still displays the name of a built-in scheme when you click OK. The next time you return to this dialog box, the Color Schemes entry will be blank (indicating that you're using an unnamed color scheme), and the built-in scheme that was there when you saved will still be intact.

If you hit upon a color scheme that pleases your eye, it's best to name it before you save it. That way, you'll be able to switch back and forth between your own design and one of the ones supplied by Windows—or between several of your own making.

To save a named color scheme, simply click the Save Scheme button and supply a name. Windows adds your name to the bottom of the Color Schemes list box.

If you tire of your named color scheme, you can easily remove it. Simply select its name, and click the Remove Scheme button.

Customizing the Color Palette

To the 16 gray shades or 48 colors of your basic palette, Windows lets you add up to 16 custom colors—colors that you define yourself by mixing red, green, and blue elements.

To define a custom color, start by clicking the Define Custom Colors button. Windows opens the Custom Color Selector.

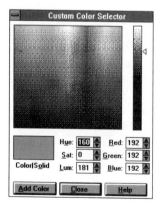

If you have a mouse, you can specify a custom color by dragging selection cursors within the two color scales—the big square one and the vertical bar. If you don't have a mouse, you can enter numbers in either or both of the two scales at the lower right corner of the Custom Color Selector. Whichever method you use, it's probably useful to have a little background information about the terms in which colors are defined.

How Colors Are Defined

Colors in Windows are recorded as a combination of three parameters: hue, saturation, and luminosity. Roughly speaking, the basic quality of a color—its redness, blueness, or whatever—is defined by its *hue*. The purity of a color is defined by its *saturation*; a lower saturation value means more gray is mixed in. And the brightness or dullness of a color is defined by its *luminosity*.

Hue, saturation, and luminosity are the parameters that Windows uses internally, but your video display hardware lives by a different set of numbers. Images on a color monitor are formed from a combination of dots, or *pixels*. (A pixel is the smallest dot that can be displayed on your screen.) To make each pixel visible, a beam of electrons is fired at three tiny spots of phosphor—one red, one green, and one blue. The result is three points of distinctly colored light so close together that they're perceived as a single light source. The apparent color of that light source is determined by the relative intensities of its red, green, and blue components.

Every combination of hue, saturation, and luminosity, therefore, is translated by Windows into varying levels of energy directed at those spots of red, blue, and green phosphor.

Thus there are two scales in the lower right corner of the Custom Color Selector—one for the parameters used by Windows, the other for the relative red, green, and blue intensities. You can define a custom color by modifying the numbers in either scale.

To set a custom color with the mouse, you adjust the position of two pointers—the cross-hair in the big square grid and the arrowhead to the right of the vertical scale. For every possible position of those pointers, Windows displays a sample of the selected color in the two boxes at the lower left corner of the Color Selector.

Why two sample boxes? Because your system isn't capable of displaying every possible combination of the three color parameters. Windows uses dithering to approximate the colors that your system can't display directly. The sample box on the left (the one marked *Color*) displays the dithered color; the one on the right (marked *Solid*) displays a closely related color your system can display without dithering.

Experimenting with Color

The vertical scale on the right controls luminosity (brightness). As you move this pointer higher, the color becomes lighter. Putting the pointer at the top of the scale creates pure white, no matter where the other pointer may be; putting the pointer at the bottom produces jet black.

The square grid controls hue and saturation. Moving the cross-hair higher increases the saturation; moving it from side to side changes the hue.

To see the range of "pure" colors available, start by putting the luminosity pointer about halfway up the vertical scale. Then put the cross-hair pointer at the upper left corner of the square grid. This combination gives you a fully saturated red of medium luminosity. Now slowly drag the pointer across the top of the grid; as you do, you'll move from red through yellow, green, blue, violet, and back to red again. (Alternatively, you can click the upward arrow in the Hue box to step the Hue parameter from 0 to 239.)

To see the effect of luminosity on color, double-click the Solid sample box or press Alt-O. This moves the cross-hair to the nearest position where you see a pure color in both sample boxes. Then move the luminosity pointer up and down the scale (or click the arrows in the Lum box). To test the effect of saturation, put the luminosity pointer back in the middle of the scale and drag the cross-hair straight up and down in the square grid (or click the arrows next to the Sat box).

Adding Custom Colors to Your Palette

When you find a color you like, you can add it to your Custom Color palette by clicking the Add Color button. (If you prefer to add the solid color, double-click the solid box or press Alt-O first.) Windows adds the color to the first available Custom Color box. If you want to add it to a specific box in your custom palette (for example, if you want to replace a custom color), select that box with the mouse before clicking the Add Color button.

When you've filled out the custom palette to your satisfaction, click the Close button. Now you can assign your custom colors to the screen elements exactly as you did the basic colors.

CONFIGURING SERIAL PORTS

A *serial port* is a physical connection between your computer and some peripheral device, such as a printer, modem, or scanner. Your computer probably has at least one serial port and may have as many as four. Serial ports are named COM1, COM2, COM3, and COM4.

To *configure* a serial port means to tell Windows how you want information transferred across the port to your peripheral device. For each port your system uses, you can set five communications parameters:

- Baud rate
- Data bits
- Parity
- Stop bits
- Flow control

Baud rate refers to the speed at which data flows across the port. Baud rate is also sometimes expressed as *bits per second* (bps).

Data bits and *stop bits* refer to the way in which characters are "framed" as they're sent through the serial port. A character consists of data bits (usually seven or eight), which are sent one at a time (serially). Stop bits mark the beginning and ending of each character.

Parity is a form of error checking employed by certain peripheral devices. If used, it comes in four "flavors": *even, odd, mark,* and *space.*

Flow control refers to the way your computer and the external device let each other know they're ready (or not ready) to communicate. Flow control is also often referred to as *handshaking.*

To set communications parameters for a serial port, double-click the Ports icon in Control Panel or pull down the Settings menu and choose Ports. Windows displays the following dialog box.

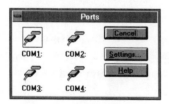

Select the name of the port you want to configure, and then click the Settings button (or press Alt-S). Windows presents the Settings dialog box for the selected port, as shown in the illustration on the following page.

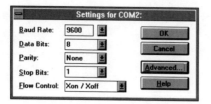

For the proper settings for your serial ports, consult the documentation for the devices you're using.

The Advanced button in the communications settings dialog box produces an additional dialog box that you can use to change a communications port's base address or interrupt request (IRQ) line. You won't ordinarily need to do this, however, and you *shouldn't* change either setting unless you know what you're doing!

 WINDOWS TIP: The communications settings you assign with Control Panel become the defaults for your serial ports. You can override these defaults temporarily with communications programs such as Terminal. Therefore, if you use your modem to communicate with several different services, each requiring different parameters, you don't have to return to Control Panel each time you switch services. For more information, see Chapter 15.

CUSTOMIZING THE MOUSE

The Mouse section of Control Panel lets you tailor the behavior of your mouse or other pointing device to suit your personal tastes. You can adjust the mouse's *tracking* and *double-click* speeds, and you can reverse the functionality of the left and right buttons. You might find it handy to reverse these buttons if you're left-handed; by reversing the button functions, you can put the mouse on the left side of your keyboard and still use your index finger for most mouse commands.

You can refine your mouse's behavior in some additional ways by making changes directly to your WIN.INI file. See "Fine-Tuning the Mouse," later in this chapter.

The Mouse section of Control Panel also includes a check-box option called Mouse Trails, which is handy if you use Windows on a laptop computer. Depending on how you have set your window background and desktop colors, your mouse pointer might be hard to see on an LCD display. If you select the Mouse Trails option, your pointer leaves a temporary trail on screen as you move it. Thus, if you lose track of the pointer you can simply move your mouse (or track ball, or other pointing device) and you should be able to locate the pointer with no difficulty.

To make mouse adjustments, start by double-clicking Control Panel's Mouse icon. Or pull down the Settings menu and choose Mouse. Windows displays the following dialog box.

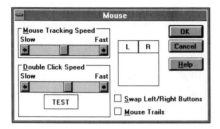

The term *tracking speed* refers to the relationship between movement of the mouse on your desktop and movement of the pointer on screen. With a faster tracking speed, it takes less mouse movement to move the pointer.

If you often find your mouse pointer overshooting its target as you select commands or objects in Windows, you'll probably find it helpful to select a slower tracking speed. On the other hand, if you find yourself "rowing"—picking the mouse up, bringing it back through the air, and then sliding it over the desktop again merely to get the pointer from one side of the screen to the other, try increasing the tracking speed.

To lower the tracking speed, click the arrow at the left side of the Mouse Tracking Speed scroll bar. To increase it, click the arrow on the right side. Alternatively, you can drag the box in either direction in the scroll bar. Be careful, though; even a small adjustment in the position of the scroll box has quite an effect on mouse behavior.

MOUSE TIP: Windows gives you immediate feedback about changes you make to the mouse tracking speed. That way you can tell whether you've made the right adjustment before you click OK to return to Control Panel. If you regret a change you make, you can click the Cancel button to restore your former setting.

The double-click speed specifies the time interval within which two mouse clicks have to occur to be interpreted by the system as a double-click. You can adjust this parameter the same way you adjust tracking speed—by clicking the arrow at either end of the Double Click Speed scroll bar or by dragging the box within the scroll bar.

To test the double-click speed you set, try double-clicking the box labeled TEST. If your two clicks are read as a double-click, the box changes from light to dark or from dark to light.

To reverse the functioning of your mouse buttons, check the Swap Left/Right Buttons check box. Windows confirms the change by reversing the letters *L* and *R* in the diagram above the check box.

Note that if you reverse the button functions and then change your mind, you will have to click the check box with the *right* button to undo the swap.

CUSTOMIZING YOUR DESKTOP

The term *desktop* refers to that part of your Windows screen that lies outside any particular windows or icons. It's the background area within which you create and work with windows. Control Panel's Desktop section has a number of options that affect the appearance and behavior of your desktop.

- The Pattern feature lets you cover your desktop with a repeating dot pattern—either one that you create yourself or one that Windows supplies. Doing this is somewhat like throwing a tweed tablecloth over your screen; just the ticket, perhaps, if you get bored with solid colors or grays.

- For a more pictorial backdrop, you can add "wallpaper" to your desktop. The wallpaper can be a small image repeated as many times as necessary to fill the screen (in the manner of true wallpaper), a single image centered on the desktop, or a single image that covers the entire screen.

- To protect your screen while you're away from your computer, you can install a *screen saver*. Windows supplies several screen-saver modules to choose from. If you've installed a third-party screen saver on your system, you might be able to use Control Panel to switch between the built-in saver modules and your third-party saver.

- A check box in the Desktop dialog box lets you specify whether you want long icon labels to be displayed on two or more lines. (This option is normally turned on.)

- A Granularity option lets you control the positions of objects on your desktop by activating an invisible set of grid lines. With grid lines in place, Windows and icons automatically align on the nearest grid line.

Also included in the Desktop section are commands for increasing or decreasing the cursor-blink speed, for setting the width of your icons, and for adjusting the thickness of window borders.

To customize your desktop, start by double-clicking Control Panel's Desktop icon—or pull down the Settings menu and choose Desktop. The following dialog box appears.

Setting a Background Pattern

To apply a background pattern to your desktop, click the downward arrow in the Pattern box, select one of the patterns listed, and click the OK button. If you want to look at the available patterns without applying any of them, start by clicking the Edit Pattern button. You'll get the Edit Pattern dialog box. Now, by pressing the Down direction key, you can cycle through the pattern list and see a sample of each. The illustration on the following page, for example, shows what the Thatches pattern looks like.

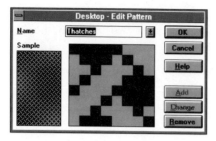

If you find a pattern to your taste, you can apply it to the desktop by clicking OK two times—first in the Edit Pattern dialog box, and then in the Desktop dialog box.

Editing Background Patterns

The big square in the center of the Edit Pattern dialog box represents the "cell" of which the selected background pattern is made. The cell is an eight-by-eight grid of dots; each dot is either dark or light. You can edit the background pattern by changing one or more dots from light to dark or dark to light. To do that, simply click the mouse on whatever dots you want to change. (Unfortunately, there's no keyboard equivalent for this procedure.)

As you make changes to the dot pattern in the background cell, you can see the effect of those changes in the Sample box to the cell's left. When you're satisfied with your editing of the pattern, click the Change button to save the revised pattern. Then click OK to select it.

Adding New Background Patterns

The easiest way to create a new background pattern is to edit an existing one (as explained in the previous paragraphs) and give it a new name. When you replace the text in the Name text box (in the Edit Pattern dialog box), Windows grays out the Change button and activates the Add button. Click the Add button, and your new pattern joins the list of existing patterns. At this point, you can apply it to your desktop by clicking OK twice.

Changing the Behavior of Alt-Tab

Ordinarily, when you switch between Windows programs by pressing Alt-Tab, Windows displays a box in the center of your screen that shows the name and icon of the program you're about to switch to. This method of telling you where you're going is new in Windows 3.1. In earlier versions, as you held down the Alt key and pressed Tab, Windows displayed the window borders and title bar of each program in turn.

Most users find navigating between programs a lot easier with the Windows 3.1 approach to Alt-Tabbing. But if you prefer the old style, you can easily reinstate it. Simply invoke the Desktop section of Control Panel and deselect the Fast "Alt+Tab" Switching check box.

Choosing a Screen Saver

Cathode-ray-tube (CRT) displays used by desktop computers create images by firing electron beams at phosphor-coated screens. If the same picture or text remains on a screen for a long period of time, the phosphor coating can be damaged, leaving a faint but permanent image on the screen. Screen savers reduce this hazard by monitoring screen activity. Whenever your screen has not changed for a specified length of time, the screen saver puts its own constantly varying image on the screen. As soon as you press a key or (with most savers) move the mouse, the screen saver restores the image that was there before.

That's the ostensible purpose of a screen saver, at any rate. In truth, with current display technology, the probability that you'll ruin your CRT with a burned-in image is pretty remote. But screen savers have other values, as well. They're fun to watch, and they can prevent others in your office from prying while you're away from your machine. Many screen savers have "save now" and password options. The save-now option lets you display the saver pattern on demand, either by pressing a certain keyboard combination or by moving the mouse to a particular corner of the screen. With a password option you can ensure that only you are able to restore the underlying display. If your screen saver has these features, you can display the saver image any time you walk away from your computer and be reasonably confident that no one will invade your privacy in your absence. (Someone determined to snoop can, of course, reboot your machine.)

In the Desktop section of Control Panel, you can choose from several screen-saver modules supplied with Windows (the default choice is None). If you use a third-party screen-saver program, such as After Dark or Intermission, you might find its modules in the Screen Saver drop-down list, alongside the Windows-supplied modules. (To be listed, a third-party product must use a data file with the extension SCR, and that file must be stored in your Windows directory or its SYSTEM subdirectory.)

The default screen-saver module is None. The Name list also includes a module called Blank Screen. This one simply blanks the screen (no pattern is displayed).

Below the screen-saver name list, you'll find a setting called Delay. This specifies the length of idle time the saver will wait before going into action. The default value is two minutes. You can increase or decrease this amount by clicking on the arrows or typing in a new number.

 WINDOWS TIP: Setting a Delay time of zero disables the screen saver. This option is a convenient way to turn off the screen saver temporarily. If you want to be rid of it permanently, choose (None) in the Name list.

To the right of the Name list and the Delay time, you'll find command buttons labeled Test and Setup. The Test button lets you see the appearance of a saver module without committing to it. The Setup button lets you assign options specific to the current saver. These options can significantly vary the appearance of a saver module. For example, the Marquee module displays a moving line of text on your screen. Its Setup options allow you to specify the font, color, speed, position, and content of the text message.

The Setup button also allows you to assign a password to the current saver module. To do this, click Setup, select the Password Protected check box, and then click the Set Password command button. In the next dialog box, you'll be asked to enter your password twice (to ensure that you haven't made a typing mistake).

To turn off password protection temporarily, revisit the Setup dialog box and remove the check from the Password Protected check box. To remove password protection permanently or to change your password, click the Set Password button again. On the top line of the next dialog box, type the password as it now stands. Then, to remove the password, simply click OK. To set a new password, type it twice—exactly as you did when you assigned the first password.

Be careful when assigning passwords. If you forget your password, you could find yourself forced to reboot to regain control of your computer.

 WINDOWS TIP: The Windows-supplied screen savers do not work with non-Windows applications running under Windows. Many third-party savers offer this functionality, however.

 WINDOWS TIP: Do not assign a screen saver in Control Panel if a third-party screen saver, such as Intermission, is already running.

Wallpapering Your Desktop

If you want to drape your desktop with something livelier than a simple dot pattern, try the wallpaper option. This feature lets you display a picture as a backdrop to everything you do in Windows. Here's what your desktop might look like when covered with one of the wallpaper files supplied with Windows:

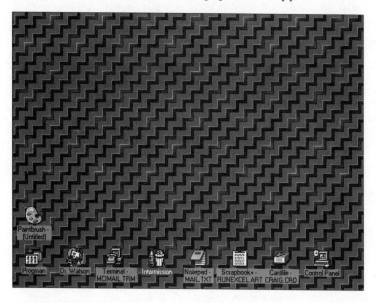

To try out the various wallpaper selections at your disposal, click open the Desktop section of Control Panel, and then click the downward arrow in the Wallpaper box. In the list box that unfolds, you'll find the names of each file in your Windows directory that has the extension BMP. To wallpaper your desktop, select a filename and click the OK button. To remove the wallpaper, follow the same procedure but select (None) in the drop-down list.

 WINDOWS TIP: You can also type the name of a BMP file stored in a different directory. As long as that directory is in your MS-DOS path, in your Windows directory, or in the SYSTEM subdirectory of your Windows directory, Windows will find and use the file you specify. (You don't have to include the full path in your specification.) You can also specify the full path of a BMP file not stored in one of the path directories. In this case, however, Windows responds by copying the file into your Windows directory—unnecessarily reducing your free hard disk space in the process.

Some wallpaper files produce a single image that covers your entire desktop. Others produce smaller images that can either be displayed once—typically in the center of the desktop—or repeated as many times as necessary to fill the screen. If you want the image to appear once only, select the Center option button; otherwise, select Tile.

WINDOWS TIP: You can make an image appear in a location other than the center of your desktop by modifying the WIN.INI file. If you use a company logo or a picture of your family as wallpaper, for example, you might want to have it in a corner of the screen (where you can see it more often), rather than right in the middle (where it will usually be covered by applications you're working with). The procedure for offsetting a wallpaper image are described later in this chapter; see "Specifying a Wallpaper Offset."

Using Wallpaper to Customize Your Desktop

You can personalize the appearance of your Windows system by designing your own custom wallpaper. Any image recorded in the Windows bitmap (BMP) format can serve as a backdrop to your system. Store the file in your Windows directory and its name will appear in the Wallpaper list box.

You can create BMP files using drawing commands in Paintbrush (see Chapter 16). You can also use a scanner to import such images as photographs and company logos, provided your software can output the image as a BMP file.

 WINDOWS TIP: Many public bulletin-board systems (BBS's) have wallpaper images that you can download. The WINNEW forum on CompuServe is a particularly good place to find public-domain wallpaper files. For more about the Windows forums on CompuServe, see Appendix C.

Wallpaper and Display Resolution

A bitmapped image, such as a BMP file, specifies the relative position of each pixel in the image. A BMP file that fills a standard 640 × 480 VGA screen maps 307,200 (640 multiplied by 480) pixels. Such an image will not fill a higher-resolution screen, such as an 800 × 600 or 1024 × 768 Super VGA. Instead the image appears smaller and is centered on the display. Conversely, an image designed to fill an 800 × 600 or 1024 × 768 display overflows a standard VGA screen. The upper left corner of the image appears in the upper left corner of your screen, but areas on the right and lower edges of the images are not displayed at all.

It's a good idea to check the resolution of an image before downloading it from a bulletin-board service (this information is usually provided as part of the description of the image).

Controlling the Appearance of Icons and Their Labels

By default, Windows 3.1 wraps long *icon labels*—the text beneath icons in Program Manager and on the desktop—onto two or more lines. If you'd rather have your labels all on one line, simply invoke the Desktop section of Control Panel and deselect the Wrap Title check box.

If you find your program-item icons are crowded together too tightly in Program Manager's windows, you might want to increase the number in the Icon Spacing box. The value here specifies the width of each icon. The Icon Spacing value also determines how closely icons will be positioned at the bottom of your desktop when you minimize windows or use Task List's Arrange Icons command.

The Icon Spacing value sets the icon width in pixels. (The width of the pixel depends on your screen's resolution; the higher the resolution, the smaller the pixel.) The largest value allowed is 512; the smallest depends on screen resolution. On a VGA screen, the minimum is 32 pixels. At this setting, your icons will stand shoulder-to-shoulder.

Turning on the Size-and-Position Grid

The Granularity value in the Sizing Grid section of the Desktop dialog box controls the spacing of an invisible set of grid lines on your desktop. These grid lines can help you control the positioning and alignment of windows (but not icons) on your desktop. With grid lines turned on, whenever you size or move a window, it automatically snaps into place along the nearest horizontal and vertical grid lines.

A higher granularity value creates a coarser grid with fewer available positions for windows. You can see this for yourself by entering a value such as 25 and clicking OK. After you do that, try clicking the mouse on Control Panel's title bar and dragging Control Panel around the desktop. On a standard VGA screen, only six possible positions exist for the Control Panel window with the granularity set at 25.

You can set the granularity to any number from 0 through 49. Setting it to 0 turns the grid lines off. Unless you're using a high-resolution display or you have a special need for a coarse grid, you'll probably want to keep the granularity set somewhere between 0 and 5.

Setting Border Width

The Border Width option allows you to fatten up or reduce the borders of all sizable windows. (A few programs—Windows Calculator is one of them—appear in windows of fixed size. Such nonsizable windows also have fixed-width window borders.)

Thicker borders can make it a little easier to size windows with the mouse. On the other hand, they waste screen space. You can set the border width from an anorexic 1 through an obese 49.

Setting the Cursor Blink Rate

If the rate at which the Windows cursor blinks seems too fast or too slow for your taste, open the Desktop section of Control Panel and experiment with the Cursor Blink Rate scroll bar. The vertical line that appears below this scroll bar shows the cursor blink rate before you make any changes. When you make changes with the scroll bar, the blinking line shows the new cursor blink rate.

SETTING COUNTRY-SPECIFIC OPTIONS

The International section of Control Panel lets you tailor your system for use in a variety of countries. Here, for example, you can tell Windows such things as what currency symbol you want to use (and whether it appears in front of or behind numbers), how you expect to see dates and times formatted, what measurement system to use, and so on.

If you work in the United States, Windows is probably already set up with the country-specific settings that you need. Even so, you may find this section of Control Panel useful if you travel with your computer or if you need to correspond with overseas business associates. Most Windows applications automatically base their display of dates, times, and currency symbols on the settings in the International section of Control Panel.

 WINDOWS TIP: If a Windows application does not seem to be conforming to your current international settings, it's probably because you started that application before making your changes in Control Panel. Try closing and restarting the application.

To change Windows' international settings, double-click Control Panel's International icon or pull down the Settings menu and choose International. You'll see this dialog box:

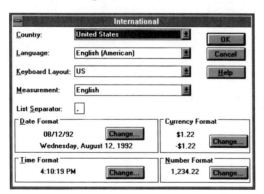

The easiest way to work with this dialog box is to start with the Country drop-down list. Click the downward arrow to open the list, and then pick the country whose settings you want to adopt. For example, if you're going to be working in Sweden, you would select Sweden in the Country list. Control Panel would then adjust the settings in the Measurement, Date Format, Time Format, Currency Format, and Number Format sections of the dialog box, like this:

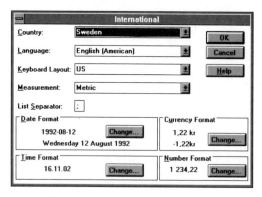

Normally, those settings should be correct for the country you've chosen. But, in case you need to make any adjustments, you can click the appropriate Change button in the bottom section of the dialog box. Each Change button brings up its own separate dialog box. Here, for example, is what you'll see if you ask to change the date format:

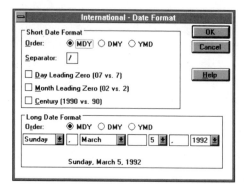

Before clicking OK to leave the International dialog box, you may need to adjust the Language and Keyboard Layout settings. Control Panel does not automatically change these settings when you modify the Country setting.

Choose a different Keyboard Layout if you want to be able to type accented characters directly from the typewriter keyboard. (You can also type accented characters with the help of the Alt key and the numeric keypad or with Character Map. See Chapter 7 for details on using Character Map.) Choose a different Language if you need to perform a language-specific task, such as sorting or case conversion.

> **NOTE:** *If you change either the Language or the Keyboard Layout setting, Windows may ask you to insert one of your original distribution disks so that it can get a file of information specific for your chosen language.*

ADJUSTING THE KEYBOARD REPEAT RATE

The Keyboard section of Control Panel allows you to modify the "typematic" behavior of your keyboard. When you double-click the Keyboard icon, Control presents this dialog box:

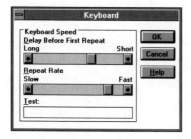

Whenever you hold down a key, your system waits for a moment, and then begins repeating the character you pressed. The upper scroll bar in this dialog box lets you change the length of time the system waits before repeating. The lower scroll bar lets you change the repeat speed.

If you want to test a new setting before clicking OK, tab to the Test line, and then hold down any alphabetic or numeric key. The character you press will appear in the Test box, and you'll be able to judge whether the delay and repeat rate are satisfactory.

SETTING THE DATE AND TIME

Control Panel provides a simple way to adjust the date and time, in case the system time is not set correctly. You'll find this feature handy if you transport your computer into a new time zone.

To set the date or time, double-click Control Panel's Date/Time icon or pull down the Settings menu and choose Date/Time. You'll see the following simple dialog box.

To change a date or time setting with the keyboard, press Tab until the number you want to change is highlighted. Then type a new number. In the illustration above, for example, you could change the date to 8/13/92 by tabbing once (to highlight the 12) and typing the number 13.

To change a date or time setting with the mouse, click the number you want to increase or decrease. Then click the upward or downward arrow to the right of the number.

INSTALLING AUDIO DRIVERS

If your computer is equipped with a sound board, such as a Creative Labs Sound Blaster or a Media Vision Thunder Board, you may need to use Control Panel's Drivers icon to install the appropriate driver for that board. (Note: Some vendors of audio hardware supply their own driver-installation routines. If your sound board works correctly now, you probably don't need to concern yourself with the Drivers section of Control Panel.)

Double-clicking the Drivers icon produces a simple dialog box that lists all currently installed media drivers:

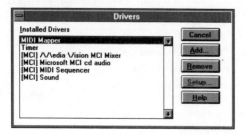

To add a new driver, click the Add button, choose a driver from the next list that appears, and follow the prompts. If the driver you need to add does not appear in the list, select the item labeled Unlisted or Updated Driver. Windows then prompts you to insert a disk with the unlisted driver in drive A.

If the driver you install offers configuration options, the Setup button in the Drivers dialog box is enabled (not grayed out). Click that button and fill out the dialog box that appears.

MAPPING SOUND FILES TO SYSTEM EVENTS

If your computer is equipped with a sound board and you have installed the correct driver for it, you can set up Windows to respond to various events with sound files (files with the extension WAV) instead of its normal beep. When you double-click the Sound icon, Windows lists the "mappable" events in the following dialog box.

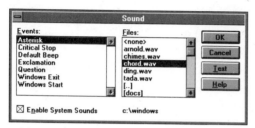

Alongside the Events list is a listing of all WAV files in your Windows directory. To hear what any of these files sounds like, select a filename and click the Test button. (This button is grayed out if you have not installed an appropriate audio driver.) To map a system event to a WAV file, simply select the event in the list at the left and the filename in the list at the right.

Turning the Sound Off

Windows normally sounds a warning beep or plays the sound file mapped to the default beep when you try to take an action that it deems inappropriate. In the unlikely event that you've never been so rewarded, you can experience this signal for yourself as follows:

1. Double-click Control Manager's Sound icon, or pull down the Settings menu and choose Sound.

2. After the dialog box appears, click the mouse anywhere in the Control Panel window, outside the dialog box.

If you find the beep or sound file annoying, deselect the Enable System Sounds check box in the Sound dialog box.

SETTING NETWORK OPTIONS

If you're connected to a network, Control Panel includes an icon marked Network. Double-clicking this icon displays a dialog box specific for your network. Depending on your network, it lets you do such things as log onto the network, modify your user identification and password, and send messages to other network users. Here's what the dialog box looks like for a Microsoft-compatible network (one that uses Netbios protocols):

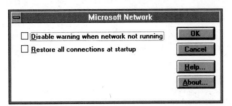

Note the Restore All Connections At Startup option in this dialog box. If this check box is selected (its default state), Windows keeps track of all the network drives you're connected to and restores those connections at the beginning of each session. If you deselect this check box, you will need to use the Network Connections command in File Manager to reconnect your network drives each time you restart Windows.

MODIFYING THE INI FILES DIRECTLY

Windows records vital information about your preferences and your system in two initialization files, called WIN.INI and SYSTEM.INI. Many Windows applications (including several of the Windows desktop accessories) also use "private" initialization files for similar purposes. These initialization files have certain things in common: They're ASCII text files, they're stored in your Windows directory, and they're crucial to the functioning of your system. The SYSTEM.INI file, because it spells out the nature of your hardware, is a particularly critical component. If you accidentally delete or damage SYSTEM.INI, you could be forced to reinstall Windows.

Earlier versions of Windows often required users to make direct modifications to WIN.INI and SYSTEM.INI in order to customize their systems. Fortunately, this is almost unnecessary in Windows 3.1. Unfortunately, there may still be times when you need to edit one or another of the INI files.

 WINDOWS TIP: For details about all the standard settings in your WIN.INI and SYSTEM.INI files, use Write to read the files WININI.WRI and SYSINI.WRI. These files should be in your Windows directory.

We'll look at a few details a moment. But first, a short sermon on the importance of backing up.

If you do nothing else in the way of routine backup, you would be wise to copy your INI files occasionally, particularly after you make any changes to your hardware or switch from one display resolution to another. One way you could to this is to create a small MS-DOS batch file similar to the following:

```
@echo off
c:
cd\windows
win
copy c:\windows\*.ini *.bak
```

Name this file W.BAT, store it in a directory that's included in your MS-DOS path, and then start Windows each day by typing *w* instead of *win*. If you do this, then any time you quit Windows, your INI files will automatically be copied to similarly named files with the extension BAK. This procedure is not nearly as good as backing up to some form of removable media. But it's better than doing nothing at all.

How the INI Files Are Structured

Here's what the beginning of a typical WIN.INI file looks like:

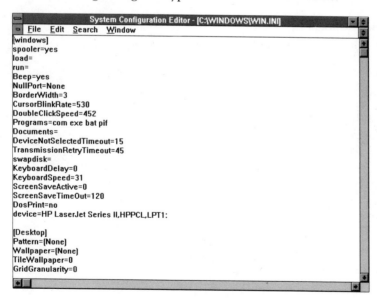

As you can see, much of the information in this file concerns preferences that are normally specified via Control Panel. The line *Beep=yes*, for example, records our desire to hear the bell when we err, the *BorderWidth=3* line tells Windows how fat to make the window borders, and so on.

The WIN.INI file has several sections, each headed by a word enclosed in brackets. The first section in the file illustrated above—it's probably the first section in yours, as well—is called [windows]. The second is [Desktop], the third [Extensions], and so on.

Under each bracketed heading, you'll find a number of lines beginning with a single word (it may be a compound word such as *CursorBlinkRate*) and an equal sign. These are called *keywords*; each keyword controls some aspect of the way your Windows system functions. On the right side of the equal signs are values that are assigned to the various keywords.

If nothing appears to the right of an equal sign, that means that Windows has assigned a default value to the keyword. If a keyword itself (or a whole section of keywords) doesn't appear in the file, its absence also means that a default value has been assigned. For example, if you're using the Windows Default color scheme, you might not find a [colors] section in your WIN.INI file.

The order in which the sections appear is not critical. Nor is the order in which keywords appear within a section.

How to Edit an INI File

The two principles to remember when changing the contents of any INI file are:

- Make a backup copy of the file before you begin.

- Do not use a "formatting" editor.

Copying the file before you embark gives you a way to recover if you make a serious mistake. A formatting editor is one that adds formatting information to the file—information about fonts, page dimensions, indents, and so on; most word processors fall into this category. Such information will almost certainly corrupt your INI file.

Introducing Sysedit

Sysedit is a program included with your Windows package. You won't find it in any program group (unless you put it there yourself), and the Windows documentation is not likely to say anything about it. But it's the ideal tool for editing four important files: AUTOEXEC.BAT, CONFIG.SYS, WIN.INI, and SYSTEM.INI. Sysedit automatically creates a backup copy of any files you edit. And it's a plain-text editor, so it won't corrupt your files with formatting information.

To run Sysedit, pull down the File menu in either Program Manager or File Manager. Then type *sysedit* and click OK. The program looks like this:

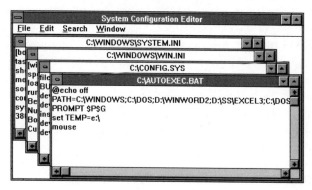

Sysedit is essentially a multi-document version of Notepad, except for two important differences: It automatically backs up any files you change (using the extension SYD), and it can be used only with the four files named above.

Changing Your Default Shell

To change your default shell (the program that starts and ends your Windows sessions), open the SYSTEM.INI file and look for the line that begins *shell=*. You'll find it under the [boot] heading.

Remove whatever filename appears there now (progman.exe, for example), and add the name of your new shell's executable file. To make File Manager the default shell, for example, make the *shell=* line read

shell=winfile.exe

Then save your modified SYSTEM.INI file. Your new default shell will be in place at the start of your next Windows session.

 WINDOWS TIP: Many third-party shell programs take care of the SYSTEM.INI modification for you automatically, if you choose to make them the default shell.

Changing Mouse Behavior in a Windowed MS-DOS Application

When you run an MS-DOS (non-Windows) application in a window in 386 enhanced mode, Windows 3.1 normally lets your MS-DOS application use the mouse exactly as it would if you were running that program outside of Windows. The price of this convenience is that when you want to copy information from this program to the Windows Clipboard, you must first use the Control menu's Mark command before selecting the data to copy (see Chapter 8). In earlier versions of Windows, you could select data to copy immediately (without first using the Mark command), but you could not use the mouse for choosing commands in the MS-DOS application.

If you prefer the way the older Windows versions worked, you can make a simple modification to your SYSTEM.INI file. In the [NonWindowsApp] section, look for a line that reads *MouseInDosBox=1* and change the 1 to a 0. (If you don't find such a line in your [NonWindowsApp] section, add it.) Then save the file and restart Windows.

Using WIN.INI to Start Programs Automatically

In earlier versions of Windows, the only way to make a program start automatically at the beginning of each Windows session was to modify the *run=* or *load=* line in WIN.INI. If you use Program Manager as your default shell, you no longer have to make this WIN.INI edit. You can start programs automatically by including them in a program group called Startup.

It's possible you'll still want to specify startup programs in WIN.INI, however. You might want to reduce the number of your program groups (by eliminating the Startup group) or ensure that particular programs are loaded first, ahead of any in your Startup group. Windows starts any programs listed in WIN.INI first. Then it loads the items in your Startup group, beginning with the icon in the upper left corner of the group and proceeding left to right, row by row.

To specify startup programs in WIN.INI, look for the lines *run=* and *load=*. You'll find both lines under the [windows] heading. (Usually that heading is near the top of the file). If you don't see either line there, simply add it.

Programs named on the *run=* line start as open windows. Those on the *load=* line start minimized.

On the right side of the equal sign, type the name of the executable file for each program you want to run or load. (Include the full path if the file is not stored in your Windows directory, its SYSTEM subdirectory, or a directory included in your MS-DOS path.) Separate program names with spaces. You can include up to 127 characters on each line.

Fine-Tuning the Mouse

The Mouse section of Control Panel lets you make some basic adjustments to the behavior of your mouse. You can make further adjustments by modifying your WIN.INI file. In particular, you can do the following:

- Specify the amount of vertical and horizontal pointer movement that Windows allows between the two clicks of a double-click

- Change the acceleration characteristics of your mouse

- Change the number of pointer images that Windows displays when the Mouse Trails option is selected

Redefining the Double-Click

For two mouse clicks to be interpreted by Windows as a double-click, they have to occur within a certain time interval, and the pointer must not move more than a certain amount. The default parameters are 452 milliseconds for the time interval and 4 pixels (in both the horizontal and vertical directions) for the spatial interval. As mentioned earlier in this chapter, you can adjust the time interval by using the Mouse section of Control Panel. If you want to relax the spatial requirement, you need to modify your WIN.INI file directly.

The WIN.INI lines to change are *DoubleClickWidth=* and *DoubleClick-Height=*.

To the right of the equal sign, enter the number of pixels of horizontal and vertical movement that you want Windows to allow within a double-click.

If you have never adjusted the double-click settings, you probably won't find these lines in your WIN.INI file. In that case, you'll need to add them. Both lines must be in the [windows] section.

Changing Acceleration Characteristics

Three lines in the [windows] section of your WIN.INI file control the manner in which Windows relocates the mouse pointer on screen as you move the mouse on your desk. Those three lines are *MouseSpeed=*, *MouseThreshold1=*, and *MouseThreshold2=*.

The MouseSpeed parameter—which can be 0, 1, or 2—determines whether Windows accelerates the pointer as you move the mouse. If MouseSpeed is set to 0, then the speed of the pointer's movement maintains a constant relationship to the speed of the mouse's movement; nudge the mouse a given number of centimeters and your pointer travels a fixed number of pixels. If MouseSpeed is set to either 1 or 2, this relationship between mouse and pointer movement is no longer constant.

If MouseSpeed equals 1, Windows looks to see whether, in the interval between two mouse interrupts, you have moved the pointer more than the number of pixels specified by the MouseThreshold1 parameter. (Your mouse sends signals known as *interrupts* at regular, minuscule, time intervals. The absolute value of the interrupt interval varies from computer to computer and is not crucial to this discussion.) If the pointer movement between interrupts exceeds the value of MouseThreshold1, Windows multiplies the pointer movement by 2.

If MouseSpeed is set to 2, Windows multiplies pointer movement by 2 when it exceeds the value of MouseThreshold1, and it multiplies the pointer movement by 4 when it exceeds the value of MouseThreshold2. In short, with MouseSpeed at 0, you get no acceleration. At 1, you get a bit of acceleration, and at 2 you get a whole lot. The point at which the acceleration "kicks in" is determined by the two threshold parameters.

Control Panel's Mouse Tracking Speed scroll bar (shown in the figure on page 213), gives you a selection of seven mouse settings. Putting the scroll box at the left edge of the scroll bar sets MouseSpeed at 0. The next three scroll-bar positions set MouseSpeed to 1, and the rightmost three set MouseSpeed to 2. As you move the scroll box to the right, the values of the two threshold parameters come down.

If none of Control Panel's seven settings quite meets your taste, you can fine-tune the one that comes closest by modifying the WIN.INI file. Unlike the mouse settings you make with Control Panel, however, those that you make by modifying WIN.INI directly do not take effect until the next time you start Windows.

Customizing the Mouse Trail

Control Panel's Mouse Trails check box, if selected, causes Windows to display a ghost trail of pointer images as you move the mouse. It's designed to facilitate the use of Windows on LCD screens, where finding the pointer can sometimes be a challenge. By default, the mouse trail consists of seven pointer images. If you like the trail but find that a smaller ghost will suffice, you can reduce this value by modifying the *MouseTrails=* line, in the [windows] section of WIN.INI.

You can set MouseTrails to any value from 1 through 7. Note that if you set this value to something other than the default 7, and you subsequently deselect

the Mouse Trails check box in Control Panel, Windows remembers your preference and restores it the next time you select that check box. For example, if you
change the *MouseTrails=* line from 7 to 4, then turn the feature off altogether in
Control Panel, Windows simply puts a minus sign in front of the 4 in your WIN.INI
file. The next time you select the Mouse Trails check box, it removes the minus
sign, giving you a four-image ghost once again.

Changing the Icon Font

Windows normally uses 8-point MS Sans Serif to display the text below Program
Manager program-item icons and the icons of minimized applications. Three
settings in the [Desktop] section of WIN.INI let you override that choice. If you're
having trouble reading the icon descriptors on your screen, or if you want your
Windows system to look a little different from your neighbor's, you can select
another typeface, size, and style. The lines to modify are *IconTitleFaceName=*,
IconTitleSize=, and *IconTitleStyle=*.

If you've never changed these parameters, you probably won't find these
lines in your WIN.INI file. Be sure to add them under the [Desktop] heading;
otherwise, Windows ignores your request.

On the *IconTitleFaceName=* line, put the name of any screen font available
on your system. (You can find out what names are available by opening the Fonts
section of Control Panel.) On the *IconTitleSize=* line, put any available point size.
And on the *IconTitleStyle=* line, enter 0 for normal type or 1 for bold.

Note that to restore the default typeface, size, and style, you need to delete
these lines from your WIN.INI file.

Specifying a Wallpaper Offset

If you are displaying wallpaper on your desktop with the Tile option (see "Wall-
papering Your Desktop," earlier in this chapter), you can adjust the position of
the wallpaper images by adding (or altering) two lines in WIN.INI. The lines are
WallpaperOriginX= and *WallpaperOriginY=*, and they appear in the [Desktop]
section.

The default value for both lines is 0, which means that Windows normally
begins tiling your wallpaper at the upper left corner of the screen. To move the
wallpaper display to the right, enter a positive value for *WallpaperOriginX=*. To
move the display downward, specify a positive value for *WallpaperOriginY=*. The
numbers you specify on these lines specify offsets in pixels.

The values specify the position at which the wallpaper starts tiling. The
entire desktop is still covered with wallpaper, but the starting point is moved.

WINDOWS TIP: The wallpaper offset values also affect the position of centered wallpaper. To place your wallpaper in the upper left corner of the screen, use 1 for both values, because 0 (the default value) centers the image on the desktop.

Removing Screen-Saver Password Protection

If you forget a password assigned to a Windows-supplied screen saver, all is not lost. Open the file CONTROL.INI (you'll need to use Notepad, rather than Sysedit). Look for all lines that read *PWProtected=1* and, in each case, change the 1 to 0. This disables the password protection without removing the password assignment. To remove the password assignment, look for the line that begins *Password=* and delete everything to the right of the equal sign.

Changing Performance Characteristics with SYSTEM.INI

You can use SYSTEM.INI to control the following:

- The disk on which Windows stores application swap files in standard mode

- The disk on which Windows stores temporary swap files in 386 enhanced mode

- The maximum size of a temporary swap file in 386 enhanced mode

- The minimum amount of free disk space reserved when Windows is using a temporary swap file in 386 enhanced mode

These matters are all discussed in Chapter 19.

CONFIGURATION CHANGES
THAT REQUIRE WINDOWS SETUP

If you equip your computer with a new printer, you can give Windows the information it needs by running Control Panel. Similarly, if you upgrade from a 1200-bps modem to a 9600-bps modem, you can make the necessary configuration changes to your serial port with the help of Control Panel.

But if you add a mouse to your system, change your video display, switch to a different type of keyboard (not a different key layout, but a different physical device), or attach your computer to a network, you'll need to run Windows Setup, not Control Panel. Windows Setup and Control Panel perform similar functions, but they have different areas of jurisdiction (see Table 9-1).

Windows Setup is discussed in Appendix A.

If You Install or Change	*Use This Program*
Keyboard	Setup
Keyboard layout	Control Panel (International)
Modem	Control Panel (Ports)
Mouse	Setup
Network drive	Control Panel (Network), File Manager
Network printer	Control Panel (Printers)
Network software	Setup
Printer	Control Panel (Printers)
Sound board	Control Panel (Drivers)
Swap file (virtual memory)	Control Panel (386 Enhanced)
Video display	Setup

Table 9-1.
Programs for customizing Windows.

10
Automating Windows with Recorder

A *macro* is a recorded sequence of keystrokes and mouse actions that can be played back with a single keystroke or keystroke combination. The content of the macro can be one or more commands to Windows or an application program, or it can be information, such as text, entered into an application—or both.

For example, you can use a macro to start or quit one or more programs, to copy information from one program to another, to type *boilerplate* text (words that you use repeatedly in different contexts), and to perform any number of other routine tasks. Any sequence of actions that you carry out repetitively in Windows is a candidate for a macro.

Windows includes a program called Recorder that enables you to create and play back macros. We'll explore the use of Recorder in this chapter.

STARTING RECORDER

You'll find a program-item icon for Recorder in Program Manager's Accessories group. To start Recorder, simply double-click the Recorder icon.

 WINDOWS TIP: If you use macros regularly, you'll probably want to set Windows up so that Recorder starts automatically. We'll see how to do that later in this chapter.

Recorder's initial screen looks like this:

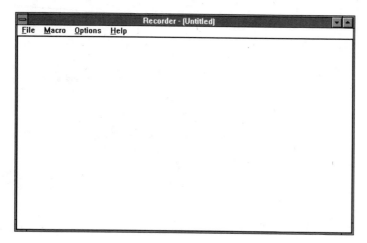

The big open workspace looks like a place for you to type, but it's not. Recorder uses this window to display the names of macros you create. Here, for example, is what your Recorder window might look like after you have created a handful of macros:

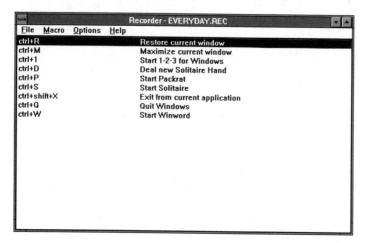

The column on the left in the illustration lists the *shortcut keys* for each macro, and the column on the right lists the macros' names. The shortcut key for each macro is the keyboard combination you press to execute that macro.

Macros are stored in files with the extension REC. The preceding illustration shows the contents of a macro file called EVERYDAY.REC. The number of macros you can put in a file depends on the complexity of the macros you create. When the size of your macro file reaches 64 KB, Recorder won't accept any more macros. You can create as many macro files as you like, but you can have only one file in memory at a time.

RECORDING A MACRO

The best way to see how macros are recorded is to record a few of them. So in a moment, we'll create two macros—a very simple one and another that's slightly more complex. But first, let's look at the general procedure for creating *any* macro. The steps are as follows:

1. Prepare the application in which you want your finished macro to be played back.

    For example, if you wanted your macro to execute one or more commands in Notepad, you would begin by starting Notepad and making sure that Notepad is in an open window.

2. Activate the Recorder window, pull down Recorder's Macro menu, and choose Record. A dialog box appears.

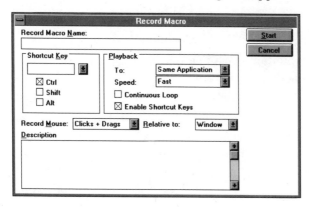

3. Supply a name for the macro (in the Record Macro Name box) or a keyboard shortcut (in the Shortcut Key box), or both. It's best to supply both.

    Assigning a keyboard shortcut lets you play the macro back with a simple keystroke or keystroke combination. If you don't assign a keyboard shortcut, it takes a little more work to play your macro back.

The macro name provides a short description of the macro to help you keep track of what each macro does. You can type up to 39 characters in the Record Macro Name box.

4. If you need more than 39 characters to describe your macro, add text to the Description box.

There's enough room to write a small essay in the Description box.

5. In the remaining sections of the dialog box, select the recording and playback options you want to use.

These settings tell Recorder what kind of mouse actions to record (if any), whether the location at which mouse "events" (clicks and drags, for example) occur should be recorded relative to the current window or the entire desktop, whether you want the macro played back at full speed or at recorded speed, and whether you want the macro to work only with a particular application. The illustration above shows the default settings for all these options. Most of the time, the default settings should serve you well.

We'll look at each of the available recording and playback options later in this chapter.

6. Click Start to begin the recording.

When you click Start, Recorder minimizes itself and blinks its icon—to let you know the "tape" is running. From now until you press Ctrl-Break, your actions are recorded for posterity!

7. Carry out the actions you want your macro to perform for you.

It's best to record as much of your macro as possible with keyboard actions, rather than mouse actions. That way, the macro plays back correctly, regardless of the size and positions of windows and icons at playback time.

8. Press Ctrl-Break to stop the recording.

Recorder presents a small dialog box, as shown on the following page.

9. If you've made a mistake and want to start over, you can select Cancel Recording. If you want to do a few things off-the-record, so to speak, you can ignore the dialog box for the moment (click anywhere outside it), do what you need to do elsewhere, and then come back to the dialog box (click on the Recorder icon) and select Resume Recording. But if you have finished recording, you would:

10. Select Save Macro and click the OK button.

11. Double-click Recorder's icon to restore the window.

   An entry for your new macro appears in Recorder's window. You can now play the macro back by typing your keyboard shortcut.

12. Use Recorder's Save or Save As command (they're on the File menu) to save the current macro file.

   You must save your macros in a disk file if you want to use them again at a subsequent Windows session.

Creating a Simple Macro

Now let's try creating a very simple macro. We'll record a macro that does nothing more than execute the Select All command on Notepad's Edit menu. In effect, what we'll be doing is creating a keyboard shortcut for a menu command that doesn't already have one. Here are the steps:

1. Start Notepad as an open application window.

2. Choose the Record command on Recorder's Macro menu.

3. In the Record Macro Name box, type

   Choose Select All in Notepad

4. In the Shortcut Key box, type *S*.

   Note that the check box marked Ctrl, below the Shortcut Key box, is checked.

   That means our keyboard shortcut will be Ctrl-S. The Record Macro dialog box now looks like this:

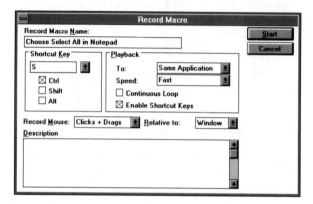

5. Be sure the recording and playback options are set as shown in the illustration above. Then click the Start button.

   The default recording and playback options are fine for this example.

6. If Notepad is not the current Window now, use Alt-Tab or Alt-Esc to make it the current window.

7. Press Alt, E, A to choose the Select All command on Notepad's Edit menu.

   Because the Select All command will always be in the same position relative to the upper left corner of the Notepad window, no matter what the size and position of the Notepad window might be, you can use the mouse to choose Select All if you prefer. But if you use the mouse, your macro might not run on a system that uses a different kind of display. Your best bet when recording macros is to acquire the habit of using keyboard actions exclusively.

8. Press Ctrl-Break.

NOTE: *On some keyboards, the Break key is the same as the Pause key; on others, it's the same as the Scroll Lock key. Look for the label on the front of the key.*

9. Select Save Macro and click the OK button.

    It's fine to use the mouse when you're telling Recorder to save your macro because this action isn't part of the macro itself.

10. Restore the Recorder window, pull down Recorder's File menu, choose Save As, and supply a filename.

That's all there is to it. Now you have a keyboard shortcut—Ctrl-S—for Notepad's Select All command.

Creating a Slightly More Complex Macro

Now let's try something just a little more ambitious. We'll record a macro to activate Program Manager and start an application—Cardfile—in a maximized window. What makes this example more complex is the fact that we can't know whether Program Manager will be open or minimized at the time we play the macro back. We'll therefore add an explicit step to restore Program Manager (even if it doesn't need restoring when we make our recording). Here goes:

1. Activate Recorder and choose the Record command.

2. In the box marked Record Macro Name, type

    Start Cardfile in a Maximized Window

3. In the box marked Shortcut Key, type *C*. Check the Shift check box.

    Our keyboard shortcut will be Ctrl-Shift-C.

4. Check to see that the recording and playback options are set as shown in the following illustration.

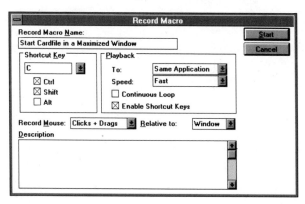

Again we'll use the default settings.

5. Click the Start button.

6. Press Alt-Tab as many times as necessary to make Program Manager the active window. If Program Manager is already active, press Alt-Tab to cycle through all applications on your desktop until Program Manager is active again.

   This step ensures that the macro will run, even if Program Manager is minimized.

7. Press Alt, F, R. Then type *cardfile* and press Enter.

   Here we definitely need to use keyboard commands. If instead we double-clicked the Cardfile icon, the macro would not work—unless that icon was in exactly the same spot (relative to the upper left corner of the Program Manager window) each time we played the macro back.

8. Press Alt, Spacebar, X.

   The Cardfile window is maximized.

9. Press Ctrl-Break.

10. Choose Save Macro and click OK.

11. Switch back to Recorder and save the current macro file, with the Save or Save As command.

 WINDOWS TIP: Recorder's macros are intended to be used only with Windows applications. But you can use the procedure just described to start a non-Windows program as well. You won't be able to record anything that happens inside your non-Windows application, but you at least can get it started.

When you record the step that starts your non-Windows program, Recorder suspends the recording. When you quit your non-Windows program, you'll find a blinking Recorder icon on your Windows desktop. You can either continue recording or press Ctrl-Break.

PLAYING A MACRO BACK

To play back a macro, simply press its keyboard shortcut. You don't have to make Recorder active to do this. All that's necessary is for Recorder to be somewhere on your desktop and for the macro in question to be listed in Recorder's window.

You can play back a macro in two other ways:

- Activate Recorder, and double-click the entry for the macro you want to run.

- Activate Recorder, select the macro you want to run (using keyboard or mouse), and choose the Macro menu's Run command.

You can use either of these methods to run a macro that doesn't have a keyboard shortcut.

If the Playback Doesn't Work

If something goes wrong during the playback of a macro, you will see an error message like this:

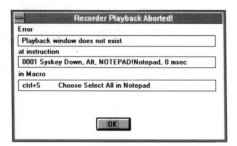

NOTE: *If Recorder is minimized when the error occurs, its icon will blink. When you double-click the blinking icon, the error message will appear.*

The error message has three components:

- A description—in English!—of the problem

- The location and content of the macro instruction that could not be played back

- The keyboard shortcut and name of the macro that failed

The first item is your clue about what went wrong. In the preceding illustration, for example, you can discern from the error message that the macro failed because the application in which it was supposed to operate was nowhere to be found. In other words, you tried to use a macro to execute a Notepad command, but there were no Notepad windows on the desktop.

The second item may not be much help to you, because Recorder doesn't let you see or edit the code it records. You should write down the information on this line if you're planning to call Microsoft for technical assistance.

The third item, the macro name, is useful if you happen to be creating macros that run other macros. If you experience a playback failure with a set of chained macros, this information will tell you which link in the chain caused the problem.

Unfortunately, Recorder macros can't be revised. You can change their names, keyboard shortcuts, descriptions, and playback options, but you can't modify the commands they perform. Therefore, the best thing to do with a macro that generates playback errors is delete it (use the Delete command on the Macro menu) and try again.

OPTIONS FOR RECORDING

Now let's look in more detail at the options Recorder provides for recording macros.

Keyboard Shortcuts

Practically any key—with or without Ctrl, Alt, or Shift—can be used as a keyboard shortcut. The best shortcuts are ones that have a mnemonic connection with the macros they trigger (Ctrl-Shift-C for starting Cardfile, for example), but you're free to use almost any exotic connection you can think of.

To see what keys are available (in addition to the letters and numbers on your keyboard), use Recorder's Record command, and then click the downward arrow to open the Shortcut Key drop-down list box. The list that unfolds includes Backspace, Caps Lock, Delete, the various direction keys, Enter, Esc, all the function keys, and assorted other non-alphanumeric keys. To choose one of these, simply click it with the mouse.

Below the Shortcut Key list box are three check boxes, marked Ctrl, Shift, and Alt. You can use these singly or in combination—or you can use none at all. To designate the F10 key by itself as a keyboard shortcut, for example, you would remove the checks from all three boxes, and put F10 on the Shortcut Key line.

WARNING: *Recorder will let you assign Ctrl-Alt-Del as a keyboard shortcut, but don't do it! Pressing this key combination will reboot the current application.*

It's also a good idea to avoid reassigning any of the standard keyboard shortcut combinations used by Windows. For example, if you assign Alt-F4 to a macro, you will no longer be able to use that combination to quit a Windows application.

Recording Mouse Actions

You have three choices regarding the recording of mouse actions. You can have Recorder:

- Record all mouse positions
- Disregard the mouse entirely
- Record mouse positions only when a mouse button is pressed

The third choice is the default. In the Record Mouse box, the default is identified as Clicks + Drags.

To make a different choice, click the downward arrow at the right of the Record Mouse box. Choose Everything to have Recorder track all mouse movement or Ignore Mouse to have Recorder ignore all mouse movement.

As we've said, the safest way to record macros is to use the keyboard exclusively. If you're taking that approach, it doesn't matter how you set the Record Mouse option.

Some Windows applications include procedures that are either difficult or impossible to carry out without a mouse or other pointing device. If you're writing macros to operate in this kind of application, you will need to choose either Clicks + Drags or Everything. You should pick Clicks + Drags unless your program actually responds in some way (other than simply changing the shape of the mouse pointer) when you move the mouse without pressing any buttons.

Recording Positions Relative to Window or Desktop

If you're going to be recording mouse actions, you need to make a decision in the box marked Relative To. Here your choices are Relative To Window (the default) and Relative To Screen.

When Recorder records a mouse action, it records both the nature of the "event" (button down or button up, for example) and the position at which it occurs. The position at which the event occurs is measured as an offset from the upper left corner of either the current window or the entire desktop (screen).

Normally, you want to use the Window option, because that choice ensures that the macro will work regardless of where your applications may be positioned at playback time.

The Effect of Screen Resolution on Mouse Playback

Mouse positions are measured in units specific to the display adapter on which the macro is recorded. Therefore, if you record mouse actions on, say, a VGA display, you probably will not be able to play them back on, for example, an EGA display. This is one more reason to avoid recording mouse actions altogether, if possible.

PLAYBACK OPTIONS

Recorder offers several options that affect the way macros are played back. These options can be chosen either before the macro is recorded or at any time afterward. To select playback options before you record the macro, use the Playback section of the Record Macro dialog box. To select them afterward, use the Properties command on the Macro menu. (We'll look at the Properties command later in this chapter.)

Same Application or Any Application

The Playback To option determines whether a macro can be played back only in the application(s) in which it was recorded or in any application. Because most macros you create are likely to be application-specific, the default choice for this option is Same Application—which means the macro can be played back only where it was recorded.

When you play back a macro with the Same Application option in effect, Recorder starts by looking for the application in which the macro was recorded. It will find that application regardless of how many programs happen to be open on the desktop. If two or more copies of the program in question are open on your desktop, Recorder plays back the macro in the first copy it finds.

Note that selecting Same Application does not preclude creating macros that operate on more than one application. For example, the second macro we created earlier in this chapter executed commands in both Program Manager and Cardfile; it started Cardfile in Program Manager, and then it issued a Maximize command in Cardfile. You can work with as many applications as you like in a macro, and—provided Recorder can find the applications at playback time—the Same Application option will work just fine.

If you choose the Any Application option, Recorder will play your macro back in the current window—unless the current window happens to be Recorder itself. If Recorder is the active window when you play the macro back, the macro affects the "next window in line"—that is, the window you would be activating if you pressed Alt-Tab or Alt-Esc.

Playback Speed

Macros can be played back either at the system's top speed or at the speed at which they were recorded. Normally, you want the macro to do its work as quickly as it can, so the default setting is Fast. The Recorded Speed option is useful primarily for creating self-running demonstrations.

The Continuous Loop Option

If you check the Continuous Loop check box, Recorder plays your macro over and over again. Like the Recorded Speed option discussed in the previous paragraph, this option is useful not for everyday work but for demos.

To stop a continuously running macro, press Ctrl-Break.

Preventing the Chaining of Macros

Recorder ordinarily allows one macro to play back another. For example, if one of your macros has Ctrl-S as its shortcut and another has Ctrl-T, you can use the first macro to run the second by pressing Ctrl-T as the last action in the first macro. You are allowed to link up to five macros this way.

You can "break apart" a chain of connected macros by removing the check from the Enable Shortcut Keys check box. In the example above, if you wanted to run the Ctrl-S macro by itself, you remove the check from the Enable Shortcut Keys check box for the Ctrl-S macro.

The Enable Shortcut Keys check box has no effect on Windows' built-in keyboard shortcuts, which will always work in your macros.

CHANGING A MACRO'S PROPERTIES

After you have recorded a macro, you may change its name, keyboard shortcut, description, or playback options. To make any of these changes, open the Recorder window and select the name of the macro you want to alter. Then pull down the Macro menu and choose the Properties command. You'll see a dialog box like the one in the illustration at the top of the following page.

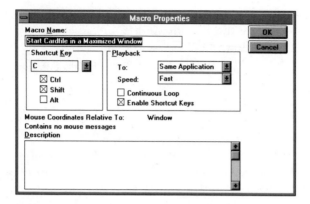

Simply choose options in this dialog box the same way you did when you created the macro.

Note that the Properties dialog box includes information about whether you've recorded mouse actions (Recorder calls them "mouse messages") and whether your mouse and keyboard positions were recorded relative to the current window or the entire screen. You might find this information useful if you're trying to understand why a macro isn't behaving as you expect it to.

CHANGING THE DEFAULT OPTION SETTINGS

If you find yourself frequently overriding some of Recorder's default settings for recording and playback options, you might want to change the defaults. You can do that by choosing the Preferences command on Recorder's Options menu. This command summons the following dialog box.

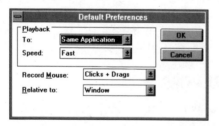

Options can be selected in this dialog box exactly as in the Record and Properties dialog boxes discussed earlier in this chapter.

OTHER RECORDER OPTIONS

In addition to Preferences, Recorder's Options menu has three other commands you can use to modify its behavior. The Options menu looks like this:

The Control+Break Checking setting determines whether you can interrupt a macro by pressing Ctrl-Break. Remove the check mark next to this setting before playing back a demonstration macro (a macro that runs continuously) if you want to prevent viewers from stopping the demo. With Ctrl+Break Checking disabled, you have to turn off your computer to stop a continuous macro, and you must click on the Recorder icon to stop recording a macro.

The Shortcut Keys setting determines whether Recorder starts a macro when you press its keyboard shortcut. You might want to remove the check mark from this setting if you run an application that uses a keyboard shortcut you assigned to a macro. For example, Notepad uses the F5 key as a shortcut for its Time/Date command. If you've set up a macro to start when you press F5, you might want to disable Recorder's response to shortcut keys while you run Notepad.

With shortcut keys turned off in Recorder, you can still use your macros. Simply activate the Recorder window, select the macro you want to play back, and use the Macro menu's Run command. (Or double-click the name of the macro.)

The Minimize On Use setting, if checked, causes Recorder to minimize itself (if it isn't already minimized) whenever you run a macro. If you're creating a series of macros, you might want to remove the check from this setting. That way, you'll be able to return to Recorder's window without first having to restore Recorder.

WORKING WITH MACRO FILES

The commands on Recorder's File menu work exactly like their counterparts in practically all other Windows applications. Use Save and Save As to store your macro files on disk. Use New to begin a new macro file and Open to load an existing file into memory.

The one unusual command on this menu, Merge, allows you to combine macro files. For example, if you have a file called OLDMACS.REC and you create another file called NEWMACS.REC, you can use the Merge command to combine the two. You would do that as follows:

1. Use the Open command to load one file into memory.

2. Use the Merge command and select the name of the other file.

    If the file you name in step 2 includes macros whose shortcut keys are already in use in the other file, Recorder removes those shortcuts from the incoming file. The macros themselves are not deleted or altered, but you'll need to use the Macro Properties command to assign new shortcuts. You will see the following message.

    Click OK to acknowledge the message.

3. Use the Save or Save As command to save the combined file.

If you use the Save command, the merged file retains the name of the file that you opened in step 1. Use Save As if you want to assign the combined file a new name.

STARTING WINDOWS WITH RECORDER AND A PARTICULAR MACRO FILE

If you tend to use the same set of macros every day, you will probably want to set up Windows so that it always starts with Recorder and your favorite macro file in place. To do that, start by using File Manager to be sure that all files that have the extension REC are associated with the application RECORDER.EXE. (See Chapter 6 for information about associating document files with applications.) Then do either of the following:

■ Start Windows every day by typing

    win filename.rec

at the MS-DOS command line (substitute the name of your macro file for *filename.rec*). You can put this instruction in your AUTO-EXEC.BAT file if you want to start Windows automatically each time you turn on your computer.

■ Create a program item for your macro file in Program Manager's Startup group. (Or add the name of your macro file on the *load=* line in WIN.INI.)

Either way, your macros are readily accessible each time you begin working in Windows.

PART IV

PRINTING

Getting the most out of Windows' printing capabilities requires an understanding of three topics: printer drivers, Print Manager, and fonts. These are the subjects of the next three chapters.

A printer driver enables Windows to translate output from its own internal graphics language into the language used by your printer. Before you can print, you have to install and set up a printer driver. Chapter 11 tells you how.

Chapter 12 introduces Print Manager, the Windows program that manages information on its way to your printer. Print Manager lets you continue working in Windows applications while your printer is printing.

Fonts enable you to add typographic variety to your printing. Windows comes with a set of fonts you can use on any supported printer, and most printers augment these with additional typefaces and styles. Chapter 13 provides background on font terminology and the typographic resources supplied by Windows.

11

Installing and Setting Up Printer Drivers

When you pull down a Windows application's File menu and choose Print, you set in motion a complex chain of events:

- First, your application generates codes in *Graphics Device Interface* (GDI), Windows' internal graphics language. These codes specify everything Windows needs to know about the content and formatting of your document, but they don't tell your printer how to print the document.

- Data is then handed off to a *printer driver*, which converts the GDI code into instructions that your printer understands.

- This printer-specific information is then passed to a Windows application called Print Manager, a traffic cop that handles all jobs on their way to all printers attached to your system. Print Manager stores the printer-specific information temporarily on disk in a *spool file*. If you create spool files for a particular printer faster than that printer can turn them into output, Print Manager maintains a *print queue*.

- When the print job in question arrives at the front of its queue (when all jobs ahead of it have been printed), Print Manager sends the contents of the spool file to your printer by way of a particular *port*, and then erases the spool file from disk.

- Your printer receives the information from Print Manager and turns it into printed output.

For all this to work, a few details need to be in order before you pull down the File menu and choose Print. Specifically, you need to do the following:

- *Install* a printer driver appropriate for your printer.

- *Connect* the printer driver to the correct port.

- *Set up* the printer driver for the options you intend to use most often.

If you print by way of a serial port, you also need to configure the port so Windows knows how fast to send data to your printer, whether to use parity checking, and so on. And if you use more than one printer, you need to let Windows know which will be your *default printer*—the printer you'll be using most of the time.

This may sound like an imposing to-do list, but unless you use a number of printers and frequently switch between them, you won't have to perform most of these steps more than once.

This chapter steps you through the details of installing, connecting, and setting up printer drivers; configuring your printer port; and choosing a default printer.

INSTALLING PRINTER DRIVERS

When you first used the Windows Setup program to install Windows on your hard disk, you were given an opportunity to install one or more "printers" (actually, printer drivers) on your system. If you took advantage of that opportunity, you probably don't need to concern yourself with the next page or two of this book. (You can skip ahead to "Connecting Printer Drivers to Printer Ports.") If you did not install a printer at that time, if you are having trouble printing from Windows, or if you'd now like to install another printer, follow along.

To begin the printer installation process, run the application called Control Panel (for a complete description of Control Panel, see Chapter 9). If you're using Program Manager as your Windows shell, double-click the Control Panel icon, which is probably in the Main program group. If you're using File Manager, start Control Panel by double-clicking CONTROL.EXE in the directory containing your Windows files.

Double-click the Control Panel's Printers icon, or pull down the Settings menu and choose Printers. Windows presents the Printers dialog box. If you don't currently have any printers installed, the dialog box looks like the one shown at the top of the following page.

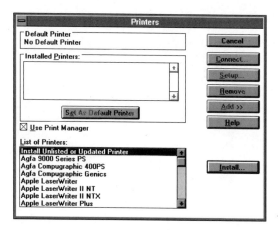

If you already have one or more printers installed, the dialog box looks something like this:

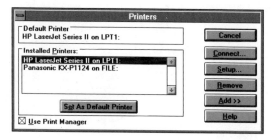

(It probably doesn't look *exactly* like this, but it should have the same basic components.)

If you're installing your first printer, Control Panel presents the list of available printer drivers at the bottom of the dialog box. If you have a printer installed already and you're now installing another, click the Add button to display the printer list.

Scroll through the printer list to find the entry that most closely describes your printer. (If you don't find a suitable entry for your printer, see "If Your Printer Is Not Listed," below.) When you find the appropriate entry, select it and click the Install button (or press Alt-I).

At this point, you might see a message asking you to insert a disk in drive A. If the format of your Windows distribution disks requires you to use drive B, type *b:* in the dialog box, in place of A:\. Then insert the requested disk and press Enter.

 WINDOWS TIP: Note that the message asks you to insert one of the Windows distribution disks *or a disk containing an updated driver file.* Printer vendors often revise and improve their driver files. You might want to contact the dealer from whom you bought your printer to see if the driver file supplied on your Windows disks is the latest version available.

After you have inserted the appropriate disk(s) (depending on the printer, you might be asked for a second disk containing font files), you will find yourself back in the Printers dialog box, with the name of the printer you just installed displayed in the Installed Printers list box.

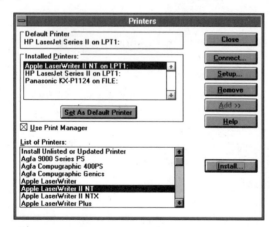

If Your Printer Is Not Listed

If Windows doesn't appear to include a driver for your printer, you should do the following:

- First, check your printer's documentation to see if your printer includes an *emulation* of a Windows-supported printer. Many printers can be set up (via switches or menu commands) to behave like other printers. If your unlisted printer, for example, has an IBM Graphics Printer emulation mode, set it up to use that mode and install the IBM Graphics Printer driver.

- Second, call Microsoft to request the current Driver Library Disk. Microsoft will be adding drivers as time goes by; if your printer wasn't supported when you bought Windows, it might be supported now. Microsoft's Supplemental Driver Library is also available for downloading from CompuServe; see Appendix C for more information.

- Third, contact the dealer from whom you bought your printer to see if a Windows driver is available from the printer's manufacturer. If you obtain a driver from your printer vendor (or other third party), choose Install Unlisted Or Updated Printer in Control Panel's list of printer drivers. You'll be prompted to insert the disk containing your printer driver file(s).

- If no driver for your printer is available from any source, install the driver labeled Generic / Text Only. You won't be able to print graphics, but you will be able to print text. (See "Using the Generic / Text Only Printer," later in this chapter.)

CONNECTING PRINTER DRIVERS TO PRINTER PORTS

After you install a printer driver, the next thing you need to do is tell Windows what printer port you'll be using for that driver. Start by selecting the name of the driver in the Installed Printers list box. Then click the Connect button. Windows presents a small dialog box.

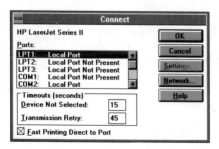

The main business of this dialog box is to connect a printer driver to a particular port. But you need to be aware of a couple of *timeout* options, as well. First, let's look at the Ports list.

A *port* is a physical point of connection between your computer and some external device, such as a printer, scanner, or modem. Printers are generally attached to either serial ports or parallel ports. Serial ports have names such as COM1, COM2, and COM3, and parallel ports are called LPT1, LPT2, and so on.

All the ports supported by your system, including both local and network ports, are listed in the Ports list box. Some ports might be described in the list as "not present." These may include ports that are recognized by Windows and MS-DOS but that don't actually exist in your hardware, as well as serial ports that are in use by another device.

The illustration above, for example, shows a computer with one parallel port and two serial ports. A mouse is attached to the first serial port (COM1). Because Windows and MS-DOS recognize three parallel ports, the list box includes LPT1 through LPT3; the ports LPT2 and LPT3 are identified as "not present." COM1 is also marked "not present," because that port has already been claimed by the mouse.

The default printer port is LPT1. If your printer is attached to LPT1, therefore, you don't need to concern yourself further with the Ports list box. If your printer is connected to a different port, scroll through the list box and select that port.

Assigning a Printer Driver to a Network Printer Port

To assign a printer driver to a network port, begin by clicking the Network button in the Connect dialog box (pictured above). You'll see a display similar to the following.

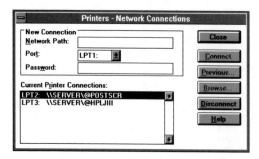

This dialog box has two sections, labeled New Connection and Current Printer Connections. In the latter, you'll find a list of network printer queues already available to you. To assign your printer driver to a new network device, you need to fill out the New Connection section. Type the appropriate network path in the first text box, select a port from the Port list, and enter any required password. Then click the Connect button. When you've finished with the Network Connections dialog, click Close to return to the Connect dialog.

Printing to a File

If you want to send printed output to a disk file instead of to a physical printer, connect your printer driver to the port called FILE. When you print to this driver, Windows prompts you for a filename. Windows then creates a disk file containing exactly the same information it otherwise would have sent to your printer.

> **NOTE:** *The file created by printing to a disk file is not suitable for viewing with Notepad or another editor; it contains printer commands, which can make it virtually unreadable.*

Later you can get hard copy from this file by copying it to your printer port. For example, if your printer is attached to LPT1, you could turn the print file into hard copy with File Manager. Select the filename in a File Manager directory window, choose File Manager's Copy command, and then enter LPT1 as the destination for the copy. Or you could enter the following command at the MS-DOS prompt.

copy *filename* lpt1

If you frequently print to a file, you might want to install a second copy of your printer driver. Attach one copy to the physical port your printer uses and the other to FILE.

Timeout Options

After you select a port, you can turn your attention to the timeout options. Timeout options tell Windows how many seconds to wait before bothering you with an error message if it's unable to get your data printed.

The Device Not Selected value sets the length of time that Windows waits before notifying you that your printer is unplugged, turned off, or off line. The default value of 15 seconds is reasonable; it gives you a chance to switch the printer on if you notice after issuing a Print command that it's turned off.

The Transmission Retry value sets the length of time Windows waits if the printer is on line but "busy." Printers can't handle information as fast as computers can send it to them. They store data in memory buffers while they print, and when the buffer gets full, they send a signal to the computer to hold up until further notice. When they're ready for more, they send another signal, telling the computer to resume. The Transmission Retry setting of 45 seconds means that Windows will give up and issue an error message if it doesn't get a resume signal from the printer after 45 seconds of waiting. This should be an ample period of time, except possibly under one or more of the following conditions:

- If you're using a serial port (Serial ports don't transmit data as quickly as parallel ports.)

- If you're printing on a network printer and there's lots of network traffic

- If you're printing complex graphics (It takes longer to process graphics than ordinary text.)

- If you're using a PostScript printer

If you find yourself getting timeout error messages when nothing is wrong with your printer or its connection to your computer, try increasing the Transmission Retry timeout value.

The Fast Printing Direct To Port Option

To improve printing performance, Windows 3.1 bypasses the normal MS-DOS printing routines. Thus, the Fast Printing Direct To Port check box is selected by default. This setting should work with most of your applications. It is possible that this setting might pose problems for certain unsupported networks. If you experience difficulty printing to a driver that has this check box selected, try returning to Control Panel and deselecting it.

WINDOWS TIP: If the list of printer ports that appears when you click the Connect button includes names with the suffix DOS (for example, LPT1.DOS), you can use these ports as an alternative method of forcing Windows to use the MS-DOS printing interrupts. Printing to a port named LPT1.DOS, for example, is equivalent to printing to LPT1 and deselecting the Fast Printing Direct To Port check box.

Configuring a Serial Port

If you have assigned a printer driver to a serial port (COM1, COM2, COM3, or COM4), you need to tell Windows how to specify communications settings for that port. To do that, select the port in the Ports list box, and then click the Settings button. You'll see the dialog box on the following page.

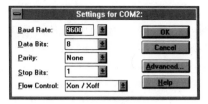

(To change the settings for a printer driver you've already installed, run Control Panel and double-click the Ports icon. Then double-click the icon for the port you want to configure. This is an alternative way to reach the dialog box shown above.)

As the illustration shows, you have five settings to concern yourself with: Baud Rate, Data Bits, Parity, Stop Bits, and Flow Control. Choose the appropriate settings for your printer (consult your printer manual if you're not sure what these terms mean or what settings to choose), and then click the OK button.

CHOOSING YOUR DEFAULT PRINTER

After you have installed drivers for all the printers you intend to use, you need to tell Windows which one you expect to use most often—that is, which will be your default printer. The names of all your installed drivers will appear in Control Panel's Installed Printer list box, like this:

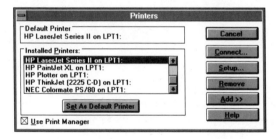

To make a printer the default, simply double-click its name in this list box. Or select the name and click the Set As Default Printer button.

When you use an application's Print command, your output goes to the default printer unless you specify otherwise. In most applications, you can print to a nondefault printer by choosing a Print Setup, Select Printer, or other similarly named command. In some applications, this action also resets the default printer. In others, it does not.

Note that you may install as many printer drivers as you please, and you can even assign multiple printer drivers to the same printer port. Unlike Windows 3.0, Windows 3.1 does not treat some printer drivers as active and others as inactive. All installed printer drivers are available at all times.

CHOOSING SETUP OPTIONS FOR YOUR PRINTER DRIVERS

Whenever you install a new printer driver, you should visit the driver's Setup dialog box to see what options it presents. Drivers are always installed with a default set of options to cover the most common printing needs. But you should familiarize yourself with the choices available to you.

To get to the Setup dialog box, select the appropriate printer driver in Control Panel's Installed Printers list box, and then click the Setup button. The dialog box you see next can be simple or complex, depending on the printer. Here's what the Epson LQ-2550's Setup dialog looks like:

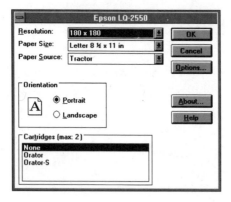

Note that this dialog box includes a button labeled Options. Clicking this button produces a second setup dialog box that looks like this:

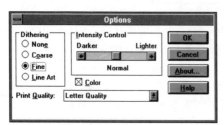

The Setup dialogs for many of the Windows printer drivers include secondary dialog boxes like this one. Be sure to check out these additional dialog boxes to see what all of your options are.

Some Common Setup Options

Setup options vary considerably from printer to printer. Let's explore some of the choices you might encounter with your printer.

 WINDOWS TIP: With many setup options, such as Resolution, you'll want to switch settings as needs dictate. Fortunately, you can get to your printer's Setup dialog box directly from within many Windows applications; you won't have to restart Control Panel to change a printing option. Typically, you display the Setup dialog box by choosing a command called Print Setup, or Select Printer, on the application's File menu. If you want to change a printer's port or timeout settings, however, you'll need to return to Control Panel.

Resolution

Most printer drivers allow you to choose between two or more levels of resolution for printing graphics. These options are expressed in terms of the number of dots per inch (dpi) the printer can create. With higher resolution numbers, you get finer graphics output; with lower numbers, your output is coarser. The trade-off for quality is speed; the more dots the printer has to put on the paper, the longer it takes it to do its job.

Orientation

Many printers offer two orientation choices—Portrait and Landscape. In Portrait orientation, lines of text run perpendicular to the paper's direction of travel through the printer; with most paper, this means the page is taller than it is wide. In Landscape orientation, text lines are parallel to the paper's travel; the page is normally wider than it is tall. (Landscape orientation is sometimes called *sideways* printing.)

Memory

The Memory box initially displays the default memory value for the printer model you select in the Printer box. If you're not sure how much memory your printer has, it's best to assume it has the default value.

WINDOWS TIP: Hewlett-Packard LaserJet printers (and many compatible printers) can print a self-test sheet that shows how much memory is installed. Press the printer's Test button, or refer to the printer's documentation for complete instructions on printing a self-test sheet.

Copies

The Copies box specifies the number of uncollated copies you'll get each time you use a Windows application's Print command. For example, if you put a 2 in this box and print a multipage document, you'll get two copies of page one, then two copies of page two, and so on. Note that this setting is different from the Copies setting that appears in some applications' Print dialogs. If you print a document in Microsoft Word for Windows and ask for two copies in Word's Print dialog box, Word will print all pages of the first copy, followed by all pages of the second copy.

Cartridges

If your printer accepts font cartridges, you will see a cartridge list box in your setup dialog. If your printer model supports more than one cartridge, the dialog box will allow you to select as many as the printer allows. Simply click the name of each cartridge you're planning to use. To deselect a selected item, click it a second time. (If you're using the keyboard, press the Spacebar to select a cartridge; press it again to deselect.)

Dithering

Some printers include four dithering options, labeled None, Coarse, Fine, and Line Art. These settings govern the way Windows prints bitmapped images on black-and-white printers.

Dithering is a process by which a device, such as a printer or video display, approximates colors that it cannot generate directly. For example, if you're using a 16-color display, and you draw a rectangle in the light tan color that appears in the upper right corner of Paintbrush's default palette (see Chapter 16), Windows produces this shade by mixing red, white, and yellow dots.

Most printers can produce only one color—black. A page printed on the typical printer, therefore, is made up entirely of black areas and white areas (assuming the paper itself is white). When you print a color bitmap on a monochromatic printer, your printer driver uses dithering to translate colors other than black and white into shades of gray. The four dithering options that are available with certain printer drivers govern the method by which these drivers do their dithering.

If you choose None, the printer driver translates all colors in the bitmap to either black or white. (Note, however, that if the original color in the bitmapped image is itself dithered, some elements of that color might be translated to white and others to black; your printed image in this case might appear dithered, even though you have chosen the None option.) The Coarse and Fine options produce relatively larger and smaller dot patterns, respectively. And the Line Art option uses a dithering method optimized for images that don't have large blocks of solid colors.

In general, you'll probably want to avoid the None and Line Art choices, except in special circumstances. (You might choose None if you want to emphasize contrast in a printout at the expense of shades of gray.) When a bitmapped image has closely related colors (see, for example, the file TARTAN.BMP supplied on your Windows disks), those colors will usually be easier to distinguish if you print with the Coarse setting, rather than Fine. But the best policy is to experiment. Try all the options to see what generates the most satisfactory results with your images and your printer.

Print TrueType as Graphics

When you print a document formatted with TrueType fonts on a Hewlett-Packard LaserJet or compatible printer, your printer driver normally downloads the font information to your printer's memory. Downloading the font(s) in this manner gets your document printed in the shortest possible time. Under one circumstance, however, you might want to override the default arrangement and have your text printed as a page of bitmapped graphics.

If your document includes graphic objects overlying text, downloading the fonts might cause the text to "bleed through" the graphics, producing a document that doesn't match what you see on screen. For example, if you print a Microsoft Excel document that includes a chart embedded on the worksheet, text that is not visible on screen might appear in your printout.

To correct this problem, select the check box labeled Print TrueType As Graphics. Note that printing the TrueType fonts as graphics will slow your printer down considerably, because Windows will have to compute a bitmap for your entire printed page (instead of relying on your printer's intelligence to render the text). Therefore, you'll probably want to leave this option deselected most of the time and override the default only as needed. Remember that, with most applications, you can do that by choosing a Printer Setup command in the application itself; you don't need to return to Control Panel.

Basic Setup Options for PostScript Printers

The Windows PostScript printer drivers offer myriad setup options, some of which are beyond the scope of this book. The basic choices you'll confront include some of those in the preceding section, as well as the following, which appear when you click the Options button.

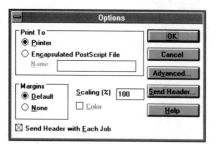

Scaling Factor

The Scaling option allows you to generate printouts that are smaller or larger than normal. For example, if you enter 50 in this box, everything appears half as large as it would with the default setting of 100.

Printing in Color

If your PostScript printer offers color printing, put a check in the Color box to take advantage of this feature. The Color box is gray if your printer does not support color printing.

Downloading the PostScript Header

A PostScript printer has to read a set of generic instructions before it can process any print request. Normally, these instructions are sent in the form of a header at the beginning of each print job. (The header gets its name from the fact that it appears at the top of each file sent to the printer.) Processing the header adds about twenty seconds to the time required to print a job.

You can save those twenty seconds per print job by sending the header to the printer only once—at the beginning of a Windows session. Unless the printer is turned off or the header information is wiped out by another user on a shared network printer, the header will remain in the printer's memory and won't be needed for subsequent printouts.

You can do this in either of two ways: by copying the header to a separate file, and then copying it to the printer; or by copying the header directly to the printer. The first way sounds like more work, but in the long run it's not. We'll look at that method first.

Copying the PostScript Header to a File. To copy the PostScript header to a file, follow these steps:

1. Click the Options button in the PostScript Setup dialog box.

2. In the Options dialog box, click the Header button.

3. In the Header dialog box, select the Already Downloaded option button.

4. Still in the Header dialog box, click the Download button.

5. In the Download Header dialog box, select File and then click OK.

   At this point, you'll be prompted for the complete pathname of your header file.

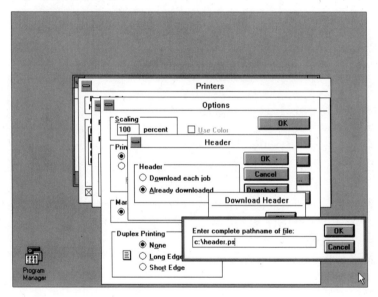

6. Enter a name such as the one shown in the illustration above, and then click OK.

   Windows creates your header file.

7. Finish filling out the PostScript Setup dialog box, and click OK to return to Control Panel.

8. Open Notepad and load the file C:\AUTOEXEC.BAT.

9. Add the following line to AUTOEXEC.BAT:

```
COPY C:\HEADER.PS COM1
```

10. In place of C:\HEADER.PS, substitute the path and name of your header file if you used a different name. In place of COM1, substitute the name of the port to which your printer is attached if it's not attached to COM1.

11. Use Notepad's Save command to save your modified AUTO-EXEC.BAT file.

Now, each time you start your computer, your PostScript header will automatically be sent to the printer.

 WINDOWS TIP: If you use your AUTOEXEC.BAT to copy the PostScript header to your printer, you must be sure to turn on the printer *before* starting your computer each day.

Copying the PostScript Header Directly to the Printer. If you don't want to take the trouble of modifying your AUTOEXEC.BAT file, you can still avoid sending the PostScript header to the printer with each printout. Follow these steps:

1. At the beginning of each Windows session or before the first printout, start Control Panel, double-click the Printers icon, select your PostScript printer driver, and then click Setup.

    This puts you back in the Setup dialog box for your PostScript printer driver.

2. Click the Options button.

3. In the Options dialog box, click the Header button.

4. In the Header dialog box, select Already Downloaded.

5. Still in the Options dialog box, click the Download button.

6. Select Printer, and then click OK.

7. Click OK in each dialog box until you're back in the Printers dialog box; then press Close to return to Control Panel.

Creating an Encapsulated PostScript (EPS) File

An encapsulated PostScript (EPS) file is a file format that can include a bitmapped graphics image as well as PostScript instructions. EPS files provide a means of transferring images from a program such as Paintbrush to another program capable of importing the EPS format.

To print to an EPS file, choose the Encapsulated PostScript File option in the dialog box shown on page 272. Then enter a filename in the Name text box.

USING THE GENERIC / TEXT ONLY PRINTER

Along with all its drivers for specific printers, Windows includes a general-purpose "roll your own" printer driver called Generic / Text Only. As its name suggests, this driver doesn't handle graphics. But you can use it to print text, and you can set it up to handle the idiosyncrasies of your own printer.

When you install the Generic / Text Only driver and click the Setup button, you'll see the following dialog box.

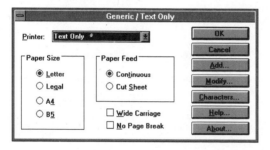

As you can see, this dialog gives you the usual options regarding paper size (narrow or wide carriage, letter or legal length), paper feed (continuous or cut sheet), and whether to observe page breaks. In addition, the generic driver has customizing options that let you, in effect, create a driver appropriate for your own printer. If you click the Add button, Windows presents the following dialog box.

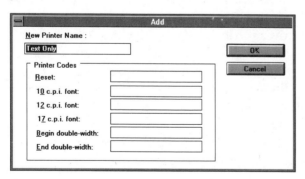

Here you can substitute your printer's real name for "Text Only." More important, you can supply the codes associated with six common printing features: selecting three character pitches (10, 12, and 17 characters per inch), invoking double-width printing, canceling double-width printing, and restoring your printer's default settings. Check the manual for your printer to see if it supports these features and what codes invoke these features. Then enter the codes shown in your manual.

You can enter printer codes either as decimal character values or as Ctrl codes. For example, if your printer manual lists a code as Ctrl-O, you can enter this value in the dialog box by holding down Ctrl and typing O.

NOTE: *You can enter an Escape code by pressing Ctrl-[.*

If your manual provides a three-digit decimal value for the code you want, you can enter that value as follows:

1. Hold down the Alt key.

2. On the numeric keypad, type *0* (zero). Continue to hold down the Alt key.

3. On the numeric keypad, type the three digits listed in your printer manual.

4. Release the Alt key.

Note that the initial 0 (step 2) is required because Windows uses ANSI, rather than ASCII, character values.

If your printer manual lists feature codes only in hexadecimal notation, you will need to convert the values from hexadecimal to decimal before entering them in the Setup dialog box. (Hexadecimal to decimal conversions are easy with Calculator's scientific mode; see Chapter 7.)

You can set up as many generic printers as you like. Simply give each one a different name.

The generic printer driver also lets you specify the way characters with ASCII values between 128 and 255 (the "high-bit" characters) are printed. From the first Setup dialog box, select the name of the printer you want to adjust (if you have only one generic printer, this step is unnecessary). Then click the Characters button. You'll see the display on the following page.

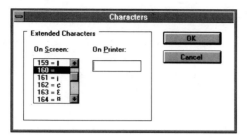

In the On Screen list box, Windows shows you the ANSI values for each high-bit character it can display on screen. (Windows uses the ANSI character set, not the IBM Extended ASCII set; see "Character Map" in Chapter 7.) By default, the generic driver "maps" each high-bit screen character to a printer character in the "low-bit" ASCII range—0 to 127. That way, the driver can accommodate printers, such as daisy-wheels, that aren't capable of printing high-bit characters. For example, the generic printer driver translates a British pound symbol (ANSI 163) on screen to a pound sign (#) on your printout.

If your printer can handle high-bit characters, you might want to edit this "translation table." For example, if your printer can produce a true British pound symbol, you can select 163 in the On Screen list, and then replace the pound sign in the On Printer box with the character value that generates the pound symbol on your printer.

If the character value that produces a pound symbol on your printer is 156, you would do the following:

1. Select 163 in the On Screen list box.

2. Erase the pound sign in the On Printer box.

3. Hold down the Alt key.

4. Type *0156* on the numeric keypad.

5. Release the Alt key.

To learn what high-bit character values your printer uses, you'll need to find a character table in your printer's documentation.

12

Printing with and Without Print Manager

Normally, when you print a Windows document, the data you print passes from your application to your printer driver. From there the data goes to a Windows utility called Print Manager, which feeds it to your printer. The presence of Print Manager in this sequence allows you to send several documents on their way to the printer at the same time. Print Manager acts as a traffic officer, gathering the data from each document you've asked to print, keeping an orderly *print queue* so that documents arrive at the printer in the order you choose, and reporting on the status of all jobs waiting to be printed.

Print Manager can handle as many printers as you have attached to your system. If you print several documents to one printer and several others to another, Print Manager maintains a separate queue for each and feeds the data to each printer as appropriate.

For users running Windows on a network, Print Manager can perform some additional services. Provided the network software permits, Print Manager can show you the status of each print queue on each network printer—even those to which your own computer is not currently attached. You can decide for yourself which of the network's printers is most likely to get your job done the quickest, and then you can use Control Panel to attach your computer to that printer.

Print Manager can be a great convenience, particularly when you need to do a lot of printing from several different Windows applications. (Print Manager does not get involved when you print from non-Windows applications.) But there may be times when you'll find it advantageous to print directly, leaving Print Manager out of the picture. If you bypass Print Manager, you'll be able to complete a particular print job more quickly, but you'll have to wait until the document is printed before doing any further work on that document. And you won't be able to use the Print command from any other application as long as the printer is busy.

In this chapter we'll look at the commands and options for using Print Manager—both on a local printer (one attached directly to your computer) and a network printer. We'll conclude with a few words about printing without Print Manager.

STARTING PRINT MANAGER

Print Manager is a self-starter. As long as you haven't chosen to bypass its services, Print Manager appears automatically on your desktop as soon as you use a Windows application's Print command. You'll see the Print Manager icon at the bottom of your screen.

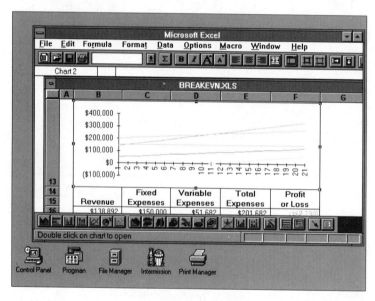

If you don't open (restore) the icon, Print Manager will depart from your desktop (freeing up the memory it was using) as soon as all pending print jobs have been sent to their respective printers.

If you want to invoke Print Manager manually (for example, if you want to inspect your network print queues), you can do so by double-clicking its program-item icon in Program Manager. You'll find that icon in the Main program group, if you haven't moved it or renamed the program group.

WINDOWS TIP: You can print some Windows documents by dragging filenames from a File Manager window and dropping them onto the Print Manager icon (see Chapter 6 for details). If you find yourself using this "drag-and-drop" printing feature often, you might want to put a copy of your Print Manager program item in your Program Manager Startup group. That way, the drag-and-drop target will always be available on your desktop.

PRINT MANAGER'S DISPLAY

If you open the Print Manager icon while a document is being printed, you'll see a display something like this:

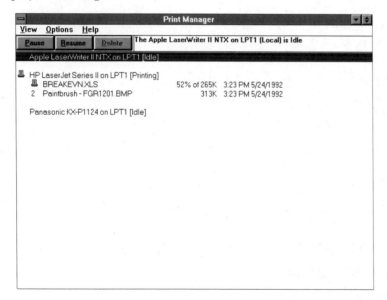

In the example shown above, Print Manager is telling us the following:

- Three printer drivers are installed on this computer: an Apple LaserWriter II NTX, an HP LaserJet Series II, and a Panasonic KX-P1124. All are connected to the computer's first parallel port, LPT1.

- The LaserJet is busy printing.

- The other two printers are idle.

- The LaserJet is currently printing a document called BREAKEVN.XLS. A second document, FGR1201.BMP, is awaiting its turn at the LaserJet. Both jobs were entered into the queue at about the same time, at 3:23 P.M. on May 24.

Note that Print Manager does not display the names of any printer drivers attached to FILE. Print Manager does not handle printer output sent to a disk file. (For information about printing to a file, see Chapter 11.)

The numbers on the right side of the LaserJet queue indicate that the spool files for BREAKEVN.XLS and FGR1201.BMP are 265 KB and 313 KB in size, respectively, and that 52 percent of the BREAKEVN.XLS spool file has been sent to the printer. (A *spool file* is a temporary file that holds your data while it's in transit to the printer.) In Windows 3.1, these numbers also indicate that printing of the first document is about half finished. (In earlier versions of Windows, the size of the spool file often continued to grow, even after Print Manager began despooling the file to the printer. The percentage figure indicated only how much of the accumulated spool file had been despooled, not how much of the total job had been processed.)

If you wish, you can simplify Print Manager's display by pulling down the View menu and deselecting the first two commands—Time/Date Sent and Print File Size. Print Manager's menu commands and command buttons allow you to do a number of other useful things as well. We'll come back to those presently, but first a few more words about spool files.

CREATION OF THE SPOOL FILE

Immediately after you choose an application's Print command (and fill out any associated dialog boxes), the application presents an information window, like this:

This window remains on screen for as long as it takes your application and printer driver to generate the complete spool file for your document. During that time, you will not be able to do any further work in that application. You can, however, switch to another Windows application. In that case, the spool file might not generate as quickly (because Windows will have to share your computer's processor time between Print Manager and the program you switched to), but you won't have to sit on your hands and stare at the screen.

As soon as your application has turned over the entire spool file to Print Manager, you'll be free to go back to work in that application.

NOTE: *During the spooling/despooling process, Print Manager creates temporary files on disk. The names of these files all begin with the tilde character (~) followed by the letters SPL. Do not delete any of these files! Print Manager will delete them itself as soon as it has finished printing.*

REARRANGING A PRINT QUEUE

Print Manager lets you change the order of jobs in a print queue. Simply open Print Manager's window, select the name of the print job whose position you want to change, and then drag it upward or downward in the queue. Print Manager renumbers the queue when you release the mouse button. You can't move the current print job (the one with the small printer icon next to it).

To reorder a queue with the keyboard, do the following:

1. Select the name of the job you want to move.

2. Hold down the Ctrl key.

3. Use the Up or Down direction key to move the job to a new position in the queue.

4. Release the Ctrl key.

USING THE PAUSE AND RESUME BUTTONS

If you need to interrupt a local printout for any reason—to change a ribbon or add paper, for example—open Print Manager, select the name of the printer you want to interrupt, and click the Pause button (or press Alt-P). Print Manager's display will indicate that the selected printer is "paused."

To restart the printout, click the Resume button or press Alt-R.

You might or might not be able to interrupt and resume printing on a network printer. It depends on your network software.

DELETING JOBS FROM A PRINT QUEUE

You can remove a job from any of Print Manager's queues at any time. Simply select the item you want to remove (using keyboard or mouse) and click the Delete button or press Alt-D. Print Manager asks you to confirm your intentions.

The item you remove can be either a document that's already in the process of being printed or one that's waiting in line.

If you delete a document at the head of a queue—that is, a document that's currently being printed—you might need to reset your printer before printing another document.

CHANGING THE BACKGROUND PRIORITY GIVEN TO PRINT MANAGER

Normally, Print Manager acts as a *background* application. That is, it does its work behind the scenes while you interact with another application—the *foreground* application. Whenever you have two or more applications running, Windows usually splits your computer's processing time in such a way that the foreground application gets the largest share and each background application gets a smaller share.

Unlike other programs that happen to be running in the background, however, Print Manager includes commands that let you increase or decrease its share of the computer's processing time. These commands are located on the Options menu, which looks like this:

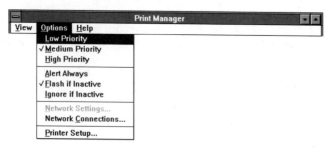

For the fastest printing that Print Manager can supply, choose High Priority. If you're in no hurry for hard copy and don't want to sacrifice the responsiveness of your foreground application, choose Low Priority. Otherwise, simply accept Print Manager's default setting—Medium Priority.

IF PRINTING IS INTERRUPTED

If Print Manager is unable to complete a print job for some reason—the printer runs out of paper, someone turns the printer off, the data cable falls off the back of your computer, or whatever—Print Manager displays the following message:

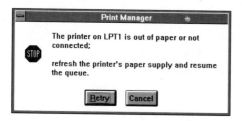

Correct the problem that interrupted your printout, and then click the Retry button.

The appearance of other Print Manager messages—for example, the ones you'll see if you've set up your print for manual page feeding—depend on which setting you've chosen in the second section of Print Manager's Options menu.

With the default setting, Flash If Inactive, in effect, Print Manager displays the problem message only if its window is both open and active. If Print Manager is minimized, it beeps and blinks its icon. If Print Manager is an open window but not the active window, it beeps and blinks its title bar. Either way, you simply need to activate Print Manager to read the message.

If you choose Alert Always, Print Manager always interrupts what you're doing and displays its message. If you choose Ignore If Inactive, Print Manager doesn't bother notifying you of a printing problem unless it happens to be the active window.

PRINTING ON A NETWORK

When you print on a network printer (a printer that's not attached directly to your own computer), information is fed from your computer to a print queue managed by the network software. Typically, the network queue includes jobs sent by other users on the network, as well as those you send yourself. The network software handles the transfer of print jobs from the network queue to the network printer.

Using or Bypassing Print Manager

By default, Print Manager is set up so that print jobs are passed directly to the network queue, without first becoming part of a local (Print Manager) queue. With this arrangement, your print jobs arrive at the network queue as quickly as possible, and Print Manager can still give you information about where your jobs stand in the network queue.

If you prefer, however, you can let Print Manager form a local queue of print jobs on their way to the network queue. Your jobs might take a little longer to reach their final destination—the network printer—but you'll be able to get some work done while Print Manager is queuing up your spool files.

To use Print Manager's local queuing services when printing to a network printer, do the following:

1. Open Print Manager.

2. Open the Options menu and choose Network Settings.

3. In the dialog box that appears, remove the check from Print Net Jobs Direct and click OK.

Options for Displaying Network Queue Status

Regardless of how the Print Net Jobs Direct option is set, Print Manager can keep you informed about the status of network print queues. If the network software permits, Print Manager offers the following reporting options:

- It can display the names of all jobs pending on a network queue or only those you have sent yourself.

- It can display the status of all print queues on the network or only those to which your own computer is connected.

- It can update its status displays as often as the network makes the information available or only on demand from you.

In all cases, the tradeoff for information is speed. At times of peak network use, you might want to opt for less information to minimize traffic on the cable.

Viewing All Jobs on a Network Queue

To see the entire contents of a network queue, not only those jobs you yourself have added to the queue, do the following:

1. Open Print Manager.

2. Select the name of the network queue.

3. Open the View menu and choose Selected Net Queue.

You'll see a window that lists the jobs in the network queue.

Viewing Network Print Queues to Which You Are Not Connected

Looking at the status of network print queues to which you are not currently attached can help you determine which printer is likely to get your work printed the soonest. To view the status of a queue that you're not currently attached to, do the following:

1. Open Print Manager.

2. Open the View menu and choose Other Net Queue.

3. Fill out the dialog box with the name of the queue you want to inspect.

After you have determined which queue you want to join, you still need to attach your own computer to that queue. You can do that either with Control Panel (see "Assigning a Printer Driver to a Network Printer Port," in Chapter 11) or by choosing the Network Connections command on Print Manager's Options menu. The results are the same in either case.

Disabling Automatic Update of Network Queue Status

Updating Print Manager's reports about the status of network print queues adds traffic to the network. If you don't need this information and want to help minimize network gridlock, you can do the following:

1. Open Print Manager.

2. Open the Options menu and choose Network Settings.

3. Remove the check from Update Network Display.

With network display update turned off, Print Manager displays the names of jobs you send to the network but doesn't tell you about their standing in the network queue. You can update Print Manager's network information manually with the View menu's Refresh command.

PRINTING WITHOUT PRINT MANAGER

The quickest way to get a job printed is not to use Print Manager. When you leave Print Manager out of the picture, your document goes directly from your application to your printer driver, and from there directly to the printer. You save the processing time that would be required for Print Manager to spring onto your desktop, set up the print queue, and so on.

While your job is being printed, you won't be able to use the application that's doing the printing. You will be able to use other Windows applications, but doing so will put the printing application into the background and delay your print job. If you're really in a hurry, you should disable Print Manager, use your application's Print command, and simply wait until the printing is finished.

To disable Print Manager, do the following:

1. Close Print Manager if it's now on your desktop as an open window or icon.

2. Open Control Panel and choose Printers.

3. In the Printers dialog box, remove the check from Use Print Manager.

4. Click OK to return to Control Panel.

You won't be able to open Print Manager again until you go back to Control Panel and reselect the Use Print Manager option.

13
Using Fonts in Windows Applications

Windows offers the ability to print documents in a variety of typefaces and styles. Even with inexpensive dot-matrix printers, many Windows applications make it easy for you to generate reports, letters, and memos whose impact is enhanced by the power of typography.

Understanding the basics of font terminology and technology will help you get the most out of your work in Windows. To help you acquire that understanding, this chapter will focus first on some of the terms used to describe fonts, font sizes, styles, and so on. Then we'll look at the ways in which fonts can be used in Windows applications. We'll conclude with a survey of the font options available with certain major classes of printers.

TYPOGRAPHICAL TERMINOLOGY

A *font* is a complete set of characters in one size and one typeface. For example, all the letters, numbers, punctuation marks, and other symbols available in 12-point Courier New bold italic constitute one font. The same set of characters in another size constitutes another font.

Fonts are identified by their size, typeface family, weight, and style. In the name "12-point Courier New bold italic," for example, 12-point is the size, Courier New is the typeface family, bold is the weight, and italic is the style. When the weight is "normal" and the style is "roman," these terms are usually omitted.

Font Size

A font's size is usually measured in points and expressed as a "point size." A *point* is a printer's measurement, equal to $^1/_{12}$ of a *pica*, or approximately $^1/_{72}$ of an inch. A font's point size is approximately the distance in points from the top of its highest character to the bottom of its lowest character. (This definition applies to a font's printed size only. On screen, point size has no absolute significance at all, because of the differences in screen size. A 10-point font on a 16-inch screen might be larger than a 12-point font on a 14-inch screen—and so on.)

Point size is a rough measure of a font's height but says nothing about width. Many font families come in *compressed* and *expanded* variants, as well as in normal widths. The PostScript font Helvetica-Narrow is an example of a compressed font.

Fonts designed for dot-matrix and daisy-wheel printers are typically measured not by point size but by their widths, in characters per inch (cpi). A 10-cpi (also called *10-pitch*) font, for example, measures 10 characters to the inch. You might also encounter the terms *elite* and *pica* to describe font size; an elite font measures 12 cpi, and a pica font measures 10 cpi.

Style and Weight

The most common *style* variants for fonts are roman and italic. Roman characters are the "normal" kind, with straight up-and-down strokes predominating. Italic characters, forward slanting and often more rounded, are used for emphasis, titles of books, and so on.

The term *weight* refers to the thickness of a font's strokes. The most common weights are normal (also called regular) and bold, but some font families also include other weights, such as thin, light, heavy, ultra, and black.

Serif and Sans Serif Fonts

Most fonts fall into one of two categories—serif and sans serif. Serif fonts have fine lines that finish off the main strokes—for example, at the bottom of a capital *T* or the ends of the *T*'s crossbar. These "finishing strokes," called *serifs*, are absent in sans serif fonts. Serif fonts, such as Times New Roman, are generally considered more suitable for conventional text, such as what you read in a newspaper or book. Sans serif fonts, such as Helvetica and Arial, have a more modern appearance and are often used in headlines, tabular material (such as spreadsheet reports), and advertising.

Monospaced and Proportionally Spaced Fonts

Fonts in which every character takes up the same amount of space are called *monospaced*. Fonts in which some characters (such as *m* and *w*) are wider than others (*i* and *t*, for example) are described as being *proportionally spaced*. Proportionally spaced fonts produce a more typeset appearance and are generally considered easier to read. Monospaced fonts are often preferred for such printouts as legal documents, which have traditionally been produced on typewriters.

Arial and Times New Roman are examples of proportionally spaced fonts. The most commonly used monospaced font is Courier.

Note that, although the widths of letters in a proportionally spaced font vary, the widths of numerals are all the same—so that numbers can be aligned in tables.

Scalable and Nonscalable Fonts

Fonts can be described as being either *scalable* or *nonscalable*. Scalable fonts are fonts that can be used at any number of different point sizes. Nonscalable fonts are designed for use at particular sizes; enlarging or reducing them generally produces unattractive distortions (serrated diagonal lines, for example).

Nonscalable fonts are sometimes described as *bitmapped fonts*. That's because the form in which they're stored on your hard disk (or in a printer cartridge) records the relative position of each dot comprising each character. For example, a capital *I* might be stored as a column of twelve dots plus two six-dot crossbars. To generate a character from a bitmapped font, your video or printing hardware simply reproduces the bitmap at the desired location.

Most scalable fonts are stored as outlines; such fonts, therefore, are often called *outline fonts*. An outline is a mathematical description of each character in the font. Before characters from an outline font are rendered on your screen or printer, font-management software converts them to bitmaps, using a process called *scan conversion*. To avoid jagged lines and other distortions in the final rendering, particularly at smaller point sizes, the font-management software also employs *hints*—algorithms that modify the scan-conversion process to produce optimal looking characters.

Because outline fonts are stored as mathematical descriptions, rather than as fully realized bitmaps, they can be scaled to a wide range of point sizes. They can also be slanted, rotated, compressed, extended, inverted, and otherwise manipulated. Their *metrics* (character-width specifications) can also be modified as needed to produce kerned or letterspaced typography. The one small disadvantage of outline fonts is that the scan-conversion process takes a modest amount of processing time. The first time you use an outline font at a given point size, therefore, you might encounter a slight delay while your system performs the calculation required to convert the font's outline into the appropriate set of bitmaps. After the bitmaps have been rendered, however, they're stored in an area of memory called a *cache*. When you need to reuse the font, Windows simply grabs the bitmaps out of cache memory, avoiding the original calculation delay.

FONTS SUPPLIED WITH WINDOWS 3.1

Incorporated into Windows 3.1 is a font-management technology called True-Type, which Microsoft has licensed from Apple Computer. Along with this font-management technology, Windows 3.1 includes five TrueType typeface families—Arial, Times New Roman, Courier New, Symbol, and Wingdings. Arial is a sans serif typeface that's similar to Helvetica. Times New Roman is a serif face similar to Times Roman. Courier New is a monospaced serif face, and Symbol is a serif face consisting of the Greek alphabet, plus a few mathematical and phonetic symbols. Wingdings is a collection of icons, symbols, and "dingbat" characters that you can use to enliven your documents. The Windows-supplied TrueType typefaces are each available in four styles—roman, italic, bold, and bold italic.

In addition to the five TrueType families, Windows 3.1 also includes three *stroke* fonts, called Modern, Roman, and Script, and three sets of bitmapped fonts—MS Serif, MS Sans Serif, and Courier.

Like outline fonts, stroke fonts are scalable. But they're based on a simpler scaling technology and produce much less satisfactory results. Their single virtue is that they produce characters consisting only of straight lines and hence can be used on non-raster output devices (devices that do not operate by positioning dots on an output medium) such as plotters. (Because stroke-font characters consist only of straight lines, such fonts are also commonly called *vector* fonts.)

The bitmapped fonts are provided for compatibility with earlier versions of Windows. (Two of them have been renamed; MS Sans Serif was previously known as Helv, and MS Serif is the former Tms Rmn.) They're available only in particular point sizes, and you can't use them on laser printers.

Along with this assortment of Windows-supplied font resources, you might find additional fonts available to you, courtesy of particular applications that you have installed. If you use Microsoft Word for Windows 2.0, for example, you will likely see a TrueType font named Fences listed in Word's Format Character dialog box. This font, used by Word's equation editor, is one of several that become part of your Windows system automatically when you install Word. Other applications similarly install other fonts for their own use; typically, these fonts become available from any of your Windows applications.

THIRD-PARTY FONT RESOURCES

A number of type vendors provide fonts and font-management systems compatible with Windows 3.1. These third-party font resources fall into two broad categories: fonts that are stored on your hard disk as bitmaps for specific point sizes and fonts that are stored as outlines and scan-converted as needed. MicroLogic Software's MoreFonts is an example of the first category. Adobe's Adobe Type Manager (ATM), Hewlett-Packard's Intellifont-for-Windows, and Bitstream's FaceLift are examples of the latter. For more about these specific third-party font resources, as well as other font-related products, see Chapter 17.

Because TrueType font technology is also built into the Apple Macintosh's System 7 operating system, TrueType fonts designed for the Macintosh should also work, without conversion, in Windows 3.1—and vice versa. You might, therefore, be able to share public-domain and shareware TrueType fonts with colleagues and friends who use Macintoshes. For more information about public-domain and shareware software resources, see Appendix C.

YOUR PRINTER'S OWN FONT RESOURCES

In addition to the fonts that Windows supplies and any additional fonts that you install in Windows, you can take advantage of any of your printer's internal font resources. Your printer driver tells Windows what fonts the printer provides, and those fonts appear in the Font dialog boxes used by your applications.

When you use your printer's own fonts, Windows doesn't have to download font information (or turn each page of your document into a bitmap—a time-consuming process), so printing is likely to be quicker. In trade for this speed increase, however, you might have to sacrifice some degree of correspondence between the appearance of your document on screen and its appearance on paper.

When you format a document with an internal printer font, Windows displays the same font on screen—if it can. For example, if you're printing to an HP LaserJet III (or a compatible PCL-5 laser printer) and you have installed Hewlett-Packard's Intellifont software, Intellifont generates screen fonts that match your printer's internal fonts.

If Windows does not have a screen font to match the printer font you select, it gives you the closest match that it can. For example, if you choose the Courier font that's built into your LaserJet Series II, Windows formats your text on screen with its own TrueType Courier font (Courier New). If you select your PostScript printer's Avant Garde font (and you have not installed Adobe Type Manager and the Avant Garde screen font), Windows uses the nearest TrueType equivalent (Arial) on screen. Both are sans serif fonts.

Even if the screen font used by Windows doesn't exactly match the printer font you select, Windows applications attempt to show you where your lines will break on the printed page. The correspondence of line endings on screen to line endings on paper might not always be perfect, however, and some applications do a better job of this than others. If precise text positioning is critical, it's always best to avoid printer fonts that don't have equivalent screen fonts.

VIEWING, ADDING, AND DELETING FONTS WITH CONTROL PANEL

The Fonts section of Control Panel provides you with a way to look at samples of all fonts installed in your Windows system. When you run Control Panel and double-click the Fonts icon, you see a display similar to this:

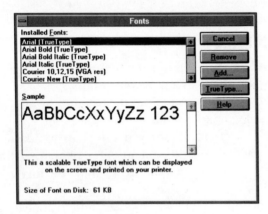

In the upper half of this dialog box, you'll see a list of all your installed fonts. Note that this list includes only those fonts that Windows can display on screen. Printer-resident fonts do not appear on the list.

As you select each name in the installed-font list, Windows displays a sample in the lower half of the dialog box. With TrueType and stroke fonts, you see only one point size; with bitmapped fonts, you see a sample of each size available on your system. The bitmapped fonts are identified in the font list by the available point sizes and the resolution of your display; in the figure above, for example, "Courier 10,12,15 (VGA Res)" denotes a bitmapped font in VGA resolution, available in point sizes of 10, 12, and 15.

Adding Fonts

You can also use the Fonts section of Control Panel to install new fonts. You might not need to do this with commercial font packages because such packages typically include their own installation routines. With public-domain or shareware fonts, or other fonts that don't include installation programs, you can invoke Control Panel's Fonts section and select the Add button. You can also use this command to restore native Windows fonts that you have previously deleted.

Control Panel's Add button displays a dialog box like this:

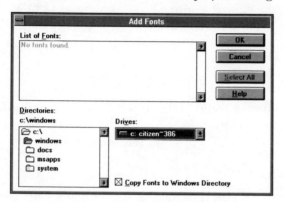

Select the directory that contains your font files. Then select one or more files in the Fonts list and click OK. (Or, if you want to install all the fonts in the selected directory, simply click the Select All button and then click OK.)

These steps copy the selected font files to the SYSTEM subdirectory of your Windows directory and make the appropriate modifications to your WIN.INI file. If you do not have enough space on your hard disk to store the selected font files, you can skip the file-copying part of this process by deselecting the Copy Fonts To Windows Directory option. Windows then retrieves font information from your source directory (presumably a network drive or floppy disk) as needed. You must, of course, ensure that the specified directory is always available.

Deleting Fonts

If you're running low on disk space, or if you find you never use certain fonts, you can take advantage of Control Panel's Remove button. When you select a font name and click this button, Windows modifies your WIN.INI file to make the selected font unavailable. Note that the font file itself is not deleted from your hard disk unless you check the Delete Font File From Disk check box.

NOTE: *Windows uses MS Sans Serif for many of its dialog boxes. You should therefore not delete this font, even if you never use it in your applications. You should also be careful not to delete any font files whose names do not appear in the [fonts] section of your WIN.INI file. (If you do, you might inadvertently get rid of fonts that Windows needs to display non-Windows applications.)*

The procedure just described can be used to delete only the fonts that are actually installed in your Windows system. Fonts that are generated by a font-management application, such as Adobe Type Manager, do not appear in Control Panel's font listing (or in the [fonts] section of your WIN.INI file). To remove such fonts from your hard disk, consult the documentation that came with your font-management software.

USING FONTS WITH SPECIFIC TYPES OF PRINTERS

The way in which font information is translated into printed output depends on the kind of printer you use. Understanding how Windows works with *your* printer will help you get the most out of your system's font resources.

Dot-matrix and Inkjet Printers

Unless you format with resident (internal) printer fonts, Windows creates output on dot-matrix and inkjet printers by converting each page to a bitmap and invoking your printer's graphics mode. Printing with internal fonts will therefore be considerably quicker than using Windows TrueType or bitmapped fonts, but you will not see the same fonts on screen as you see on paper. The Windows TrueType fonts also offer the significant advantages of being available at all point sizes and in both landscape and portrait orientation. (Internal fonts are available in portrait mode only.)

 WINDOWS TIP: For the optimum mix of speed and quality, you might want to format headings with TrueType fonts and body text with your printer's internal fonts.

HP LaserJet Series II and Compatible Printers

LaserJet Series II and compatible printers can use the following kinds of fonts:

- Internal (permanently built-in) fonts
- Cartridge fonts (fonts supplied via plug-in cartridges)

- The Windows stroke fonts

- "Soft" (downloaded) fonts, including TrueType fonts

The Windows bitmapped fonts are not available on LaserJet printers.

Internal and cartridge fonts are nonscalable and orientation-specific. That is, they come in fixed point sizes and are designed for portrait or landscape orientation, but not both. (Fonts on the LaserJet IID and LaserJet IIP, although designed for one orientation, can be used for both orientations.)

Your printer's font resources might include several fonts in each orientation. If so, when you use your printer driver's Setup dialog box (either in Control Panel or from within an application) to switch from one orientation to the other, the menus and dialog boxes of your applications will change to reflect the fonts available for the current orientation. In effect, your programs act as though you had two separate printers housed in the same physical device.

The Windows stroke fonts—Modern, Roman, and Script—can be printed in either orientation in sizes from 4 through 127 point. Windows prints these fonts in graphics mode, as bitmaps.

TrueType fonts will be scan-converted in your computer and downloaded as "soft" fonts. This means that Windows converts the font outlines to bitmaps and downloads the information to your printer's memory. Your printer then uses its own intelligence to render characters onto paper.

If you wish, however, you can force Windows to print TrueType characters as bitmaps instead of downloading font information to the printer. As mentioned in Chapter 11, you might want to do this if your document includes graphic objects (pictures or diagrams, for example) that intentionally obscure some of your TrueType text. Because the LaserJet II family of printers is capable of generating text and graphics in separate "bands" (separate passes through the page), the normal mode of TrueType printing can produce printouts that don't match what you see on screen. To force Windows to print TrueType fonts as bitmaps, invoke your printer's Setup dialog box (either in Control Panel or from within your application), click the Options button, and then select the Print TrueType As Graphics check box.

HP LaserJet III and Compatible Printers

Font options for LaserJet III and compatible printers are comparable to those for the LaserJet Series II, except that the LaserJet III has the ability to perform scan conversion from internal font outlines. If you use a LaserJet III, you will probably want to avail yourself of Hewlett-Packard's Intellifont font-management software.

PostScript Printers

PostScript printers include built-in outline font technology and a set of Type 1 outline fonts. (Type 1 is the name of outline font technology used by the Post-Script page-description language.) When you format your documents with any of these resident fonts, the scan conversion is performed at the printer. What you see on screen, meanwhile, depends on whether or not you are using Adobe Type Manager. If you are, ATM creates screen fonts on the fly that faithfully match your printer fonts. If you are not, Windows uses TrueType to give you its best imitation of what you'll see on paper. Practically speaking, that means you get Arial if you select a sans serif PostScript font, Times New Roman if you select a serif font, Courier New if you choose PostScript Courier, and Wingdings if you format with Zapf Dingbats.

If you format your documents with TrueType fonts, the situation is a little more complicated. At smaller point sizes (up to 15 point), Windows scan-converts its TrueType outlines in your computer and sends your printer a bitmap. (In Postscript terminology, it downloads a "Type 3" instead of a "Type 1" font.) At larger point sizes, Windows converts its TrueType outlines to Type 1 and downloads a Type 1 font, allowing your printer to perform the scan conversion. This dual approach allows you to avoid the lengthy delays occasioned by the downloading of large bitmaps.

If you wish, you can override Windows' normal way of working and have all TrueType characters downloaded as Type 3 bitmaps. To do this, first invoke your printer's Setup dialog box—either through Control Panel or from within an application. Then click the Options button. In the next dialog box that appears, click Advanced. You'll see a display similar to the following.

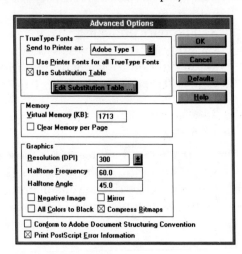

Open the drop-down list labeled Send To Printer As, and select Bitmap (Type 3).

You can also choose to have TrueType fonts mapped automatically to native PostScript fonts. To do this, invoke the Setup dialog box, choose Options, and then choose Advanced. You'll see the dialog box shown in the previous figure. In the TrueType Fonts section of this dialog box, select the check box labeled Use Substitution Table. Then click the Edit Substitution Table button. You'll see two lists—your TrueType fonts on the left and your PostScript fonts on the right.

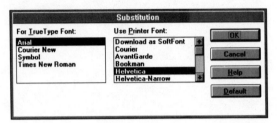

Now you can step through the list on the left and indicate which PostScript font you want to substitute for each TrueType font. If you want Windows to substitute PostScript fonts for some (but not all) of your TrueType fonts, choose Download As SoftFont for those fonts that you don't want substituted.

PART V

USING APPLICATIONS

Part V takes up the topic of applications—the programs you use to get your work done in Windows. Chapters 14, 15, and 16 describe Write, Terminal, and Paintbrush, the three major applications that come with your Windows package. Write is a word processor, Terminal is a communications program, and Paintbrush is a program you can use to create and manipulate images.

Chapter 17 provides brief descriptions of major Windows applications that are not supplied with Windows. These vignettes will give you an idea of how certain programs take advantage of the Windows environment.

Chapter 18 tells you how to run your non-Windows applications, with or without program information files (PIFs). And Chapter 19 provides details about setting up Windows for optimal capacity and performance.

14
Using Write

This chapter introduces Write, the word processor that comes with Windows. Write lets you create highly formatted documents that can include pictures as well as text. You can format individual paragraphs to be flush left, flush right, centered, or justified, and you can choose from three line-spacing options. Documents can be printed with multiline headers or footers that may include automatic page numbering. Write also supports object linking and embedding as a client application.

Even if you subsequently adopt an even more powerful Windows word processor, such as Microsoft Word for Windows or WordPerfect for Windows, you will find working in Write a valuable introduction to word processing in a graphical environment. And, of course, the documents you create in Write can be transferred by way of the Clipboard to many other Windows applications.

STARTING WRITE

To start Write, double-click its program-item icon. You'll find it in the Accessories program group, unless you have moved it to another group.

Write's opening display looks like this:

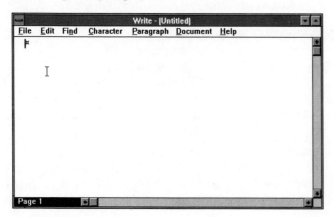

You'll see the following symbols as you work in Write:

Insertion point: The flashing vertical line is the *insertion point*. It indicates the place where your next character will appear.

End mark: The small object to the right of the insertion point in the preceding illustration is the *end mark*. As its name suggests, the end mark appears beside the last character in your document; when you start creating a Write document, it sits right next to the insertion point.

I-beam: The I-shaped pointer below and to the right of the end mark in the illustration is the *I-beam*. Your mouse pointer becomes an I-beam when you work in a Write document. The I-beam allows you to relocate the insertion point. If you don't have a mouse, you won't see an I-beam, but you'll be able to move the insertion point with the keyboard.

On the right and bottom edges of your Write window, you'll find scroll bars. And in the lower left corner, Write displays the current page number. Don't be disconcerted if this counter remains at 1 while you create a lengthy document. As soon as you print or repaginate your document, the page numbers will be reported accurately.

(If you have used Write already, you might see a "ruler" at the top of your window. The use of Write's ruler is discussed later in this chapter.)

SELECTING A PRINTER

The first command you should acquaint yourself with in Write is Print Setup, on the File menu. Write adjusts its screen display and its Fonts dialog box to reflect the currently selected printer, so whenever you start a new Write document be sure you're set up for the printer you want to use.

The Print Setup command presents the following dialog box.

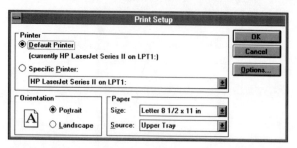

When you start Write, the program is always set to use the default printer set by Control Panel. To use a different printer, click the arrow to the right of the

Specific Printer box and choose from the list that unfolds. Write automatically adjusts the dialog box to display the paper size and paper source options available for the printer you select. Be sure those options are set as you want them, click OK, and you're ready to get to work.

WINDOWS TIP: Be sure that your printer is set for the correct orientation—portrait or landscape. Write adjusts the dimensions of the document you're working on to reflect the printer's orientation. In portrait orientation on letter-size paper, the default text area is 6 inches wide; in landscape orientation, it's 8.5 inches wide. And with most printers, your font options also depend on your printer's orientation.

You can change printers after you've begun working on a Write document. Later in this chapter, we'll see how Write handles such a change.

ENTERING TEXT

To enter text in Write, simply type. As you do so, Write measures the lengths of your document's lines *as they will appear when printed.* It knows the printed width of each character in each available font. When your text reaches the right margin, Write starts a new line for you. You don't have to press the Enter key until you come to the end of a paragraph. If a word is too long to fit entirely on one line, Write moves the entire word to the next line.

If you want a blank line between paragraphs, press Enter twice at the end of each paragraph. If you want each paragraph to start with an indent, you can work in either of two ways. You can simply press the Tab key at the beginning of each new paragraph. Or you can use the Indents command, on the Paragraph menu, to automatically move the first line in a specified distance. The Indents command is discussed later in this chapter.

Using Soft Hyphens

Write does not ordinarily hyphenate words at the right margin. If you want to allow the program to hyphenate, you can insert *soft hyphens* wherever hyphenation is acceptable. To enter a soft hyphen, type Ctrl-Shift-Hyphen. Unlike a normal hyphen, a soft hyphen is ignored unless it occurs at the end of a line.

For example, suppose you're nearing the right margin and the next word in your document is *mononucleosis.* You type that word and Write breaks the entire word down to the next line, leaving your document with a very ragged right edge. You might want to go back and insert a soft hyphen after the second *o* (or at some other appropriate hyphenation point). If the portion of your word to the left of the soft hyphen fits on the previous line, Write moves it back.

Soft hyphens remain invisible unless Write actually uses them to divide words.

EDITING TEXT

As you'll recall from Chapter 3, the insertion point in Windows documents always lies *between* characters. To insert text into existing text, simply position the insertion point where you want the new material to go. You never have to concern yourself with issuing an "insert" or "overstrike" command, as you do in many MS-DOS word processors.

To replace existing text with new text, start by selecting the text you want to replace. You can do that with either the mouse or the keyboard. (We'll review the procedures for selecting text in a moment.) Then type; the words you selected disappear, and the new words you type take their place.

To erase a small amount of text, position the insertion point either before or after the text you want to erase. Then press Backspace or Del. Backspace erases the text to the left of the insertion point; Del erases text to the right of the insertion point.

To erase a large amount of text, start by selecting the text. Then press the Del key. If you want to delete a block of text but preserve it on the Clipboard, select the text and then use the Edit menu's Cut command. (As a keyboard shortcut for the Cut command, you can press Ctrl-X.) Keeping the deleted text on the Clipboard gives you the option of putting it right back in the place you removed it from (if you should change your mind) or reusing it in another context.

USING THE UNDO COMMAND

Write's Edit menu includes a versatile and valuable Undo command. Undo enables you to recover from many kind of accidents: deletions, overtyping, formatting changes that don't produce the desired effect, and even search-and-replace operations of which you immediately repent. As you will note if you pull down the Edit menu, the Undo menu item is *dynamic*; that is, it changes to indicate what kind of action it's able to undo at any given moment. Right after you make a formatting change, for example, the command reads Undo Formatting.

As a keyboard shortcut for the Undo command, press Ctrl-Z.

USING THE KEYBOARD TO MOVE THE INSERTION POINT

All the procedures described in Chapter 3 (see "Entering and Editing Text in Windows Documents") for moving the insertion point in a Windows text document work in Write. In addition, Write makes use of the 5 key on your numeric keypad as a "Go To" key. You can press the 5 key followed by the Down direction key, for example, to move directly to the next paragraph. Pressing 5 followed by Up takes you to the previous paragraph.

> **NOTE:** *The Go To key does not work when your keyboard is in its Num Lock state. If pressing Go To puts a 5 in your document, erase the 5, press the Num Lock key, and then try again.*

The keystrokes used by Write for moving the insertion point are summarized in Table 14-1 on the next page. Note that the Go To, PgDn and Go To, PgUp keystroke combinations do not function until a document has been printed or paginated. See "Printing a Write Document," later in this chapter.

> **NOTE:** *Keystrokes that move the insertion point to a previous location, such as Go To, Left (which moves to the beginning of the previous sentence), have a two-step action. The first time you press Go To, Left, the insertion point moves to the beginning of the current sentence. Press it again to move the insertion point to the beginning of the previous sentence.*

KEYBOARD TIP: Don't use Tab, the Spacebar, or Backspace when all you want to do is move the insertion point. The Tab key and the Spacebar add blank space to the content of your document, and the Backspace key erases the character to the left of the insertion point.

Keystroke(s)	Moves the Insertion Point
Right	To the next character
Left	To the previous character
Down	To the next line
Up	To the previous line
Ctrl-Right	To the next word
Ctrl-Left	To the previous word
Ctrl-Down	To the next line (and scrolls the window)
Ctrl-Up	To the previous line (and scrolls the window)
PgDn	Down one windowful
PgUp	Up one windowful
Ctrl-PgDn	To the last line in the current window
Ctrl-PgUp	To the first line in the current window
Home	To the first character in the current line
End	To the last character in the current line
Ctrl-Home	To the first character in the document
Ctrl-End	To the end mark of the document
Go To, Right	To the beginning of the next sentence
Go To, Left	To the beginning of the previous sentence
Go To, Down	To the beginning of the next paragraph
Go To, Up	To the beginning of the previous paragraph
Go To, PgDn	To the beginning of the next page
Go To, PgUp	To the beginning of the previous page

Table 14-1.
Navigation keystrokes in Write.

SELECTING TEXT IN A WRITE DOCUMENT

Write uses the same procedures for selecting text that were described in Chapter 3 (see "Entering and Editing Text in Windows Documents"). You can do either of the following:

- Put the mouse at one end of the area you want to select, press and hold down the mouse button, drag the mouse to the other end of the area to be selected, and then release the mouse button.

- Put the insertion point at one end of the area you want to select, press and hold down either Shift key, navigate to the other end of the area to be selected, and then release the Shift key.

Additional procedures, specific to Write, allow mouse users to quickly select the current line, the current paragraph, or the entire document. To use any of these procedures, start by positioning the mouse pointer in the area to the left of your text. You'll see the mouse pointer change from an I-beam to a "northeast"-pointing arrow.

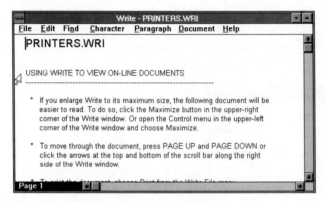

Now you can do any of the following:

- Click once to select the current line

- Double-click to select the current paragraph

- Hold the Ctrl key down and click once to select the entire document

COPYING AND MOVING TEXT WITH THE CLIPBOARD

You can use the Clipboard procedures described in Chapter 8 to copy or move text from one place to another within a Write document, from one Write document to another Write document, or from a Write document to a document created in a different application.

For details about using these procedures, see Chapter 8.

USING WRITE'S FIND COMMAND

Write's Find menu offers a handy set of commands for finding and changing text. The Find menu looks like this:

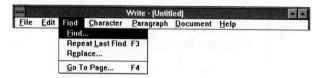

The Find command helps you locate a particular combination of letters or words. You type the text you're looking for in the Find What text box of the following dialog box.

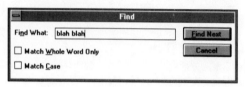

You can specify up to 255 characters in the Find What box.

Including Wildcards in Your Search Text

If you include a question mark in your search text, Write interprets it as a *wildcard* that can stand for any single character. For example, if your search string looks like this:

?ray

Write will find *bray, Cray, fray, gray, pray, tray,* and *ray.* (Write finds *ray* because the space before it matches the wildcard.)

To search for an actual question mark in your document, specify the search text like this:

^?

To type the caret character on a keyboard with the standard U.S. layout, press Shift-6.

Including White Space Characters in Your Search Text

Write also lets you search for particular kinds of "white space," such as tab characters or paragraph endings. The following codes are recognized by Write's Find command:

^w	Any kind of space — a space between words, a tab character, a paragraph ending, or a manual page break
^t	A tab character
^p	A paragraph ending
^d	A manual page break (Manual page breaks are discussed later in this chapter.)

So, for example, if you wanted to find all examples of the word *agenda* (followed by a period) that fell at the end of a paragraph, you could specify the following as your search text:

agenda.^p

To search for a caret character, specify the search text like this:

^^

Options for Searching

Before beginning the search, you can select either or both of the check-box options in this dialog box.

If you check Match Whole Word Only, Write ignores any instances of your search text that are not complete words. For example, if you search for *graphic* with the Whole Word option selected, Write ignores the words *graphical*, *graphics*, and *typographic*.

If you check Match Case, Write finds only those examples of your search text that are typed with the same capitalization you use in the Find What text box.

Starting the Search

After you have filled out the Find What text box and chosen your search options, you can start the search by clicking the Find Next button or pressing Enter. Write searches in the forward direction, starting at the current position of the insertion point. If Write reaches the end of your document without finding your search text, it continues the search starting at the top of the document.

As soon as Write has found an example of your search text, it selects the text and stops searching. The dialog box remains on screen, however. At this point, you have several options:

- If you have found what you're looking for and don't want to do any more searching, you can remove the dialog box by pressing Esc or Alt-F4 or by clicking the dialog box's Cancel button.

- If you want to search for the next example of the same search text, click Find Next again.

- If you want to search for different text or use different search options, fill out the dialog box again and click Find Next.

Repeating the Search

If you want to resume working on your document but you think you might need to search for the same text again, you can either:

- Move the Find dialog box to a position on your screen where it won't be in your way. Then click outside the dialog box (or press Alt-F6) to return to the document. When you're ready to repeat the search, simply click the Find Next button again (or press Alt-F6 to return to the Find dialog box, and then Alt-F to choose the Find Next command).

- Remove the dialog box. When you want to repeat the search, press F3 (or open the Find menu and choose Repeat Last Find).

USING WRITE'S REPLACE COMMAND

The Find menu's Replace command lets you replace one set of characters or words with another. You can confirm each change, or you can have Write change every occurrence of the search text automatically. You can apply the command to an entire document or to the current selection only.

When you choose the Replace command, Write presents the following dialog box.

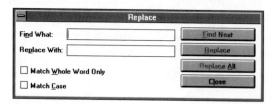

Telling Write What to Change

To specify the text you want to change, fill out the Find What text box. This line works exactly the same way as the corresponding line in the Find dialog box.

Specifying Search Options

The Match Whole Word Only and Match Case check boxes work exactly the same way in the Replace command as they do in the Find command.

Telling Write How to Change It

To specify your replacement text, fill out the Replace With text box.

Although a question mark in the Replace With text box does not function as a wildcard character, the four white-space codes—^w, ^t, ^p, and ^d—behave the same way they do in the Find What text box. That means, for example, that if your document has a blank line between each pair of paragraphs, you could remove that blank line by specifying *^p^p* as your search text and *^p* as your replacement text.

Limiting the Change Command to a Text Selection

By selecting an area of text before you choose the Find menu's Replace command, you can restrict the operation of that command to the selected text. If no text is selected when you choose the Replace command, the command is applied to the entire document. Write scans through the document in the forward direction, starting with the current position of the insertion point. When it gets to the end of the document, it continues at the beginning.

Replacing Selectively or Automatically

When you've filled out the Replace dialog box, you can start the Replace operation in either of two ways:

- To replace all occurrences of the search text automatically, click Replace All. (If you have selected an area of text before issuing the Replace command, this button will say Replace Selection.)

- To have Write pause for confirmation before making each change, click Find Next.

If you click the Find Next button, Write stops as soon as it finds your search text. At that point you can do any of the following:

- If you do *not* want Write to change this occurrence of the search text, click Find Next.

- If you want Write to change this occurrence and continue searching for further occurrences, click Replace, and then click Find Next.

- If you want Write to change all occurrences, click Replace All (or Replace Selection).

- To stop the Replace operation without making any further changes, press Esc or Alt-F4, click the dialog box's Close button, press Alt-F6, or click anywhere outside the dialog box.

If you press Alt-F6 or click outside the dialog box, the dialog box remains on screen. You can use it again at any time by pressing Alt-F6 again or clicking within the dialog box.

FORMATTING YOUR DOCUMENT

Write arranges its formatting commands on three menus: Character, Paragraph, and Document.

Commands on the Document menu apply to a whole document. You can use these commands to do any of the following:

- Display or remove a ruler at the top of your document

- Create a header or footer that prints at the top or bottom of each page

- Define tab stops

- Specify left, right, top, and bottom margins

- Tell Write to begin numbering pages at a number other than 1

- Specify inches or centimeters as Write's default measurement unit

Commands on the Paragraph menu apply to individual paragraphs or selections of consecutive paragraphs. You can use these commands to do any of the following:

- Set a paragraph-alignment style (flush left, flush right, centered, or justified)

- Choose a line-spacing option (single-spaced, double-spaced, or halfway between single and double)

- Apply indents

Commands on the Character menu apply to individual characters or selections of characters. You can use these commands to do any of the following:

- Choose fonts and point sizes

- Apply boldface, italics, or underlining

- Have characters displayed as superscripts or subscripts

Displaying a Ruler

To display a ruler at the top of the document, pull down the Document menu and choose Ruler On. The ruler looks like this:

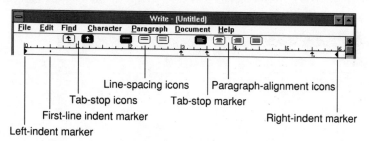

As you move through a document, the ruler shows you what line spacing, paragraph-alignment style, indents, and tab stops are currently in effect. It also gives you a simple way to change any of these settings with the mouse.

The ruler has three groups of icons, directly above the inch (or centimeter) markings. The two icons in the leftmost group provide mouse shortcuts for setting ordinary and decimal tab stops. The three icons in the middle group indicate the current line spacing and provide a mouse shortcut for changing the line spacing. The four icons in the rightmost group show the current justification style and provide a mouse shortcut for changing that style.

Three markers on the ruler itself show the current position of left, right, and first-line indents. They also provide a convenient way to change indent settings with the mouse; simply drag the marker to the desired location.

Choosing Your Measurement System

Write normally measures indents, margins, and tab-stop positions in inches, unless you have used Control Panel's International command (see Chapter 9) to specify metric as your preferred measuring system. You can switch from inches to centimeters—or vice versa—by choosing the Page Layout command on Write's Document menu. Select inch or cm in the lower left corner of the dialog box.

Specifying a Header

A *header* is one or more lines of text that are printed at the top of each page. You can have one header in each Write document, and you can insert page numbers into a header.

To specify a header, choose the Header command on Write's Document menu. The Page Header dialog box appears on your screen.

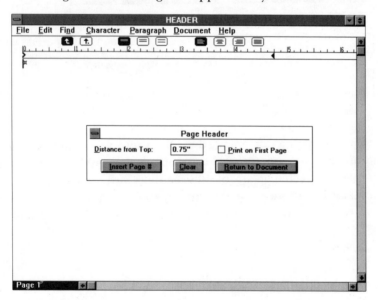

Notice that behind the dialog box, you now see a window titled Header. This window looks in every way like an ordinary window for creating a Write document. You see an insertion point, an end mark, an I-beam (if you're using a mouse), and—if you've turned on the ruler display—a ruler at the top of the window.

Type your header text in this window in exactly the same way you would type ordinary document text. You can use any of Write's formatting commands as you do so. Don't type any page numbers, though; we'll see how to add page numbers in a moment.

When you've finished typing your header text, you're ready to select or confirm a few simple options in the Page Header dialog box. Before you go to the dialog box, though, put the insertion point where you want the page number to appear—if you're going to include a page number in your header. Then click the mouse inside the dialog box or press Alt-F6.

The Distance From Top setting in the dialog box indicates the amount of space that Write will leave between the top of your header and the top edge of your pages. The default is 0.75 inch; you can specify a different value.

The Print On First Page check box indicates whether or not your header will appear atop page one. The default is no; put a check in the box if you want a header on the first page.

To add page numbers to your header, click the Insert Page # button, or press Alt-I. The word *(page)* will appear in your header at the place where you left the insertion point. When your document is printed, Write replaces that marker with the appropriate page numbers. Page numbering begins at 1, unless you ask to have them begin at some other number. You can do that in the Page Layout dialog box, which we'll come to in a moment.

When you're satisfied with your header, click the Return To Document button. If you want to start over and create a new header, click Clear.

Specifying a Footer

A *footer* is one or more lines of text that are printed at the bottom of each page. You can have one footer in each Write document, and a footer can include page numbers.

The procedure for specifying a footer is exactly like that for specifying a header. See the preceding section.

Setting and Using Tab Stops

Write offers two kinds of tab stops: *ordinary* and *decimal.* An ordinary tab stop produces left alignment of text at the position of the tab stop. Decimal tab stops are designed for use with numbers; the decimal points in a column of numbers align at the tab-stop position, and the whole-number and fractional portions appear to the left and right of the tab stop.

By default, your Write document has ordinary tab stops every 0.5 inch. You can replace those default stops with tab stops of your own—as many as 12—wherever you like. You can do this by filling out a dialog box or by using the tab-stop icons on the ruler. When you set your own tab stops by either method, Write removes its 0.5-inch tab stops to the left of your tab stops. (It leaves 0.5-inch tab stops in place to the right of your rightmost stop.)

Tab stops in Write apply to entire documents; you can't have different stops in effect for different paragraphs.

To set tab stops with a dialog box, open the Document menu and choose Tabs. The dialog box looks like this:

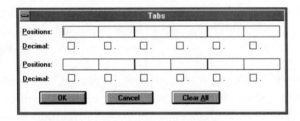

In the wide boxes on the lines marked Positions, type the distance from the left margin where you want each tab stop to be. Write assumes your numbers mean inches if the measurement unit in effect is inches, or centimeters if the current measurement unit is centimeters. (See "Choosing Your Measurement System," earlier in this chapter.) You can override the default measurement system by including the units in the Positions boxes; for example, if the measuring system in effect is inches, you could enter a tab stop such as 5.08 cm. Write converts the measurement units to the default unit when you click OK.

To set a decimal tab stop, click the box below the tab stop position. Write assumes all tab stops are ordinary unless the associated Decimal box is checked.

To remove a tab stop, redisplay the dialog box, select the stop you want to remove, press the Del key, and click OK. To remove all tab stops at once, click Clear All in the Tabs dialog box.

To set tab stops with the ruler's tab-stop icons, first display the ruler. Then do the following:

1. Click the mouse pointer on the appropriate tab-stop icon—the bent arrow for an ordinary tab stop, the straight arrow with a period next to it for a decimal tab stop.

2. Position the tip of the mouse pointer directly below the ruler position where you want the tab stop, and then click. The appropriate tab marker will appear on the ruler.

To adjust the position of any tab stop, drag the tab marker along the ruler.

To remove a tab stop by using the ruler, simply drag the tab marker away from the ruler and release the mouse button.

Setting Margins

Write's default top and bottom margins are 1 inch. The default left and right margins are 1.25 inches. To override any of these settings, choose the Document menu's Page Layout command and fill out the ensuing dialog box.

Note that margins apply to an entire document. If you want particular paragraphs to be offset a greater distance from the left and right edges of your paper, apply indents to those paragraphs.

Setting the Starting Page Number

Write normally numbers pages starting at 1. If you want to use a different starting number, choose the Document menu's Page Layout command. Specify your new number in the box marked Start Page Numbers At.

APPLYING PARAGRAPH FORMATTING

The commands on the Paragraph menu let you choose paragraph-alignment styles, line spacing, and indention values.

To assign a paragraph format to new text, simply position the insertion point where you're about to type, and then issue your formatting command. To apply a format to an existing paragraph, put the insertion point anywhere in that paragraph, and then choose your command. To apply a format to a group of existing paragraphs, select at least some of the text in each paragraph, and then issue your command.

Choosing a Paragraph-Alignment Style

Write offers four paragraph-alignment styles:

- Flush left (left margin straight, right margin ragged)
- Centered (both margins ragged, last line of each paragraph centered between the margins)
- Flush right (left margin ragged, right margin straight)
- Justified (both margins straight)

You can apply any of these options either from the Paragraph menu or by clicking one of the ruler's paragraph-alignment icons.

Choosing Line Spacing

Write offers three line-spacing options: single, one-and-a-half, and double. You can apply one of these options either from the Paragraph menu or by clicking one of the ruler's line-spacing icons.

Using Indention

You can use three kinds of indention in the paragraphs of a Write document:

- An indent from the left margin that applies to all lines in a paragraph
- An indent from the right margin that applies to all lines in a paragraph
- An indent from the left margin that applies only to the first line in a paragraph

The last of these options can be used to set up automatic paragraph indenting or to create paragraphs with hanging indention. See "Using Hanging Indention," below.

Like tab stops, indents can be set by means of a dialog box or the ruler.

To set one or more indents using a dialog box, choose the Paragraph menu's Indents command. The dialog box looks like this:

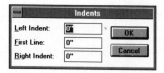

Simply fill out the appropriate boxes and click OK.

On the ruler, the right-pointing triangle marks the position of the left indent; it sits at 0 if no indent is in effect. The left-pointing triangle marks the position of the right indent; if no indent is in effect, it indicates the position of the right margin. The first-line indent is indicated by a dot; if no first-line indent is in effect, the dot and the left-indent symbol are superimposed.

To apply or change an indent setting using the ruler, simply drag the appropriate symbol to the ruler position of your choice.

Using Hanging Indention

A paragraph is said to have *hanging indention* when all of its lines *except* the first are indented. This style is useful for such things as bulleted or numbered lists. To set up a hanging indent, simply specify a positive left indent and a negative first-line indent.

With a left indent of 2 inches and a first-line indent of –2 inches, for example, all lines except the first will appear two inches from the left margin. The first line will start at the left margin.

Selecting Default Paragraph Settings

You might have noticed one more command on the Paragraph menu: Normal. This command provides a shortcut for returning to Write's default paragraph settings. Paragraph alignment is set to Left, line spacing is set to Single Space, and all indents are set to zero.

APPLYING CHARACTER FORMATTING

The commands on the Character menu let you assign typefaces, point sizes, and typographic styles. These formatting options are not shown on the ruler.

All of the character-formatting commands can be applied either to a selection of existing text or to new text that you're about to enter. If you select a character or group of characters before choosing one of the formatting commands, your command is applied to the selection only. If you do not select text before choosing the command, the command is applied to everything you type ahead of the current insertion-point position—but not to existing text.

Choosing a Typeface and Point Size

To assign a typeface in a particular point size, pull down the Character menu and choose the Fonts command. The dialog box that appears, shown on the next page, gives you the full range of font and point-size options available on your printer.

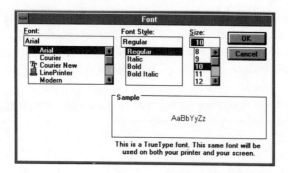

Fill in or choose a font and a point size, and then click OK. To specify a point size that doesn't appear in the list box, simply type a number in the Size box.

Changing Point Size

The most precise way to change a point size is to choose the Fonts command and select a size from the Size list box. As a shortcut that's usable under some circumstances, Write provides the Reduce Font and Enlarge Font commands on the Character menu.

The Reduce Font and Enlarge Font commands step you down and up through a predefined set of point sizes. The point-size sequence, which is the same for all fonts, is as follows:

4 6 8 10 12 14 18 24 30 36 48 72 127

Some of these sizes might not be appropriate for particular typefaces on your printer. Therefore, exercise some caution using the Enlarge Font and Reduce Font commands.

Applying Typographic Styles

Write's styling options include Bold, Italic, Underline, Superscript, and Subscript. Commands for all five are located near the top of the Character menu. You can use these styles singly or in conjunction with one another (except Superscript and Subscript, which cannot be used together). Write displays a check next to each styling option currently in effect.

To remove all styling options from the current selection or from text you're about to type, choose the Character menu's Regular command.

KEYBOARD TIP: You can press Ctrl-B, Ctrl-I, or Ctrl-U as keyboard shortcuts for bold, italic, and underlining, respectively. As a shortcut for the Regular command, you can press F5.

NOTE: *Unfortunately, although Write is aware of most of your printer's capabilities and limitations, it won't warn you if you apply a styling command that's not available on your printer. For example, if you're using a LaserJet with a font cartridge that includes 14-point Helvetica in roman but not italic, Write lets you format text in 14-point Helvetica italic. It appears italic on screen, but roman on your printout. You might want to experiment to be sure you know all your printer's capabilities before creating extensively formatted documents in Write.*

INCLUDING PICTURES IN WRITE DOCUMENTS

Write documents can include pictures as well as text. To incorporate a graphic image in a Write document, do the following:

1. Create the image in a Windows graphics program, such as Paintbrush (or load an existing image from disk into a program such as Paintbrush).

2. In the graphics program, select the area of the picture that you want to use in your Write document.

3. Use the graphics program's Copy or Cut command to put the image on the Windows Clipboard.

4. In your Write document, move the insertion point to the place where you want the picture to appear.

5. Use the Paste command, on Write's Edit menu, to insert the picture.

If your source program has put the graphic on the Clipboard in more than one format, the Paste Special command, on Write's Edit menu, will also be available. You can use this command to choose between the available formats. (See "Controlling a Pasted Object's Format," later in this chapter.)

Repositioning a Picture

When you first paste a picture into a Write document, the picture is aligned flush with the left margin. You can center the picture or align it against the right margin with the help of Write's Paragraph menu:

1. Select the picture by clicking it with the mouse or by using the direction keys.

2. Open the Paragraph menu and choose Centered or Right.

You can also adjust the horizontal position of a picture with the Edit menu's Move Picture command. When you select your picture and choose this command, Write puts a square cursor in the center of the picture, like this:

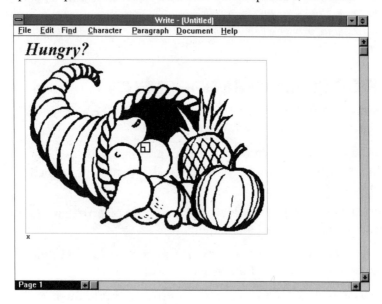

Use the Right and Left direction keys to relocate your picture, and then press Enter. If you change your mind about the move, press Esc before pressing Enter.

To move your picture with the mouse, simply move the mouse left or right. When the outline is where you want your picture, click the mouse button.

Resizing a Picture

You can also change the size of a picture after importing into Write. To do this, select the picture and choose the Edit menu's Size Picture command. Like the Move Picture command, Size Picture plants a square cursor in the middle of your image. At the same time, it displays sizing information in the lower left corner of the Write window (where the current page number is usually displayed).

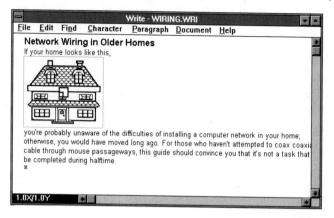

You can size your picture with the mouse, the keyboard, or both. The mouse might be quicker, but the keyboard is more effective for precise adjustments.

To size with the mouse, simply move the pointer. When you're satisfied with the new size, press the mouse button.

To size with the keyboard's direction keys, first move the square cursor to the edge of the picture that you want to move. For example, if you want to stretch or compress the picture from the right edge, start by pressing Right. Then use Right, Left, or both, to adjust the right edge of the picture.

If you want to adjust two sides at once, move the cursor to the corner between the two sides.

When you're satisfied with the new size of your picture, press Enter.

 WINDOWS TIP: The X and Y numbers in the lower left corner of the window indicate the picture's current size relative to its size when you first imported it into Write. If you make the picture wider, the X value increases; if you make it taller, the Y number increases. To avoid distorting the shapes of the objects depicted in your image, it's best to modify the X and Y dimensions evenly. On the other hand, if you want to create fun-house-mirror effects, you're free to change one dimension more than the other.

CONTROLLING A PASTED OBJECT'S FORMAT

Sometimes when you copy a graphic image to the Clipboard, the source program puts the image on the Clipboard in more than one format. It might, for example, store the image on the Clipboard in both *picture* format and *bitmap* format. (See Chapter 8 for more information about data formats and the Clipboard.) Whenever the data to be pasted is available in more than one format, Write's Paste command gives you the most information-rich format. But in these cases Write also enables the Paste Special command, allowing you to make your own choice about which format to use.

Here, for example, is how the Paste Special dialog box looks when a graphic is available in picture and bitmap formats:

Simply select the format you prefer, and then click the Paste button.

Usually, Write's Paste command makes the best choice for you automatically. For example, when the available formats are picture and bitmap, it chooses picture—and, generally speaking, the picture format gives you more satisfactory results. (In particular, because the picture format is not tied to the resolution of a specific output device, it usually gives you a much better printed image than the bitmap format.) However, the Paste Special command is there, just in case you want to override the default choice.

When the source application happens to be an OLE server, Write's Paste command automatically embeds the data stored on the Clipboard. (See "Embedding and Linking in Write," below.) If you want your pasted image to be a static object, rather than an embedded object, you will need to use the Paste Special command instead of Paste. Paste Special's dialog box in this case will look something like this:

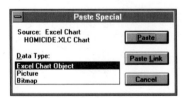

Its position at the top of the list tells you that Write will embed this Excel Chart Object by default. Embedding the image doesn't add any more bulk to your file than pasting it in as a static object, and it allows you to edit the image quickly and easily. (To change a static image, you'd have to copy it back into your graphics package manually, delete it from your Write document, make your edits, and then copy it back into Write—a far more laborious process.) But the Paste Special command gives you the means of vetoing Write's standard procedure.

EMBEDDING AND LINKING IN WRITE

As mentioned, Write is capable of acting as an OLE client application. This means that you can embed or store links to the following kinds of data, among others, in your Write documents:

- Graphic images copied to the Clipboard from OLE server programs, such as Paintbrush or Ami Pro

- Charts or worksheet "pictures" copied from Microsoft Excel

- Sound annotations copied from the Windows Sound Recorder accessory

- Packages copied from the Windows Object Packager accessory

To embed data from the Clipboard, simply use Write's Paste command. If the data's source application is an OLE server, the data will automatically be embedded. To link the data instead of embedding it, choose the Paste Link command. (For a complete discussion of linking and embedding, the differences between the two, and the advantages and disadvantages of each, see Chapter 8.)

Alternatively, you can embed or link data by choosing the Paste Special command (see "Controlling a Pasted Object's Format," above). If the data on the Clipboard came from an OLE server, the Paste Special dialog box indicates what type of data it is and which program it came from (see the preceding illustration). The first format in the list of format choices will also include the word *object.* To embed the data, select the first choice in the list of formats and click the Paste command. To store a link to the data's source, select the format you want to use and click the Paste Link button.

WINDOWS TIP: If the Paste Special dialog box indicates that the Clipboard's data came from an OLE server, but the Paste Link button is grayed out, that probably means the data has never been saved in the source application. To create a link to OLE server data, you must first have saved that data in a disk file.

Moving and Sizing Embedded or Linked Objects

For display purposes, Write handles embedded and linked objects the same way it handles static graphic images. You can move and size such objects using the same procedures you would use with static objects. For details, see "Repositioning a Picture" and "Resizing a Picture," earlier in this chapter.

 WINDOWS TIP: If you double-click an embedded image after changing its size in Write, the image appears for editing—at its original size—in the source application. When you update the Write document after making your edits, however, the image reappears at the modified size.

Activating, Playing, and Editing Embedded or Linked Objects

When you select an object in a Write document that was embedded or linked from an OLE server, the Object command, near the bottom of Write's Edit menu, becomes available. It also changes to reflect the kind of object you select. The following illustration, for example, shows how the Object command appears if you select a graphic embedded from Paintbrush.

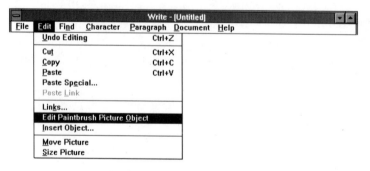

Choosing this command activates the object's source application—Paintbrush in this example—and allows you to edit the object. (A simpler way to edit an embedded image is to double-click it.)

If the embedded or linked object is a graphical representation of a nongraphical data type, such as a sound annotation or a package, the Object command presents a small cascading submenu, like this:

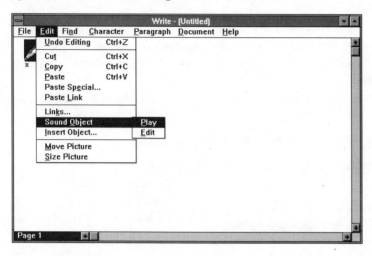

Choosing Play "renders" the object (lets you hear the sound annotation, for example), while choosing Edit invokes the object's source application. Double-clicking in this case is a shortcut for the Play command. If you want to edit the object, you have to use the menu command.

Embedding with the Insert Object Command

The Insert Object command, near the bottom of Write's Edit menu, lets you initiate the embedding or linking process from within your Write document, instead of from within an object's source application. When you choose this command, Write presents in a dialog box all the "linkable" and "embeddable" object types listed in your Windows system's registration database:

Choose the kind of object you want to link or embed, and then click OK. Write activates the object type's source application, allowing you to create an object (or load one from a disk file).

Modifying Links with the Links Command

When you link an object, as opposed to embedding it, Write does not store the object in your file. Instead, it stores a "pointer" to the object's source—the name of the source application and the file in which the object is stored, for example. If you subsequently rename or move the object's source file, the stored link will no longer be valid. In that case, you can repair the link with the help of Write's Links command.

The Links command, on Write's Edit menu, lists all objects linked into the current Write document:

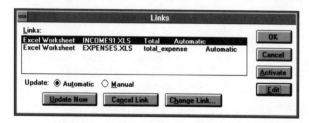

To change the source file for a link, select the link you want to modify, and then click the Change Link command. Write presents a file-browser dialog box, allowing you to pick the file you need.

The Links command also allows you to change a link from automatic to manual, or vice versa. Links are always automatic by default, which means that any changes in the source data are reflected as soon as possible in your Write document. If you prefer to have them updated only on demand, choose the Links command, select the link you want to change, and then click the Manual option button.

SAVING AND RETRIEVING FILES

Write uses the same procedures for saving and retrieving files as most other Windows applications. (For more information about these procedures, see "Creating, Opening, and Saving Files," in Chapter 3.) Use the following File-menu commands:

- Save, to save the current file
- Save As, to save the current file under a new name or to choose different file-saving options
- New, to remove the current file from memory and begin creating a new one
- Open, to load an existing file from disk into memory

Write's normal file extension is WRI. If you don't specify an extension, Write automatically uses WRI. You may use other extensions—or no extension—if you want. To save a file with no extension, include a period at the end of its name.

Backing Up When You Save

When you save a file the first time, Write presents the Save As dialog box.

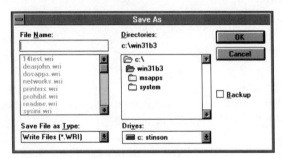

If you check the Backup box, with each subsequent save, Write preserves the file as it stood the last time you saved it. That way, if you regret the changes you make, you can return to the previous version.

Write's backup files are saved with the extension BKP. To reopen a backup file, use the File menu's Open command and specify your filename with the extension BKP.

Saving a Text File

To save your file as plain (unformatted) text, choose Save As, and then open the Save File As Type drop-down list. In the list that unfolds, choose either Word For DOS/Txt Only or Text Files (*.TXT). Either way, Write saves the words in your file but removes all character, paragraph, and document formatting. Your file also loses any embedded or linked data and any pictures pasted in as static objects. You might want to save your document as a text file under these conditions:

- If you need to transmit the document over a modem to a system that cannot accept a binary file transfer (see Chapter 15 for a discussion of binary and text file transfers)

- If you need to transfer your document into a non-Windows word processor that cannot read a formatted Write document

 WINDOWS TIP: If you need to transfer a Write document into a Windows word processor that doesn't accept files with the extension WRI, use the Windows Clipboard.

Saving a Microsoft Word File

To save your Write document in a format that can be read by the non-Windows version of Microsoft Word, choose Save As and open the Save File As Type drop-down list. Choose Word For DOS (*.DOC). All paragraph formatting and document formatting will be preserved. Provided the printer driver you're using in Word is the same as the one you're using in Windows, your character formatting will also be preserved. If the printer drivers differ, Word will make appropriate font substitutions.

Any linked or embedded data and any pictures in your Write document will be lost when you save the file in Microsoft Word format.

If you check the Backup box when saving a file in Microsoft Word format, the backup file will be stored with Word's backup extension—BAK.

Opening a Text File

A text file is a file that contains text characters only, without formatting information. Examples include files created by Notepad or by the MS-DOS text editor, Edit. Most word processors, both Windows and non-Windows, include options for saving documents as text files.

You can use Write to read and edit text files. When you've finished working with such a file, you can save it again as a text file or convert it to a formatted Write file.

To open a text file, simply specify the name of the file in the Open dialog box. As soon as Write begins reading the file into memory, it recognizes that it's a text file, and you'll see the following dialog box.

You need to convert the file to Write's format only if both of the following are true:

- Your text file contains special characters, such as accented letters; mathematical symbols; trademark, copyright, or registration symbols; or line-drawing characters.

- Your file was created in a non-Windows application.

If you do not convert a non-Windows text file that contains special characters, those characters will be incorrect when they appear in your Write window.

Opening a Microsoft Word File

Write can work with files created in the MS-DOS version of Microsoft Word. You don't need to convert your Word files to plain text before loading them into Write.

To open a Word file, simply specify the name of the file in the Open dialog box. As soon as Write begins reading the file into memory, it recognizes that it's a Word file and you'll see the following dialog box.

Click the Convert button to load the file or the Cancel button to abandon the whole idea.

Paragraph and document formatting in your Word file will be preserved in Write. Character formatting will be preserved to the extent that your Windows printer driver supports it. If the driver you're using in Windows is different from the driver you used when creating the Word file, some of your original font specifications might be lost.

Write does not translate Microsoft Word style sheets.

PAGINATING AND PRINTING A WRITE DOCUMENT

To print your document, simply pull down the File menu and choose Print. You'll see a dialog box like this:

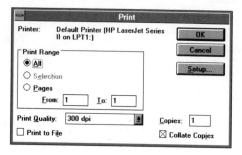

If you want more than one copy, change the number in the Copies box. If you want to print a selection of pages, instead of the entire document, fill in the page numbers you want in the From and To boxes.

As it prints, Write decides where to divide your document into pages. If you want to know where those page breaks will be, or if you want to exert some control over where the pages will be broken, choose the File menu's Repaginate command before choosing Print. You'll see this dialog box:

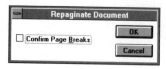

If you want to be able to modify Write's page-break choices (for example, to avoid a page break between a heading and its associated text or in the middle of a table), put a check in the Confirm Page Breaks box before clicking OK. With the Confirm option on, Write stops at each proposed page break and presents the following:

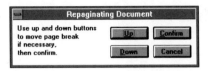

Click the Up button if you want to move the page break up. With each click, Write moves the proposed page break up one line.

Click the Down button if you have already moved the proposed page break up and you want to lower it again. (You can't move the page break any lower than Write's initial proposed location.)

When you're satisfied with the location of the break, click Confirm. If you override Write's initial proposed location, a "manual page break" will be inserted into your document at the location you choose.

Manual page breaks are represented in your document by dotted lines. "Soft" page breaks—page breaks chosen by Write, not by you—are identified by a chevron symbol in the left margin.

If you edit your document and print it or repaginate it, the soft page breaks will probably appear in different locations. Your manual page breaks will remain where you put them, however. Therefore, if you edit a document that already contains manual page breaks, you might want to paginate it again before printing, to ensure that the manual page breaks you chose earlier are still appropriate.

IF YOU CHANGE PRINTERS

As mentioned earlier in this chapter, Write formats documents with the current printer driver in mind. The selection of fonts and point sizes presented in the Fonts dialog box, as well as the locations of line and page breaks, all depend on the characteristics of the current printer. If, after creating a Write document, you switch to a different printer or switch between portrait and landscape orientations, your line breaks will almost certainly move, and the contents of the Fonts dialog box will change.

If you select a block of text that was originally formatted with a font not available on the current printer, Write's Font dialog box will look something like the illustration at the top of the following page.

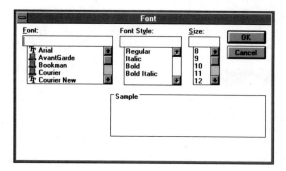

The Font, Font Style, and Size boxes will all be blank. If you print your document now without assigning a different font to this text block, Write will print the block in the supported font that's closest in style to your original choice. If you return to the printer driver for which the document was originally formatted, your original font specifications will be restored.

15

Using Terminal

Terminal is a program that allows your computer to communicate with other computers. You can use it to do such things as retrieve data from a company mainframe, explore an online information service such as CompuServe, or send electronic mail (e-mail) over a public e-mail network such as MCI Mail.

To communicate with a remote computer using Terminal, you need to have a modem attached to one of your computer's serial ports. The modem converts signals from your computer into a form that can be transmitted over telephone lines. The party with whom you're communicating must also have a modem to reconvert the telephone signals into the form understood by computers.

This chapter tells you how to use Terminal's features. You'll learn to set up a communications link, send and receive files, use Terminal's error-checking options, create printed transcripts of your communications sessions, and so on. You'll also find out how to save "settings" files that are tailored for the various computers and services you communicate with regularly.

A TYPICAL SESSION

A typical communications session using Terminal goes something like this:

1. Start Terminal.

2. Load or create a "settings" file.

    Before establishing a communications link, you have to supply a number of "communications settings." These settings tell Terminal what number you'll be dialing, the speed at which you'll be transmitting and receiving, what kind of *parity*—if any—you want to use (parity is a form of error-checking), and so on. Several of these settings might be different for each computer or service you connect with.

    Usually, the service or host computer with which you're communicating will tell you what settings it requires, so it's not a serious problem if you don't understand all the technical details about each setting.

To save you the trouble of reentering settings each time you start a communications session, Terminal lets you create settings files. These files store all the information Terminal needs to connect with a particular computer or service. So, for example, if you frequently get stock quotes or other news from the Dow Jones/News Retrieval service, you might create a settings file called DOWJONES.TRM. Any time you want to log onto Dow Jones, then, you can simply load DOWJONES.TRM into Terminal and you'll be ready to go.

3. Use the Dial command.

Terminal uses your modem's built-in dialing capability to establish a telephone connection with your party. After a connection has been established, whatever you type in Terminal's window is sent across the data link. If the person or computer at the other end of the line sends information back, it appears in Terminal's window as though someone behind the screen were typing.

You can continue to use Terminal's menu commands after you have established connection with the other computer. Your interaction with Terminal's menu system is *not* transmitted.

4. Log onto the host computer or service.

If you're communicating with a mainframe or an information service, you'll probably be required to enter your name and a password as soon as the connection is established. This process is called *logging on*. To simplify this and other routine procedures, Terminal lets you assign strings of characters to your keyboard's function keys. The function-key assignments are saved in your settings files, so you can have a different set of assignments for each service you use.

5. Interact with the party you're connected to.

Your conversation might consist of nothing more than simple messages typed at the keyboard. Or you might transmit a great deal of information at once by pasting it into Terminal from the Clipboard.

You can also exchange files with the host computer. Terminal lets you send and receive two kinds of files—text files and binary files. We'll see what the differences are and what procedures are used for file transfers later in this chapter.

 WINDOWS TIP: If you're receiving or sending a lot of information, you might want to let Terminal do its work in the background while you focus your attention on a different application. If you're running Windows in 386 enhanced mode, you can use either Windows or non-Windows applications while Terminal operates in the background. If you're running in standard mode, Terminal will be suspended if you switch to a non-Windows application.

6. Log off the remote computer or service.

7. Use Terminal's Hangup command to break the telephone connection.

    When you log off, the host computer might break the telephone connection itself. Terminal will not know that, however, so it's best to use the Hangup command regardless of what the other party does.

8. Quit Terminal.

    If the telephone line is still open (or if Terminal thinks it is), Terminal prompts you to close the connection before quitting.

CREATING A SETTINGS FILE

The procedure for creating a new settings file is as follows:

1. Start Terminal.

    Double-click the Terminal icon in Program Manager. If it hasn't been moved, you'll find it in your Accessories program group.

NOTE: *The first time you start Terminal, a Default Serial Port dialog box appears. Simply select the port to which your modem is attached and click OK.*

2. Select the appropriate options on Terminal's Settings menu. The Settings menu looks like this:

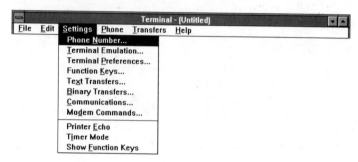

The first eight commands on this menu all bring up dialog boxes. All the choices you make in these dialog boxes are saved in your settings file. Each settings file can have a different arrangement of choices. (The bottom three commands are *toggles*—options that are either turned on or turned off. Your choices here are not recorded in your settings files.)

3. Pull down the File menu, choose Save As, and supply a name for the file. Terminal uses the extension TRM if you don't specify one.

We'll look at each of the Settings menu's many details now.

Modem Commands

We'll start with Modem Commands, because the settings you assign there should be appropriate for every settings file you create. The Modem Commands dialog box, shown below, tells Terminal what signals it needs to send to your modem to originate a call, prepare to receive a call, dial the telephone, and hang up.

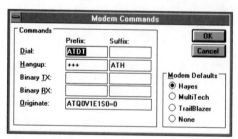

The dialog box is initially filled out with the settings required by a Hayes or Hayes-compatible modem. If your modem fits that description and your telephone system uses tone dialing, the default modem commands will be correct for all your settings files.

If your telephone uses pulse (rotary) dialing, change the Dial Prefix setting from ATDT to ATDP.

If you're using a MultiTech or TrailBlazer modem, click the appropriate option button under Modem Defaults. The settings in the rest of the dialog box will change appropriately.

If your modem conforms to none of the three supported standards—Hayes, MultiTech, and TrailBlazer—click the None button and consult your modem's documentation to fill out the rest of the dialog box.

Terminal Preferences

The Terminal Preferences dialog box lets you specify about a dozen options, each of which has something to do with the way your system behaves while connected to another computer.

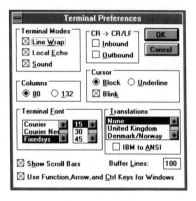

Terminal Modes

The Terminal Modes section of the dialog box includes three check boxes: Line Wrap, Local Echo, and Sound.

Check the Line Wrap option if the host computer sends lines that are too long for your computer to display. With this option set, a long line will be "wrapped" to the next line on your screen, as it would in a word processing program.

If, after you've established connection with a remote computer, the characters you type are not displayed on your screen, put a check in the Local Echo check box. On the other hand, if every character you type appears twice on your screen, remove the check from this check box.

If the Sound check box is checked, your system will beep if the remote system sends a "bell" character (Ctrl-G). Unless you object to the sound, it's probably best to leave this option checked.

Translate CR to CR/LF

The CR → CR/LF options govern how line endings (carriage returns) are handled by your computer and the remote computer. If everything sent by the host computer appears on a single line on your screen, put a check in the Inbound box. If the party you're communicating with complains that everything on his or her system is displayed on one line, put a check in the Outbound box.

Obviously, if you're communicating with an information service, a bulletin board, an electronic mail service, or some other unattended system, there won't be anyone on the other end of the line to complain to you. But if you're not communicating successfully with the remote system, try putting a check in the Outbound box to see if that helps.

80 or 132 Columns

If your screen can display 132 characters on a line, and if the system you're communicating with sends more than 80 characters per line, select the 132 button in the Columns section of the dialog box. Otherwise, accept the default setting of 80 columns.

Cursor Shape and Blink

You can choose between two cursor shapes: block and underline. You can also decide whether you want the cursor to blink or not. You might want to experiment to see which cursor style you like best.

Terminal Typeface and Size

Terminal can display your communications session in any font installed on your system. However, Terminal looks best if you use one of the three monospaced typefaces—Courier, System, or Terminal. On a VGA screen, System and Terminal appear a little darker than Courier and seem marginally easier to read. Size choices range from 12 point to an overwhelming 60 point.

Like the cursor choice, your decision about typeface and size is strictly a matter of taste. The font you pick has no impact on your communications session.

Translations

The Translations setting is used for communicating with a computer in another country. It allows the data you send to be formatted in the character set used by the host computer. Retain the default setting, None, if you're going to be communicating only within your own country.

Buffer Size

A *buffer* is an area of memory used to store something temporarily. While you're connected to another computer, everything you send and receive is stored in a buffer and displayed in Terminal's window. The buffer gives you a way to review what you send and receive, without capturing the "conversation" in a disk file or generating a printed transcript. As long as the buffer's capacity has not been exceeded, you can scroll up and down in the Terminal window to reread everything that has passed back and forth over the telephone line. (There is one exception: Any binary files you send or receive are not recorded in the buffer.) You can also select any text stored in the buffer and copy it to the Clipboard; to do so, use the Edit menu's Copy command, as you would in most other Windows applications.

When the buffer reaches its capacity, each new line replaces the oldest line already in the buffer. For example, if the buffer size is set at 100 lines, when the 101st line arrives, the first line is discarded.

You can set the buffer size at anywhere from 25 through 399 lines. If you have plenty of memory, you might want to reserve a full 399 lines; if memory is scarce, choose a smaller size. If you don't have enough memory for the buffer size you request, Terminal gives you as much as it can.

 WINDOWS TIP: The buffer is convenient because it lets you reread material that has scrolled off your screen. But if you want a complete record of your communications session, consider sending a copy of it to your printer or recording it in a text file. See "Creating a Transcript of Your Communication Session," later in this chapter.

Scroll Bars

Terminal normally displays scroll bars to help you read lines that have disappeared off the top of Terminal's window or that extend beyond the right edge. You can get rid of the scroll bars by removing the check from the Show Scroll Bars check box. Doing so increases the size of Terminal's window slightly.

Special Keys

In its default state, Terminal is designed to let Windows capture function-key keystrokes, Ctrl-key combinations, and the various direction keys (the arrow keys, PgUp and PgDn, Home and End). These keystrokes are not normally transmitted to the remote computer. You can change this state of affairs by toggling the check box labeled Use Function, Ctrl, And Arrow Keys For Windows. You might find it convenient to change the state of this check box, for example, if you frequently need to send a Ctrl-C to the service you're communicating with.

Note that certain function keys and Ctrl-key combinations are processed by Windows (rather than being transmitted), regardless of the state of this check box. For example, whichever way the check box is set, the F1 key still invokes the Help system, F10 gets you to the menu bar, Ctrl-Esc summons Task List, and keyboard shortcuts defined in Program Manager continue to perform as usual.

Communications Parameters

The settings in the Communications dialog box govern the way your data is packaged and sent over the telephone line. For communication to be successful, most of the settings in this dialog box need to be identical to those of the system you're communicating with.

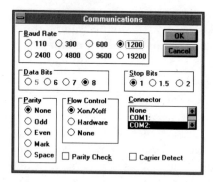

Connector

In the Connector list box, select the serial port to which your modem is attached. Your choices are COM1, COM2, COM3, and COM4.

> **NOTE:** *If you're communicating directly with another computer via a null modem cable, see "Communicating Without Telephone Lines," later in this chapter.*

Baud Rate

Baud rate is the speed, in bits per second, at which information is transmitted and received. The speeds most commonly used by the current generation of modems are 2400 baud and 1200 baud.

Data Bits, Stop Bits, and Parity

In a typical asynchronous communications link (the kind used by Terminal), each character transmitted consists of seven or eight bits of data, followed by one stop bit. The stop bit is used as a timing signal to tell the receiving computer where one character ends and another begins. Some older systems use fewer than seven data bits and more than one stop bit, but such systems are now rare.

Systems that use seven (or fewer) data bits might also employ an error-checking method called *parity*. Different systems use different types of parity checking—hence the Odd, Even, Mark, and Space options in the Parity section of this dialog box.

The most common arrangement of these parameters for use with mainframe computers and online information services is 7-E-1, which means seven data bits, Even parity, and one stop bit. Public bulletin-board systems (BBS's) are more likely to require 8-N-1, or eight data bits, no parity (None), and one stop bit.

Parity Check

The check box marked Parity Check tells Terminal what to do if you're using any parity setting other than None and a parity error is detected. If you check this box, Terminal displays a question mark in place of any incorrectly received character. Otherwise, Terminal displays whatever character it received, which is probably incorrect.

Flow Control

When information sent by the remote computer fills Terminal's buffer to capacity, Terminal has to tell the remote system to pause momentarily before sending any more characters. Otherwise, incoming data would be lost. When Terminal is ready to receive again, it sends another signal to the remote computer. A similar pair of signals is used by the remote computer to control the flow of data being sent by Terminal.

These "pause" and "resume" signals are known as *handshaking*. The method of handshaking used is determined by the Flow Control setting.

Terminal's default choice, Xon/Xoff, is the method most commonly used today. A few older systems still use hardware handshaking. If you're not sure what method is used by the system you're going to communicate with, try Xon/Xoff.

If the remote system has no handshaking capability, choose None.

 WINDOWS TIP: If characters you transmit are being lost by the remote system, regardless of your Flow Control choice, you can try sending a character at a time or a line at a time. See "Options for Transferring Text," later in this chapter.

Carrier Detect

If you check the Carrier Detect box, Terminal relies on a hardware signal from your modem to determine whether you've established connection with the remote computer. This option is normally off; if you're having trouble connecting, try turning it on.

Terminal Emulation

The Terminal Emulation setting determines how your screen behaves when it receives "formatting" information (such as commands to position the cursor or to erase characters) from the system with which you're communicating. It also determines what characters are sent to the remote computer when you press function keys, direction keys, and so on.

When you choose the Terminal Emulation command, you see the following dialog box.

In the default setting, shown here, Terminal makes your keyboard and screen behave like a VT-100 terminal from Digital Equipment Corporation (DEC). This is a popular standard, and many mainframe computers and online information services base their interaction with you on the assumption that you're either using or emulating this terminal. Therefore, it's best to try this setting first if you're not sure what's required of you.

Alternatively, you can make your system emulate a DEC VT-52 terminal or a TTY ("dumb") terminal. A TTY terminal recognizes no formatting codes except Carriage Return, Line Feed, Tab, and Backspace.

Assigning Strings of Characters to Function Keys

Terminal's Function Keys command lets you create as many as thirty-two miniature macros to perform routine typing chores. The command is called Function Keys because each macro you create can be executed with the combination of Ctrl-Alt plus one of the first eight function keys (F1 through F8). You can also display the names of your macros at the bottom of the screen and execute them by clicking the mouse.

When you choose the Settings menu's Function Keys command, you see the following dialog box.

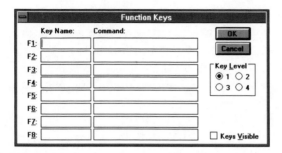

In the boxes on the left, under the heading Key Name, you can assign a name for each key you want to use. In the boxes on the right, under the heading Command, you enter the keystrokes you want the macro to type for you. You can enter as many as 41 characters per function key.

If you need more than eight function-key assignments, you can switch to a different "level" by clicking one of the numbers in the Key Level box. With each new level, you get a fresh set of macro slots.

If the Keys Visible check box is checked when you click OK to leave the dialog box, Terminal displays your function-key assignments—eight at a time—in the buttons below the horizontal scroll bar. You can also display the function-key assignments by choosing Show Function Keys from the Settings menu. Here's how your Terminal window might look, for example, if you assigned some of the most common MCI Mail commands to function keys:

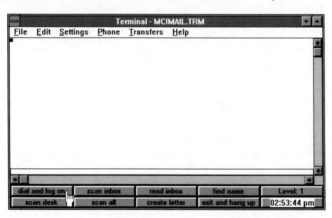

The function-key assignments are shown starting with F1 in the upper left corner of the display ("dial and log on," in the preceding illustration). Below F1 is F2, to the right of F1 is F3, and so on.

347

When you position the mouse pointer over one of these function-key windows, it changes from an arrow to a hand (see the preceding illustration). You can execute the character sequence assigned to any function key by putting the finger on its button and clicking. You can also switch between any of the four function-key levels that have keys defined by clicking the button marked Level, on the right side of the function-key display.

If you don't have a mouse, you execute function-key character sequences by holding down the Ctrl and Alt keys while pressing the relevant function key. To switch to a different level of the function-key display, you can go back into the Function Keys dialog box and click a different Key Level button. But you can also assign a level-switch code (^$L1, ^$L2, ^$L3, or ^$L4) to one of the function keys at each level; this technique is described below.

Assigning Special Codes to Function Keys

In addition to ordinary characters, you can assign control characters and a few commands to your function keys. Table 15-1 lists the available commands and their effects.

Code	Effect
^A through ^Z	Sends Ctrl plus the associated letter. To send Ctrl-M, for example, enter ^M.
^$C	Dials the telephone. This is a shortcut for the Phone menu's Dial command. It dials the number entered in the Phone Number dialog box.
^$H	Hangs up the telephone. This is a shortcut for the Phone menu's Hangup command.
^$B	Sends a 117-millisecond break code.
^$D*nn*	Pauses for *nn* seconds. Two digits are required; use a leading 0 for numbers less than 10.
^$L1 through ^$L4	Switches function-key levels. To switch to level 2, for example, use ^$L2.

Table 15-1.
Special codes available in function-key assignments.

So, for example, to dial and log onto an information service, you might use a function-key assignment like this:

^$C^M^$D02*name*^M^$D02*password*^M

This sequence would start by dialing whatever number you had entered in the Phone Number dialog box. When the remote computer answered, your computer would send a Return character (sending Ctrl-M is equivalent to pressing the Enter key; the character sent is called Return).

Your system would then pause two seconds, allowing the remote computer to respond to your Return character. After the two-second delay, your system would send your name, followed by another Return character. After another two-second delay, your system would send your password followed by one more Return character.

You might have to experiment with a sequence like this to get the timing right; how much delay is needed depends on the responsiveness of the remote computer. Note, however, that you do not need to include a delay to allow your own system to dial or the remote system to answer. After reading the dialing code (^$C), Terminal does not send the next characters in the sequence until connection with the remote computer is established.

KEYBOARD TIP: If you don't have a mouse and you're using all four function-key levels, you'll probably want to reserve one assignment at each level (F8, perhaps) as a level-switcher. Assign ^$L2 to that key at level 1, ^$L3 at level 2, and so on.

Suppressing the Function-Key Display

If you're not using the function keys, or if you temporarily need to see as many lines of Terminal's buffer as possible, you might want to suppress the function-key display. You can do that by opening the Settings menu and choosing Hide Function Keys.

Phone Number

The Phone Number dialog box tells Terminal what number to dial. The dialog box looks like this:

You can enter the telephone number with parentheses and hyphens if you like. Terminal ignores those punctuation marks when it dials. You must include all the digits that need to be dialed, however. For example, if your number is in a different area code, be sure to include the 1—or whatever other prefix your long-distance carrier requires.

If you need to dial a 9 or some other number to get an outside line, include that as well. And if you want the modem to pause after requesting the outside line (to allow time for the outside dial tone to appear), include one or more commas in the dialing sequence. Each comma results in a delay of about two seconds. So, to have your modem dial 9, wait four seconds, and then dial 357-0971, you would enter the following:

    9,,357-0971

The Phone Number dialog box specifies your choices regarding three other options, in addition to the phone number itself. The Timeout If Not Connected In box tells Terminal how long to wait before giving up if no one answers the phone. The default value, 30 seconds, is also the minimum value that Terminal will accept.

If you check the Redial After Timing Out check box, Terminal tries again if at first it doesn't succeed. The interval between retries will be the same as Timeout If Not Connected value. You can interrupt the retry sequence at any time by clicking a Cancel button.

A check in the Signal When Connected box tells Terminal to beep when it reaches your party. It's a good idea to check this box. That way, if you switch to a different program while Terminal dials, the beep tells you when to switch back.

Options for Transferring Text

The standard Xon/Xoff handshaking system (discussed earlier, under "Flow Control") usually ensures that all characters you send are received and processed by the remote system. If you find that the remote system is losing characters nevertheless, try sending characters a line at a time or a character at a time. (For more information about transmitting text, see "Transmitting Data from the Clipboard or the Buffer" and "Sending and Receiving Files," later in this chapter.)

To override the standard handshaking system, choose the Settings menu's Text Transfers command. You'll see this dialog box:

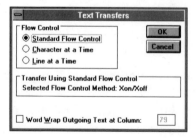

Wrapping Words at a Specified Screen Position

The remote system might be losing characters because the lines you're sending are too long. You can have Terminal automatically "break" lines at a specified column (position on screen) by putting a check in the Word Wrap Outgoing Text At Column check box. The default word-wrap column is 79, because most screens can handle 80-character lines. But you can change that to some other value.

If the Word Wrap option doesn't solve your problem, try choosing Line At A Time. Transmission will be slower, but the remote system might be able to process all your data that way. When you choose Line At A Time, the dialog box changes to reveal two additional options.

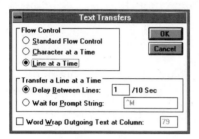

You can specify a timed delay between lines (in increments of a tenth of a second), or you can tell Terminal to pause after each line until it receives a specific character or string of characters from the remote system. If you choose the Wait For Prompt String option, the dialog box displays ^M (the Return character) as the default prompt string. That should work fine with systems that "echo" everything you send (many systems do). If the remote system does not echo and a person is available on the other end of the line to interact with you, you can try a different prompt string, such as "OK."

To slow down your transmission still more (increasing the likelihood that every character you send will be received and processed), try the Character At A Time option. As with Line At A Time, you can set this mode of transmission to proceed in either of two ways.

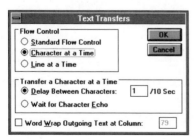

You can enter a timed delay between characters, in tenths of a second, or you can tell Terminal to wait for an echo (confirmation) of each character sent.

Options for Transferring Binary Files

Terminal offers two error-checking methods (protocols) for transferring binary files—XModem/CRC and Kermit. The default choice is XModem/CRC. If you regularly use Kermit when communicating with a particular remote system, choose the Settings menu's Binary Transfers command, and then choose Kermit in the dialog box. Your preference for Kermit will then be recorded in your settings file.

For more information about transferring binary files, see "Sending Binary Files" and "Receiving Binary Files," later in this chapter.

Saving and Retrieving Settings Files

To save a settings file, use the File menu's Save or Save As command. These commands work exactly the same way in Terminal as they do in other Windows applications. Terminal uses the extension TRM unless you supply a different extension.

Note that the contents of Terminal's window are not saved in your settings file. Only the selections you make in the Settings menu's dialog boxes are saved.

To retrieve an existing settings file, use the File menu's Open command. To begin creating a new settings file (removing the current one from memory), use the File menu's New command.

INITIATING A TELEPHONE CALL

To initiate a telephone call, load the settings file for the system you want to contact. Then open the Phone menu and choose Dial.

Even if you don't have a settings file for the party you want to call, you can choose the Dial command. Terminal prompts you for the number to dial.

While Terminal is dialing, you see a display like this:

At the same time, the dialing command sent to your modem is displayed in Terminal's application window.

When the remote system answers, the message box disappears and your system beeps (unless you have cleared the Signal When Connected check box in the Phone Number dialog box). Depending on your modem and the baud rate at which you're using it, you might also see a message in Terminal's window indicating that a connection has been established.

If the remote system does not answer, Terminal leaves the line open for the length of time specified in the Phone Number dialog box (see "Phone Number," earlier in this chapter), and then hangs up. Then, if the Redial After Timing Out option (in the Phone Number dialog box) has been selected, Terminal redials. You can stop this sequence at any time by clicking Cancel.

ANSWERING A CALL INITIATED BY THE REMOTE SYSTEM

When someone at another computer is going to initiate a data link with your computer, you can put your modem in *auto-answer mode*. When the phone rings, then, your modem will answer and establish the connection.

To put your modem in auto-answer mode, you need to type a particular sequence of characters in Terminal's window. To find out what to type, check your modem's documentation.

For example, if you're using a Hayes or Hayes-compatible modem, you would type

ATS0=1

This character sequence sends a command to the modem, telling it to pick up the phone on the first ring. (To have the modem pick up on a different ring, substitute a different number for the 1 in the above command.)

If your modem is not in auto-answer mode but you are working in Terminal, the word *RING* might appear on your screen when someone dials your telephone number. You can have your modem answer the call then by typing *ATA* and pressing Enter. (This sequence works for Hayes and Hayes-compatible modems.)

WINDOWS TIP: If you often use your modem in auto-answer mode, you might want to assign the command string to a function key. For a Hayes or Hayes-compatible modem, you can use the command string *ATS0=1^J^M*. (The *^J^M* characters are added so you don't have to press Enter.)

353

HANGING UP THE TELEPHONE

When you're through communicating, use whatever command the host computer requires to log off. Then pull down the Phone menu and choose Hangup.

CREATING A TRANSCRIPT OF
YOUR COMMUNICATIONS SESSION

You can create a transcript of some or all of any communications session in either of two ways. You can "echo" everything that's sent and received to your printer. Or you can "capture" everything in a text file on disk.

To create a printed transcript, open the Settings menu and choose Printer Echo. A check mark will appear beside the Printer Echo menu command, and Print Manager will appear on your desktop.

To record your session in a text file, open the Transfers menu, choose Receive Text File, and fill out the dialog box. The Receive Text File command includes some options; see "Receiving a Text File," later in this chapter.

You can begin copying your session to the printer or a disk file at any time before or after you dial the telephone. And you can end the copy at any time, as well. To stop the printer echo, open the Settings menu and choose Printer Echo a second time. To stop saving information in a text file, pull down the Transfers menu and choose Stop, or click the Stop button that appears at the bottom of Terminal's window.

TIMING A COMMUNICATIONS SESSION

If you have chosen to make your function-key assignments visible at the bottom of Terminal's window (see "Assigning Strings of Characters to Function Keys," earlier in this chapter), you'll see a set of buttons at the bottom of the Terminal application window. In the lower right corner of this display, Terminal shows you either the current time of day or the number of minutes and seconds that have elapsed since the beginning of your most recent connection. The latter information might be particularly useful if you're connected to an information service that charges by the minute.

If you have a mouse, you can switch the time window from time of day to elapsed time—or back—by clicking on the time window. If you have don't have a mouse and Terminal is showing the time of day, choose the Timer Mode command on the Settings menu to see the elapsed time.

If the function-key assignments and the time window are not visible, open the Settings menu and choose Show Function Keys.

INSPECTING AND SELECTING TEXT IN TERMINAL'S BUFFER

As mentioned earlier, you can move back and forth in Terminal's window to see text that has been sent or received. The entire contents of Terminal's buffer, including whatever portion of it has scrolled off the screen, is available for you to look at and use. As soon as the buffer is filled, however, Terminal begins deleting the earliest lines in the buffer to make room for new material.

You can select text in the buffer the same way you can select text in other Windows applications—by dragging the mouse, or by positioning the insertion point and using the direction keys while holding down the Shift key.

Selected text can be copied, but not cut, to the Clipboard. From there, you can paste the selection into a word processor, a spreadsheet, or some other application.

A text selection cannot be deleted from the buffer. If you select a block and press the Del key, Terminal merely deselects the block. You can empty the entire buffer at once, however, by choosing the Edit menu's Clear Buffer command. You might want to do this after finishing one communication session and before beginning another—provided you no longer need the material in the buffer.

TRANSMITTING DATA FROM THE CLIPBOARD OR THE BUFFER

Any text stored in the Windows Clipboard can be transmitted to a remote computer. Simply use the Edit menu's Paste command after establishing connection with your party. The Clipboard's text appears in Terminal's window exactly as though you were typing it.

You can also transmit material stored in the buffer. Simply select it, and then choose the Edit menu's Send command. You might want to use this technique if you get a message from one party that you want to forward to another.

SENDING AND RECEIVING FILES

Commands on Terminal's Transfers menu allow you to send and receive two kinds of files: text files and binary files.

A *text file* is a file containing nothing but letters, numbers, punctuation symbols, and "control codes." (Control codes are characters with values in the range of 1 through 31. They include such functions as carriage returns, line feeds, tabs, form feeds, and escape codes.) Examples of text files include the following:

- Any document created in Notepad or in a plain-text editor such as Edlin or the MS-DOS 5 Edit program

- Any document created in a word processor and saved with a "text file," "text only," or "unformatted" option

- Any report formatted for the printer but redirected to a disk file (a Lotus PRN file, for example)

- A database file saved in a "comma-delimited," "comma-and-quote-delimited," or "fixed-length-record" format

- An MS-DOS batch file (a file with the extension BAT)

 WINDOWS TIP: If you're not sure whether a file is a text file, try loading it into Notepad. If you can read all of it in Notepad, it's a text file.

A *binary file* is any file that's not a text file. Examples include:

- An executable program file (one with the extension COM, EXE, or PIF)

- A program "overlay" file (such files often have the extension OVL)

- A "dynamic link library" file (one with the extension DLL)

- A formatted word processing document, such as the kind Write saves if you don't use the "text only" option

- Any file containing graphics information

- Any file that was saved with a file-compression utility

Text files are typically transmitted without any special error-checking protocol (other than parity, if you have selected a parity-checking option in the Communications dialog box). This is not because errors are less likely to occur, but because they're more easily detected. Usually, you can tell by context whether a character has been transmitted incorrectly.

Binary files, on the other hand, are almost always sent and received with the help of some kind of error-checking routine. Terminal lets you choose between two protocols: XModem/CRC and Kermit. Again, the reason is detectability. A transmission mistake in a binary file might be difficult to find. (Mistakes in binary files might also have more serious consequences; even a slight corruption of a program file could render it worthless.)

In fact, though, you *can* use one of Terminal's error-checking protocols when sending or receiving a text file. To do so, follow the procedures for working with a binary file. You might want to do this if you're using a "noisy" telephone line and getting a lot of obvious transmission errors.

Similarly, you *can* exchange binary files without error checking (by sending them as text files); this is not a good idea, however!

Sending a Text File

To send a text file, open the Transfers menu and choose Send Text File. You'll see a dialog box like this:

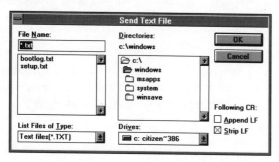

Specify the file you want to send, choose either of the options under Following CR, if appropriate, and click OK.

The Following CR options tell Terminal how to handle line endings in your file. If the remote system receives your file with an extra line space at the end of each line (double-spaced, for example, when your file is in fact single-spaced), put a check in the Strip LF check box (it is selected by default). If everything arrives at the remote computer on a single line (or is single-spaced when your document is double-spaced), put a check next to Append LF.

While your document is being sent, you'll see a display at the bottom of Terminal's window, like the one in the illustration on the following page.

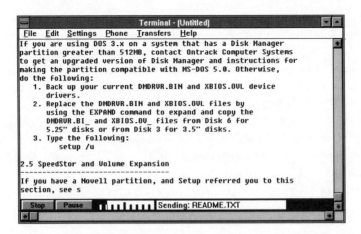

On the left side of this display is a Stop button. Click this if you don't want to send any more of the file. Next to the Stop button is a Pause button. You can interrupt the transmission of your text file by clicking this button; after you click Pause, the button says Resume. (Keyboard users will find equivalents for these buttons on the Transfers menu.)

The document bar, to the right of the Pause/Resume button, indicates how much of your file you've sent and how much remains. In the preceding illustration, you can see that about 20 percent of the file has already been transmitted.

The last element in this display confirms the name of the file that Terminal is sending.

When all of your text file has been sent, Terminal removes the buttons, document bar, and filename from the screen.

Viewing a Text File

Terminal includes a handy command that lets you inspect a file before you send it (or after you have received it). To use this command, open the Transfers menu, choose View Text File, and fill out the dialog box. Terminal scrolls your file into the buffer as though it were transmitting it, but nothing is sent.

Receiving a Text File

To receive a text file, choose Receive Text File from the Transfers menu. You'll see the dialog box shown in the illustration at the top of the following page.

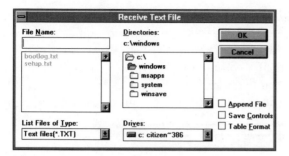

Specify the name of the file you want to receive, check any appropriate options, and click OK. You can choose all, some, or none of the following three options: Append File, Save Controls, and Table Format.

Append File

Choose Append File if you want the incoming file to be *added* to an existing file on disk. If you do not check this box and you specify the name of a file that already exists, you'll see the following warning message:

If you click Yes, your new file will replace the existing file.

Save Controls

The Save Controls option, when checked, allows the receipt of control codes. Some applications include control codes for text formatting—even when you save a file as "text only." If you do not select Save Controls, control codes other than Carriage Return and Line Feed are "stripped" from the file as it is received. When you're receiving files that truly contain only text, the setting of this option has no effect.

Table Format

If you choose the Table Format option, Terminal replaces blocks of two or more spaces in the incoming file with tab characters. This option might enable you to create a neatly structured table from mainframe data in which numbers are separated by spaces instead of tabs.

Choosing Receive Text File puts Terminal in a "capture" mode, in which all characters passing through the buffer—those you send as well as those you receive—are copied to the specified file on your disk. Thus you can use this command to transcribe all or part of a communication session, as well as to receive text documents sent by the remote computer.

While Terminal is capturing text to a disk file, you see a display like this:

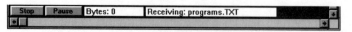

The Stop and Pause buttons allow you to terminate or interrupt the capture. If you select Pause, the button changes to read Resume. Equivalent commands are also provided on the Transfers menu, for the benefit of keyboard users.

You need to use the Stop button or Stop command when you have captured all the text you want to capture. Otherwise, Terminal remains in capture mode until you quit Terminal.

Choosing a Protocol for Binary File Transfers

As mentioned, Terminal offers two error-detecting protocols for the transmission of binary files: XModem/CRC and Kermit. You select the protocol you want in the Binary Transfers dialog box (on the Settings menu).

XModem/CRC is a faster protocol than Kermit, so you should use it if the system with which you're communicating also supports it. Choose Kermit if the remote system supports Kermit but not XModem/CRC.

Sending a Binary File

To send a binary file, open the Transfers menu, choose Send Binary File, and supply the name of your file in the ensuing dialog box. There are no other options to be concerned with.

Before file transmission can begin, the party with whom you're communicating must prepare his or her system to receive your file—using the same protocol that you have chosen. If you issue the Send Binary File command before your party is ready, Terminal waits for a ready signal from the remote computer.

While the file transfer is in progress, you will not see any data move through the buffer, but you will be able to track the progress of the transmission by looking at the display at the bottom of your window.

You can stop the transfer by clicking the Stop button (or choosing its equivalent on the Transfers menu), but you cannot pause a binary-file transfer.

Next to the Stop button, Terminal displays a document bar to show the progress of your file transfer. To the right of the document bar, you'll find the name of the file you're sending.

With both XModem/CRC and Kermit, if any transmission errors are detected, the block of data in which the error occurred is resent. The Retries number, to the right of your filename at the bottom of Terminal's window, indicates the number of times Terminal has had to resend a block of data.

When the entire file has been sent, the buttons, document bar, filename, and retry counter are removed from your screen.

If Terminal is unable to send or receive a block of data correctly after six consecutive retries, Terminal notifies you that the file transfer has been aborted. Try again on a different telephone line or at a different time of day.

Receiving a Binary File

To receive a binary file, open the Transfers menu, choose Receive Binary File, and supply the name under which you want to store the incoming file. There are no other options to be concerned with.

While the file is being sent to you by the remote computer, you will not see any data moving through the buffer. You can track the progress of the file transmission by watching the byte counter in the display that appears at the bottom of your window.

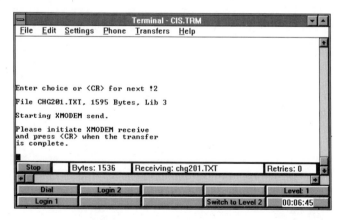

This display looks and functions exactly like the one shown above for a binary send, except that Terminal reports the number of bytes received instead of showing you a document bar. If you know the file's total size in bytes, you can use the counter to predict how long the transmission will take.

COMMUNICATING WITHOUT TELEPHONE LINES

You can use Terminal to communicate data directly from one computer to another, without a modem. Here's how:

1. Connect the serial ports of the two computers with a *null modem cable.*

2. In the Communications dialog box (on the Settings menu), choose the Connector your null modem cable is attached to.

3. In the Communications dialog box, set all the options the same on both computers. Set the Baud Rate to 19200.

4. Because your computers are directly connected, you won't need the Dial command. Use the rest of Terminal's commands and functions as though you were communicating over telephone lines.

5. You may need to change the Local Echo or CR $\rightarrow$ CR/LF options in the Terminal Preferences dialog box so that you can see what you are typing.

16
Using Paintbrush

Paintbrush is a program that lets you create and edit graphics images. You can use it to produce anything from simple text banners and line diagrams to complex works of art. You can start with a blank canvas, or you can modify an image generated by a scanner or imported from another Windows program—such as a chart from Microsoft Excel. Any graphics information that can be copied to the Clipboard as a bitmap can be pasted into Paintbrush.

Paintbrush replaces Paint, the drawing program that was included in versions of Windows before 3.0. If you used Paint, you will appreciate the following improvements in Paintbrush:

- Images created in Paintbrush can be in color or black and white.

- Paintbrush offers a more extensive set of drawing tools and editing commands than Paint.

- In addition to its default file format (BMP), Paintbrush reads and writes PCX files—a format that can be generated by many scanning software packages and incorporated into a number of non-Windows word processing programs (such as Microsoft Word and WordPerfect).

Images saved in Paint's file format (MSP) can be read into Paintbrush, but you can't save a Paintbrush image as a Paint file.

PAINTBRUSH AND OLE

Version 3.1 of Paintbrush supports object linking and embedding as a server application. That means that pictures created or edited in Paintbrush can be embedded in documents created by OLE client applications, such as Write and Cardfile. For an example showing how to use embedded objects with OLE client applications, see Chapter 8.

STARTING PAINTBRUSH

To get Paintbrush running, double-click its program-item icon. (It's in the Accessories program group, if you haven't moved it.) If you're using File Manager as your shell, double-click PBRUSH.EXE in your Windows directory.

Paintbrush's opening screen looks like this:

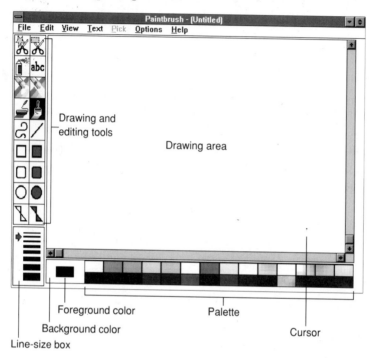

NOTE: *This illustration, like all others in this chapter, is a black-and-white representation of a color VGA screen. On a color display you will see a palette of colors along the bottom of the window instead of the shades of gray shown here.*

The blank area that makes up most of Paintbrush's window is your *drawing area*. The icons to the left of the drawing area are *drawing and editing tools*. You'll use these tools to draw and edit images in the drawing area.

Immediately to the left of the color/pattern palette, Paintbrush displays the current *foreground and background color* selections. In the illustration above, Paintbrush's foreground color is black, and its background color is white.

In the lower left corner of Paintbrush's window is the *line-size box.* The setting in the line-size box determines the thickness of the lines that Paintbrush will draw.

The dot in the lower right corner of the drawing area is your *cursor.* Like the insertion point in a word processing program, the cursor indicates where your next drawing action will take place.

OTHER CURSOR SHAPES

The cursor's shape depends on the drawing or editing tool you're using. Paintbrush's default tool is the brush, and the cursor shape corresponding to that tool is the dot shown in the preceding illustration (you can make the dot appear bigger by choosing a broader brush). At other times during your work in Paintbrush, you will see the following cursor shapes:

When you work with text in Paintbrush, the cursor is replaced by an insertion point and an I-beam. These look exactly like the insertion point and I-beam you've seen in Write and Notepad.

THE SIZE OF THE PICTURE

The actual size of your picture may be larger or smaller than what you see in Paintbrush's drawing-area window. When you first start Paintbrush, the program determines an optimum picture size, based on the type of display you're using and the amount of memory your computer has. But you can choose a larger or smaller canvas if you want.

The size of a picture is determined when you first begin to create the picture. You can't make a picture larger or smaller after you've begun. (You can enlarge or reduce selected sections of a picture, however.)

The following illustration shows a picture that is much smaller than Paintbrush's drawing-area window.

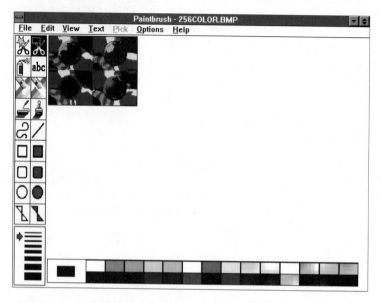

And here's a picture that's considerably larger:

SEEING THE LARGER PICTURE

Paintbrush offers three ways to see more of a large picture at once. You can:

- Use the View Picture command.
- Remove the tools, line-size box, and palette.
- Use the Zoom Out command.

The View Picture Command

The View Picture command, on the View menu, temporarily removes Paintbrush's toolbox, line-size box, palette, and scroll bars, giving the maximum possible space to your picture. After you use this command, your very next keystroke or mouse click returns the display to its previous state, so you can't do any work with your picture in this mode. It's a useful command, though, when you want to see those parts of your picture that lie just off-screen.

MOUSE TIP: As a mouse shortcut for the View Picture command, double-click the Pick tool—the scissors with the rectangle in the upper right corner of the toolbox.

KEYBOARD TIP: As a keyboard shortcut for the View Picture command, press Ctrl-P. Then press any key to return to the normal display.

Removing the Toolbox, Line-size Box, and Palette

To work with the largest possible area of your picture, use the Tools And Linesize command and the Palette command (both are on the View menu). Choosing Tools And Linesize extends the drawing-area window to the left edge of Paintbrush's application window. Choosing Palette extends the drawing-area window to the bottom of the application window.

Both commands are toggles. Choose Palette once, for example, to make the palette go away. Choose it again when you want to reuse the palette.

Zooming Out to Get the Whole Picture

To see an entire large picture at once, you can use the View menu's Zoom Out command. Here's how the doll maker in the previous illustration looks after being zoomed out:

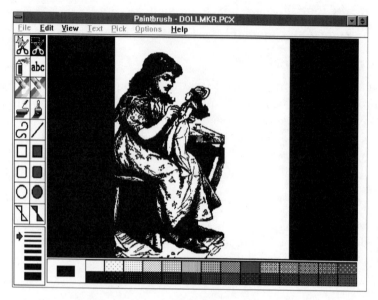

When you zoom out, Paintbrush reduces your picture so that everything fits in the window—no matter how large the picture.

In addition to letting you see your entire picture, the Zoom Out command serves another valuable purpose: It allows you to select a larger area of your picture than would normally fit on the screen. For example, if you wanted to copy all of the doll maker—from head to toes—you would need to zoom out first, use the Pick tool to select the entire image, and then copy it to the Clipboard.

To return to Paintbrush's normal view after using the Zoom Out command, pull down the View menu again and choose Zoom In.

 KEYBOARD TIP: Ctrl-N and Ctrl-O are keyboard shortcuts for Zoom In and Zoom Out, respectively. After you've zoomed out, Ctrl-N restores the normal display. A second Ctrl-N takes you to a closeup view. Similarly, after you've zoomed in, you can press Ctrl-O once to restore the normal view and a second time for the panoramic overview.

WINDOWS TIP: When you paste an image into Paintbrush, only the data that fits in the current drawing area is accepted. Anything that doesn't fit within that space is "clipped" from the pasted image. To paste an image larger than the size of your screen, therefore, you need to do the following:

1. Use the Image Attributes command (on the Options menu) to specify a canvas size large enough to accommodate the image you're about to paste.
2. Use the View menu's Zoom Out command.
3. Paste the image.
4. Click anywhere outside the image area.
5. Use the Zoom In command.

NAVIGATING ON A LARGE CANVAS

Paintbrush displays scroll bars whenever the entire picture won't fit in the drawing area. If you have a mouse, you can click the scroll bars to move the cursor to a different part of a large picture. For example, in the doll-maker graphic shown on the previous page, it takes only a couple of clicks on the vertical scroll bar to bring the doll maker's skirt and shoes into view.

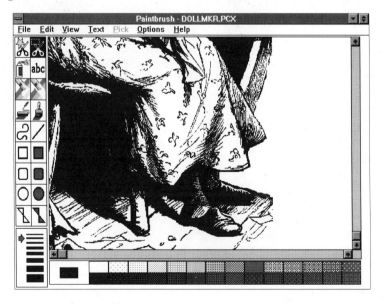

If you don't have a mouse, you can scroll the window with the keystrokes listed in Table 16-1.

Keystroke	Effect
Shift-Right	Moves right one space
Shift-Left	Moves left one space
Shift-Down	Moves down one line
Shift-Up	Moves up one line
Shift-PgDn	Moves right one screen
Shift-PgUp	Moves left one screen
PgDn	Moves down one screen
PgUp	Moves up one screen
Home	Moves to the top of the picture
End	Moves to the bottom of the picture
Shift-Home	Moves to the left edge of the picture
Shift-End	Moves to the right edge of the picture

Table 16-1.
Navigation keystrokes in Paintbrush.

PRECISE CURSOR POSITIONING

For certain kinds of work in Paintbrush, it's helpful to know precisely where the cursor is. For example, if you're trying to draw two vertical lines of exactly the same length, you might find it convenient to know how far the beginning and end of the first line are from one of the picture's edges. The View menu's Cursor Position command can provide the information you need.

When you choose Cursor Position, Paintbrush displays the x and y (horizontal and vertical) coordinates of the current cursor position in a small window near the upper right corner of the Paintbrush window.

In the illustration on the following page, the center of the cross-hair cursor has x and y coordinates of 312 and 280, respectively. One tip of the cursor rests on the southern extreme of Baldwin Avenue. To add another street running parallel to Baldwin and extending the same distance south of the 210 Freeway, we would simply maintain a y coordinate of 280 while moving the cursor the appropriate distance to the east or west of Baldwin. Then we'd draw another straight vertical line from that new position up to the 210.

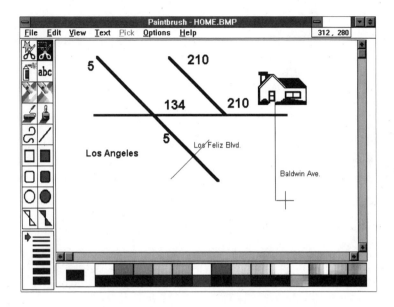

The cursor position is reported by Paintbrush as an offset in *pixels* from the upper left corner of the picture. (A pixel is the smallest dot your screen can display and the smallest increment by which you can move the cursor.) So, for example, the coordinate pair 312, 280 represents a point 312 pixels to the right of and 280 pixels below the upper left corner of the picture. Note that the 0, 0 point is always the upper left corner of the picture, not the upper left corner of the drawing-area window.

As long as the Cursor Position display is on, Paintbrush updates your cursor coordinates almost as fast as you can move the cursor. If you get tired of looking at those constantly changing numbers, you can pull down the View menu and choose Cursor Position again. Or simply double-click the Control-menu icon in the corner of the cursor-position window.

WORKING WITH MOUSE AND KEYBOARD

You can do almost anything in Paintbrush with either the mouse or the keyboard. Generally, the mouse is easier to use, but for certain actions—such as positioning the cursor in a critical location prior to drawing a line—you might want to rely on the keyboard. It's difficult to move the cursor a mere pixel or two with the mouse; on the other hand, it's laborious to draw a line halfway across the canvas by leaning on a direction key.

371

Paintbrush uses both mouse buttons for commands. (If you use a three-button mouse, "both" refers to the left button and the right button; the middle button is inactive.) For example, to change the foreground color, you click the left button on the palette. To change the background color, you click the right button.

 MOUSE TIP: If you have used Control Panel to reverse the behavior of your mouse buttons, the term *left button* in this chapter always means *right button* to you—and vice versa.

Many drawing and editing procedures in Paintbrush involve clicking or dragging the mouse in the drawing area. If you don't have a mouse, you can simulate these actions with the keyboard equivalent shown in Table 16-2.

If you are working without a mouse, you can use the Tab key to move from the drawing area to the toolbox. Press Tab again to move to the line-size box, and press a third time to get to the color/pattern palette.

Mouse Action	Keyboard Equivalent
Click left button	Press Ins
Click right button	Press Del
Double-click left button	Press F9-Ins
Double-click right button	Press F9-Del
Drag, holding left button	Hold down Ins and use direction keys
Drag, holding right button	Hold down Del and use direction keys

Table 16-2.
Keyboard equivalents for mouse actions.

SETTING UP FOR A NEW PICTURE

Before beginning a new picture, you have to prepare your canvas. In particular, you need to decide the following:

- The background color or pattern that will be used for your entire picture

- The dimensions of the picture

- Whether you want to work in color or black and white

After you have applied the first brush strokes to a new picture, you can't change any of these factors.

NOTE: *If your Windows system is set up for a monochrome display (such as Hercules monochrome, CGA, or VGA with monochrome display), you can't create color pictures. You can load a color picture into Paintbrush, but Paintbrush reduces it to black and white.*

Choosing a Background Color or Pattern

Paintbrush uses one color (or black-and-white pattern) as its default background color. You might think of this as the color of the canvas before you start to paint. You can override the background color any place you choose, with any color you choose. But after you've started a picture, you can't change the color of the canvas as a whole.

To choose a background color or pattern, put the cursor on the color of your choice (in the color/pattern palette) and click the right mouse button.

NOTE: *If the last picture you created was in color and you want your next one to be in black and white, proceed as follows: First choose Black And White in the Image Attributes dialog box. Choose a black-and-white background pattern, as described in the preceding paragraph, and then choose New on the File menu. Paintbrush performs a similar reduction if you open a 256-color bitmap on a system that uses a 16-color display. The 256 colors of the original file are displayed in the nearest available 16 colors, and if you save the file to disk, Paintbrush saves it as a 16-color file.*

 MOUSE TIP: As a shortcut for the New command, you can double-click the Eraser tool, which is the third tool down on the right side of the toolbox—directly under the tool marked *abc*.

Establishing the Size and Shape of Your Picture

To specify the dimensions of your picture, choose Image Attributes from the Options menu. You'll see a dialog box like the illustration on the following page.

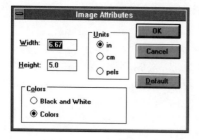

Specify the width and height you want for your picture, in whatever units you find most convenient to work with. You can choose inches, centimeters, or *pels*; the term *pel* is a synonym for *pixel*.

To revert to the picture dimensions that Paintbrush considers optimum for your display and the amount of memory in your system, click the Default button.

Choosing Color or Black and White

The Image Attributes dialog box is also the place where you decide whether your image will be in color or black and white. (If you're working at a monochrome display, the Colors option is grayed out.)

When making this choice, it's a good idea to consider the medium in which you're most likely to output your new image. Color is unquestionably more interesting to work with than black and white, but if you're going to send your image to a black-and-white printer, you'll get better control of the final product by working in black and white.

Installing Your New Canvas

When you have made your dimension and color choices, click OK in the Image Attributes dialog box. Paintbrush then presents a new, blank picture with the attributes you selected. (If you have an unsaved picture when you click OK, Paintbrush gives you a chance to save it before proceeding.)

DRAWING BASICS

After you've set up your canvas as described in the previous section, you're ready to start drawing. In general terms, the process of putting an object on the canvas goes as follows:

1. Select a drawing tool.

    Each drawing tool is specialized for a particular kind of object. For straight lines, for example, you choose the Line tool; to create a rectangle, select one of the rectangle tools—and so on.

The properties of the various tools are described in "Exploring the Toolbox," later in this chapter.

To select a tool, click on it.

2. Choose a line width from the line-size box.

You can draw with lines from one pixel wide through nine pixels wide. Simply click the width you want to use.

3. Choose a foreground color.

To choose a foreground color, use the mouse to point to the appropriate box in the color/pattern palette, and then click the left button.

If you don't find the color or pattern you want on the palette, you can create it with the Edit Colors command. See "Working with Custom Color/Pattern Palettes," later in this chapter.

4. Choose a background color.

Some tools make use of the current background color as well as the foreground color. Others use the foreground color only. You only need to concern yourself with this step if the tool you're about to apply makes use of the background color.

To choose a background color, use the mouse to point to the appropriate box in the palette, and then click the right button.

5. Draw.

At this stage, before the new object is "pasted down," you can touch it up by pressing Backspace or remove it altogether with the Edit menu's Undo command. See "Quick Fixes: Backspace and the Undo command," below.

6. When you're satisfied with the new object, paste it down to make it a permanent part of your picture.

An object that has been pasted down can still be erased or edited, but it can't be removed in one fell swoop with the Undo command or touched up with Backspace. To paste down the object you draw in step 5, do any of the following:

☐ Select another tool (or reselect the same one).

☐ Use any command on the View menu except Cursor Position.

☐ Scroll the picture.

☐ Change the size of the Paintbrush application window.

❑ Change the position of the Paintbrush application window.

❑ Switch to a different application.

As soon as you take any of these actions, the Undo command appears grayed out on the Edit menu.

QUICK FIXES: BACKSPACE AND THE UNDO COMMAND

Immediately after you draw a new line, circle, rectangle, or other object, Paintbrush gives you two easy ways to make adjustments to it. These quick-fix options—the Undo command and the Backspace key—become unavailable as soon as you paste your new object down.

Touching Up with the Backspace Key

When you press Backspace after drawing a new object, the cursor turns into a square with an *X* inside. This new cursor is a special-purpose eraser that can rub out any part of your new object but has no effect on objects already pasted down. You'll find the Backspace eraser handy for such tasks as shortening lines that went farther than you intended.

To touch up an object before you've pasted it down, press Backspace. Then drag the eraser over any part of the new object that you want to remove.

 WINDOWS TIP: You can change the width of the Backspace eraser by selecting a different line in the line-size box. For very careful erasing, choose the narrowest line width.

Note that the Backspace key works differently when you're using the Text tool—the one marked *abc*. In that context, it simply erases the character to the left of the insertion point—exactly as it does in most word processing programs.

Radical Surgery with the Undo Command

The Edit menu's Undo command wipes out everything you've added to your canvas since the last time you pasted an object down. Because some of Paintbrush's drawing tools may not always give you exactly what you have in mind the very first time you use them, you're likely to find the Undo command invaluable.

WINDOWS TIP: Be sure to paste down any object that you're completely satisfied with. That way, you won't inadvertently remove good work the next time you use Undo or the Backspace key. Remember, you can always use Paintbrush's other editing procedures to alter your pasted-down objects later.

Another excellent way to protect yourself against accidental erasures is to save your picture on disk at regular intervals. Paintbrush's Save command is described later in this chapter.

EXPLORING THE TOOLBOX

Paintbrush's toolbox includes the following eighteen tools. You can use:

The Scissors tool to select an irregularly shaped *cutout* (A cutout is a selection that can be cut, copied, moved, and manipulated in a number of other ways. See "Working with Cutouts," later in this chapter.)

The Pick tool to select a rectangular cutout

The Airbrush to create "spray-paint" effects

The Text tool to add letters, numbers, and words in various typefaces, sizes, and styles

The Color Eraser to change an object's foreground color

The Eraser to remove objects from a picture

The Paint Roller to fill enclosed shapes with the foreground color

The Brush to create freehand shapes

The Curve to draw smooth curves

The Line to draw straight lines

The Box to create unfilled rectangles

The Filled Box to create rectangles filled with the foreground color

The Rounded Box to create unfilled rectangles with rounded corners

The Filled Rounded Box to create rectangles with rounded corners filled with the foreground color

The Circle/Ellipse to create unfilled ellipses or circles

The Filled Circle/Ellipse to create circles and ellipses filled with the foreground color

The Polygon to create irregular closed shapes

The Filled Polygon to create irregular closed shapes filled with the foreground color

You might think of the Scissors, the Pick, the Color Eraser, and the Eraser as editing tools, and the rest as drawing tools. We'll look at the drawing tools first; then we'll take up the editing tools.

Using Paintbrush's Drawing Tools

Drawing with Spray Paint: the Airbrush Tool

The Airbrush tool deposits a circular pattern of dots in the foreground color. To get a wide dot pattern, select a wide line in the line-size box; for a narrow pattern, choose a narrow line width.

To draw with the Airbrush, hold the left mouse button down and drag the mouse. The speed with which you move the mouse affects the density of the line; the slower you move, the denser the line you get.

Freehand Drawing: the Brush Tool

The Brush tool works somewhat like a normal paintbrush. To use the Brush, hold down the left mouse button and drag the mouse across the canvas. Paintbrush deposits the foreground color along the path of the Brush.

You can modify both the width and the shape of the Brush to get different kinds of brush strokes. To change the width, select one of the lines in the line-size box. To change the shape, open the Options menu and choose Brush Shapes. You'll see the following dialog box.

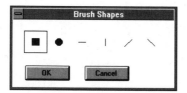

The default brush shape is the one on the left in the illustration—which produces strokes of even width in all directions. (Note that the big square around the little square is not part of the brush shape; it merely indicates that the shape on the left is currently selected.) If you're adept at calligraphy, try one of the diagonal shapes with a broad brush width; that combination will give you narrow strokes in the direction parallel to the Brush's own shape and broad strokes in the perpendicular direction.

 MOUSE TIP: As a shortcut for the Brush Shapes command, you can double-click the Brush tool icon (the fourth icon down on the right side of the toolbox).

To draw with the Brush, hold down the left mouse button and drag.

The Brush is primarily intended for freehand drawing. If you want straight lines, it's best to use the Line tool instead of the Brush (unless, of course, you want to take advantage of one of the non-square brush shapes).

You can, however, draw perfectly straight horizontal and vertical lines with the Brush. To do that, hold down the Shift key as you draw. And you can get perfect right angles as follows:

1. Hold down the Shift key.

2. Draw the horizontal or vertical leg of the right angle.

3. Move the cursor in the direction of the other leg of the right angle while still holding down the mouse button and the Shift key.

4. Release the Shift key. A straight line appears between the cursor and the first line.

Straight Edges: the Line Tool

The Line tool creates straight lines in the foreground color. The current setting in the line-size box determines the width of the line.

To use the Line tool, put the cursor where you want the line to begin, press and hold down the left mouse button, move the cursor to the place where you want the line to end, and then release the mouse button.

Paintbrush always gives you the straightest, smoothest line possible on your display. For a perfect horizontal, vertical, or 45-degree diagonal stroke, hold down the Shift key as you draw.

Smooth Curves: the Curve Tool

The Curve tool lets you create a line with either one or two curves in it. Follow these steps:

1. Put the cursor where you want your curved line to begin.

2. Hold the left mouse button down and move the cursor to the place where you want the curved line to end. Release the mouse button.

    At this point, you have a straight line.

3. Put the cursor near the part of the line that you want to bend. Hold down the left mouse button and move the cursor in the direction you want to bend the line.

    Now you have a line with one curve.

4. If you want to bend the line only once, click again without moving the cursor. If you want a second bend, repeat step 3.

It might take some practice to get accustomed to the behavior of the Curve tool. If your curve isn't shaping up the way you want it, you can click the right mouse button any time before finishing the second bend to remove the line and start over.

Like the Line, Brush, and Airbrush tools, the Curve tool does its work in the current foreground color. Your choice in the line-size box determines the width of the curved line.

Perfect Rectangles: the Box and Filled Box Tools

To create rectangles and squares, use either the Box tool or the Filled Box tool. The Box tool draws an open rectangle in the current foreground color. The Filled Box draws a rectangle in the current background color and fills it with the current foreground color. The width of the rectangle's borders is determined by the line-size setting.

To use either tool, first put the cursor where you want one corner of your rectangle to be. Then hold down the left mouse button and drag the mouse toward the diagonally opposite corner. As you move the mouse, Paintbrush expands the rectangle. When you get to the place where you want the opposite corner, release the mouse button.

To draw a perfect square, hold down the Shift key as you drag the mouse.

Beveled Rectangles: the Rounded Box and Filled Rounded Box Tools

To draw open or filled rectangles with rounded corners, use the Rounded Box tool or Filled Rounded Box tool. These tools work exactly like their unrounded counterparts, described under the previous heading.

Ovals and Circles: the Circle/Ellipse and Filled Circle/Ellipse Tools

To create ellipses or circles, use the Circle/Ellipse tool or Filled Circle/Ellipse tool. The Circle/Ellipse tool draws an ellipse or circle in the current foreground color. The Filled Circle/Ellipse tool draws an ellipse or circle in the current background color, and then fills it with the current foreground color.

To use either tool, first put the cursor where you want the corner of an imaginary rectangle that will contain your figure. Then hold down the left mouse button and drag the mouse to expand the figure. When the figure reaches your desired size, release the mouse button.

To draw a perfect circle, hold down the Shift key while you move the mouse.

Irregular Closed Shapes: the Polygon and Filled Polygon Tools

To create any kind of closed shape other than a rectangle, square, ellipse, or circle, use the Polygon tool or the Filled Polygon tool. With these tools, you can draw as many straight line segments as you want. Each segment begins where the last one ended. When you double-click the left mouse button, Paintbrush closes the figure by connecting the end of your last line segment with the beginning of your first.

You can create anything from simple triangles to complex shapes with overlapping lines. If you choose the Polygon tool, Paintbrush draws the lines in the foreground color. If you choose Filled Polygon, Paintbrush draws with the background color and fills the resulting figure with the foreground color. In either case, the width of the lines is determined by the current line-size setting.

To draw with either polygon tool, follow these steps:

1. Put the cursor where you want your first line segment to begin.

2. Hold down the left mouse button, and move the mouse to the end of your first line segment. Release the mouse button.

3. Move the cursor to the place where you want your next line segment to end, and then click the left mouse button.

4. Repeat step 3 until you reach the end of the next-to-last line segment in your figure.

5. Double-click the left mouse button to close the figure.

For perfect horizontal, vertical, or 45-degree diagonal line segments, hold down the Shift key as you click the mouse button at the end of the segment.

 MOUSE TIP: The right mouse button cancels any drawing made with the Line, Curve, Box, Filled Box, Rounded Box, Filled Rounded Box, Circle/Ellipse, Filled Circle/Ellipse, Polygon, and Filled Polygon tools—as long as the drawing action isn't completed. Therefore, for all except the Curve, Polygon, and Filled Polygon, you must click the right mouse button while still holding the left button to cancel the action.

Filling an Enclosed Shape: the Paint Roller Tool

The Paint Roller tool allows you to fill any enclosed portion of your picture with the current foreground color. When you select this tool, the cursor changes to look like this:

Simply position the tip of the roller anywhere within the space you want to fill. Then click the left mouse button.

Note that if the space you want to fill has any gaps—even a gap of a single pixel—the rolled-on paint will leak through the gap. If that happens, wait until the roller has finished painting, use the Undo command, patch the leak, and try again. To patch a very small leak, you might want to use the Zoom In command, described later in "Fine-Tuning Your Image with Zoom In."

Letters, Numbers, and Words: the Text Tool

Paintbrush's Text tool is a special kind of implement. You don't really draw with this tool; instead you select typefaces, styles, and point sizes, and then insert characters from the keyboard or the Clipboard. Nevertheless, after you've pasted down your text characters, they behave exactly like any other component of your Paintbrush image.

The general procedure for adding text to a Paintbrush picture is as follows:

1. Select the Text tool.

    The cursor becomes an I-beam.

2. Choose your typeface, point size, and style.

3. Put the I-beam at the place where you want your text to begin, and then click the mouse.

    An insertion point appears.

4. Type. If you want to enter text from the Clipboard, choose Edit Paste or use its keyboard shortcut, Ctrl-V.

5. Paste down the text you just typed.

You can paste your text down using any of the methods described earlier in this chapter, or by clicking the mouse to move the insertion point.

Until you paste your text down, you can still change its typeface, size, or style. You can also erase it a character at a time by backspacing over it.

To choose a typeface, style, and size, choose the Fonts command from the Text menu. You can select among any of the fonts installed on your system.

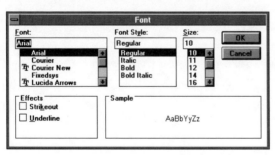

You can choose some styles directly from the Text menu.

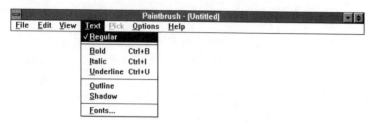

The Bold, Italic, and Underline styles may be used singly or in combination. To deselect a style, choose it again; to deselect all styles, choose Regular.

The Outline and Shadow styles are mutually exclusive but may be used in conjunction with Bold, Italic, or Underline. When you choose Outline, Paintbrush draws a one-pixel-wide border around each character, using the current background color. When you choose Shadow, the program adds a drop shadow to the left of and beneath each character, again using the background color.

The following illustration shows the effect of using Outline and Shadow. Note that the background color for these characters is solid black, even though the background chosen as a default for the canvas as a whole is white.

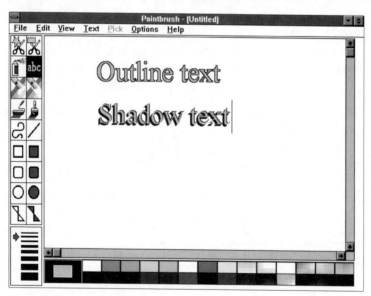

Using Paintbrush's Editing Tools

Changing Colors: the Eraser and the Color Eraser

Your toolbox includes two tools for erasing objects: an Eraser tool and a Color Eraser tool. The Eraser tool "erases" objects of any color, and the Color Eraser tool "erases" only those objects drawn in the current foreground color.

 WINDOWS TIP: When you're working with a black-and-white picture, the Eraser and the Color Eraser perform the same function.

The word *erases* is in quotation marks, because neither of these tools works quite like the rubber tip at the end of your pencil. When you erase something in Paintbrush, what you're doing is changing its color from whatever it is now to the current background color.

You can use the eraser tools to "remove" objects from your Paintbrush picture. Simply set the current background color to match the default background color—the color of your entire canvas before you started drawing on it. Then choose the appropriate eraser tool and go. The objects you erase become invisible because they blend in with the background.

But you can also use either eraser tool as a color-switcher rather than an object-remover. Simply set the current background color to some shade other than the default background.

When you choose the Eraser tool, your cursor becomes an open square. Choosing the Color Eraser changes the cursor to a square with a cross in it.

To erase an object (or change its color), put the eraser cursor at one end of the object, press and hold the left mouse button, and drag the mouse. Whatever the cursor passes over is erased. If you change your mind, choose the Edit menu's Undo command before selecting your next tool, scrolling the Paintbrush window, or taking any other action that "pastes down" your erasure.

You can make the eraser fatter or thinner by changing the selection in the line-size box. For careful work, choose the top line in the box. When you want to wipe out large areas with a few broad strokes, pick a line near the bottom.

For careful work in a color picture, choose the Color Eraser tool and set the foreground color to match the object you want to erase. That way, if your eraser strays onto an object in a different color, that object is not affected.

The Color Eraser has a global option that can be used to change all objects of one color into another color at once—much like a search-and-replace command in a word processor. To use this option, double-click the color eraser.

> **WINDOWS TIP:** Be careful using the Color Eraser's global-switch option when the current foreground color is a *dithered color*. Because a dithered color is actually a mixture of pixels in two or more solid colors, the Color Eraser under these circumstances modifies each component color. As a result, areas of your picture that you wanted to leave alone might change color.
>
> To be safe, save your work before you use any command—such as a global color switch—that has the potential to alter your picture radically. Then check the results after you use the command. If you don't like what you see, use Undo. If you discover a problem after it's too late to use Undo, use File Open to reload the picture you saved.

So, for example, if you grow tired of looking at red lines in your picture and decided you'd rather see green, you could make red the foreground color and green the background. Then you would double-click the Color Eraser tool.

This global option works on only the portion of your picture that you can see in Paintbrush's drawing-area window. If your picture extends beyond the window, you need to scroll each section into view and repeat the global switch.

The Color Eraser and Eraser have almost identical toolbox icons, but you can tell them apart by remembering the difference between the two tools.

Color eraser   Eraser

The Eraser tool alters all objects in its path, regardless of their color. Hence the Eraser's icon shows a white stripe across several strips of contrasting colors. The Color Eraser affects nothing but the current foreground color. Hence its icon shows the colored strips without a white swath.

Defining Cutouts: the Scissors and the Pick

The tools at the top of the toolbox—the scissors with the star and the scissors with the rectangle—are used for specifying *cutouts*—defined areas of a picture that can be manipulated in various ways. (See "Working with Cutouts," later in this chapter.) Though a pair of scissors dominates the icon for each of these tools, Paintbrush calls only the tool on the left the Scissors tool; the one on the right is called the Pick tool.

With the Pick, you can define any rectangular area of your picture as a cutout. With the Scissors, you can define an area of any shape.

With both tools, your cutout can be no larger than the drawing-area window. To define an area that extends beyond the window, use the Zoom Out command. (See "Zooming Out to Get the Whole Picture," earlier in this chapter.)

The Scissors tool is particularly useful when you want to select an irregularly shaped object and you don't want to include any of the surrounding canvas. For example, if you want to work with one branch of holly from the following illustration, the Scissors is the appropriate tool.

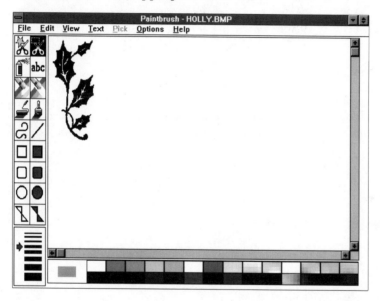

To use the Scissors, start by clicking the Scissors tool icon. Then put the cross-hair cursor somewhere along the edge of the object you want to select. Press and hold down the left mouse button, and then drag the cursor around the object. Paintbrush displays a solid line in the path of the cursor. When you have the object completely surrounded, release the mouse button. (You don't actually have to close the selection; when you release the mouse button, Paintbrush connects the current cursor position to the place where you started.) When you release the mouse button, Paintbrush displays a dotted line around the object you've selected.

WINDOWS TIP: You might find the keyboard more effective than the mouse when you need to select a convoluted shape such as the holly shown on the preceding page. To use the Scissors tool with the keyboard, position the cursor near an edge of the object to be selected. Hold down the Ins key while you use direction keys to encircle your object. Release the Ins key when you've completed the selection.

When the object you want to select is rectangular in shape or when it doesn't matter if you pick up a little background canvas along with the object, the Pick tool will do fine. And it's a lot easier to use than the Scissors.

To use the Pick tool, position the cursor at one corner of the object you want to select. Press and hold down the left mouse button, and then drag the mouse toward the diagonally opposite corner. When you get there, release the mouse button.

 MOUSE TIP: The right mouse button cancels any selection made with the Scissors and Pick tools—as long as the editing action isn't completed. Therefore, you must click the right mouse button while still holding the left button to cancel the action.

WORKING WITH CUTOUTS

After you've defined a cutout, you can do any of the following with it:

- Cut it to the Clipboard
- Copy it to the Clipboard
- Copy it to a separate disk file as a bitmap
- Move it to another place within the current picture
- Copy it to another place within the current picture
- "Sweep" it across your picture, leaving a trail of copies in the wake of your mouse
- Change its size or shape
- Flip it horizontally

- Flip it vertically
- Tilt it
- Reverse its colors

Cutting or Copying a Cutout to the Clipboard

To put your cutout on the Clipboard, pull down the Edit menu and choose Cut or Copy. If you choose Cut, Paintbrush removes it from the current picture and transfers it to the Clipboard. If you choose Copy, Paintbrush puts a copy of the cutout on the Clipboard and leaves the current picture unchanged.

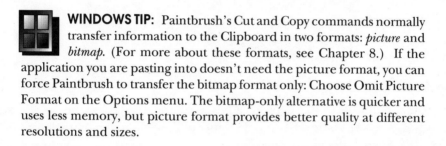

WINDOWS TIP: Paintbrush's Cut and Copy commands normally transfer information to the Clipboard in two formats: *picture* and *bitmap*. (For more about these formats, see Chapter 8.) If the application you are pasting into doesn't need the picture format, you can force Paintbrush to transfer the bitmap format only: Choose Omit Picture Format on the Options menu. The bitmap-only alternative is quicker and uses less memory, but picture format provides better quality at different resolutions and sizes.

When you remove a cutout to the Clipboard by using the Cut command, the area of the current picture occupied by the cutout assumes the current background color. If you want this area to look like blank canvas after the cutout is gone, be sure the current background color matches your initial (default) background color.

Copying a Cutout to a Disk File

You can copy your cutout to a separate disk file as well as to the Clipboard. It's a good idea to do this if you think you might want to paste your cutout into a variety of different pictures on different occasions, if you're planning to use it in another application (such as Cardfile or Write), or if you want to use your cutout as wallpaper for your Windows desktop.

To save your cutout as a separate disk file, use the Edit menu's Copy To command and fill out the dialog box that appears. The dialog box is identical to the one presented by the Save As command—the command you use to save your entire picture for the first time (or to save it under a new name). That dialog box is described later, under "Saving and Opening Paintbrush Files."

Pasting a Cutout from the Clipboard

To paste a cutout from the Clipboard into the current picture, choose the Edit menu's Paste command. Your cutout will appear in the upper left corner of your drawing area, surrounded by a dotted line. At this point, you can move the cutout by dragging it to the place where it fits in your picture. Or you can copy it, sweep it, or manipulate it in any of the other ways described below.

Note that pasting in Paintbrush is a little different from pasting in other kinds of applications. In a word processor, for example, you position the insertion point at the place where you want the Clipboard's contents to appear; then you choose Paste. In Paintbrush you choose the Paste command first; then you position the pasted object.

NOTE: *Paintbrush handles Clipboard text differently from graphics. When you paste text from the Clipboard, you must position the insertion point first; then choose the Paste command.*

Pasting from a Disk File

To paste a cutout that has been saved as a separate disk file, choose the Edit menu's Paste From command, and then fill out the dialog box that appears. The dialog box is the same as the one used by the File menu's Open command.

 WINDOWS TIP: The dialog box that appears when you choose Paste From includes an Info button. This button presents size and color-format information about any selected file. You might want to check this information if you think the file you want to paste might be too large for the picture you're currently working in.

When you use the Paste From command, Paintbrush displays your cutout in the upper left corner of the current picture, surrounded by a dotted line. At this point, you can move the cutout to the place where it belongs in your picture. Or you can copy it, sweep it, or manipulate it in any of the other ways described below.

Moving a Cutout

To move a cutout from one place to another in a picture, put the cursor anywhere within the dotted line that encircles the cutout. Then press and hold down the left or the right mouse button while you drag the cutout to its destination.

When you move a cutout, the area of the current picture occupied by the cutout assumes the current background color. If you want this area to look like blank canvas after the cutout is gone, be sure the current background color matches your initial (default) background color.

Moving Transparently or Opaquely

The mouse button you press while dragging the cutout determines whether the move is *transparent* or *opaque.*

When you move a cutout transparently, any part of the cutout drawn in the current background color assumes the underlying color of the location to which it's moved. When you move a cutout opaquely, all parts of the cutout retain their colors at the new location.

To move a cutout transparently, drag it with the left mouse button. To move it opaquely, drag it with the right mouse button.

Copying a Cutout within a Picture

To copy a cutout from one place to another within the same picture, place the cursor anywhere within the dotted line that encircles the cutout. Then hold down the Ctrl key while you drag the cutout copy to its destination.

To copy the cutout transparently, drag it while holding down the left mouse button. To copy it opaquely, drag it while holding down the right mouse button.

Sweeping a Cutout

To "sweep" a cutout means to create a trail of copies with it as you pass the mouse across your canvas. In the illustration on the following page, for example, a wagon-wheel cutout has been swept across the canvas.

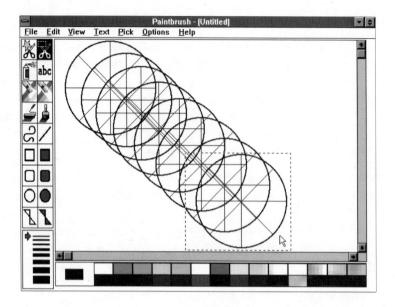

To sweep a cutout, first move the cutout to the place where you want to begin the sweep (if it's not there already). Then put the cursor anywhere within the dotted line that encircles the cutout and hold down the Shift key while you drag the cutout. To sweep transparently, drag the cutout while holding down the left mouse button. To sweep opaquely, drag the cutout while holding down the right mouse button.

The speed at which you move the mouse determines the number of copies that result from the sweep.

Modifying a Cutout with the Shrink + Grow Command

The Pick menu's Shrink + Grow command allows you to expand or contract a cutout. In the process you can either maintain the cutout's original ratio of width to height or change it—as you choose. Your resized cutout can either replace the original cutout or appear in another location on the picture as a modified copy of the cutout.

Note that all these transformations produce *opaque* replicas of your original cutout.

Making a Copy in a New Size and Shape

To make a copy of a cutout in a new size and shape, follow these steps:

1. Use either the Scissors tool or the Pick tool to define your cutout.

2. Pull down the Pick menu. If a check appears next to the Clear command, choose Clear to remove the check.

3. Choose the Pick menu's Shrink + Grow command.

4. Put the cursor at one corner of the position where you want the resized and reshaped copy to appear. Then hold down the left mouse button and drag the mouse toward the diagonally opposite corner. A dotted-line rectangle follows the path of your mouse to show you the size and shape your cutout is about to assume.

   At this point, your picture might look something like this:

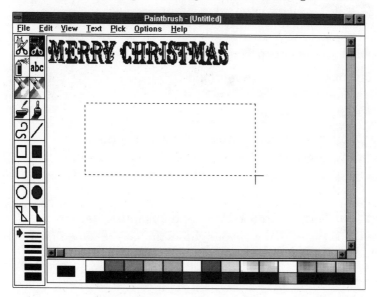

5. Release the mouse button.

   Paintbrush draws your copy.

6. To make another copy, repeat steps 4 and 5.

You can make as many resized and reshaped copies as you want. When you've made enough, paste your work into the picture by any of the methods described earlier in this chapter.

Making a Copy in a New Size and the Original Shape

To maintain the original shape of your cutout while you make a copy in a new size, follow steps 1 through 6 above, but hold down the Shift key during steps 4 and 5.

Replacing Your Cutout with a Resized and Reshaped Version

To change the size and shape of your cutout and at the same time remove the original cutout from the picture, follow these steps:

1. Use either the Scissors tool or the Pick tool to define your cutout.

2. Pull down the Pick menu. If a check does not appear next to the Clear command, choose Clear.

   The Clear command must be checked if you want to replace the original cutout with your new version.

3. If a check does not appear next to the Pick menu's Shrink + Grow command, choose the Shrink + Grow command.

4. Put the cursor at one corner of the position where you want the resized and reshaped copy to appear.

   If you want the new version to appear in the same place as the original, start with your mouse at one corner of the original.

5. Hold down the left mouse button and drag the mouse toward the diagonally opposite corner. A dotted-line rectangle will follow the path of your mouse to show you the size and shape your cutout is about to assume.

6. Release the mouse button.

Replacing a Cutout with a Resized Version in the Same Shape

To maintain the original shape of your cutout while you create a new resized version, follow steps 1 through 6 above, but hold down the Shift key during steps 5 and 6.

 MOUSE TIP: The right mouse button cancels any change made with the Shrink + Grow command—as long as the editing action isn't completed. Therefore, you must click the right mouse button while still holding the left button to cancel the action.

Modifying a Cutout with the Tilt Command

The Pick menu's Tilt command lets you distort your cutout by slanting one edge of it. For example, you can use Tilt to change the shape of a cutout from a rectangle to a parallelogram.

The Tilt command works like the Shrink + Grow command, described in the previous section. Start by defining the cutout you want to modify. Then choose Clear on the Pick menu if you want to replace your original cutout with the modified version. Be sure to deselect (remove the check from) Clear if you want to maintain the original and produce a modified copy. Then choose the Tilt command.

After choosing Tilt, put your cursor at the place where you want the upper left corner of your tilted version to appear. Press the left mouse button, and Paintbrush displays a dotted outline of your cutout.

Continue to hold down the left mouse button while you move the mouse to the left or right. As you do this, the shape of the dotted outline changes, as shown in the illustration on the following page.

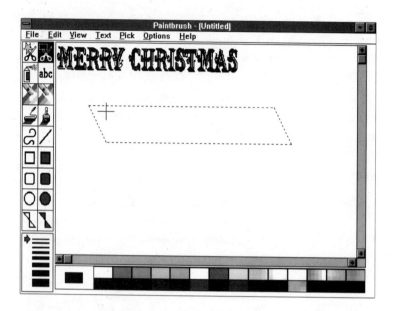

When the outline has assumed the shape you want, release the mouse button. Paintbrush will redraw your cutout to fit the new shape.

You can make as many tilted copies of your cutout as you please.

MOUSE TIP: The right mouse button cancels any change made with the Tilt command—as long as the editing action isn't completed. Therefore, you must click the right mouse button while still holding the left button to cancel the action.

Flipping a Cutout Horizontally or Vertically

With the Pick menu's Flip Vertical and Flip Horizontal commands, you can flop or invert any image. Simply define the image as a cutout, and then choose the appropriate Flip command. Here's how our Christmas banner would look after you had used the Flip Horizontal and Flip Vertical commands:

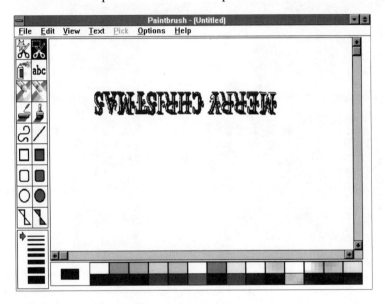

Reversing the Colors of a Cutout

The Pick menu's Inverse command "reverses" the colors of your cutout. Blacks become whites, whites become blacks, and colors switch to their opposite numbers on the red-green-blue color wheel.

If you apply the Inverse command to a dithered color, each component of the color is inverted separately. The result might be a color different from any you now have on your palette. You might want to experiment to see what effects you can achieve with this command.

Working with Large Cutouts

If you want to define a cutout larger than Paintbrush's drawing-area window (that is, a larger image than you can see on screen without zooming out), you must first pull down the View menu and choose the Zoom Out command. The same is true if you want to paste an image (from a file or from the Clipboard) that's larger than the drawing-area window. If you paste a large image without first using the Zoom Out command, Paintbrush pastes only as much of the image as it can fit in the drawing-area window.

When you use the Paste or Paste From command after zooming out, Paintbrush displays the pasted image as a hatched shape in the upper left corner of the window, like this:

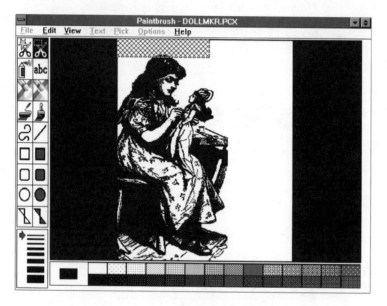

Drag the hatched cutout to the place where you want to put it, and then click anywhere outside the cutout. Paintbrush then removes the hatch marks. The following illustration shows the result.

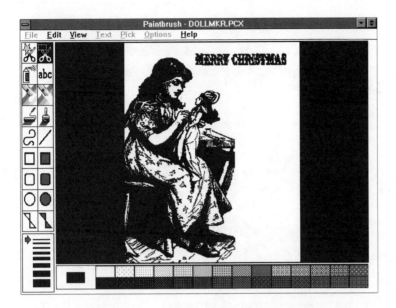

Use the View menu's Zoom In command to return to the normal view.

FINE-TUNING YOUR IMAGE WITH ZOOM IN

Paintbrush stores the images you create as *bitmaps*. As you might recall from the discussion of bitmapped fonts in Chapter 13, a bitmap is a data structure that records the relative position of each visible dot on screen. The individual dots are called pixels.

You might not normally be aware of separate pixels as you create and modify your Paintbrush images. But when you want to see and edit the image pixel by pixel, Paintbrush will accommodate you.

Simply choose the View menu's Zoom In command. Paintbrush then turns your cursor into small rectangle. Position the rectangle over the portion of the image that you want to zoom in on, and then click the left mouse button.

Here's an example of an image that has been zoomed in:

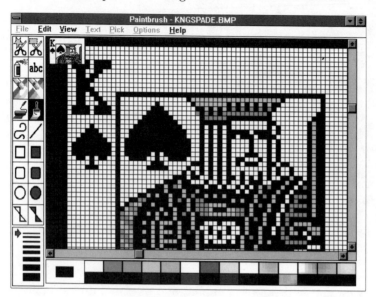

Each little square in this view represents one pixel of the image. You can change any pixel to either the foreground or background color by positioning the mouse on the pixel in question and clicking. To put the current foreground color in a pixel, click the left button; to put the current background color in, click the right button.

You can "paint" a group of pixels at once in either the foreground or background color by holding down the appropriate mouse button and dragging the mouse. Be careful not to move too quickly when you do this, though, or some of the pixels in your path might not be painted.

 MOUSE TIP: To paint straight horizontal or vertical lines in zoom-in mode, hold down the Shift key while dragging the mouse.

When you're ready to return to the normal view of your image, open the View menu again and choose Zoom Out.

WORKING WITH CUSTOM COLOR/PATTERN PALETTES

Paintbrush gives you a set of 28 default colors or patterns to use in your pictures. Sixteen of these are solid colors. The remaining 12 are dithered—mixtures of two or more solid colors.

You can create additional custom colors or patterns by choosing the Option menu's Edit Colors command. Each new color or pattern replaces one color or pattern in your palette, but you can use as many different colors or patterns as you want.

Note that pictures that use more than 16 solid colors can be imported into Paintbrush, and—provided your display adapter permits—all solid colors will be displayed. You cannot use more than 16 solid colors to modify such pictures, however.

Creating a New Color or Pattern

To create a new color or pattern, do the following:

1. Put the cursor on the color or pattern you want to replace, and then click the left mouse button.

2. Open the Options menu and choose Edit Colors.
   You'll see this dialog box:

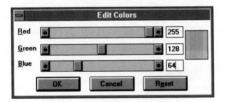

3. Use the scroll bars to adjust the red, green, and blue levels.
   Note that when you're using Paintbrush in black and white, the three scroll bars are locked together; when you adjust one, the other two are adjusted at the same time.

   As you experiment with different levels of red, green, and blue, you can see the result of your mixture in the sample box to the right of the scroll bars.

4. When you achieve the color you're looking for, click OK.

If you change your mind and want to reinstate the color you started with, click Cancel instead of clicking OK. If you change your mind after clicking OK, choose Edit Colors again. Then click Reset and OK. The default (standard) color will be reinstated.

MOUSE TIP: To edit one of the current palette colors, simply double-click it in the palette. Doing so immediately displays the Edit Colors dialog box.

Saving and Retrieving Custom Palettes

If you create a color or pattern you particularly like, you can save your modified palette with the Save Colors command, on the Options menu. You'll be asked to supply a file name for your custom palette; Paintbrush uses the extension PAL.

At the start of your next Paintbrush session, you can replace the standard palette with the custom palette you saved. To do this, choose the Options menu's Get Colors command.

SAVING AND OPENING PAINTBRUSH FILES

To save a Paintbrush image for the first time, choose the Save As command. To save it subsequently, choose Save. Both commands are located on the File menu. You'll see the following dialog box when you choose Save As:

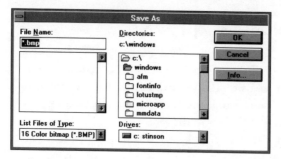

File Format Options

Paintbrush provides five file-format options. To see your choices, click the arrow at the right of the List Files Of Type list box, shown in the following illustration.

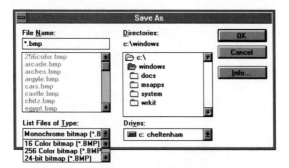

The two basic file formats used by Paintbrush are PCX and BMP. But, as the illustration shows, the BMP format is available in four flavors: monochrome, 16-color, 256-color, and 24-bit.

You should save your file in the PCX format if you want to be able to import it into a non-Windows application that does not support BMP files. Such applications currently include a number of non-Windows word processors, such as Microsoft Word and WordPerfect 5.1.

Use one of the BMP (bitmap) formats if any of the following is true:

- You want to use your picture as wallpaper for your Windows desktop. (See "Customizing Your Desktop," in Chapter 9.)

- You want to incorporate the picture into a document created under the OS/2 Presentation Manager (version 1.2 or later).

- You want to incorporate your picture into another Windows application that supports BMP files, but not PCX files.

If you're not concerned about using your picture as Windows wallpaper or importing it into another application, you can take your choice between PCX and BMP. If you choose BMP, pick your flavor according to the following guidelines:

- If your picture is black and white, choose Monochrome Bitmap.

- If your picture uses no more than 16 solid colors, choose 16 Color Bitmap. (All color pictures created in Paintbrush fall into this category.)

- If you have created or imported a picture into Paintbrush that uses more than 16 but no more than 256 colors, choose 256 Color Bitmap.

- If you have created or imported a picture into Paintbrush that uses more than 256 colors, choose 24-Bit Bitmap.

NOTE: *If you're not sure how many colors your picture uses, click the Info button in the Save As dialog box. The Info button also shows the size of the picture you're working on.*

Opening a Paintbrush File

To open an existing Paintbrush file, choose the Open command. You'll see the following dialog box.

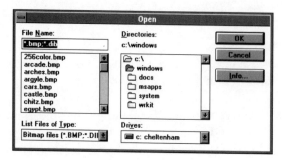

This dialog box works like its counterparts in other Windows applications, except that you need to specify a file type, and you can click a button to get information about a file you might want to open. The Files box lists only those files that have the selected format. If you don't find the file you're looking for with BMP selected, try selecting MSP or PCX.

The MSP option in the List Files Of Type box allows you to import a file that was created in Paint, the drawing program included in versions of Windows before 3.0. Paint files are black and white only. You can edit them in Paintbrush, but you can't save them again in MSP format. Choose PCX or Monochrome Bitmap to save a modified Paint file.

You can click the Info button to get size and color-format information about a selected file.

PRINTING YOUR PAINTBRUSH IMAGE

To print your Paintbrush image, first be sure your printer is set for the graphics resolution and orientation you want to use. To change resolution or orientation—or to switch to a different printer, use the File menu's Print Setup command. This command works exactly the same way in Paintbrush as it does in Write, Terminal, and the Windows desktop accessories.

Paintbrush normally prints with half-inch margins on all four sides. You can change any of these margins by choosing the File menu's Page Setup command.

The dialog box for this command, shown below, also gives you an opportunity to specify a header and header and footer for your printout.

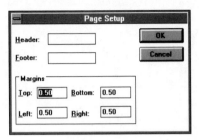

You can use codes to specify the position of your header or footer, or to insert the current date or time, the name of your file, or the page number. The codes used by Paintbrush are the same as those used by the desktop accessories; for details, see "Notepad's Printing Commands," in Chapter 7.

When you're ready to print, open the File menu again and choose Print. The Print dialog box looks like this:

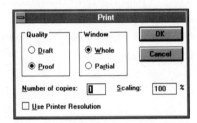

As you can see, you have some choices to make before printing.

Draft or Proof Quality

If your printer offers a draft mode, you can choose Draft for fast printing and low quality, or choose Proof for the opposite.

Whole or Partial Printout

By default, Paintbrush prints your entire image. If you want only some of it, choose Partial. When you choose OK to start the printout, Paintbrush adjusts the screen to display your entire image. Put the cursor at one corner of the area you want to print, press and hold down the left mouse button, and drag the mouse to the diagonally opposite corner.

Number of Copies

Change the value in this box if you want more than one copy of your artwork.

Resolution and Scaling

As we've noted, your Paintbrush picture is stored by the Paintbrush program as a bitmap—a data structure that represents the relative position of each pixel in your picture. When you print, that bitmap is simply transferred to your printer and reproduced with dots on paper instead of points of light on a video screen. The size of the dots used by your printer is determined by its *graphics resolution.* The higher the resolution, the smaller the dots.

By default, Paintbrush prints at *screen resolution.* That means it uses a resolution that approximates what you see on your video display. If you're not satisfied with the printed image you get at screen resolution, put a check in the Use Printer Resolution check box.

Selecting printer resolution usually produces smaller output than screen resolution (because the dots on most printers are smaller than those on most screens). If neither the screen resolution nor any of your printer's own resolution options produces the image size you're trying to achieve, pick the setting that comes closest. Then enter a scaling factor in the box marked Scaling. To make the image larger, enter a value greater than 100; to make it smaller, enter a value less than 100.

When you enter a scaling factor other than 100, Paintbrush adds or removes dots from your image's bitmap to produce the size modification you request. Scaled-up images, as a result, might have unacceptably jagged diagonals and curves, and scaled-down images might lose detail. For these reasons, it's better to achieve a desired image size by changing resolution than by applying scaling.

17

A Sampling of Major Windows Applications

In word processing, spreadsheets, desktop publishing, presentation graphics, and every other major application category, many of the most advanced and powerful programs are now being written specifically to run in the Windows environment. In fact, there has been such an explosion of Windows application development since the arrival of Windows 3.0 in May, 1990, that it is no longer possible to give any kind of broad overview of what's available. Instead, this chapter presents vignettes of some of the leading Windows programs in major business application categories. These programs were all available at the time of (or very shortly after) the announcement of Windows 3.1.

WORD PROCESSING

Ami Pro 2.0

Ami Pro was the first major word processor written for the Windows environment. In its current revision, 2.0, it still qualifies as the most mature product of its kind. It's also arguably the most fully powered Windows word processor you can buy, although its claim to that distinction is now under serious challenge from both Microsoft Word for Windows 2.0 and the Windows version of WordPerfect.

Because Samna Corporation (the original developer of Ami Pro) was acquired by Lotus Development Corporation in 1990, Ami Pro now shares certain design characteristics with other Lotus Windows applications, such as 1-2-3 for Windows and Freelance Graphics for Windows. For example, all three of these programs feature a SmartIcon palette—a customizable toolkit of mouse shortcuts for whatever commands you use most often. You can assign any menu item or macro to a SmartIcon, thereby saving yourself the time and trouble of wading through menus and dialog boxes to get at frequently used commands. More important, perhaps, the suite of Lotus Windows applications is designed to "play well" together. If you're using Ami Pro on a network, for example, you can seamlessly send messages to and receive messages from users of Lotus's cc:Mail and Lotus Notes products.

Feature highlights of Ami Pro 2.0 include the following:

- Support for the Windows multiple-document interface (MDI)
- Formatting by style sheets, with "style by example"
- Support for DDE and OLE (as a client or a server application)
- Integrated charting and drawing modules
- The ability to modify the brightness or contrast of imported TIFF images
- An equation processor
- A powerful macro language, with a macro recorder, editor, and debugger
- The ability to embed text and graphics frames within documents and flow text around them
- Outlining
- The ability to embed "power fields" in documents, such as the current date and time, the name of the document's creator, the number of words in the document—and many others
- Workgroup features, including revision marking, password protection, and the ability to embed "sticky notes" in documents
- Footnotes, end notes, indexing, spell-checking, and a thesaurus
- Automatic sequence numbering and cross-referencing
- Four levels of Undo

Ami Pro is shipped with Adobe Type Manager, 13 Type 1 fonts, and a variety of clip-art images.

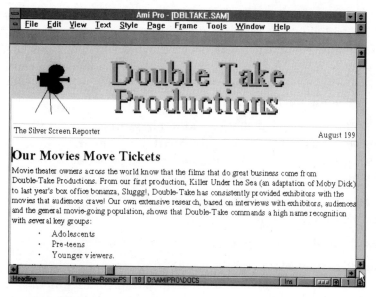

Ami Pro 2.0
Lotus Development Corporation
55 Cambridge Parkway
Cambridge, MA 02142
(617) 577-8500
$495 standalone; $195 per network node

Microsoft Word for Windows 2.0

Like Ami Pro, Microsoft Word for Windows is an enormously feature-rich graphical word processor that takes advantage of the Windows environment to show you exactly how documents will look when printed. You can use multiple fonts in multiple sizes and styles and never have to make mental translations between the text you see on screen and the output you expect on paper. You can lay out pages with multiple columns, heads across columns, sidebars, text flowing around graphic elements, and so on.

Also like Ami Pro, Word for Windows employs style sheets to simplify formatting tasks and ensure stylistic consistency. But a style sheet in Word for Windows is just one component of a document *template*, a file that serves as a model for a particular kind of document. Templates can also include a *glossary* (a collection of boilerplate text that can be reused in any context) and macros. The macros can be used, among other things, to customize the Word for Windows menu system. So with template files, you can tailor the entire Word for Windows working environment to suit particular document types, such as reports, memos, book chapters, or letters.

Version 2.0, released in October, 1991, brings major enhancements to Word for Windows, including the following:

- A customizable tool bar that provides mouse shortcuts for file saving and retrieving, creating bulleted and numbered lists, accessing the program's drawing and charting modules, spell checking, printing, and whatever other features you use often

- The ability to copy and move text or graphics by dragging and dropping with the mouse

- Support for OLE as a client or a server application

- An intelligent envelope printer that finds names and addresses in your document and positions them automatically on the envelope

- A "print merge helper" that assists you in creating form letters

- Single-step creation of bulleted lists, with more than 100 bullet styles to choose from

- A grammar checker

- A graphical file finder that lets you see long file names, the subject, or the contents of a document on screen before opening it

- The ability to create tables by clicking on the tool bar, then modify column widths by clicking and dragging

- The ability to create text effects, such as curved, rotated, or inverted characters

- Drawing and charting modules

- An equation editor

- Optional (extra-cost) spelling checkers for a variety of foreign languages

- A dedicated help facility for WordPerfect émigrés

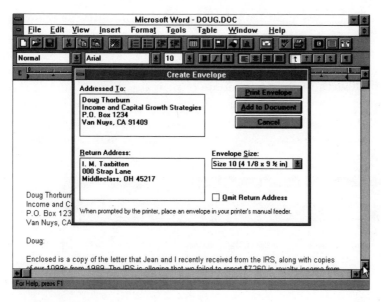

Microsoft Word for Windows 2.0
Microsoft Corporation
One Microsoft Way
Redmond, WA 98052
(800) 426-9400
$495

WordPerfect for Windows 5.1

As its name suggests, WordPerfect for Windows 5.1 is a faithful implementation of WordPerfect 5.1 in the Windows environment. Compatibility with its market-leading MS-DOS counterpart is this product's greatest strength. If you're accustomed to WordPerfect 5.1's function-key-oriented user interface, for example, you can continue to use those keystrokes to interact with the Windows version. (You can also choose to operate WordPerfect for Windows with pull-down menus and dialog boxes.) Both the Windows and MS-DOS versions use exactly the same file formats, and WordPerfect Corporation's licensing arrangement even allows you to keep and use both versions with a single license.

The Windows version of WordPerfect includes a customizable "button bar," somewhat like the tool bars of Word for Windows and Ami Pro. You can attach your most frequently used menu commands, or even your own macros, to the button bar and save yourself the trouble of navigating through menus and dialog boxes. WordPerfect for Windows also includes an easy table generator that makes effective use of the graphical environment. You can create a table with a single mouse click and then modify column widths with simple clicks and drags.

Other highlights include an elaborate file-management utility, complete with file viewers; the ability to view and manipulate graphic images without invoking a print-preview mode; and WordPerfect Corporation's own set of printer drivers. These drivers in many cases provide faster performance than the drivers supplied with Windows.

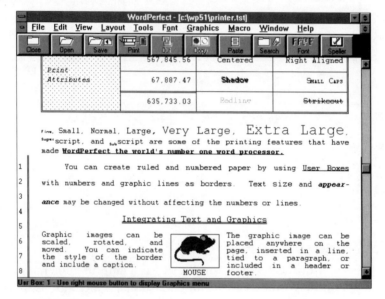

WordPerfect for Windows 5.1
WordPerfect Corporation
1555 N. Technology Way
Orem, UT 84057
(800) 451-5151
$495

SPREADSHEETS

Microsoft Excel 4.0

Microsoft Excel is the original graphical spreadsheet program. Developed first for the Macintosh, it has been available in the Windows environment since 1987.

Microsoft Excel takes advantage of the Windows environment in many ways. It allows you to keep multiple worksheets on screen in separate document windows that can be individually sized and positioned. A movable and customizable Toolbar lets you perform everyday formatting and charting tasks with simple mouse clicks. Gallery-style menus allow you to choose from more than fifty chart styles and customize charts by clicking on whatever chart element you want to change. A "drawing layer" lets you add emphasis and design to spreadsheet reports, using arrows, geometric shapes, freehand drawing, and imported graphics.

Microsoft Excel also offers a number of other unusual spreadsheet features, including worksheet outlining; the ability to create custom menu bars, menus, and dialog boxes; a flexible worksheet-consolidation command; and exceptionally sophisticated range-naming options.

Among the features added in version 4.0 are the following:

- True three-dimensional worksheets (including a "workbook" feature that automatically creates a table of contents for a stack of worksheet pages)

- A scenario manager that lets you create and switch between named alternative values for selected cells

- Full support for OLE as both server and client

- An extensive set of analysis tools (see illustration) that let you (among other things) create histograms, apply moving averages and exponential smoothing to data, create random-number sets that meet particular distribution parameters, and generate a wide variety of descriptive statistics

- The ability to create multiple named reports

- The ability to scale printouts to fit a page on any supported printer

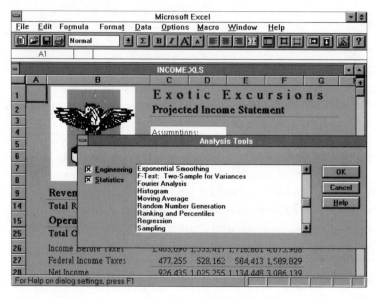

Microsoft Excel 4.0
Microsoft Corporation
One Microsoft Way
Redmond, WA 98052
(800) 426-9400
$595

Lotus 1-2-3 for Windows 1.0a

Lotus 1-2-3 for Windows is a graphical spreadsheet product with features comparable to those of Lotus 1-2-3 Release 3.1+ for the MS-DOS environment. The program allows you to build three-dimensional models consisting of up to 256
separate worksheet pages. A charting module includes a variety of three-dimensional chart types, in addition to the complete set of charting options offered by
Release 3.1+. The database component of the program gives you the ability to
access external SQL and dBASE files via Datalens drivers.

To simplify your transition from any MS-DOS version of 1-2-3, the Windows
version offers a choice of a "Classic" menu or a Windows-style set of drop-down
menus and dialog boxes. If you press the slash key, 1-2-3 for Windows pops up a
small window that replicates the menu tree of 1-2-3 Release 3.1. A similar display
of the Wysiwyg add-in's menu tree appears when you press the colon key. Thus,
if you're already a 1-2-3 user, you can access practically all of 1-2-3 for Windows'
features by means of familiar keystrokes.

Like other Windows applications from Lotus, 1-2-3 for Windows features a SmartIcon palette, with which you can tailor the program to provide shortcuts for your most-needed menu commands and macros. The SmartIcon palette can be positioned at any edge of the screen or made to float on top of your worksheet window.

Lotus 1-2-3 for Windows version 1.0a supports DDE but not OLE. Lotus has promised OLE support for its next version. Lotus 1-2-3 for Windows is shipped with Adobe Type Manager.

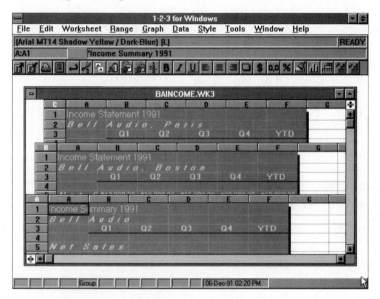

Lotus 1-2-3 for Windows 1.0a
Lotus Development Corporation
55 Cambridge Parkway
Cambridge, MA 02142
(617) 577-8500
$595

Quattro Pro for Windows 1.0

Quattro Pro for Windows is a three-dimensional implementation of Borland International's popular MS-DOS spreadsheet program. Like Lotus 1-2-3 for Windows, it allows you to build worksheet models consisting of up to 256 pages. In Quattro Pro for Windows, such a file is called a *notebook*. To assist you in navigating through a three-dimensional worksheet structure, Quattro Pro for Windows displays customizable tabs along one edge of the notebook, much like the tabs on a set of index cards or file folders. You can put a descriptive title on each tab, and then use simple mouse clicks to move between worksheet pages.

Like Microsoft Excel (but unlike 1-2-3 for Windows), Quattro Pro for Windows includes a "drawing layer" on the worksheet. You can use this layer to display graphs alongside worksheet data or to annotate data (or graphs) with drawings or imported graphic images. Quattro Pro for Windows also includes a slide-show utility and a light-table view to assist you in organizing presentations.

Quattro Pro for Windows offers a completely customizable menu system. Application developers can create their own menu bars and dialog boxes, as well as custom functions. Macros can be attached to menu commands or to buttons embedded in the worksheet.

Quattro Pro for Windows reads and writes worksheets in all Lotus formats through 1-2-3 for Windows 1.0 and Microsoft Excel formats through version 3.0. Formatting specified via the Lotus Allways and Wysiwyg add-ins is automatically converted to Quattro Pro formatting, and macros written for the Lotus MS-DOS spreadsheets run without a translation step.

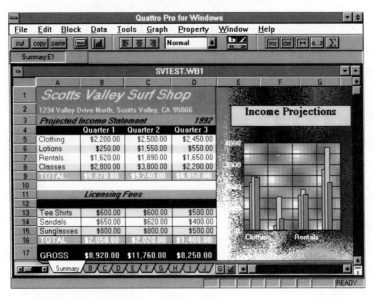

Quattro Pro for Windows 1.0
Borland International
1800 Green Hills Road
P.O. Box 660001
Scotts Valley, CA 95067
(408) 438-5300

PRESENTATION GRAPHICS

Freelance Graphics for Windows 1.0

Lotus Development Corporation's Freelance Graphics for Windows has little beyond name and file compatibility in common with the company's MS-DOS versions of Freelance Plus. The Windows product takes a much more visual approach to presentation graphics than did its popular forerunners. Rather than filling out tables and forms to create slides and handouts, you can manipulate graphic elements directly and immediately see the results of your work.

At the heart of Freelance Graphics for Windows is a set of sixty "SmartMaster" templates. These not only provide a consistent, well-designed look to a presentation; they also guide you through the process of creating slides and charts. Each SmartMaster defines a spatial layout for nine common slide formats (title screen, bullet chart, data chart, and so on), a color palette, a background style, and a set of font choices. You can override any of these elements as needed, and you can create your own SmartMasters to augment the default set.

Other highlights of Freelance Graphics for Windows include the following:

- Support for DDE and OLE, plus automatic linking to WK1, DBF, ASCII, and SYLK files

- A bidirectional outliner (changes to the outline are reflected on slides and vice versa)

- A charting module with 96 predefined chart styles

- Extensive drawing tools

- A spelling checker

- A ten-level Undo command

- 500 clip art images

- A screen-show facility

- Tight integration with the Lotus mail products, cc:Mail and Lotus Notes

- A SmartIcon palette that provides mouse shortcuts for the menu commands you use most often

Freelance Graphics for Windows is shipped with Adobe Type Manager and 13 Type 1 fonts.

Freelance Graphics for Windows Release 1.0
Lotus Development Corporation
55 Cambridge Parkway
Cambridge, MA 02142
(617) 577-8500
$495

Claris Hollywood 1.0

Hollywood is a richly featured presentation graphics program with particular strengths in the areas of data charting and text manipulation. The program includes a runtime slide-show utility, a communications module for the MAGI-Corp slide service bureau, and an extensive set of clip art. The special text effects—including rotations, shadows, kerning, and letterspacing—can be applied to any Bitstream Speedo-format font; three such fonts (Dutch, Swiss, and ITC Zapf Dingbats) are included in the package. Text can be imported directly from ASCII, WordPerfect, and DisplayWrite files. A built-in outliner facilitates creation of bullet and numbered-list slides.

Hollywood's spreadsheet module supports automatic links to Microsoft Excel and Lotus 1-2-3 (WK1) files. Data charts can include up to 24 series and 400 points per series. The program offers some unusual chart types, such as multiple pies with proportionally scaled radii.

Hollywood originally appeared in 1991 under the banner of IBM's Desktop Software unit. Marketing responsibilities for the product were transferred to Claris Corporation later in the year.

Claris Hollywood 1.0
Claris Corporation
5201 Patrick Henry Drive
Santa Clara, CA 95052
(408) 727-8227
$499

FONT MANAGERS

Adobe Type Manager 2.0

Adobe Type Manager (ATM) is a utility that generates printer and screen fonts from Type 1 PostScript font outlines. The program creates fonts on the fly, as needed. The first time you specify an ATM font in a document, you might experience a momentary delay while the font is rendered. The resulting bitmap is then stored in a memory cache that remains available for the balance of the working session. A Control Panel program lets you adjust the size of the cache (as well as turn ATM on or off).

ATM works with any printer supported by Windows, including HP LaserJets and dot-matrix printers as well as PostScript printers. LaserJet users have the option of creating bitmapped fonts in advance. These result in faster downloading but consume disk space.

ATM is shipped with 13 scalable font outlines—4 styles each of Helvetica, Times Roman, and Courier, plus a Symbol font. A large assortment of additional Type 1 fonts is available from Adobe as well as from third-party type vendors.

ATM is currently bundled with a number of Windows applications from Lotus Development Corporation. If you're considering adopting Lotus applications as well as ATM, check to see if the font manager is already included with one of the applications you're planning to buy.

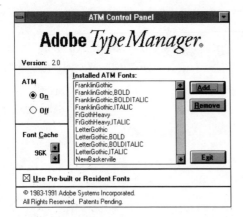

Adobe Type Manager for Windows 2.0
Adobe Systems, Inc.
1585 Charleston Road
Mountain View, CA 94039
(800) 833-6687
$99

FaceLift 2.0

FaceLift is a type manager that generates screen and printer fonts on the fly from outlines that use Bitstream's proprietary Speedo technology. The program is shipped with 13 font outlines, including Swiss (comparable to Helvetica), Dutch (comparable to Times Roman), and 4 decorative faces (Park Avenue, Cooper Black, Brush Script, and Formal Script 421). Many more fonts are available from Bitstream.

Like Adobe Type Manager, FaceLift includes a Control Panel program that allows you to turn the utility on and off and set options. Unlike ATM, FaceLift can be turned on and off for specific printers.

FaceLift, Version 2.0
Bitstream, Inc.
215 First Street
Cambridge, MA 02142
(800) 522-3668
$99

SHELLS AND UTILITIES

The Norton Desktop for Windows 1.0

The Norton Desktop for Windows combines a shell program (an alternative to both Program Manager and File Manager) with a thick packet of valuable accessories. Included in the set is a complete implementation of Norton Backup for Windows (a product also sold separately for nearly the list price of the Norton Desktop), as well as a batch language and an extremely versatile file finder.

Like Program Manager, the Norton Desktop's shell program (called Quick Access) lets you create a startup program group and assign keyboard shortcuts to program-launch icons. But it also allows you to nest program groups within one another and to copy frequently used launch icons to the desktop itself (out of particular program groups). Thus, if you use a particular set of programs every day, for example, you can make their launch icons permanent fixtures of your Windows desktop.

Like File Manager, the Norton Desktop provides a drag-and-drop printing capability. But it also includes an extensive set of file viewers, allowing you to look at spreadsheets, text, and graphics without having to open the application that created a file. Frequently used directory listings, moreover, can be stationed separately on the desktop for easy access.

The accessory suite includes a utility to recover accidentally deleted files, a utility that diagnoses disk problems, a file "shredder," a pair of calculators, a tool for launching programs or batch tasks at prescribed times, and much more.

> The Norton Desktop for Windows 1.0
> Symantec
> 10201 Torre Avenue
> Cupertino, CA 95014
> (800) 441-7234
> $149

Power Launcher 1.0

Power Launcher is a set of program-launch and resource-management tools aimed at "power users." Intended as an adjunct to, rather than a replacement for, your current Windows shell, it allows you to create "enhanced commands" for launching applications and documents. An enhanced command can specify the starting position and size of windows, modify windows' title bars (for example, you can give Solitaire a respectable title such as BUDGET.WRI), and specify that a program be launched at a particular time of day. To help you manage desktop clutter, Power Launcher also lets you hide and unhide windows and create a virtual workspace up to 64 times the dimensions of your normal screen. Power Launcher also includes its own macro recorder.

Three "Microapps" included with Power Launcher allow you to remap your keyboard, customize your mouse buttons, and create a floating toolbar of mouse shortcuts. Keyboard and mouse modifications can be tailored for specific programs or applied to your entire Windows environment.

Power Launcher 1.0
hDC Computer Corporation
6742 185th Avenue NE
Redmond, WA 98052
(206) 885-5550
$99.95

ProKey for Windows 1.0

ProKey for Windows is a versatile replacement for the Windows Recorder accessory. Unlike Windows' native macro recorder, ProKey allows you to edit macros and provides a trace mode to help you do so. ProKey macros can also include delays and user prompts and can accept user input (of fixed or variable length) during playback. Macros can be executed via hot keys or by clicking on a floating script palette.

ProKey also provides a Clipboard alternative to facilitate macro-driven cutting and pasting. Unlike the built-in Windows Clipboard, in which each new entry replaces the current contents, ProKey's offers multiple "vaults." Thus, with a

ProKey macro, you could grab data from several different sources, and then paste them as a unit into a target application.

ProKey for Windows 1.0
RoseSoft, Inc.
P.O. Box 70337
Bellevue, WA 98007
(206) 562-0225
$99.00

HOME AND SMALL BUSINESS ACCOUNTING

Microsoft Money 1.0

Microsoft Money is an easy-to-use single-entry bookkeeping and check-printing system suitable for home or small-business use. It allows you to track multiple checking, credit-card, asset, and liability accounts. Transactions can be entered either in a ledger or check format. A "SmartFill" feature compares the entry you're currently making against previous transactions and greatly reduces the time and effort required to record recurrent transactions. A "SmartReconcile" feature points out suspicious entries (misplaced decimal points, for example) to help you ferret out reconciliation errors.

Money also allows you to record future transactions (bills to be paid on specified dates, for example), prints checks automatically, and generates a variety of budget, income, and expense reports.

423

Microsoft Money 1.0
Microsoft Corporation
One Microsoft Way
Redmond, WA 98052
(800) 426-9400
$69.95

Quicken for Windows 1.0

Quicken for Windows is a Windows implementation of the best-selling small-business accounting system for MS-DOS. Like its MS-DOS counterpart, it allows you to keep track of multiple checking, credit-card, asset, and liability accounts; print checks automatically; generate a multiplicity of useful reports; record future transactions; be reminded of bills due; and more. Like Microsoft Money, Quicken for Windows memorizes prior transactions for easy reentry and includes an intelligent reconciliation troubleshooter. Unlike Microsoft Money, Quicken for Windows also has a built-in interface with the CheckFree electronic bill-paying system, supports DDE links with other Windows applications (such as Microsoft Excel or Lotus 1-2-3 for Windows), and offers two levels of password protection.

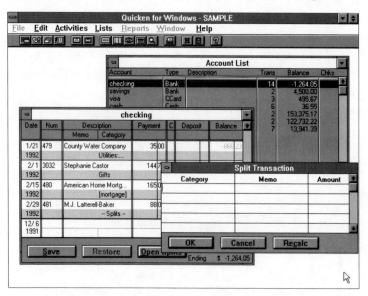

Quicken for Windows 1.0
Intuit
P.O. Box 3014
Menlo Park, CA 94026
(800) 624-8742
$69.95

18

Running Non-Windows Applications

Many of the best programs in all major categories of application software are now written specifically for Windows. As time passes, you might find yourself moving more and more toward the exclusive use of such Windows applications.

But if you're like many other Windows users, you probably already have a major investment in programs that were written for the standard MS-DOS environment. Such non-Windows applications can be run right alongside your Windows programs. You can switch between them using the same commands you use to switch between Windows programs, and you can transfer data between them with the Windows Clipboard.

In this chapter, we'll focus on the techniques for running non-Windows applications in the Windows environment.

RUNNING NON-WINDOWS PROGRAMS IN STANDARD MODE

If you're running Windows in standard mode, your use of non-Windows applications is subject to a few limitations:

- A non-Windows application can be run in the full screen only.

- Other applications are suspended when a non-Windows application is running.

- Your non-Windows application is suspended when you switch back to Windows or to a different non-Windows application.

- Data can be copied from a non-Windows application to the Clipboard only a screenful at a time.

For more about the use of the Clipboard with non-Windows applications in standard mode, see Chapter 8.

RUNNING NON-WINDOWS APPLICATIONS IN 386 ENHANCED MODE

If you're using Windows in 386 enhanced mode, you can run non-Windows applications either in a window or full screen. If you choose to run a program in a window, you have the advantage of being able to see two or more programs at the same time. But your non-Windows programs run more quickly and use less memory when run full screen.

 KEYBOARD TIP: You can switch between full-screen and windowed display at any time while running a non-Windows program by pressing Alt-Enter.

Windows' 386 enhanced mode provides some additional flexibility for non-Windows applications:

- You can run a non-Windows application in the foreground or background. In the background, your non-Windows program continues to run even while you're working in another application. You can start a sorting or indexing operation, for example, and then switch back to Windows to work on something else until the operation has finished.

- You can control the relative amount of your computer's processing time that's devoted to each individual non-Windows application.

- You can copy data from your non-Windows program to the Windows Clipboard without having to copy an entire screen.

- You can set up shortcut keys that make it easier to switch between several running applications.

- You can use a mouse in a non-Windows application whether it's running full screen or in a window. This feature, new in Windows 3.1, makes some non-Windows applications "feel" like true Windows applications. See "Mouse Support in a Windowed Display," later in this chapter.

- You can choose among several fonts when displaying non-Windows applications in a window, allowing you to strike a balance between legibility and screen-space conservation. See "Changing Fonts in a Windowed Display," later in this chapter.

STARTING A NON-WINDOWS APPLICATION

To run a non-Windows application, you can do any of the following:

- Create a Program Manager program item for the non-Windows application, if the Setup program hasn't already done that for you. Then double-click the program-item icon.

- Choose the File menu's Run command in either Program Manager or File Manager.

- Double-click a filename in one of File Manager's directory windows.

 WINDOWS TIP: You can also run a non-Windows application by double-clicking the MS-DOS Prompt program-item icon in Program Manager. This action puts the MS-DOS command prompt on your screen, allowing you to run your program the same way you would outside Windows. For more about this approach to running non-Windows applications, see "Running Non-Windows Applications from the MS-DOS Prompt," later in this chapter.

PROGRAM INFORMATION FILES (PIFS)

When you set up a program item for a non-Windows application, or when you start such an application with the File Run command, you need to give Windows the name of an executable file for your application. That name can be either the full name of the file you would use to run the program outside of Windows (123.EXE, for example, for Lotus 1-2-3 Release 2.3) or the name of a Program Information File (PIF) set up for your application.

A PIF is a special file that provides Windows with certain details about your program—how much memory it needs, how it uses certain resources (the screen, your communications ports, and the keyboard), what directory should be current when the program begins to run, and so on. Your Windows package comes supplied with PIFs for many popular non-Windows applications. If you chose to let the Setup program install non-Windows applications for you, program items for some—perhaps all—of your non-Windows applications are in a program-group window called Applications. Each of those icons was created by Setup and associated with one of the PIFs that came in your Windows package.

You can customize those standard PIFs if you like, and you can also create additional PIFs for other non-Windows applications. To do this, you use a program called PIF Editor that's included in your Windows package. Much of the remainder of this chapter is devoted to a tour of PIF Editor and your options for creating and customizing PIFs.

If the program item you use to start your non-Windows program is associated with an MS-DOS executable file (an EXE, COM, or BAT file) rather than with a PIF, Windows runs your program using a default Program Information File. The default file is called _DEFAULT.PIF. You can use PIF Editor to modify the contents of _DEFAULT.PIF the same way you would edit any other PIF.

For example, if you're using Windows in 386 enhanced mode and you want to run most of your non-Windows programs in a window, you can arrange that by making a minor modification to _DEFAULT.PIF.

INSTALLING OTHER PREDEFINED PIFS

Some non-Windows software packages are supplied by their vendors with PIFs to make it easier for you to run these programs under Windows. If you buy a program that comes with a PIF, copy the PIF to your hard disk and set up a program item to run the application from its PIF. (See Chapter 5 for information about creating a new program item.) You might find it easiest to store the PIF in your Windows subdirectory, because that's where Windows put any PIFs that were installed by the Setup program. But you can store a PIF in any subdirectory; be sure the Command Line text box of the Program Item Properties dialog box lists the path of the directory in which you store your PIF.

If you received a PIF with your non-Windows software package, chances are it's set up to run your program correctly. But, of course, you can modify that PIF with PIF Editor if you need to.

USING TWO OR MORE PIFS FOR THE SAME APPLICATION

If you run some of your programs with different start-up options, you might find it convenient to create a separate PIF for each way you use your program.

For example, if you use the non-Windows word processor Microsoft Word, you might create three separate Word PIFs:

- One PIF to start the program with no command-line options

- Another PIF to start the program with the /L option, which reloads the last document file you worked with

- A third PIF to start the program and prompt you for the name of a document file—or for another command-line option

You could create a separate program-item icon for each of these PIFs.

STARTING PIF EDITOR

You'll find a program-item icon for PIF Editor in your Main program group (if you haven't moved it). To start PIF Editor, double-click that program-item icon. Or choose the Run command on Program Manager's or File Manager's File menu, and type *pifedit.exe*.

Creating a PIF is a matter of filling out and saving a form, but the information you supply to create a PIF depends on the Windows operating mode you're using.

 WINDOWS TIP: You can get detailed help with any PIF setting by selecting that setting in the PIF Editor window and pressing the F1 key.

USING PIF EDITOR'S FILE COMMANDS

PIF Editor's File menu has the usual New, Open, Save, and Save As commands. When you're ready to save a new PIF for the first time, choose Save As. When you want to edit an existing PIF, choose Open, make your changes to the file, and then choose Save (to resave it under its current name) or Save As (to assign a new name).

Note that you must save an edited PIF and restart the associated application before your changes can take effect.

EDITING _DEFAULT.PIF

When you run a non-Windows application from its executable file (an EXE, COM, or BAT file) instead of running it from a PIF, Windows uses the settings in _DEFAULT.PIF. To change these settings, use PIF Editor to edit _DEFAULT.PIF.

This PIF is like any other except for one idiosyncrasy: You must enter a "dummy" filename in the Program Filename text box. It doesn't matter what filename you put here (as long as it's a legal MS-DOS name), but you can't leave the line blank.

CREATING A PIF TO RUN IN STANDARD MODE

In standard mode, PIF Editor's initial display looks like this:

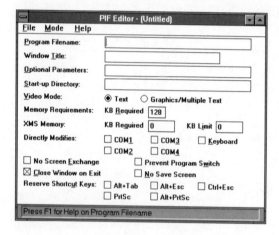

Now let's look at each of the options for creating a standard-mode PIF. (If you run Windows exclusively in 386 enhanced mode, you don't need this information. You can skip ahead to "Creating a PIF to Run in 386 Enhanced Mode.")

Program Filename

In the Program Filename text box, type the complete path and filename of your application's executable file. Be sure to include the extension. The extension must be BAT, COM, or EXE. The Program Filename text box is the one PIF Editor box you must fill out; PIF Editor won't let you save a PIF without appropriate information in this box.

You can omit the path of your program's executable file if that file is stored in your Windows directory, the Windows directory's SYSTEM subdirectory, or in any directory included in your MS-DOS path.

Window Title

When you switch from a non-Windows application back to your Windows desktop, your application appears as an icon. The identifying text under the icon will be whatever you type in PIF Editor's Window Title text box. If you leave this box blank, Windows uses the name of your program's executable file.

> **NOTE:** *The Description setting in Program Manager's Program Item Properties dialog box overrides the Window Title setting. Therefore, if you have a program item defined for this application, the Window Title setting appears only if you start this application by using the File Run command or double-clicking the PIF filename in File Manager.*

Optional Parameters

In the Optional Parameters text box, you can include any filenames or other parameters that you would type when starting your non-Windows program under MS-DOS. For example, if you typically start Lotus 1-2-3 with a SET file named ASCII, you might put 123.EXE in the Program Filename text box and ASCII in the Optional Parameters box. Running this PIF would then be equivalent to typing

    123.EXE ASCII

at the MS-DOS command prompt.

 WINDOWS TIP: If you want to be prompted for parameters each time you start a non-Windows application, put a question mark in the Optional Parameters box.

> **NOTE:** *If you enter anything after the program's filename in the Command Line box of Program Manager's Program Item Properties dialog box (even a space character), the Optional Parameters setting is ignored.*

Start-up Directory

You can use the Start-up Directory text box to have Windows make a specified directory current as soon as it starts your non-Windows application. That way, you can automatically save documents in the directory you name.

If you save a given application's documents in different directories depending on the kind of document you're creating (personal correspondence in one directory and business correspondence in another, for example), you might want to create several PIFs for the same application—one for each directory you use.

Some programs must be run from the directory in which their files are stored. To run a program of this kind, you must supply the name of the program's directory in the Start-up Directory box.

If you leave the Start-up Directory box blank, the directory that's current when you start your non-Windows application remains current after the program starts. For example, if the current directory is C:\WINDOWS when you run QUICKEN.PIF, and your PIF for Quicken doesn't specify a start-up directory, C:\WINDOWS will still be the current directory when Quicken starts.

Some non-Windows applications—Microsoft Word 5.5 and Lotus 1-2-3 Release 2.3, for example—include commands to specify a default data directory. The Start-up Directory box in your PIF does not override these default data directory commands.

NOTE: *The Working Directory setting in Program Manager's Program Item Properties dialog box overrides the Start-up Directory setting in PIF Editor.*

Video Mode

On the Video Mode line, choose Text if your application runs only in text mode. Choose Graphics/Multiple Text if it runs in graphics mode or if it uses multiple "screen pages" in text mode.

When you switch from a non-Windows application to a different non-Windows application or back to the Windows desktop, Windows saves the contents of your screen so it can restore your context when you switch back. Windows has to reserve a certain amount of memory for this purpose. Saving a graphics-mode screen takes considerably more memory than saving a text-mode screen, so if you select Graphics/Multiple Text on the Video Mode line, less memory will be available to your program.

If you're not sure which mode to choose, try Text first. If you select the wrong mode, you'll be able to run your program, but you won't be able to switch to another program. If you press Alt-Tab, Alt-Esc, or Ctrl-Esc and nothing happens, try the following:

1. Quit your program.

2. Return to PIF Editor.

3. Use PIF Editor's File Open command to reopen your PIF.

4. Change the Video Mode setting to Graphics/Multiple Text.

5. Use the File Save command to resave your PIF.

6. Restart your program and try again.

Memory Requirements

The Memory Requirements: KB Required box tells Windows the bare minimum amount (in kilobytes) of memory your program must have before it can start. Windows always allocates as much memory as it can to your program, but if the amount available is less than the amount specified in this box, it won't even try to run your program. (Instead you'll get an insufficient-memory message from Windows.)

If you're not sure what to put in this box, try a relatively low value first. The default is 128 KB, and that's not a bad place to start. If you don't get an insufficient-memory message from Windows but your program doesn't run, increase the KB Required value and try again.

Note that minimum memory requirement stated by your software vendor (on the outside of the original package or in the documentation) is likely to be higher than the number you need to put in your PIF. That's because the value stated by the vendor often includes (in addition to memory used by the program) memory used by the operating system. In your PIF, you need to state only the minimum amount of memory required by the program itself.

XMS Memory

The XMS Memory boxes (KB Required and KB Limit) tell how much *extended* memory Windows needs to allocate to your application. You should leave these values set at 0 unless your non-Windows application can use extended memory. Most non-Windows programs cannot.

A few non-Windows programs—Lotus 1-2-3 Release 3.1 is an example—*require* extended memory. When creating a PIF for this kind of application, specify the minimum amount of extended memory needed to run the program in the KB Required box. In the KB Limit box, specify the maximum amount of extended memory that you want to allocate to your program. If you don't want to set a limit on the amount of extended memory given to your program, put −1 in the KB Limit box.

In standard mode (and 386 enhanced mode), Windows itself uses extended memory. So if you put too high a value (or –1) in the KB Limit box, you might rob your Windows programs (including Program Manager) of memory they need to run smoothly. If you find your Windows applications moving at a glacial pace while you run a non-Windows program that uses extended memory, quit your non-Windows program, reduce the KB Limit value in its PIF, and try again.

Directly Modifies

The check boxes in the Directly Modifies section tell Windows whether your program is "well behaved" in its use of your computer's serial ports and keyboard. A well-behaved program is one that communicates with these resources using standard MS-DOS procedures. Many programs are "ill-behaved" programs, which means they bypass standard procedures in an effort to gain performance.

Nearly all non-Windows programs directly modify the hardware that controls your video display. PIF Editor assumes your program does this. But only a few programs communicate directly with serial ports or the keyboard.

If you happen to run two communications programs at the same time, both of which interact directly with the same serial port, you could transmit or receive garbled data—or you could lose data in transmission. If you find yourself in these circumstances, put a check in the appropriate Directly Modifies box (COM1, for example, if the trouble occurs with programs using your first serial port). Windows then arbitrates the use of that port; while one program is using it, others will not be allowed to.

If you run a non-Windows program that communicates directly with the keyboard, you won't be able to switch from your program to another non-Windows program or to the Windows desktop. Windows won't know you want to switch, because the keystrokes you press (Alt-Tab, Alt-Esc, or Ctrl-Esc) will be intercepted by your program.

If one of your non-Windows programs falls into this category, you should put a check in the Keyboard check box. You still won't be able to switch from this program, but you'll free up memory that Windows otherwise would have reserved to allow you to switch. (To switch to another window, you'll have to quit this program.)

Before putting a check in the Keyboard box, however, be sure you haven't checked the Prevent Program Switch box or any boxes in the Reserve Shortcut Keys section. (These options are described below.)

No Screen Exchange

If you don't mind foregoing the opportunity to copy information from your non-Windows application to the Windows Clipboard, you can save some memory by putting a check in the No Screen Exchange check box. If you sometimes find yourself low on memory and you seldom need to copy data from this program to the Clipboard, you might want to create two PIFs—one with the box checked, one without. Use the latter PIF only on those occasions when you'll need the Clipboard.

Prevent Program Switch

The Prevent Program Switch check box provides another way to be frugal with memory. Normally, Windows sets aside enough memory to preserve what's on your screen when you switch away from a non-Windows program. Putting a check in this box makes that memory available for use in your application, but you'll have to quit your program to switch back to Windows or to a different non-Windows application.

Close Window On Exit

If the Close Window On Exit box is checked (it is, by default), Windows takes you straight back to the desktop when you quit your program. If you remove the check from this box, Windows leaves your program's last display on screen when you exit; then when you press any key, the display is removed and Windows returns you to the desktop.

 WINDOWS TIP: If you're having trouble getting a non-Windows program to start, try removing the check from the Close Window On Exit check box. Your program might display an error message when it fails to start, and Windows might clear that message from the screen too quickly for you to read it.

No Save Screen

Like Prevent Program Switch (described above), the No Save Screen option conserves the amount of memory that Windows normally uses to preserve your non-Windows program's display. But with No Save Screen checked, you can still switch away from a non-Windows program. When you switch back, however, it will be up to your program to restore the state of its own display. You should use this option only with programs that are capable of saving and restoring their own displays.

Reserve Shortcut Keys

Normally, if you press Alt-Tab, Alt-Esc, Ctrl-Esc, Alt-PrtSc, or PrtSc while working in a non-Windows application, Windows "intercepts" those keystrokes and treats them as commands to switch applications, invoke Task List, or copy a screen to the Windows Clipboard. If you need to use any of those keystroke combinations in your application, put checks in the appropriate check boxes next to Reserve Shortcut Keys.

For example, if you want to be able to use the PrtSc key to print whatever your application puts on screen, put a check in the PrtSc box. That way you retain the normal MS-DOS function of the PrtSc key while working in your non-Windows application (and you still can press Alt-PrtSc to copy the screen's contents to the Windows Clipboard).

CREATING A PIF TO RUN IN 386 ENHANCED MODE

To create a PIF for 386 enhanced mode, you need to fill out a two-page form. The following dialog box appears when you invoke PIF Editor.

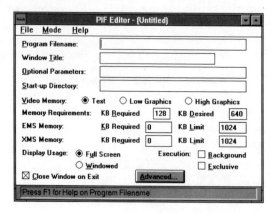

A second dialog box appears when you click the Advanced button.

Program Filename

In the Program Filename text box, type the complete path and filename of your application's executable file. Be sure to include the extension. The extension must be BAT, COM, or EXE. The Program Filename text box is the one PIF Editor box you must fill out; PIF Editor won't let you save a PIF without appropriate information in this box.

You can omit the path of your program's executable file if that file is stored in your Windows directory, the Windows directory's SYSTEM subdirectory, or in any directory included in your MS-DOS path.

Window Title

In the Window Title text box, type a brief descriptive title for your application. This title appears in the title bar of your application's window (if you run it in a window) or below its icon when the application is minimized on your desktop.

If you leave the Window Title box empty, Windows uses the name of your program's executable file.

> **NOTE:** *The Description setting in Program Manager's Program Item Properties dialog box overrides the Window Title setting. Therefore, if you have a program item defined for this application, the Window Title setting appears only if you start this application by using the File Run command or double-clicking the PIF filename in File Manager.*

Optional Parameters

In the Optional Parameters text box, you can include any filenames or other parameters that you would type when starting your non-Windows program under MS-DOS. For example, if you typically start Lotus 1-2-3 with a SET file named ASCII, you might put 123.EXE in the Program Filename text box and ASCII in the Optional Parameters box. Running this PIF would then be equivalent to typing

    123.EXE ASCII

at the MS-DOS command prompt.

 WINDOWS TIP: If you want to be prompted for parameters each time you start a non-Windows application, put a question mark in the Optional Parameters box.

> **NOTE:** *If you enter anything after the program's filename in the Command Line box of Program Manager's Program Item Properties dialog box (even a space character), the Optional Parameters setting is ignored.*

Start-up Directory

You can use the Start-up Directory text box to have Windows make a specified directory current as soon as it starts your non-Windows application. That way, you can automatically save documents in the directory you name.

If you save a given application's documents in different directories depending on the kind of document you're creating (personal correspondence in one directory and business correspondence in another, for example), you might want to create several PIFs for the same application—one for each directory you use.

Some programs must be run from the directory in which their files are stored. To run a program of this kind, you must supply the name of the program's directory on the Start-up Directory line.

If you leave the Start-up Directory box blank, the directory that's current when you start your non-Windows application remains current after the program starts. For example, if the current directory is C:\WINDOWS when you run QUICKEN.PIF, and your PIF for Quicken doesn't specify a start-up directory, C:\WINDOWS is still the current directory when Quicken starts.

Some non-Windows applications—Microsoft Word 5.5 and Lotus 1-2-3 Release 2.3, for example—include commands to specify a default data directory. The Start-up Directory box in your PIF does not override these default data directory commands.

> **NOTE:** *The Working Directory setting in Program Manager's Program Item Properties dialog box overrides the Start-up Directory setting in PIF Editor.*

Video Memory

Whenever you start a non-Windows application, Windows sets aside a certain amount of memory in which to "capture" the contents of your application's display should you decide to switch to a different application. Capturing the screen's contents this way allows Windows to restore the display instantly when you switch back to the original application.

The Video Memory line lets you tell Windows how much memory it should initially set aside for this purpose. Choose the display mode in which your program begins. If your program starts up in text mode, choose Text. If it starts in a low-resolution graphics mode, choose Low Graphics. If it starts in a high-resolution graphics mode, choose High Graphics.

If your program starts in graphics mode, but you're not sure whether it's low-resolution graphics or high-resolution graphics, choose High Graphics—unless your computer uses a single-graphics-mode display adapter such as a Color/Graphics Adapter (CGA) or Hercules Graphics Adapter. For these display types, choose Low Graphics.

If you switch from one display mode to another while working in an application, Windows adjusts its reserve of video memory appropriately. It allocates additional memory if more is needed (unless no more is available), and it releases memory if less is needed (unless you select the Retain Video Memory option, described below).

If you switch from text mode to any graphics mode, and Windows doesn't display your screen correctly, you probably need to allocate more video memory when your program starts. To do this, reopen your PIF and select Low Graphics or High Graphics. Then try again.

 WINDOWS TIP: Some high-resolution screen drivers do not permit the windowed display of a non-Windows application running in graphics mode. If you're running in 386 enhanced mode, and you've set the Video Memory option in your non-Windows program's PIF to High Graphics, but you still get error messages when you try to display the program in a window, you probably need to switch to a lower-resolution display driver—such as the standard 640 × 480 VGA driver shipped with your Windows package.

Memory Requirements: KB Required

The Memory Requirements: KB Required box tells Windows the bare minimum amount (in kilobytes) of conventional memory your program must have before it can start. Windows always allocates as much memory as it can to your program (up to the limit specified in the KB Desired box), but if the amount available is less than the amount specified in KB Required, it won't even try to run your program. (You'll get an insufficient-memory message from Windows.)

If you're not sure what to put in this box, try a relatively low value first. The default value is 128 KB, and that's not a bad place to start. If you don't get an insufficient-memory message from Windows but your program doesn't run, increase the KB Required value and try again.

Note that minimum memory requirement stated by your software vendor (on the outside of the original package or in the documentation) is likely to be higher than the number you need to put in your PIF. That's because the value stated by the vendor often includes (in addition to memory used by the program) memory used by the operating system. In your PIF, you need to state only the minimum amount of memory required by the program itself.

Memory Requirements: KB Desired

In the KB Desired box, enter the maximum amount of conventional memory your application is likely to need. Windows allocates this amount if it can.

The default KB Desired value is 640, which tells Windows to give your application all available conventional memory. If you need to conserve conventional memory for other applications, try reducing this number.

A value of −1 in the KB Desired box is equivalent to a value of 640; it's another way of telling Windows to give your program all available conventional memory.

EMS Memory

The two EMS Memory boxes let you allocate expanded memory. Windows doesn't normally use expanded memory when it's running in 386 enhanced mode, but some non-Windows programs require it. If your program won't start without a certain amount of expanded memory, specify that amount in the KB Required box. Windows then generates an error message if less than the specified amount is available when you start your program.

In the KB Limit box, specify the maximum amount of expanded memory you want your application to have. Put −1 in this box if you don't want to set an upper limit.

It's best to specify some maximum amount, because certain applications will take all they can get, whether they need it or not. Putting −1 in the KB Limit box might deprive other applications of memory they need to start or run effectively.

For more information about using expanded memory with non-Windows applications, see "Running Non-Windows Applications that Use Expanded Memory," later in this chapter.

XMS Memory

The XMS Memory options allow you to allocate extended memory to your non-Windows application. These options work exactly like the EMS Memory options described in the preceding section.

Put a nonzero amount in the KB Required box if your non-Windows application can take advantage of extended memory. In the KB Limit box, enter the maximum amount of extended memory you want your application to have (put −1 in this box if you don't want to set a limit).

Display Usage

The Display Usage section of the PIF is where you tell Windows whether you want to start your application in full-screen mode or in a window. Pick the option you're likely to use most of the time.

Running an application in a window uses more memory and is slower, but it allows you to see several windows at once, and it makes it easier to cut and paste information between applications.

Execution

Your choices in the Execution section determine whether other programs can run while you're working in your non-Windows application and whether your non-Windows application continues to run when you switch away from it. The Background and Exclusive options are check boxes; you can select either, both, or neither.

If you select neither option, other programs continue to run while you work in your non-Windows application. Your non-Windows application will be suspended when you switch away from it.

If you select Background only, other programs continue to run while you work in your non-Windows application. Your non-Windows application continues to run when you switch away from it (unless the application you switch to uses the Exclusive option).

If you select Exclusive and don't select Background, all other programs are suspended while you work in your non-Windows application. Your non-Windows application is suspended when you switch away from it.

If you select both Background and Exclusive, all other programs are suspended while you work in your non-Windows application. Your non-Windows application continues to run when you switch away from it.

To get the best possible performance from your non-Windows application, choose Exclusive (with or without Background) and run your non-Windows application in full-screen display.

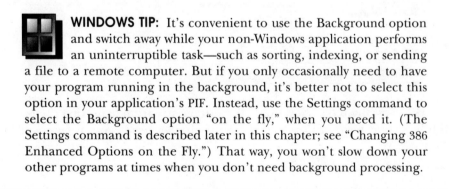

WINDOWS TIP: It's convenient to use the Background option and switch away while your non-Windows application performs an uninterruptible task—such as sorting, indexing, or sending a file to a remote computer. But if you only occasionally need to have your program running in the background, it's better not to select this option in your application's PIF. Instead, use the Settings command to select the Background option "on the fly," when you need it. (The Settings command is described later in this chapter; see "Changing 386 Enhanced Options on the Fly.") That way, you won't slow down your other programs at times when you don't need background processing.

Close Window On Exit

If the Close Window On Exit box is checked (it is, by default), Windows takes you straight back to the desktop when you quit your program. If you remove the check from this box, Windows leaves your program's last display on screen when you exit; then when you press any key, the display is removed and Windows returns you to the desktop.

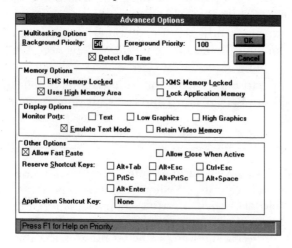

WINDOWS TIP: If you're having trouble getting a non-Windows program to start, try removing the check from the Close Window On Exit check box. Your program might display an error message when it fails to start, and Windows might clear that message from the screen too quickly for you to read it.

Advanced Options

When you click the Advanced button, PIF Editor presents a dialog box with the following additional options.

Don't let the term "Advanced" discourage you from exploring the options on this second page of the PIF form. Your choices here can have a significant impact on the way your non-Windows application performs. And at least one option on this page, the Application Shortcut Key, is not technical or advanced in any sense; it's a simple convenience feature.

Setting Multitasking Options

Your choices in the Background Priority and Foreground Priority boxes affect the performance of your non-Windows application. The Background Priority number is relevant only when your program is running in the background; if you never run it in the background, you don't need to be concerned with this box. The Foreground Priority number affects the performance of your application when it's running in the foreground—that is, when you're working directly with it in the active window.

In both cases, the higher the number, the more time Windows spends processing your application. But to see exactly what these numbers mean, we need to step back and take a broader look at how Windows apportions time among the various Windows and non-Windows applications you have running.

When you run several applications at once under Windows, your computer cycles through each application in turn, giving a brief moment of its time to the first program, then a brief moment to the next, and so on around. The process of switching applications occurs so quickly that the computer appears to be running all programs simultaneously. The time that the computer is actually running a given program during each cycle is that program's *timeslice*.

Each non-Windows application gets one timeslice, the duration of which is governed by the settings in the Multitasking Options section of the application's PIF. All your Windows applications *together* get another timeslice, the duration of which is governed by settings in the 386 Enhanced section of Control Panel. Thus, for example, if you happen to be running Program Manager, Terminal, Write, Lotus 1-2-3 Release 2.3, and WordPerfect 5.1, Windows has three timeslices to calculate—one for the three Windows programs (Program Manager, Terminal, and Write), one for 1-2-3, and one for WordPerfect.

The default priority values for non-Windows applications are 50 when the program is running in the background and 100 when it's running in the foreground. The illustration on the following page, from the 386 Enhanced section of Control Panel, shows the default priority values for Windows programs—50 in background and 100 in foreground.

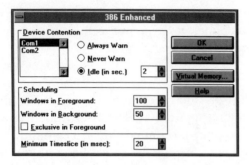

These numbers specify *relative* timeslice priorities. If WordPerfect has a priority of 50 when running in the background, for example, that doesn't mean its timeslice lasts 50 milliseconds, 50 nanoseconds, or 50 weeks. It means that Word-Perfect's timeslice is the same length as that of any other background application with a background priority of 50, half as long as any program with a priority of 100, and so on.

The next illustration shows three of the many possible ways in which processing time might be divided between some Windows applications, 1-2-3, and WordPerfect.

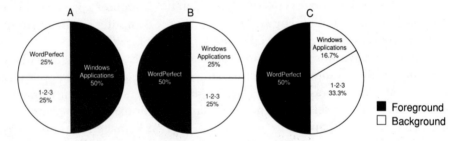

Graph A shows the Windows applications running in the foreground, with all foreground and background priorities at their default settings. The foreground value for the Windows programs is 100, and the background values for 1-2-3 and WordPerfect are both 50. The total of the priority values is 200, and because the Windows programs' foreground priority is 100, the Windows programs are receiving one-half (100/200) of the computer's time. Because both 1-2-3 and WordPerfect have background priority values of 50, they're each getting one-fourth (50/200) of the computer's time.

In the second scenario, shown in Graph B, the default priority values are retained, but WordPerfect is now running in the foreground. The total of the priority values is again 200 (50 for 1-2-3, 50 for the Windows applications, and 100 for WordPerfect). WordPerfect's share of the computer's time is now 50 percent (100/200), and 1-2-3 and the Windows programs each get a quarter share.

Graph C shows how the balance would change if WordPerfect's foreground priority were increased from 100 to 150 and 1-2-3's background priority were raised from 50 to 100. With these new settings, the total of the priority values is 300 (50 for Windows, 100 for 1-2-3, and 150 for WordPerfect). WordPerfect now gets half (150/300) of the computer's time; 1-2-3 gets one-third (100/300), and the Windows programs get one-sixth (50/300).

You can juggle these background and foreground priorities any way you want. To adjust the priorities for a non-Windows program, simply change the numbers in the Background Priority and Foreground Priority boxes on the "advanced" page of the application's PIF. To adjust the priorities for the Windows applications, open Control Panel, choose 386 Enhanced, and change the numbers in the Scheduling section of the dialog box.

 WINDOWS TIP: If you don't like the way a non-Windows application is performing while you're working in it, you can increase its foreground priority without modifying its PIF. See "Changing 386 Enhanced Options on the Fly," later in this chapter.

The Scheduling section of Control Panel's 386 Enhanced dialog box has two other options—Exclusive In Foreground and Minimum Timeslice—that affect performance when several applications are running at once.

Exclusive In Foreground

If you put a check in the Exclusive In Foreground check box, Windows handles non-Windows applications the same way it does in standard mode; it suspends each non-Windows program as soon as you switch away from it.

Minimum Timeslice

The Minimum Timeslice option doesn't change the relative amount of time the computer spends with each foreground and background application, but it does determine the frequency with which the computer switches from one program to another. Switching programs carries a small amount of overhead, so the more often you switch, the less time there is for any given program. On the other hand, the more frequently you switch, the smoother the whole system operates. The default minimum timeslice, 20 milliseconds, strikes an effective balance between smoothness and performance, but you might want to experiment with higher and lower values.

Detect Idle Time

The Detect Idle Time check box, in the Multitasking Options section of the PIF Editor Advanced Options dialog box, is normally selected (checked). This allows Windows to shorten a non-Windows application's timeslice when it's running in the background and nothing appears to be going on. It's best to leave this option selected except under unusual circumstances. If your program is taking forever to complete some operation in the background, try removing the check from the Detect Idle Time box. It's possible that Windows thinks the program is idle when it really isn't.

Setting Memory Options

Uses High Memory Area

The "high memory area" is a 64-KB block of extended memory used by some memory-resident utility programs and a few application programs. If this area is not in use when Windows starts, Windows will make it available to those non-Windows applications that request it—provided you have not removed the check from the Uses High Memory Area check box in the application's PIF. It's best to leave this option in its default setting—checked.

Locking Memory to Prevent Swapping

When memory becomes full, Windows normally "swaps" data that isn't currently being used from memory to your hard disk. This makes room for new data, allowing your hard disk to become an extension of your computer's random-access memory.

Three check boxes in the Memory Options area of your PIF allow you to prevent the swapping of data to your hard disk. Check the EMS Memory Locked box if you don't want Windows to swap from expanded memory, the XMS Memory Locked box if you don't want Windows to swap from extended memory, or the Lock Application Memory box if you don't want data swapped from conventional memory.

Putting a check in any of these boxes might improve the performance of the application whose PIF you're modifying. But this action is likely to diminish the performance of your system as a whole.

Setting Display Options

Monitor Ports

The Monitor Ports options tell Windows to monitor changes a non-Windows application makes directly to any input or output port that affect the video display. This helps Windows restore the exact appearance of your screen when you switch away from a non-Windows application, and then switch back again. The default setting on this line (nothing selected) is appropriate for most applications and most systems. If your display adapter is an EGA, however, you should check High Graphics.

If you encounter problems restoring a screen's appearance when you switch to its window, try changing the settings of the Monitor Ports options. Select the option that matches the video mode of the offending application. Select Text if the application is in text mode, Low Graphics if it uses low-resolution graphics, or High Graphics if it uses high-resolution graphics.

Emulate Text Mode

A check in the Emulate Text Mode box allows text to be displayed faster than if it is not selected. Therefore, you should leave a check in this check box unless text appears garbled on your screen, the cursor appears in the wrong location, or your application fails to run at all. In any of these events, remove the check and try again.

Retain Video Memory

Putting a check in the Retain Video Memory check box prevents Windows from releasing display memory when you switch from graphics mode to text mode, or from a high-resolution graphics mode to a lower-resolution mode. Normally, you want Windows to release this memory (so you don't want to select this option). But if you're running right at the edge of your system's memory resources and you want to be sure the program you're working with always has enough display memory, try selecting the Retain Video Memory option.

Setting Other Options

Allow Fast Paste

A check in the Allow Fast Paste check box enables Windows to transfer text from the Clipboard to your application at the fastest possible rate. This option works for most applications. If you find your program loses data when you use the Paste command, go back to its PIF and remove the check from Allow Fast Paste.

Allow Close When Active

If you try to quit Windows with unsaved work in an open Windows application, Windows warns you to save, so you don't lose your work. It can't do this, however, if you try to quit Windows when you have unsaved work in an open non-Windows application.

Normally, therefore, Windows simply doesn't allow you to quit if any non-Windows applications are still running. Instead it prompts you to close your non-Windows programs, and then use the Exit or Close command again.

If you put a check in the Allow Close When Active check box, you will be permitted to quit Windows when the affected application is still running. Checking the Allow Close When Active box also enables the Close command on the application's Control menu. You gain a little convenience, perhaps, by doing this, but you incur a risk: In a hurry to shut your system down, you might forget to save the work you just did in your non-Windows application. It's best to leave this option in its default state—unchecked—unless the application is not one in which you create data.

> **WARNING:** *Some applications do not close the file when you save your work; in these applications you can lose data even if you have "saved" your file. So we repeat: Use the Allow Close When Active option only for applications in which you do not create data.*

Reserve Shortcut Keys

Normally, if you press Alt-Tab, Alt-Esc, Ctrl-Esc, Alt-PrtSc, PrtSc, Alt-Spacebar, or Alt-Enter while working in a non-Windows application, Windows "intercepts" those keystrokes and treats them as commands to switch applications, invoke Task List, copy a screen or active window to the Windows Clipboard, invoke the application's Control menu, or switch between full-screen and windowed display modes. If you need to use any of those keystroke combinations in your application, put checks in the appropriate check boxes next to Reserve Shortcut Keys.

For example, if you want to be able to use the PrtSc key to print whatever your application puts on screen, put a check in the PrtSc box. That way you retain the normal MS-DOS function of the PrtSc key while working in your non-Windows application (and you still can press Alt-PrtSc to copy the screen's contents to the Windows Clipboard).

Application Shortcut Key

If you want, you can assign a keyboard shortcut to your non-Windows application. Then any time your application is running, you can switch to it immediately (from any Windows or non-Windows application) by pressing the keyboard shortcut.

You might, for example, assign Ctrl-W to WordPerfect 5.1, Ctrl-L to Lotus 1-2-3 Release 2.3, and so on. An application keyboard shortcut can make it much easier to work with many Windows and non-Windows applications at the same time.

The shortcut can be any combination of Alt or Ctrl with any letter, number, or function key.

 WINDOWS TIP: Be careful not to create an application shortcut key from a combination that you use elsewhere in Windows. If, for example, you assign Alt-F4 as a shortcut for switching to your favorite non-Windows application, you can use that combination to quit a Windows application only when your non-Windows program is not running.

To assign a shortcut, put the insertion point in the Application Shortcut Key text box, and then type the keystroke combination you want to use. For example, if you want to assign Alt-W, hold down the Alt key and press W.

NOTE: *The Shortcut Key setting in Program Manager's Program Item Properties dialog box overrides the PIF Editor Application Shortcut Key setting.*

SETTING PIF OPTIONS FOR THE ALTERNATE OPERATING MODE

When you start PIF Editor, the program always displays the option screen for the operating mode (standard or 386 enhanced) you're currently using. You can switch to the alternate mode by using commands on the Mode menu.

For example, if you're running in standard mode, you can create a 386 enhanced mode PIF by opening the Mode menu and choosing 386 Enhanced. If you're running in 386 enhanced mode and want to create a standard-mode PIF, open the Mode menu and choose Standard.

When you use the command on the Mode menu to switch to the mode you are not using, you'll see a warning.

Simply click OK to acknowledge the warning. Note that, despite the warning, selecting a mode in this way does not actually change the current operating mode; it merely permits you to create a PIF for use in the selected mode.

Switching PIF Editor modes allows you to create two sets of options for the same PIF—one for use in standard mode, the other for use in 386 enhanced mode.

CHANGING 386 ENHANCED OPTIONS ON THE FLY

While a non-Windows application is running in 386 enhanced mode, you can temporarily override the settings in its PIF. You might want to do this to increase the program's background or foreground priority, for example, to change from a full-screen to a windowed display, or to allow the program to run temporarily in the background.

To temporarily override the settings in your PIF, do the following:

1. Press Alt-Spacebar.

   This action opens the Control menu for your non-Windows application. If your program is running full screen, Alt-Spacebar first switches it to a windowed display, and then opens the Control menu.

2. Choose the Settings command.

   The Settings dialog box appears.

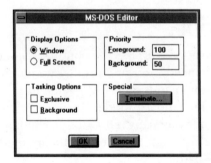

NOTE: *If you have reserved the Alt-Spacebar combination in your application's PIF, you won't be able to invoke the Settings command by pressing Alt-Spacebar. If your application is currently displayed full screen, first press Alt-Enter to switch it to windowed display. Then use the mouse to open the Control menu, and choose Settings.*

Display Options

The Display Options section of this dialog box will always be set to Window, because Alt-Spacebar switches the application to windowed display before opening the Control menu. If you want to switch back to full-screen display, select Full Screen and click OK.

 KEYBOARD TIP: You can switch a non-Windows application between full-screen and windowed display at any time, without going through the Settings dialog box. Simply press Alt-Enter.

Priority

The numbers in the Foreground and Background boxes reflect the current settings in your PIF. You can make any changes you want to these numbers. Your changes take effect immediately and last until you quit your application—or change the numbers again.

 WINDOWS TIP: If all you want to do is increase the performance of your non-Windows application for a while, and you don't mind suspending all other programs temporarily, choose Exclusive in the Tasking Options section rather than increasing the Foreground priority.

Tasking Options

The settings in the Tasking Options section reflect the current settings in your PIF. You can suspend all other applications temporarily by putting a check in the Exclusive check box. Or you can allow your program to work in the background temporarily by checking the Background check box.

Any changes you make to either tasking option last until you quit your program—or change the settings again.

The Terminate Button

The Terminate button gives you a way to quit your non-Windows application if something goes wrong and you're unable to quit by normal methods. You should not use this button except as a last resort, because it may make your Windows system unstable. ("Unstable" is a delicate way of saying that your computer might lock up at any time—causing you to lose any unsaved work.)

After terminating your program, save all your work in all other open applications. Then quit Windows, reset your computer by pressing Ctrl-Alt-Del, and restart Windows.

> **NOTE:** *If your non-Windows program locks up, first try pressing Ctrl-Alt-Del to perform a "local reboot." (For more about local reboot, see Chapter 19.) Try the Terminate button only if all else fails.*

CONTROLLING DEVICE CONTENTION IN 386 ENHANCED MODE

When you run several Windows applications at once, all of which need to use the same printer or communications port, Windows manages your resources so that only one program at a time can use each device. When one or more non-Windows applications are running in 386 enhanced mode, Windows is unable to exert the same degree of oversight, and it's possible that two or more programs might try to send or receive data over the same port at the same time.

You can ask Windows to warn you whenever there is any possibility of a mishap of this kind. To do so, open Control Panel and choose 386 Enhanced. You'll see the following dialog box.

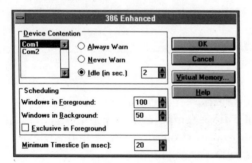

You can apply separate device contention settings to any of your serial-communication ports and parallel-printer ports. For each port, choose Always Warn, Never Warn, or Idle.

WINDOWS TIP: Unlike Windows 3.0, Windows 3.1 does not ordinarily offer to manage contention for parallel printer ports. Provided you have a driver file named VPD.386, however, you can add this capability to your system. If you have upgraded from Windows 3.0 to Windows 3.1, you might already have a copy of VPD.386 in the SYSTEM subdirectory of your Windows directory. If you do not have this file, you can get it from one of the Windows forums on CompuServe (see Appendix C) or by calling Microsoft Product Support Services and requesting a copy of the Windows Driver Library (WDL).

After you have a copy of VPD.386 in your SYSTEM subdirectory, add the following line to the [386Enh] section of your SYSTEM.INI file:

Device=VPD.386

After modifying SYSTEM.INI, restart Windows and reopen the 386 Enhanced section of Control Panel. In the Device Contention list box, you should find an entry for each of your computer's parallel ports.

If you choose Always Warn, Windows presents a message whenever a non-Windows application tries to use a port that has already been used by another open application. You will be asked to choose which program should be given control of the port. This option is the safest of the three, but it might produce unnecessary warnings.

If you choose Idle, Windows warns you if another program has used the selected port within a specified period of time. Enter the time (in seconds) in the box to the right of the Idle option button. This option should be adequate for most situations where device contention might arise.

If you choose Never Warn, you're on your own.

RUNNING NON-WINDOWS APPLICATIONS THAT USE EXPANDED MEMORY

Some non-Windows applications were designed to take advantage of any expanded memory available in the system. What these applications will find when you run them under Windows depends on how you're running Windows.

If you're running Windows in 386 enhanced mode, you'll be able to run most non-Windows applications in a window. Because Windows retains control of the system, the non-Windows application will have access to all the expanded memory under Windows' control, meaning that they can take advantage of any available expanded memory, further supplemented by Windows' virtual memory capabilities.

If you're running Windows in standard mode, Windows can't take advantage of any expanded memory installed in your system, so non-Windows applications you run under Windows will be able to detect and use any expanded memory.

MOUSE SUPPORT IN A WINDOWED DISPLAY

If your non-Windows application supports a mouse, 386 enhanced mode allows you to use the mouse with it, even when you're running in a windowed display. For example, if you're running Lotus 1-2-3 Release 2.3 in a window, you can use the mouse to select spreadsheet cells, carry out 1-2-3 menu commands, and so on. If you want to copy some information from 1-2-3's window to the Windows Clipboard, start by choosing the Edit Mark command on the 1-2-3 window's Control menu.

In order for your mouse to work with a non-Windows program displayed in a Window, however, you must have installed a mouse driver prior to running Windows. If you're not sure whether you've done this, check your CONFIG.SYS and AUTOEXEC.BAT files. If either CONFIG.SYS or AUTOEXEC.BAT installs a mouse driver file with the extension COM or SYS, you should be able to use your mouse when running non-Windows programs under Windows.

If your mouse driver is installed via CONFIG.SYS or AUTOEXEC.BAT and you can use your mouse with a non-Windows program running outside Windows, but you can't use it when running the program in a window under Windows, try making the following change to your SYSTEM.INI file: Under the [NonWindows-App] heading, add the line *MouseInDOSBox=1*. Then save your modified SYS-TEM.INI file, quit Windows, and restart.

Normally, this line in SYSTEM.INI is not needed. But if you've upgraded from Windows 3.0 to Windows 3.1 and you use a third-party screen driver, it's possible you're using a screen "grabber" (a component of your system that enables it to run non-Windows programs) designed for Windows 3.0. In this case, the MouseIn-DOSBox setting might take care of the problem.

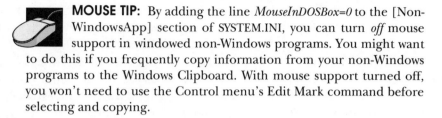

MOUSE TIP: By adding the line *MouseInDOSBox=0* to the [Non-WindowsApp] section of SYSTEM.INI, you can turn *off* mouse support in windowed non-Windows programs. You might want to do this if you frequently copy information from your non-Windows programs to the Windows Clipboard. With mouse support turned off, you won't need to use the Control menu's Edit Mark command before selecting and copying.

CHANGING FONTS IN A WINDOWED DISPLAY

The first time you run a non-Windows program in a window, Windows chooses a font that's appropriate for your system's screen driver. On a 640 × 480 VGA display, for example, Windows displays your text in an 8 × 12 font—that is, a font whose character matrix is 8 dots wide by 12 dots tall. Provided you're running the non-Windows program in text mode, however, you can pick from a variety of alternative fonts.

To change the font for a windowed non-Windows application, first launch that application and display it in a window. Then pull down the application's Control menu and choose Fonts. You'll see a display similar to the following.

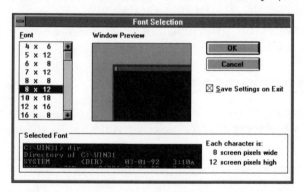

At the bottom of this dialog box, Windows shows a sample of the current font. To find the font that's easiest for you to read, check this display as you step through the various font options. Because changing the font also changes the size and shape of the application's window, the Fonts dialog box also provides you with a preview of your window's size (and position) relative to the entire desktop.

You can specify different font sizes for different non-Windows programs, if it pleases you to do so. Provided you select the Save Settings On Exit check box, Windows records your font selection in a file named DOSAPP.INI. Each non-Windows program you use gets its own entry in this file.

Certain display drivers do not permit font changes in non-Windows applications. If you find that your non-Windows programs' Control menus do not include the Fonts command, your screen driver might simply lack this capability. Before you give up on it, though, try making the following change to your SYSTEM.INI file: Under the [NonWindowsApp] heading, add the line *FontChangeEnable=1*. Then save the SYSTEM.INI file, quit Windows, and restart. (In some cases, this line will correct the inability to change fonts. In other cases, however, it will cause an incorrect display of your mouse pointer! If the latter fate befalls you, simply go back into SYSTEM.INI and remove the FontChangeEnable line.)

RUNNING MS-DOS BATCH FILES UNDER WINDOWS

A *batch file* is a text file containing one or more MS-DOS commands. When you run the batch file, each command is executed in turn, as though it had been entered separately at the keyboard. Batch files have the extension BAT.

You can run a batch file under Windows the same way you can run any other non-Windows application. You can either create a PIF for it or run it without a PIF; in the latter case, Windows applies the settings in _DEFAULT.PIF.

As the next section points out, a batch file can be a convenient way to run certain memory-resident programs.

RUNNING MEMORY-RESIDENT PROGRAMS

A memory-resident program (also sometimes called a *TSR*) is a program that remains in your computer's memory after it's no longer running. Two basic types of memory-resident programs exist:

- Programs such as network software or certain MS-DOS commands (APPEND, for example) that enable your system to run a particular way but with which you don't interact directly

- "Pop-up" programs, such as Borland International's SideKick or Lotus Metro, with which you can interact while running another application

Memory-resident programs of the first category are usually installed by your CONFIG.SYS file or AUTOEXEC.BAT file when you first turn on your computer. You should run as few of these as possible when using Windows, because they reduce

456

the amount of memory available to all your Windows and non-Windows applications.

A pop-up program can be run in any of the following ways:

- As an ordinary non-Windows application that can be accessed exactly like any other non-Windows application

- In conjunction with a particular non-Windows application, so that it can be popped up only from that application

- In conjunction with Windows applications only, so that it cannot be popped up from a non-Windows application (This option is available only in 386 enhanced mode.)

Running a Pop-Up as an Ordinary Non-Windows Application

When you run a pop-up program as an ordinary non-Windows application, you can take advantage of its services only by switching to it—the same way you would switch to any other non-Windows application. The advantage of running a pop-up this way is that you can easily quit it at any time, thereby freeing up the memory it was using.

To run a pop-up program as an ordinary non-Windows application, start it the same way you would any other non-Windows application. Either create a PIF for it, or run it directly (without a PIF, using the _DEFAULT.PIF settings).

When you start a pop-up in this manner, you see the following message from Windows.

```
      MICROSOFT WINDOWS POP-UP PROGRAM SUPPORT
  Your pop-up program is ready to run. When you have finished using
  it, press Ctrl+C to close this window and return to Windows.
```

This message simply informs you that you need to use a special procedure to quit your pop-up application. When you're ready to quit, do the following:

1. Switch to the pop-up program's window.

2. If the program has a command to quit, use it to exit the program. (You don't need to unload the program from memory; merely get back to the MS-DOS prompt.)

3. Press Ctrl-C.

Running a Pop-Up with a Specific Non-Windows Application

If you need the services of your pop-up only when you are running a particular non-Windows program, the best way to proceed is to create an MS-DOS batch file that starts the pop-up, and then starts the program with which you want to use the pop-up.

For example, if you want to use SideKick only when you are running Lotus 1-2-3, you could create the following batch file:

```
C:\SK\SK.COM
C:\123\123.EXE
```

You might name this batch file SK123.BAT.

Then create a PIF for SK123.BAT, allocating the same options (but perhaps adding a little more memory) that you would use to run 1-2-3 by itself.

If you run your pop-up this way, you can access it only while the foreground (active) application is the program with which you started the pop-up. The advantage to this approach is that the pop-up does not reduce the amount of memory (or processing time) available to any of your other applications.

Running a Pop-Up in Conjunction with Windows Applications Only

If you're using Windows in 386 enhanced mode, you can run a pop-up program so that it can be accessed only from your Windows applications and not from any non-Windows programs. To do this, create an MS-DOS batch file called WINSTART.BAT. Store this file in your Windows directory. Include a command in this batch file to start your pop-up program. For example, if you want to run SideKick, your batch file might consist of a single command—the command to start SideKick. Windows runs this batch file when it starts in 386 enhanced mode.

If you start your pop-up in this manner, you'll be able to access it the same way you would if you were not running Windows. For example, if Ctrl-Alt is the "hot-key" to pop up your program outside of Windows, you press Ctrl-Alt to pop it up from within Windows. You will not be able to pop up the program from a non-Windows application, however.

The advantage to this approach is that it does not reduce the amount of memory available to your non-Windows applications.

RUNNING NON-WINDOWS APPLICATIONS FROM THE MS-DOS PROMPT

When you first installed Windows, the Setup program created a program-item icon called MS-DOS Prompt in Program Manager's Main program group. Double-clicking its icon takes you to the MS-DOS command prompt (C>, for example), where you can start most non-Windows applications the same way you would start them if you were not running Windows.

When you're ready to quit a non-Windows program that you started from the MS-DOS prompt, do the following:

1. Use the application's normal command for quitting.

2. When you see the MS-DOS prompt again, type *exit* and press Enter.

When you double-click the MS-DOS Prompt program-item icon, Windows runs a non-Windows application called COMMAND.COM. This application is nothing other than the MS-DOS command interpreter—the component of MS-DOS that lets you enter MS-DOS commands and start MS-DOS programs.

The MS-DOS Prompt program item is set up to run full screen, with neither the Background nor the Exclusive tasking option in effect. If you are using Windows in 386 enhanced mode, you can change these settings, as well as the foreground and background priority values. After opening the window, simply press Alt-Spacebar and choose the Settings command.

The advantage of running a non-Windows application from the MS-DOS prompt is that you might find it simpler than concerning yourself with PIFs—default or otherwise. The disadvantage is that it might not work for programs that require a great deal of memory. Windows allocates sufficient memory to COMMAND.COM to run most non-Windows applications, but programs that require 512 KB or more of memory might not run from the MS-DOS Prompt program item. For these programs, you should create a PIF.

RUNNING NON-WINDOWS PROGRAMS FROM AN MS-DOS SHELL

If you're accustomed to running non-Windows programs from an MS-DOS shell program, such as XTree or the Norton Commander, you can continue to work that way under Windows. Simply create a PIF for your shell program and allocate plenty of memory to it. After you start your shell, you can then run your non-Windows applications the same way you did before you began using Windows.

19

Optimizing Windows

In this chapter, we'll look at some of the things you can do to get the maximum possible speed and capacity from your Windows system. The process of enhancing speed and capacity is called *optimizing*.

In an ideal world of limitless resources, optimizing Windows would be simple. All you would have to do is give it a ton of memory, a computer with a fast microprocessor, and a huge and speedy hard disk, and you would never complain about your system's performance.

In the real world, optimizing Windows is a matter of making the most economical use of limited resources. Among other things, that means *configuring* your memory appropriately, ensuring that nothing reduces available memory unnecessarily, performing occasional routine maintenance on your hard disk, and making sure that unneeded files don't rob Windows of vital hard-disk space. We'll look at all these optimizing measures in this chapter.

BASIC STRATEGY

A basic strategy for running Windows efficiently might look like this:

- Stuff your computer with as much extended memory as possible.

- Minimize the amount of memory used before Windows is loaded.

- Be sure you have ample hard disk space.

- Defragment your hard disks regularly.

- Use a disk-cache utility. (Windows supplies one, called Smart-Drive.)

- Use a permanent swap file if you're running in 386 enhanced mode.

- If you're running in standard mode, store your MS-DOS applications' swap files on your fastest and roomiest disk.

- If memory is plentiful, store your Windows applications' temporary files (including Print Manager's spool files) on a RAM disk.

We'll look at each of these points in turn.

THE IMPORTANCE OF EXTENDED MEMORY

Extended memory is the lifeblood of Windows. (For a discussion of the terms *conventional memory, extended memory, expanded memory,* and *virtual memory,* see Appendix B.) In both its operating modes, standard and 386 enhanced, Windows uses your computer's microprocessor in what's called "protected" mode (as opposed to the "real" mode used by MS-DOS and almost all non-Windows MS-DOS applications). Protected mode requires extended memory.

In 386 enhanced mode, when Windows needs more memory than your system can provide, it swaps information temporarily to your hard disk, thereby using the hard disk as an extension of extended memory. Transferring data to and from a hard disk is a much slower process than moving it in and out of RAM chips. Thus, swapping slows down the performance of your system. You can greatly minimize the amount of swapping required by using a disk-cache utility, as described later in this chapter. But increasing your system's extended memory is an even more effective strategy.

How Much Memory Do You Need?

Theoretically, Windows will run on systems with just under 2 MB of total memory (640 KB of conventional memory and the rest extended). Realistically speaking, though, a 2-MB machine is an unsatisfactory instrument for running Windows. If you work with only one or two applications at a time, you might find that you can get by at this memory level. (In particular, it might be fine for using Windows on a laptop, if you only perform relatively simple writing and recordkeeping tasks while away from the office.) But for most users, running Windows effectively requires a minimum of 4 MB.

Extended versus Expanded Memory

Neither Windows nor any Windows application uses expanded memory. Therefore, unless you want to reserve some expanded memory for non-Windows programs that require it, you should be sure that all memory on your system (beyond the first megabyte, which, by definition, is conventional memory) is configured as *extended*, not *expanded*. Any memory configured as expanded is simply unavailable to Windows.

If you're not sure whether the memory on your computer is configured as extended or expanded, and you're using MS-DOS version 4 or later, type *mem* at the MS-DOS command line, *before you begin a Windows session*. The MEM command tells you how much of each kind of memory you have. If you're running MS-DOS version 3, you won't be able to use the MEM command. In that case, read the messages that appear on your display as your system boots. If some of your memory is being set aside as expanded, you will probably see a boot-up message to that effect.

> **NOTE:** *If you run Windows in 386 enhanced mode, you don't need an expanded-memory manager to make expanded memory available to non-Windows programs. Provided you allocate EMS in your program's PIFs, Windows automatically uses extended memory to simulate expanded memory. Your Windows package includes a device driver named EMM386.EXE that uses extended memory to simulate expanded memory on 386 and 486 computers. But you need to install this driver only if you want to make expanded memory available to MS-DOS programs when you're not running Windows.*

MINIMIZING THE MEMORY USED BEFORE WINDOWS IS LOADED

When Windows starts, your operating system (MS-DOS or, perhaps, DR-DOS) hands it a (presumably) large pool of memory, which Windows then manipulates to its best advantage, using some very sophisticated memory-management techniques. The goal of these techniques is to ensure that the Windows programs you're using at any given moment always have enough memory to do what they need to do. What you can do to assist this process is make sure you're not unnecessarily withholding memory from the pool supplied to Windows as it starts. Basically, that means don't install any device drivers or memory-resident programs that you don't absolutely need. (Memory-resident programs are also commonly called TSRs or "pop-ups.")

If you use MS-DOS version 3 or 4, you should consider upgrading to MS-DOS 5. MS-DOS 5 can load part of itself into areas of memory that earlier versions could not access ("upper memory blocks," or UMBs), thereby making more conventional memory available before you start Windows. In addition, MS-DOS 5 can load device drivers and memory-resident programs into UMBs, freeing up the memory they would otherwise occupy.

Device drivers and memory-resident programs are usually placed in memory by commands stored in your CONFIG.SYS or AUTOEXEC.BAT files. You can find out what items are using memory in your system by reading the contents of CONFIG.SYS and AUTOEXEC.BAT. One easy way to do this is to start Windows and run the Sysedit program (Sysedit is described in Chapter 9). Using Sysedit is preferable to using Notepad or another text editor, because Sysedit's File Save command automatically creates a backup file (with the extension SYD).

The following paragraphs provide some guidelines about what you need and might not need in your CONFIG.SYS and AUTOEXEC.BAT files. This book can't tell you *exactly* what you need, however; for more information, consult your MS-DOS manuals or your company's PC support person.

The CONFIG.SYS File

The CONFIG.SYS file provides configuration information to MS-DOS (or DR-DOS, as the case may be). The operating system reads and acts on this file as soon as you boot your computer. Items you *must* have in your CONFIG.SYS file include:

- FILES=30 (If the number following *FILES*= is higher than 30, you might be able to reclaim some memory by reducing it to 30.)

- BUFFERS=20 (Reduce this number to 10 if you use SmartDrive.)

- A DEVICE= line that installs HIMEM.SYS

- A DEVICE= line that installs EGA.SYS (You need this only if your system uses an EGA display and you run non-Windows applications in standard mode.)

Items you *might* need in your CONFIG.SYS file include:

- A line that installs memory-resident network software (if you use a network)

- A line that installs EMM386.EXE (You need this only if you run MS-DOS applications that require expanded memory outside of Windows.)

- DOS=HIGH (This MS-DOS 5 command loads part of MS-DOS into high memory.)

- A line that begins with *SHELL=*

- A line that begins with *LASTDRIVE=*

The *SHELL=* line is commonly used to increase the size of the MS-DOS *environment.* If your CONFIG.SYS file has a *SHELL=* line with a /E parameter, you might be able to reclaim some memory by reducing the number that follows the /E. (On the other hand, if you find yourself getting "Out of environment space" messages from the operating system, you need to increase the /E parameter.)

The *LASTDRIVE=* line allows you to use drive letters higher than E for such devices as RAM disks, network drives, and CD-ROM drives. To conserve memory, the letter that follows *LASTDRIVE=* shouldn't be any higher than necessary; for example, don't use *LASTDRIVE=Z* unless you really need 26 drives.

Items you *might not* need in your CONFIG.SYS file include:

■ Lines that install device drivers that you can do without

■ A line that installs FASTOPEN.EXE

■ A line that begins with *FCBS=*

In particular, you can do without any line that installs a mouse driver, provided you don't need the mouse for any non-Windows applications. Windows provides its own mouse driver.

The AUTOEXEC.BAT File

The AUTOEXEC.BAT file is designed to run programs or execute MS-DOS commands automatically each time you start or reset your computer. The two items you're most likely to find in this file are a line beginning with *PATH=* and a line that invokes SmartDrive. The *PATH=* statement, which does not reduce available memory, tells MS-DOS what directories to search if you start a program that's not located in the current directory. SmartDrive is the Windows-supplied disk-cache program; it's described later in this chapter.

Other benign commands commonly found in AUTOEXEC.BAT include the following:

■ CD or CHDIR

■ DATE

■ ECHO or @ECHO

■ GOTO

■ IF

■ PAUSE

■ PROMPT

■ REM

■ SET

- TIME

- VER

- A command to start Windows

The following items in your AUTOEXEC.BAT file *might* reduce available memory and *might* be unnecessary:

- A command that runs a mouse driver (such as MOUSE.COM)

- APPEND

- FASTOPEN

- SUBST

- ASSIGN

- JOIN

- MODE

- SHARE

- Any command that starts a memory-resident program

- Any command that starts an MS-DOS shell

The MS-DOS commands APPEND and FASTOPEN reduce available memory and don't significantly enhance Windows' performance. The MS-DOS commands SUBST, ASSIGN, and JOIN are not recommended for use with Windows.

Generally speaking, you should start pop-up programs, such as SideKick or Lotus Metro, after you start Windows. See "Running Memory-Resident Programs," in Chapter 18.

MS-DOS shell programs, such as XTree and the Norton Commander, are convenient for running non-Windows programs and issuing MS-DOS commands. But if you're going to use one of these, start it after you start Windows so you don't reduce memory that Windows needs to run. (See "Running Non-Windows Programs from an MS-DOS Shell," in Chapter 18.)

ENSURING AMPLE HARD-DISK SPACE

Windows is a pretty heavy consumer of hard-disk space. A typical full installation of Windows 3.1 uses on the order of 12 MB, and many major Windows applications occupy even more than that (for example, a full installation of Microsoft Word for Windows 2.0 uses about 15 MB). Throw in a library of clip art, some digitized sound files, and a few months' worth of everyday spreadsheet documents, and you can easily overwhelm a 70-MB hard disk.

Unfortunately, to run Windows efficiently, you not only need enough room for your program and data files. You also need space for the temporary disk files that Windows creates automatically while you work. If you use Windows in 386 enhanced mode, you'll do your system a great disservice if you don't leave room for either a permanent or temporary swap file. If you run in standard mode, Windows needs to be able to create application swap files for any non-Windows programs you use. If you print with Print Manager, you should allow at least 750 KB for Print Manager's spool files. And many other Windows programs (Write, for example) also need room to create temporary files.

You can cope with this potentially discouraging situation in any of three ways (and you might want to use all three):

- Put more disk space on line.

- Use a file-compression utility to reduce amount of disk space occupied by your files.

- Unload files that you don't really need. (Either delete them or transfer them to removable media.)

The first approach is self-explanatory—and, fortunately, less costly than it used to be.

File-Compression Utilities

Essentially two kinds of file-compression utilities are available. The first type, of which PKWare's PKZIP is the most widely used example, compresses and decompresses particular files on demand. The second type, typified by Stac Electronics' Stacker, compresses and decompresses entire disk volumes "on the fly"; after you've put Stacker to work on a disk drive, all files on that drive automatically compress when you save them and decompress when you open them.

PKWare, Inc.
9025 N. Deerwood Drive
Brown Deer, WI 53223
(414) 354-8699

Stac Electronics
5993 Avenida Encinas
Carlsbad, CA 92008
(800) 522-7822

With either type of utility, the degree of compression achievable depends on the contents of the file. Large bitmaps, for example, can often be scrunched to less than 25 percent of their original size. Executable program files, because the information they contain is less patterned, are generally quite a bit less compressible.

If disk space is scarce and adding more to your system is not a feasible option, you might find a file-compression program an invaluable adjunct to your Windows system.

Unloading Files You Don't Need

The Windows-supplied games and desktop accessories are nifty, but if space is scarce, you can probably do without some of them. As you might have noticed when you installed Windows 3.1, the Setup program gives you the option of *not* installing particular Windows components if you chose the Custom installation (wallpaper files, games, accessories, and help files, among other things). If you went ahead and did a full install and now are running short of room, you can run the Setup program again (from within Windows) and ask it to *uninstall* the files you don't need. For details about this procedure, see Appendix A.

Unfortunately, Setup knows how to uninstall only the files it originally installed. It won't help you uninstall third-party or Microsoft applications. If you want to do that, and you're unsure of which files to delete, you'd be well advised to call the software vendor's technical support service before striking out on your own. Be sure to ask whether the application you're unloading has modified your WIN.INI file—and how to clean up after it if it did. Many Windows applications—particularly older ones—write configuration information in WIN.INI. If you delete such an application, you no longer need the WIN.INI data (and, in fact, an unnecessarily bulky WIN.INI can sometimes slow down your system).

DEFRAGMENTING YOUR HARD DISK

When you store files on a freshly formatted disk, MS-DOS writes each file's data in a set of adjacent disk clusters. One file might use clusters 3 through 24, for example, the next 25 through 31, a third file 32 through 34—and so on. As soon as you begin deleting files, however, this neat pattern is likely to be broken.

For example, if you deleted the file that occupied clusters 25 through 31, and then created a new file 20 clusters in length, MS-DOS would store the new file's first 7 clusters in 25 through 31 and the remaining 13 somewhere else. This new file, in other words, would be *fragmented*; it would occupy at least two noncontiguous blocks of clusters. As time went on and you added and deleted more files, the odds are good that more and more of your files would be fragmented.

Fragmentation is not a problem as far as data integrity is concerned, but it does reduce the efficiency of your hard disk. Fragmented files take longer to read and write than contiguous ones. And disk-cache programs, such as SmartDrive, can help you less when files are fragmented.

You can eliminate disk fragmentation and enhance Windows' performance with regular use of a disk defragmentation utility, or "disk optimizer." Such programs are available from a number of software vendors—usually as a part of a larger set of disk utilities. A defragmentation utility simply rearranges the files on your hard disk, storing each file in a nice neat block of adjacent clusters.

WARNING: *You must quit Windows before using your disk optimizer.*

It's a particularly good idea to optimize your hard disk at the following times:

- Before you install Windows, if you're going to be running in 386 enhanced mode and using a permanent swap file (see "Using Swap Files in 386 Enhanced Mode," later in this chapter)

- If you run in 386 enhanced mode and decide to switch from a temporary swap file to a permanent swap file or enlarge your permanent swap file

- Immediately after deleting a large number of files

Permanent swap files (used only in 386 enhanced mode) require contiguous clusters, so defragmenting your hard disk might make it possible for you to use a larger permanent swap file.

USING A DISK CACHE

A disk-cache utility, such as the Windows-supplied SmartDrive, exploits the fact that information transfers between one part of memory and another are much faster than transfers between memory and disk. Whenever your system reads information from your hard disk, a copy is stored in an area of memory called a *cache*. Later, when the system needs to read the disk again, it consults the cache first. If the cache contains a copy of the information it needs, the system can avoid reading the disk. The larger the cache, the greater the time savings that can be realized by caching.

There's a tradeoff for using a large cache, because the cache reduces the amount of memory available for other purposes. But SmartDrive works cooperatively with Windows. SmartDrive is installed with two cache-size settings—a normal size and a minimum size. If plenty of memory is available, SmartDrive uses the normal cache size. When Windows needs more memory to store the programs and documents you're working with, it reclaims some memory from SmartDrive, reducing the size of the cache.

SmartDrive continues to work when Windows is not running, but it always uses the normal cache size.

SmartDrive Settings

The Windows Setup program, by default, installs SmartDrive for you by adding a line such as this to your AUTOEXEC.BAT file:

C:\WINDOWS\SMARTDRV.EXE

NOTE: *The SmartDrive verison furnished with Windows 3.1 is an executable (EXE) file and is usually invoked via the AUTOEXEC.BAT file. Earlier versions were installable device drivers and were invoked via CONFIG.SYS. However, if your CONFIG.SYS file contains a line such as DEVICE=C:\WINDOWS\SMARTDRV.EXE /DOUBLE_BUFFER, this does not mean you are using an older version of SmartDrive. It means that the Windows Setup program has determined that it would be advisable for SmartDrive to use a feature called "double buffering" on your system. This feature, used mostly with somewhat older computers, provides additional safety at a small expense of memory and performance. You should not remove this line from your CONFIG.SYS file unless you are absolutely sure of what you're doing.*

If you have a line invoking SmartDrive in your AUTOEXEC.BAT file, the cache utility is loaded automatically every time you turn on your machine, and it uses the following default settings:

- Hard disks are both read-cached and write-cached, floppy drives are only read-cached, and all other drives (RAM disks, network drives, and CD-ROM drives) are ignored. (For a description of these terms, see "Read Caching and Write Caching," below.)

- The normal and minimum cache sizes are determined by the amount of extended memory available on your system, according to the following scheme:

Available Extended Memory	Normal Size	Minimum Size
6 MB or more	2 MB	2 MB
4 to 6 MB	2 MB	1 MB
2 to 4 MB	1 MB	512 KB
1 to 2 MB	1 MB	256 KB
Less than 1 MB	All extended memory	0 KB

You can change these parameters—and several others—by modifying the command that installs SmartDrive. For the full details about all of the SmartDrive command-line options, see your Windows documentation.

Should you change the default parameters to get optimal performance? Unfortunately, no one can tell you, because the answer depends on how you use your system. The default settings are well chosen, but experimentation might lead you to settings that achieve better performance on your system. (For a description of one testing methodology, see the book *Fully Powered Windows*, by Burton Alperson [New York: Brady Books, 1991].) Here are some points to consider if you decide to tinker with SmartDrive's settings.

Read Caching and Write Caching

Read caching occurs when the cache utility stores in memory some information that it has read *from* disk. This information then becomes (almost) instantly available the next time it is needed (provided it hasn't first been flushed from the cache). *Write caching* occurs when the cache utility stores in memory some information on its way *to* disk. SmartDrive performs write caching so that your interaction with Windows won't be slowed down unnecessarily by disk activity. As soon as you're not interacting with the system, the write-cached information is written out to disk. (It's also written to disk automatically if it has stayed in the cache memory longer than five seconds.)

Write caching hard-disk information is usually a perfectly safe procedure. Write caching floppy drives, on the other hand, is risky—because you might swap disks at the wrong time and inadvertently turn a disk file to trash. Hence, the SmartDrive defaults—write cache the hard disks, don't write cache the floppies.

If your system is prone to lockups for any reason—power failure, flaky software, or whatever—you can give yourself an extra measure of safety (at a small performance cost) by turning write caching off for your hard disks as well as your floppies. To disable write caching for a particular drive, simply add the letter of that drive to the SmartDrive command line. For example, the command line

    C:\WINDOWS\SMARTDRV.EXE C D

disables write caching on drives C and D.

To reenable write caching on those drives, either remove the drive letters from the command line or add a plus sign after each, like this:

    C:\WINDOWS\SMARTDRV.EXE C+ D+

To disable all caching (that is, read caching *and* write caching) on a particular drive, include the drive letter followed by a minus sign. For example, to turn caching off altogether on drives A through D, you could change the command line to

C:\WINDOWS\SMARTDRV.EXE A- B- C- D-

(If A through D are all the drives you have, you can accomplish the same thing by removing the SmartDrive command line from your AUTOEXEC.BAT file.)

Changing the Size of the Cache

Changing the normal and minimum cache sizes is a fruitful area for experimentation. To override SmartDrive's default settings, specify first the normal size, then the minimum, *in kilobytes*, on the command line. The following command line, for example

C:\WINDOWS\SMARTDRV.EXE 2048 512

tells SmartDrive to use 2048 KB (two megabytes) as its normal size and to reduce the cache size to 512 KB when Windows needs more memory for applications and data. (You can combine cache-size specifications with instructions to turn caching on or off for particular drives. Simply add the drive-letter instructions either before or after the cache-size instructions on the command line.)

As you experiment with different cache sizes, keep in mind that performance improvements per unit of cache size tend to diminish as the cache gets larger. For example, you would almost certainly gain more in performance by increasing the normal cache size from 512 KB to 1 MB than you would by increasing it from 1.5 MB to 2 MB. If you're fortunate enough to have more memory than you ever need for your programs and data, you can probably improve performance more by allocating some memory to a RAM disk than by boosting the cache size beyond 2 MB. (See "Storing Windows Applications' Temporary Files on a RAM Disk," later in this chapter.)

SmartDrive Versus Other Cache Programs

SmartDrive is by no means the only cache program available—nor is it the only one that shares memory cooperatively with Windows. In fact, a number of third-party cache utilities were widely considered to be "smarter" than the SmartDrive shipped with earlier versions of Windows. The SmartDrive version that comes with Windows 3.1 is considerably brighter than its predecessors, however.

If you're concerned with coaxing the absolute maximum possible performance from your Windows system, you would do well to look for comparative reviews of cache utilities in computer magazines and on the various CompuServe forums (see Appendix C). The important thing to remember, though, is that using *any* competent cache program will make Windows run dramatically better than using none at all.

USING SWAP FILES IN 386 ENHANCED MODE

In 386 enhanced mode, Windows uses your hard disk as an extension of internal memory, moving data to a swap file on disk when memory becomes full and restoring it from disk to memory as needed. This use of the hard disk is known as *virtual* memory.

You can choose between two kinds of swap files: a permanent swap file or a temporary swap file (or you can choose to have no swap file). If you set up a permanent swap file, you tell Windows how big the file should be, and its size remains constant thereafter. If you use a temporary swap file, Windows uses whatever space it needs up to a specified maximum amount.

A permanent swap file provides faster performance, because Windows uses contiguous clusters only and bypasses the normal MS-DOS procedures for reading and writing files. The disadvantage of a permanent swap file is that it consumes hard-disk space even when you're not using Windows.

Fortunately, you can easily switch back and forth between the two methods. You can create a permanent swap file when you have plenty of room on your hard disk. If your hard disk becomes crowded, you can switch to a temporary file. Later, when hard-disk space becomes more plentiful, you can go back to using a permanent file.

Two restrictions apply:

■ Permanent swap files require contiguous disk space. A highly fragmented hard disk, therefore, can reduce the size of the largest possible permanent swap file. (See "Defragmenting Your Hard Disk," earlier in this chapter.)

■ A permanent swap file cannot be stored on a network drive.

Generally speaking, storing any kind of temporary data on a network drive—a temporary swap file, a print spool file, or a temporary file created by an application—makes for poor performance and unhappy neighbors, but Windows will let you create a temporary swap file on a remote drive if you need to.

Determining What Kind of Swap File You Now Have

The Windows Setup program normally creates a swap file for you automatically when you install Windows on a 386 or 486 computer. To find out what kind of swap file it has created, what drive the file is stored on, and how large the file is, run Control Panel, double-click the 386 Enhanced icon, and click the Virtual Memory button. You'll see a display similar to the following.

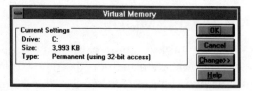

Changing the Type, Size, or Location of Your Swap File

To change anything about your swap file, click the Change button. An expanded dialog box appears.

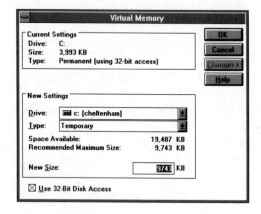

Here you can specify what drive you want to use, what type of swap file you want (permanent, temporary, or none), and how big you want the file to be. If you choose a permanent swap file, the number of bytes you specify in the New Size box will be off limits to other files for the duration—until you change this setting again. If you choose a temporary file, Windows ropes off some amount of disk space up to (but not exceeding) the amount you specify, but it makes the space available again at the end of your Windows session.

 WINDOWS TIP: If you have more than one hard disk, be sure to store your swap file on the fastest disk. Many popular utility programs, including the Norton Utilities and PC Tools, have diagnostic tools to help you determine your fastest disk.

The Space Available line in the New Settings area tells you how much unused space you have on the currently selected disk drive. The Maximum Size line reports the biggest swap file you can create—of the kind selected in the Type drop-down list. If the current setting in the Type list is Permanent, the dialog box also reports a recommended size. You can accept this size if you like, or you can change it by entering a different value in the New Size box. (If the Type setting is Temporary, Windows doesn't make a size recommendation. That's because, with temporary swap files, Windows never uses any more space than it has to.)

As soon as you make your selections in this dialog box and click OK (and answer a confirmation prompt), your new swap file will be in effect. You do not need to restart Windows.

> **WARNING:** *Never use MS-DOS commands to delete or move 386SPART.PAR, SPART.PAR, or WIN386.SWP from your hard disk. If you want to get rid of a swap file, use the 386 Enhanced section of Control Panel, click the Virtual Memory button, click Change, and then set Type to None. If you want to move a swap file, follow the same steps but change the contents of the Drive line in the New Settings portion of the dialog box.*

USING FASTDISK IN 386 ENHANCED MODE

FastDisk is a device driver that allows Windows, when running in 386 enhanced mode, to access your hard disk without using normal MS-DOS and BIOS calls. Without FastDisk, when Windows wants to read data from or write data to your hard disk, it starts by issuing a call to MS-DOS. The operating system then determines which disk sectors need to be accessed and makes a call to a routine in your ROM-BIOS. The BIOS then sends a command to your hard disk controller, which fetches or writes the data. During this sequence, your computer's processor is switched from protected mode to real mode and back to protected mode several times. FastDisk eliminates most of this overhead by making the disk-sector calculations itself and talking directly to the hard disk controller.

FastDisk offers two significant performance benefits: It speeds up all forms of disk access, and it allows non-Windows applications to make use of virtual memory. Without FastDisk, you can run only as many non-Windows applications as fit in your computer's physical (non-virtual) memory. With FastDisk, your non-Windows programs will still be limited to 640 KB apiece (unless they can also use expanded or extended memory and you've allocated such memory via their PIFs), but you'll be able to run more of them at once because they'll be able to draw on virtual memory.

The version of FastDisk shipped with Windows 3.1 works only with hard disk controllers that are 100 percent compatible with the Western Digital 1003 standard. According to Microsoft's estimates, about 90 percent of the hard disk controllers currently in use meet this criterion. But if your hard disk uses an ESDI or SCSI controller, or another controller that is not totally 1003-compatible, you will not be able to use this version of FastDisk.

How to Turn FastDisk On or Off

The Windows 3.1 Setup program, when you first installed Windows, checked your hard-drive controller to see if it appeared to be 1003-compatible. If it did appear to be compatible, the Setup program added the following three lines to the [386enh] section of your SYSTEM.INI file:

```
32BitDiskAccess=off
device=*int13
device=*wdctrl
```

It also made available a check box, labeled Use 32-Bit Disk Access, in the 386 Enhanced section of your Control Panel. This check box, shown at the bottom of the preceding illustration, allows you to turn FastDisk on and off.

To get to the FastDisk check box, open the 386 Enhanced section of Control Panel and click the Virtual Memory button, and then click the Change button. After turning FastDisk either on or off, you need to restart Windows to make the change take effect.

(Alternatively, you can turn FastDisk on or off by changing the *32BitDiskAccess=* line in SYSTEM.INI from off to on—or vice versa. Even if you take this "direct route," however, you still have to restart Windows to make the change take effect.)

The Hazards of FastDisk

As you may have noticed from the foregoing discussion, the *32BitDiskAccess=* line in SYSTEM.INI is initially set to *off* and the Use 32-Bit Disk Access check box is initially clear. The reason for this is that the Windows Setup program cannot determine with absolute certainty that it is safe to use FastDisk on your system. It can make a very educated guess, but it can be wrong. A small number of hard disk controllers appear to be 100 percent 1003-compatible but in fact are not. And, unfortunately, the consequences of misjudgment in this case can be as serious as a totally trashed hard disk.

FastDisk might also produce disastrous results on some portable computers that automatically turn off power to the hard disk when the disk is not in use.

A Rational FastDisk Strategy

The vast majority of computers running Windows 3.1 will be able to use FastDisk safely and will realize major performance gains by doing so. But the small potential for serious data loss suggests the following strategy:

- Do not use FastDisk on portable computers unless you know that the hard disk is never powered down while the system itself is running.

- If the Use 32-Bit Disk Access check box is available and unselected on your desktop computer, back up all hard disks driven by your system's primary disk controller. Then turn FastDisk on and enjoy its benefits.

- If the Use 32-Bit Disk Access check box is available and already selected (many computers that are shipped with Windows installed or that are set up by system administrators will meet this description), assume that all is well.

- Before installing any third-party memory-management software (an expanded memory manager or extended memory manager from a source other than Microsoft), check with the vendor to be sure the software does not conflict with FastDisk.

CHOOSING THE OPTIMAL LOCATION FOR STANDARD-MODE APPLICATION SWAP FILES

If you run Windows in standard mode, you won't be able to take advantage of virtual memory—and you won't have to concern yourself with the foregoing discussion about permanent and temporary swap files. There are other swap files to care about, however. Each time you switch away from a non-Windows application in standard mode, Windows stores that program's current information in an *application swap file*. (The creation of this file is what causes the momentary delay when you switch away from non-Windows programs in standard mode.) When you switch back to the non-Windows application, Windows restores the information it wrote to the application swap file. When you quit the non-Windows application, Windows deletes the application swap file.

Each non-Windows program you have open might have its own application swap file. These files can be quite large—on the order of 512 KB. Therefore, the amount of hard disk space you have available might determine the number of non-Windows programs you can have open at once. Windows will not create an application swap file if less than 512 KB of free disk space is available. (The disk space does not have to be contiguous, however.)

Windows stores application swap files in the directory pointed to by the TEMP variable in your MS-DOS environment. If your MS-DOS environment does not specify a TEMP variable, the files are stored in the root directory of your C drive—assuming that your first hard disk is C. If you have another hard disk that's either faster or roomier than C, you might want to direct Windows to store its application swap files on that other drive.

You can change the drive that Windows uses for application swap files either by specifying the drive of your choice in the MS-DOS TEMP variable or by modifying your SYSTEM.INI file.

Specifying the TEMP Variable

To specify or change the TEMP variable in your MS-DOS environment, you need to modify your AUTOEXEC.BAT file. You can do that by running Sysedit (see Chapter 9) and activating the window that displays AUTOEXEC.BAT. Look for a line that begins *SET TEMP=*. If no such line is there, add it (anywhere; it doesn't matter where in the file it appears). To the right of the equal sign, specify the drive and directory you want to use. Here's an example:

    SET TEMP=D:\SWAPDIR

Save the altered AUTOEXEC.BAT, quit Windows, reboot your system, restart Windows, and your application swap files will henceforth be stored on the drive and in the directory you specified.

Specifying a Swap Directory by Changing SYSTEM.INI

If you don't want to name or change a TEMP variable, you can choose a location for your application swap files by modifying SYSTEM.INI. You might want to do this if you want certain temporary files—Print Manager's spool files, for example—to be stored in one place (such as a RAM disk) and your application swap files somewhere else.

To specify a swap directory in SYSTEM.INI, run Sysedit and activate the SYSTEM.INI window. Search for a line that reads [NonWindowsApp]. If no such line exists, go to the end of the file and add it—exactly as shown here, on a line by itself.

Next, below the [NonWindowsApp] line, look for a line that starts *Swap-disk=*. If no such line exists, add it directly below [NonWindowsApp].

Finally, on the right side of *Swapdisk=*, add the drive and path of the directory you want Windows to use for application swap files. For example, if you want to use D:\SWAPDIR, make the line read

Swapdisk=d:\swapdir

Save SYSTEM.INI, and then quit and restart Windows.

> **WARNING:** *Application swap files are hidden files whose names begin with ~WOA. Do* not *delete these files while Windows is running. Windows will delete them itself when they're no longer needed.*

STORING WINDOWS APPLICATIONS' TEMPORARY FILES ON A RAM DISK

A RAM disk is an area of memory that's made to simulate an ordinary floppy or hard disk. When Windows (or MS-DOS) reads from and writes to a RAM disk, it acts exactly as though it were interacting with a conventional disk medium, except that the whole process takes place much more quickly. The drawbacks to using a RAM disk are two: The information stored there is lost forever unless it's eventually copied to a conventional disk, and the memory consigned to the RAM disk cannot be used for other purposes at the same time.

Because Windows needs a lot of extended memory to run well, you probably don't want to create a RAM disk unless you have a lot of memory to start with. If you do happen to have an abundance, however—say, 8 MB or more—a RAM disk can be a handy way to eke more performance out of your system. In particular, a RAM disk can be an ideal place for such things as the spool files created by Print Manager and the temporary files that many Windows applications create as you work. The RAM disk's volatility (the fact that its contents are lost when you turn off your machine) is not an issue with such files, because the files themselves are designed to be temporary.

Note that you probably do not want to create a RAM disk to store standard-mode application swap files (see the previous section). Because these files are large, setting aside enough memory to house them in a RAM disk would almost certainly be self-defeating.

To store your Windows applications' temporary files on a RAM disk, you need to do two things. First, create the RAM disk. Second, modify the TEMP variable in your MS-DOS environment. (Some programs use other MS-DOS variables, such as TMP, instead of TEMP. To find out what your programs do, you'll need to check their documentation.)

Creating a RAM Disk

Windows includes a driver called RAMDRIVE.SYS that you can use to create a RAM disk. You install RAMDrive with a line in your CONFIG.SYS file. The line has the following syntax:

DEVICE=*d:\path*RAMDRIVE.SYS [*disksize*] [*sectorsize*] [*numentries*] [/E] [/A]

NOTE: *Do not include the square brackets; they indicate optional parameters.*

d:\path is the drive and path of the directory containing the file RAM-DRIVE.SYS. Normally, this will be your Windows subdirectory.

disksize specifies the amount of memory you want to allot to the RAM disk. If you omit this parameter, RAMDrive uses 64 KB.

sectorsize specifies the sector size to be used by the RAM disk. You may specify 128, 256, 512, or 1024, or you may omit this parameter. If you omit it, RAMDrive uses 512-byte sectors. If you include a *sectorsize* parameter, you must also specify a *disksize*. (Tip: If you're going to store a great many small files, choose a small value for *sectorsize* and a large value for *numentries*. If the files you plan to store are mostly large, it's more efficient to use a larger *sectorsize*.)

numentries specifies the maximum number of files (and top-level subdirec-tories) that your RAM disk's root directory will be able to store. You may specify any value from 2 through 1024; if you omit this parameter, you'll be able to create 64 root-directory files. (The number of files you can create in subdirectories is not limited.) If you include a *numentries* parameter, you must also include *disksize*.

To store the RAM disk in extended memory, include /E. Also, be sure the line in your CONFIG.SYS file that installs RAMDrive appears *after* the line that installs HIMEM.SYS. (HIMEM.SYS is the driver that enables Windows to manage extended memory. This driver must be installed before RAMDrive can be installed in extended memory.)

To store the RAM disk in expanded memory, include /A. Also, be sure the line in your CONFIG.SYS file that installs RAMDrive appears *after* the line that installs your expanded memory manager.

The following example installs a 512-KB RAM disk with 512-byte sectors. The RAM disk allows 64 root-directory files and top-level subdirectories and is stored in extended memory.

DEVICE=C:\WINDOWS\RAMDRIVE.SYS 512 /E

After adding the *DEVICE=* line to your CONFIG.SYS file, resave the file. Then quit Windows and restart your computer. When your computer starts, RAMDrive will present a message confirming the creation of the RAM disk and telling what drive letter it uses.

You can use RAMDrive to create as many separate RAM disks as you want, and you can use these RAM disks outside of Windows as well as while Windows is running.

Modifying the TEMP Variable to Use Your RAM Disk

To store temporary files on your RAM disk, first you need to know the drive letter of your RAM disk. (If you're not sure what letter that is, read the message displayed by RAMDrive when you start your computer.) Then you need to add a line to your AUTOEXEC.BAT file. The line should look like this:

> SET TEMP=*d:*

where *d:* is the drive letter used by your RAM disk. (If your AUTOEXEC.BAT file already has a *SET TEMP=* line, modify it to specify the root directory of your RAM disk.)

COPING WITH UNRECOVERABLE APPLICATION ERRORS (UAEs)

An unrecoverable application error (UAE) occurs when a program causes a "general protection" (GP) fault. Essentially this means that a program either has tried to issue an instruction for which it doesn't have the appropriate privilege level (in your computer's "protected" mode, the operating system and other vital organs are allowed to do things that ordinary application programs may not) or has tried to access memory that belongs to a different program. With well-written software, ample memory, and ample system resources, this should never happen. But a running Windows system is a complex organism of core components, drivers, applications, and user data, and mishaps do sometimes occur.

Windows 3.1 has done away with the dreaded message "Unrecoverable Application Error" and the odious OK button that used to accompany it. But UAEs are still a fact of life, and they're no more okay now than they were in Windows 3.0. Fortunately, however, when a 3.1 application causes a UAE, you *usually* are not forced to reboot your computer. And in upgrading Windows from 3.0 to 3.1, Microsoft made a few improvements that should reduce the likelihood of your getting a UAE.

In most cases now, if an application generates an unrecoverable error, you will first see a message informing you of the fact and offering you two buttons—one marked Close, the other marked Ignore. Choose Ignore at your own risk. It's safer to click the Close button.

If you're lucky, clicking the Close button will shut down the program that was running when the error occurred but leave everything else running. At that point, the safest thing to do is save all your work in all your other running programs, quit Windows, reboot your computer, and start again. In many cases, while everything might appear to be normal after an offending program is put to rest, some other part of the complex code that runs Windows might be corrupted in some way. The best policy is to take no chances. Grit your teeth, save your work, and reset.

Local Reboot

In some cases, the offending application and its error message will remain on screen even after you click the Close button. Or the program might "freeze" your system without displaying the Close/Ignore dialog box. In either of these situations, the next thing to try is a "local reboot."

To perform a local reboot, press Ctrl-Alt-Del. This keystroke combination, which under MS-DOS resets the entire operating system, has a different effect in Windows 3.1. Windows will display a message saying that you've pressed Ctrl-Alt-Del and that your next keystroke will terminate the current application. The message will also tell you that if you press Ctrl-Alt-Del a second time, your whole system will reboot.

If the local reboot succeeds, the result will be the same as if you had received the Close/Ignore dialog box and chosen Close. The errant application will be gone, and you should proceed to save your work, shut everything down, reset your computer (from MS-DOS), and restart Windows.

Under some conditions, the local reboot will not succeed. You'll either see a message saying that Windows cannot terminate the current program or you'll see the normal local-reboot message, but your next keystroke will do nothing at all. In this case, a graceful exit is impossible. You'll simply have to reset your computer (by pressing Ctrl-Alt-Del again or pressing your computer's hardware reset button, if it has one).

Using Dr. Watson

If you get UAEs even occasionally, you should become acquainted with a Windows-supplied diagnostic program called Dr. Watson. Setup doesn't create a program-item icon for Dr. Watson, but you can create one; Dr. Watson's executable file is DRWATSON.EXE. Dr. Watson's specialty is not rescue, alas, but autopsy. Still, he's a useful fellow to have around.

If a UAE occurs while Dr. Watson is running, details about the current state of your system are automatically written into a text file named DRWATSON.LOG. After you close the foreground program (or do a local reboot), Dr. Watson himself appears in the form of a small dialog box. Here you can type a detailed description of what you were doing when your program went south. Your "eyewitness" account will then be added to the autopsy log.

If you need to contact Microsoft's or another vendor's technical support service about a recurrent UAE problem, you might be asked to supply information from your DRWATSON.LOG file. Hence, it's a good idea to keep the doctor on staff at all times. You can do that by copying his program-item icon into your Startup program group. (If you get a lot of UAEs, you'll start seeing messages from Dr. Watson saying that the log file is getting rather large. If that happens, simply rename DRWATSON.LOG and keep the renamed file. The doctor then begins a new log.)

Basic System-Level Troubleshooting Suggestions

Here are some basic troubleshooting steps you should take if you get a lot of UAEs from a variety of different applications.

Check Your System Resources

Keep an eye on the percentage of system resources available, as reported by the About command on Program Manager's Help menu. (You can also get this information from the Help menus of most of the Windows accessory programs.) If this figure drops below about 30 percent, some applications become more likely to cause a UAE. You can increase the percentage of system resources available by closing a few programs.

A *system resource* is a morsel of information stored in one of two 64-KB memory segments. Unfortunately, these segments are fixed in size, no matter how much RAM your system has. Programs that create a lot of icons, buttons, or child windows tend to consume a lot of system resource space. When you close a program, Windows reclaims the system resource space the program was using and makes it available to other programs.

The hazard of running low on system resources has been significantly reduced in Windows 3.1. The Windows programs, such as Program Manager, have been rewritten to make less demand on system resources (Program Manager in Windows 3.0 was a particularly egregious consumer), and Windows 3.1 does a better job than its predecessor of reclaiming resource space. But the size of the resource pool has not changed, and you can still create havoc by running too low.

Use CHKDSK /F—But Not While Windows Is Running

Windows runs "on top of" MS-DOS and uses MS-DOS's file system. Any files that have become "cross-linked" at the MS-DOS level can cause Windows to choke.

Therefore, it's a good idea to run MS-DOS's CHKDSK utility from time to time, to be sure the logical structure of your file system is always in order. If you include the /F switch with the CHKDSK command, CHKDSK will repair any damage it finds.

> **WARNING:** *Using the CHKDSK /F command while Windows is running can damage your data. Quit Windows first.*

Be Sure You're Running the Correct Version of MS-DOS

If the vendor of your computer supplied an "OEM" version of MS-DOS (a version with the vendor's own name on it), you should use it in preference to a generic version or to IBM's PC-DOS (unless, of course, you're using an IBM computer). Some hardware vendors make minor modifications to the generic MS-DOS code to optimize the operating system for their own equipment. Using an even slightly incompatible version could cause problems for Windows.

If the Problem Occurs in 386 Enhanced Mode, Try Standard Mode

If you get UAEs in 386 enhanced mode but not in standard mode, you might have a "page-mapping" conflict. This can occur if two or more programs or drivers are trying to access the same "upper memory block." (Upper memory blocks are areas of memory with addresses between 640 KB and 1024 KB.) Try adding the following line to the [386Enhanced] section of your SYSTEM.INI file:

    EMMExclude=A000-EFFF

Then restart Windows in 386 enhanced mode. If your problems disappear, you definitely have a page-mapping conflict. At this point, you can either leave your SYSTEM.INI file as it is (this excludes Windows from the entire upper-memory area, leaving you a bit less memory space to work with). Or you can use other diagnostic utility programs to try to pinpoint the location of the conflict. After you've located the address range where the conflict is occurring, you modify the EMMExclude line to restrict Windows from only that range. (If you have more than one region of conflict, you can use more than one EMMExclude line.)

If none of these steps alleviates your problem, or if your UAEs occur only with a particular application, your best bet is to seek technical support. Start with Microsoft's Product Support Services (or one of the Microsoft forums on CompuServe) if your problem is system-wide. If the problem occurs only with a specific application, call that application's vendor. For a brief listing of support services and other resources, see Appendix C.

PART VI

APPENDIXES

Part VI includes three appendixes and a glossary.

Appendix A describes the use of the Setup program for changing system settings, creating program items for Windows and non-Windows applications, and adding or removing optional system components.

Appendix B offers brief descriptions of the three basic kinds of memory used by personal computers: conventional memory, extended memory, and expanded memory.

Appendix C describes some of the important online and print-media resources available for Windows users.

The glossary defines nearly 200 computer terms used in this book.

A
Using the Setup Program

The Windows Setup program, for which you'll probably find a program-item icon in your Main program group, performs several valuable maintenance functions in addition to installing Windows on your computer. You can use Setup to do any of the following:

- Install a different video, keyboard, mouse, or network driver.
- Create Program Manager launch icons for Windows or non-Windows applications.
- Remove optional Windows components from your system—or add them to your system.

This appendix provides a quick overview of Setup's maintenance functionality.

CHANGING SYSTEM SETTINGS

The first item on Setup's Options menu, Change System Settings, lets you install new video, keyboard, mouse, and network drivers. The command generates a simple dialog box with four clearly identified drop-down lists.

Each list includes, in addition to all the drivers supplied by Microsoft in your Windows package, an item labeled "Other (Requires disk from OEM)." Use this item to install a driver that's not supplied with your Windows package. The Setup program will prompt you to insert a disk containing the desired driver in drive A. If you need to, you can specify a different drive or directory. For example, if your third-party video driver were stored in the DRIVERS subdirectory of C:\WINDOWS, you could point the Setup program to that directory by typing over the characters *A:* on the prompt line.

Before any driver changes can take effect, you need to quit and restart Windows. The Setup program offers to do that for you, but the restart will fail if you have any running non-Windows applications (unless you've selected the Allow Close When Active option in the applications' PIFs). Therefore, you'll want to close up all your non-Windows programs before using Setup.

 WINDOWS TIP: Some third-party drivers are furnished on a disk with a file named SETUP.INF. That filename worked correctly for adding drivers to Windows 3.0, but for successful installation in Windows 3.1, use File Manager to rename SETUP.INF as OEMSETUP.INF.

USING SETUP TO CREATE PROGRAM ITEMS

At your request, the Setup program will search your hard disk and create program items for applications—both Windows and non-Windows programs—that it recognizes. To use this feature, run Setup and choose the second item on the Options menu, Set Up Applications. Then select Search For Applications in the two-item option-button list that follows. You'll see a dialog box that looks something like this:

Click the mouse or press the Spacebar to select as many drives as you want to search. (If you want to restrict the search to those directories specified in your

MS-DOS path, choose the first item; but if you're searching your entire hard-disk system, don't select Path—because doing so will cause Setup to duplicate its efforts.)

Setup recognizes most applications by the names of their executable files. Occasionally, however, it might be unable to make a positive identification. For example, if Setup finds the program file Q.EXE, it won't know whether that file is for Quicken, Quattro Pro, or something else altogether. In such cases, you'll see a dialog box similar to the following.

Choose the appropriate program and click OK. (Or choose None Of The Above if you want Setup to ignore this application.)

The Setup program finds all Windows executable files. It also finds all non-Windows programs for which it has a PIF available. Your Windows system includes PIFs for many popular non-Windows programs, but it might not have one for every program that you use. You can create your own PIFs for those programs that Setup fails to find. (For details about creating PIFs, see Chapter 18.)

After Setup finishes searching, it gives you a list of all the programs it found and asks you which ones you want to install. You'll see a pair of list boxes, like the following.

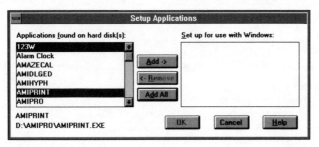

Your task is to select (by clicking or pressing the Spacebar) each item you want to install. You can select as many or as few as you wish, and you can install the whole lot by clicking the Add All button. (Generally, this is an option to be avoided. The Setup program finds every executable file related to every Windows application on your hard disk. Some of the programs it finds are likely to be accessories for which you don't need launch icons.) If you change your mind about an item while it's still in the list box on the left, simply click on it again to deselect it. When you've made your choices, click Add, and then click OK.

As you select items in the list on the left, the Setup program displays the full path of the last selected program. This information can help you figure out what certain programs in the list are. For example, in the list shown in the preceding illustration, you might not recognize the name AMIPRINT. But when you see that the file is stored in the directory D:\AMIPRO, you can tell that it's a program associated with the popular word processing program from Lotus Development Corporation.

REMOVING OPTIONAL COMPONENTS FROM YOUR SYSTEM

If your computer is running low on hard disk space, you might want to take advantage of Setup's third major option and uninstall a few files that you don't need. To do this, run Setup and choose the third item on the Options menu, Add/Remove Windows Components. You'll see a dialog box similar to the following illustration.

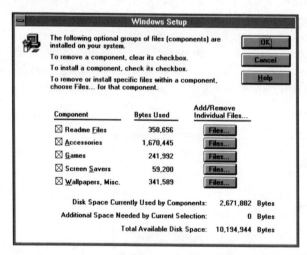

To remove all files of a particular category—all the wallpaper bitmaps, for example—simply deselect the appropriate check box. To delete some, but not all files, start by clicking a Files button. For example, if you decide you can live without Minesweeper, you start by clicking the Files button on the Games line. Setup then shows the following.

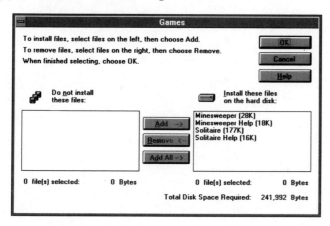

Click the two Minesweeper files (the executable and the help document), click Remove, and click OK.

If you change your mind and decide to reinstall some files, simply revisit this corner of Setup. Select the names of the files you want to install, click Add, and then click OK. The Setup program will prompt you for the appropriate distribution disks.

B

Conventional, Extended, Expanded, and Virtual Memory

Your personal computer can have three types of memory: conventional, extended, and expanded. Understanding what each type of memory is and what it's used for can help you configure the memory on your own system and set up program information files (PIFs) for running non-Windows applications.

CONVENTIONAL MEMORY

The first 640 KB of memory on any computer that uses the 8086, 8088, 80286, 80386, 80386SX, or 80486 microprocessor is called *conventional* (or standard) memory. Conventional memory is used to store the MS-DOS operating system as well as most programs that run under MS-DOS. Certain device drivers, network software, and other memory-resident programs can also use conventional memory.

Conventional memory is the most essential kind of memory for running Windows. Without at least 500 KB, you can't even start Windows. Unfortunately, the total amount of conventional memory you can have in your system is 640 KB. So it's important to keep as much of this limited resource available for Windows as possible.

EXTENDED MEMORY

Extended memory, as its name suggests, provides a straightforward extension to the amount of conventional memory in your system. The only thing that's not straightforward about it is the fact that most MS-DOS programs cannot use it! To use extended memory, your computer's microprocessor has to run in a special operating mode called *protected mode.* MS-DOS was not designed to use protected mode.

A few MS-DOS programs employ a "DOS extension" technology that allows them to take advantage of extended memory. Lotus 1-2-3 Release 3 (Lotus Development Corporation) and Paradox 386 (Borland International) are examples of such programs. So is Windows 3.1.

Computers that use the 8086 or 8088 microprocessor cannot use extended memory, because those microprocessors do not include a protected operating mode. The 8086 and 8088 operate in *real mode* only, and hence cannot run Windows 3.1.

To use extended memory efficiently, a device driver to manage the extended memory must be installed in your system. Windows provides such a driver; it's called HIMEM.SYS, and you install it by means of a command in your CONFIG.SYS file.

Extended memory is sometimes called XMS memory; XMS stands for eXtended Memory Standard. This should be distinguished from EMS, which refers to expanded memory.

EXPANDED MEMORY

When a computer is running in protected mode with extended memory available, the entire complement of conventional and extended memory is treated as a single domain. Programs can use as much or as little of this memory as they want (provided the memory is available). It's for this reason that adding extended memory to your system is the most effective way to increase the capacity of your Windows system without sacrificing speed.

Expanded memory is something quite different from extended memory. It was designed in the mid-1980s as a way of augmenting the capacity of programs running in real mode—programs that could not use extended memory.

When a program uses expanded memory, it can access only a small portion of this memory at a time. Each time a different portion of expanded memory is needed, the program must request that memory from a device driver called an Expanded Memory Manager. The Expanded Memory Manager must be installed in your system by means of a command in your CONFIG.SYS file. (Vendors who sell expanded memory boards also supply the Expanded Memory Managers.)

Expanded memory can be used on any computer that runs MS-DOS, regardless of its microprocessor. But only those applications that were written with expanded memory in mind can take advantage of this kind of memory. Windows can use expanded memory, but it runs more efficiently with extended memory.

Expanded memory is sometimes called EMS memory; EMS stands for Expanded Memory Specification. You'll also see it called LIM EMS memory; LIM stands for Lotus, Intel, and Microsoft, the three companies that jointly developed the protocol for using expanded memory. Windows supports LIM EMS versions 3.2 and 4.0.

VIRTUAL MEMORY

The term *virtual memory* refers to the use of a permanent storage medium, such as a hard disk, as though it were memory. While running in 386 enhanced mode, Windows can store some of your programs and documents in a swap file on your hard disk. This use of a swap file as an extension of memory is an example of virtual memory.

C

Resources for Windows Users

There is a huge and constantly growing amount of on-line and printed information available to assist Windows users in evaluating software and improving the efficiency of their systems. Some of the more important resources are described in this appendix.

THE WINDOWS RESOURCE KIT

Published by Microsoft, the Windows Resource Kit is a three-ring binder full of valuable technical information about Windows 3.1. The package offers a structured troubleshooting guide and a wealth of information about boosting performance, running Windows on networks, running non-Windows programs effectively, and other matters. It also includes diagnostic utilities and a few entertainment items.

The Windows Resource Kit is priced at $19.95. You can get a copy by calling Microsoft, at (800) 642-7676.

COMPUSERVE FORUMS

Through its various forums, the CompuServe Information Service (CIS) provides access to Microsoft's Windows support staff, the support teams of hundreds of third-party Windows application vendors, and the expertise and insight of thousands of other Windows users. Just about every obscure and bewildering Windows problem imaginable has been experienced, reported, and solved by some CompuServe user. In many cases, the quickest route to solving problems on your own system is a message on a CompuServe forum. For information about CompuServe's costs and procedures, call (800) 848-8990.

In addition to giving you the means to exchange ideas with other Windows users, the CompuServe forums are an invaluable source of shareware and freeware software (including wallpaper bitmaps, custom icons, and sound files) and updates to third-party device drivers.

The following CompuServe forums are of particular interest to Windows users.

WINNEW	Microsoft's forum for new Windows users. Includes sections for most of the Windows desktop accessories, plus hundreds of user-supplied wallpaper, icon, and sound files.
WINADV	Microsoft's forum for advanced Windows users. Includes sections on optimization, networks, graphics/video, memory issues, and more.
WINAPA	Third-party vendor forum. Participants include Asymetrix, Access Softek, DaVinci, Future Soft, GeoGraphix, hDC, Hi-Q, ICOM, MCAE, Meta, Micrografx, Playroom, Polaris, Pub Tech, Roykore, and Wilsonware.
WINAPB	Third-party vendor forum. Participants include Caseworks, Corel, Delrina, Echelon, Kidasa, Knowledge Garden, NBI, Owl International, Softbridge, SoftCraft, Softview, Whitewater, WUGNET, Zenographics, and ZSoft.
WINAPC	Third-party vendor forum. Participants include Abacus, Bell Atlantic, Berkeley Systems, Campbell Services, Glockenspiel, Matesys, Metz Software, Saros, Stirling Group, and Within Technologies.
ADOBE	Adobe Type Manager (ATM) and other Adobe Windows products.
BORAPP	Borland ObjectVision.
BPROGA	Borland Turbo Pascal for Windows.
BPROGB	Borland Paradox and C++ for Windows.
CENTRAL	Central Point PC Tools.
DTPFORUM	Desktop publishing products.
LOTUSA	Lotus 1-2-3 for Windows.
LOTUSB	Lotus Notes.
LOTUSWP	Lotus Ami Pro.
MSAPP	Microsoft Windows applications, including PowerPoint, Mail, Project, Works, Word, Publisher, and Money.
MSBASIC	Visual Basic.
MSEXCEL	Microsoft Excel.
MSLANG	Quick C for Windows.
MULTIMEDIA	Windows multimedia.

NORUTL	The Norton Desktop for Windows and Norton Backup for Windows.
NOVB	Novell Netware.
SPCFORUM	Software Publishing Corporation Windows applications.
SPINNAKER	PFS: Window Works and Plus for Windows.
SYMFORUM	Symantec Windows applications (other than those covered in NORUTL).
WORDSTAR	WordStar for Windows.
XEROX	Ventura Publisher.
Ziffnet: UTILFORUM	The PC Magazine Utilities forum.
Ziffnet: PCCONTACT	The PC/Computing forum.

MAGAZINE RESOURCES

Most of the major personal computer magazines have regular columns devoted to Windows topics, as well as reviews of new Windows programs, how-to articles, and other relevant material. The following are particularly noteworthy:

PC Magazine's **Windows Column.** A question-and-answer column based on letters from readers, aimed at a relatively experienced and sophisticated end-user audience. Edited by Fran Finnegan, 22 issues per year.

PC/Computing's **Windows Help Column.** A short column of end-user tips, plus a shareware "Winapp of the Month." Aimed at a beginning-to-intermediate end-user audience. Edited by Craig Stinson. 12 issues per year.

InfoWorld's **Window Manager Column.** Brian Livingston's weekly commentary and tips.

Windows Magazine. Published by CMP Publications, an entire magazine devoted to Windows reviews, columns, and features. Now in its third year of publication.

Computer Shopper's **Paul Bonner on Windows**. A monthly first-look at new Windows software.

MPC World. Published by PC World Communications, Inc., a new bimonthly magazine (first issue was February/March 1992) devoted to multimedia computing. Not exclusively Windows-centered, but contains a great deal of material that will be of interest to Windows users.

Glossary

386 enhanced mode: One of the two Windows operating modes. Windows runs in 386 enhanced mode on systems with 80386 or 80486 microprocessors and at least 2 MB of memory. The advantages of 386 enhanced mode include access to *extended memory*, the use of disk-based *virtual memory*, and the ability to run *non-Windows applications* in windows or in the *background*. See also *standard mode*.

activate: To make a window the *foreground*, or active, window.

ANSI eight-bit character set: The entire set of characters available in Windows fonts. The first 128 characters (including the *control characters*, the uppercase and lowercase alphabet, the numerals, and the standard punctuation symbols) are the same as the *IBM PC character set*. The high-bit section of the ANSI character set (the characters with values from 128 through 255) differs from the high-bit section of the IBM PC character set, however.

application swap file: A temporary disk file used by Windows to store some or all of the information used by a *non-Windows application* when you switch away from that application. Windows uses application swap files only when running in *standard mode*.

application window: One of the two main types of windows used by Windows; the other type is called a *document window*. An application window holds an entire application, or program. A document window holds a *document* used by an application.

archive attribute: One of four markers that MS-DOS can use to classify a disk file. The archive attribute indicates that a file has been modified since it was last backed up.

arrange: A synonym for *tile*. To arrange windows means to make each one as large as it can be without overlapping its neighbor.

ASCII characters: See *IBM PC character set*.

ASCII file: A file containing nothing but letters, numbers, punctuation symbols, and *control characters*. Also called a *text file*.

associate: To connect a document with the application that created it, so that the two can be opened with a single command.

attribute: A marker used by MS-DOS to classify files. See also *archive attribute, hidden attribute, read-only attribute,* and *system attribute.*

auto-answer mode: A mode in which a modem automatically answers an incoming telephone call.

AUTOEXEC.BAT: A *batch file* that runs automatically when you start your computer.

background: When Windows is running several applications at once, the one with which you are interacting is said to run in the *foreground.* All other programs run in the background.

batch file: A text file containing one or more MS-DOS commands. When you run a batch file, MS-DOS executes each of its commands in turn.

baud rate: A measure of the speed at which characters are transmitted over a serial port to a printer or modem. Equivalent to *bits per second.*

binary file: Any file that isn't a *text file.*

bitmap: A way of storing images or characters in a *font.* A bitmap records the relative position of each pixel that makes up the image or character.

bitmapped font: A *font* in which characters are stored as bitmaps. Bitmapped fonts are nonscalable and device-specific.

bits per second: A measure of the speed at which characters are transmitted over a serial port to a printer or modem. *Baud rate* is an equivalent term.

boilerplate text: A block of text designed to be reused in different contexts. Contracts, for example, often consist largely of boilerplate text.

border: Any of the four sides of a window. The borders of most windows can be *dragged* inward or outward with the mouse.

buffer: An area of memory used for the temporary storage of data.

cache: An area of memory used to hold data recently read from a hard disk. A cache improves the performance of your system by reducing the number of times Windows has to read your hard disk. See *SmartDrive.*

cache program: A program or device driver that implements a cache. The Windows cache program is called *SmartDrive.*

cascade: To stack two or more windows like a fanned hand of cards. See also *tile.*

check box: A *dialog box* element. An X in a check box means you accept the option indicated by the associated text. An empty box means you decline the option.

child window: See *document window.*

click: To position the *mouse pointer* on an object, and then press and release the mouse button once.

client: An application or document that can receive information via *DDE* or *OLE* from a *server.*

Clipboard: An area of memory that holds text, graphics, or other information cut or copied from an application. The Clipboard makes it possible for you to move and copy information between documents or within a document. See also *copy, cut,* and *paste.*

Clipboard Viewer: A Windows utility program that displays the contents of the *Clipboard.* With Clipboard Viewer, you can also save the contents of the Clipboard in a disk file or retrieve a previously saved Clipboard file.

cluster: The smallest unit of disk storage that can be allocated to a file. Also known as an allocation unit.

COM1, COM2, COM3, COM4: A computer's first, second, third, and fourth serial *ports.* Not all computers have all four serial ports.

command button: A *dialog box* element. Clicking a command button causes Windows to take an action, such as accepting the settings you have specified in the dialog box.

command-line parameter: A word, filename, or group of characters that modifies the effect of an MS-DOS command. For example, in the command *WORD /L* (which runs Microsoft Word and loads the file that was last worked on), the */L* is a command-line parameter.

communications parameters: Settings that affect the way in which information is transmitted and received over a serial port. See also *baud rate, data bits, parity,* and *stop bits.*

compressed font: A font whose characters are narrower than normal for its point size. Switching from a normal-width font to a compressed font allows you to print more words on a line.

CONFIG.SYS: A file that MS-DOS reads each time you turn on or reset your computer. Commands in the CONFIG.SYS file are used for such things as installing *device drivers,* running network software, and choosing options that affect the behavior of MS-DOS. For information about what CONFIG.SYS commands are required for Windows, see Chapter 19.

control character: A character with an ANSI value in the range 0 through 31. Control characters are not printable. Instead, they send commands to output devices such as printers and displays. Tab and Carriage Return are examples of control characters.

CONTROL.INI: A file containing definitions for Windows' built-in color schemes and patterns, as well as any custom colors you have created.

Control menu: A menu that appears in the upper left corner of all application and document windows. On *application windows,* the Control menu includes commands to move, size, *maximize, minimize, restore,* and close the window, as well as a command to invoke *Task List.* (Some application Control menus have additional commands.) On *document windows,* the Control menu usually includes a subset of these commands.

Control-menu icon: The icon used to open the *Control menu.* On an *application window,* the Control menu is a long dash; on a *document window,* it's a shorter dash.

conventional memory: See Appendix B.

copy: To transfer information from an application to the *Clipboard* without removing it from the application.

current window: The *application window* or *document window* that you're now working with. The current window is the one to which Windows applies your next keystrokes (unless those invoke *Task List* or *activate* another window).

cursor: In Paintbrush, a marker that indicates where the next action initiated by a keystroke or mouse *click* will occur.

cut: To delete information from an application and transfer the information to the *Clipboard.*

data bits: In serial communications, the number of bits that comprise each character transmitted or received.

DDE: See *Dynamic Data Exchange.*

default entry (value): A command setting that will be used unless you override it.

default filename extension: An extension that an application will use automatically unless you specify a different extension.

default shell: The *shell* program that runs automatically when you start Windows; also the program you use to end a Windows session. Initially, the default shell for Windows 3 is Program Manager. You can make a different shell program the default by modifying the *SYSTEM.INI* file.

desktop: Any part of your screen that's not within a window.

destination: The disk or window to which you copy or move a file or selection.

device driver: A program that enables Windows or MS-DOS to use a physical device (such as an external disk drive) or adds some capability to MS-DOS or Windows. Device drivers are installed by means of commands in your *CONFIG.SYS* file. Examples of Windows device drivers include *SMARTDRV.EXE, RAMDRIVE.SYS,* and *EMM386.EXE.* See also *printer driver.*

dialog box: A window that appears in response to a command and allows you to specify command options.

dingbat: A typographical term for a character that is not part of a standard character set. Dingbat characters include decorative symbols, icons, and so on.

directory pane: One of the two directory views used by File Manager (the other is *tree pane*). A directory pane displays the file and subdirectory names of a given directory.

dithered color: A color generated by a dot pattern of two or more other colors.

document: A file created with an application—for example, a letter created in a word processor or a graph created in a spreadsheet or graphics program.

document window: One of the two main types of windows used by Windows; the other type is called an *application window.* An application window holds an entire application. A document window holds a *document* used by an application. (Not all Windows programs use document windows.) Document windows are sometimes called child windows.

double-click: To press a mouse button twice in relatively quick succession, without moving the mouse between clicks.

double-click speed: The time interval within which two mouse clicks have to occur to be registered by the system as a double-click. You can use Control Panel to set the double-click speed.

drag: To drag an object means to position the *mouse pointer* on the object, then press and hold the active mouse button, then move the mouse to a new position, and then release the mouse button.

drop-down list box: A *list box* that's designed to unfold, much like a *drop-down menu.* In a *dialog box,* a drop-down list box appears as a single line of text with a downward-pointing arrow to its right. When you *click* the arrow (or press Alt-Down), the list opens.

drop-down menu: A set of commands that drops down from a *menu bar.*

duplex printing: Printing on both sides of the paper.

Dynamic Data Exchange (DDE): A set of conventions that allows information to be transferred automatically between certain Windows applications.

elite font: A twelve-*pitch* (twelve characters per inch) *font*.

EMM386.EXE: A *device driver* that allows *extended memory* on 80386 and 80486 computers to behave like *expanded memory*.

EMS: *Expanded memory* (see Appendix B). The letters stand for Expanded Memory Specification.

emulation mode: An operating mode that allows a printer to behave like a different brand of printer. For example, many non-IBM dot-matrix printers have IBM Proprinter emulation modes. See also *terminal emulation*.

end mark: A symbol used by Write to indicate the end of a document.

EPT: A printer *port* used by the IBM Personal Pageprinter and compatibles.

executable file: The file used to start a program. In Windows, an executable file must have the extension BAT, COM, EXE, or PIF.

expanded font: A *font* whose characters are wider than normal for its *point* size.

expanded memory: See Appendix B.

expanded memory emulator: A *device driver* that allows *extended memory* on 80386 and 80486 computers to behave like *expanded memory*.

expanded memory manager (EMM): A *device driver* that allows your computer to use *expanded memory*.

extended memory: See Appendix B.

extended memory manager: A *device driver* that allows your computer to use *extended memory*. The Windows extended memory manager is *HIMEM.SYS*.

FastDisk: A *device driver* that allows Windows, when running in *386 enhanced mode*, to realize significant performance gains by accessing the hard disk without using standard MS-DOS and BIOS calls.

FILE: One of the *ports* listed in Control Panel's Printers Connect *dialog box*. Connecting a printer to FILE allows you to redirect printer output to a disk file.

file fragmentation: A condition in which a disk file is not stored in contiguous clusters. A fragmented file takes longer to read and write than a contiguous file.

flow control: A system of signals that allows a receiving device (such as a printer or a communications program) to tell a sending device (such as Print Manager or another communications program) when to pause and when to resume the transmission. Colloquially known as *handshaking*.

font: A complete set of characters in one size and one typeface.

footer: Text that appears at the bottom of each page of a printout.

foreground: When Windows is running several applications at once, the one with which you are interacting is said to run in the foreground. All other programs run in the *background*.

GDI: See *Graphics Device Interface*.

Generic / Text Only printer: A printer driver that you can use with a printer that isn't explicitly supported by Windows.

Graphics Device Interface: Windows' internal graphics language.

graphics resolution: The number of dots per inch a printer can generate when printing graphics.

handshaking: See *flow control*.

hanging indention: A paragraph style in which all lines except the first are indented.

header: Text that appears at the top of each page of a printout.

hidden attribute: One of four markers that MS-DOS can use to classify a disk file. Files with the hidden attribute are not ordinarily displayed in File Manager's *directory windows*. (You can use the View menu's Include command to make them appear, however.)

high-bit characters: Characters with ANSI or ASCII values higher than 127.

HIMEM.SYS: The Windows-supplied *extended memory manager*.

hue: One of three parameters used to specify a color (the others are *luminosity* and *saturation*). Roughly speaking, the hue defines a color's basic quality—its redness or blueness, for example.

I-beam: The shape assumed by the *mouse pointer* in a *text box* or word processing document, or when using the text tool in Paintbrush. The I-beam allows you to reposition the *insertion point*.

IBM PC character set: The character set used by non-Windows applications. The first 128 characters (including the *control characters*, the uppercase and lowercase alphabet, the numerals, and the standard punctuation symbols) are the same as those the *ANSI eight-bit character set* used by Windows. The high-bit section of the

IBM PC character set (the characters with values from 128 through 255) differs from the high-bit section of the Windows character set, however.

icon: A graphic symbol used to represent a program or option. *Minimized* applications appear as icons on the *desktop.*

insertion point: The flashing vertical line that appears in *text boxes* and word processing documents (and when you're using the Text tool in Paintbrush). The insertion point indicates the place where the next character you type will appear.

keyboard shortcut: A keystroke combination that executes a menu command without opening the menu. For example, Alt-F4 is a keystroke shortcut for the *Control menu*'s Close command.

landscape mode: One of two printing modes available on most printers (the other is *portrait mode*). In landscape mode, printed lines run parallel to the paper's direction of travel through the printer.

LIM EMS: The Lotus/Intel/Microsoft Expanded Memory Specification. (See Appendix B.)

list box: A *dialog box* element that presents a set of options in the form of a list.

LPT1, LPT2, LPT3, LPT4: Your computer's first, second, third, and fourth parallel printer *ports.* Not all computers have all four ports.

luminosity: The brightness or dullness of a color; one of three parameters used to specify a color (the others are *hue* and *saturation*).

macro: A recorded sequence of keystrokes and mouse actions that you can play back with a single keystroke or keystroke combination. You can use the desktop accessory Recorder to create macros in Windows.

marquee: A dotted line used to indicate the active element in a *dialog box* (the element that will receive your next keystrokes).

maximize: To enlarge an *application window* to fill the *desktop,* or a *document window* to fill the application window in which it resides.

maximize button: The upward-pointing arrow at the right side of a window's *title bar.* Clicking a window's maximize button *maximizes* the window. (When a window is already maximized, the maximize button is replaced by a *restore button.*)

memory-resident program: A program that remains in your computer's memory after it's no longer running. Examples include *pop-up programs* (such as SideKick) and network software.

menu bar: The primary set of options offered by an application. The menu bar appears above the application's *work area*, directly below the *title bar*.

minimize: To reduce an *application window* or *document window* to an *icon*. (Some document windows can't be minimized.)

minimize button: The downward-pointing arrow at the right side of a window's *title bar*. Clicking a window's minimize button reduces the window to an *icon*.

monospaced font: A *font* in which all characters have the same width. Courier is an example of a monospaced font.

mouse pointer: The symbol that indicates where your next mouse *click* will take effect. The shape of the pointer depends on context. In menus and *dialog boxes*, it's a northwest-pointing arrow. On movable window *borders*, it becomes a two-headed arrow. In *text boxes* and word processing documents, the pointer becomes an *I-beam*—and so on.

multitasking: Simultaneous processing of two or more applications.

non-Windows application: A program not designed specifically for the Windows environment. Non-Windows applications can be run either with or without Windows.

nonscalable font: A *font* designed for one size only; a *raster font*.

null modem cable: A cable used for direct communication between two computers, without a modem.

Object Linking and Embedding: A set of conventions, introduced with Windows 3.1, that allow a *server* application to provide information automatically to a *client* application.

OEM Text: The format used by the *Clipboard* when moving text into a non-Windows application. In this format, *high-bit characters* in the *ANSI eight-bit character set* are translated to their equivalents in the *IBM PC character set*.

OLE: See *Object Linking and Embedding*.

optimizing: The process of maximizing the speed and capacity of your Windows system.

option button: A common *dialog box* element. Option buttons present a set of mutually exclusive choices. The selected option is marked by a round dark dot in a circle. Also known as *radio button*.

owner display: One of the formatting options available in *Clipboard Viewer*. In owner display, the contents of the *Clipboard* are displayed the way they were received from the sending application.

palette: A set of color or pattern options in a drawing program.

parallel port: A type of *port* most commonly used to connect a printer to a computer.

parity: A method of error checking sometimes used with printers connected to serial *ports* and with communications via modem. There are four types of parity checking, called odd, even, mark, and space.

paste: To transfer data from the *Clipboard* into an application.

pel: See *pixel*.

permanent swap file: One of the two kinds of files used for *virtual memory* when Windows is running in *386 enhanced mode* (the other kind is a *temporary swap file*). A permanent swap file provides faster performance than a temporary swap file, but it has the disadvantage of using disk space even when Windows is not running. See Chapter 19 for instructions on creating a permanent swap file.

pica: A printer's measurement, approximately equal to one-sixth of an inch. Also a synonym for 12 *pitch*.

PIF: See *Program Information File*.

pitch: Characters per inch.

pixel: The smallest dot that can be displayed on your screen. Sometimes shortened to *pel*.

point: A printer's measurement, equal to $^1\!/_{12}$ of a pica, or approximately $^1\!/_{72}$ of an inch.

pop-up program: A *memory-resident program* that can be activated while another program is running.

port: A point of connection between your computer and a device, such as a printer or modem.

portrait mode: One of two printing modes available on most printers (the other is *landscape mode*). In portrait mode, printed lines run perpendicular to the paper's direction of travel through the printer.

printer driver: A program that translates generic *GDI* information into the language understood by a specific printer. You must use Control Panel to install a printer driver before Windows can use your printer.

print queue: One or more jobs waiting to be sent to a specific printer. When you send files to the printer faster than they can be printed, Print Manager maintains a print queue of all jobs that haven't yet reached the printer.

program group: A *document window* in Program Manager. Program groups contain *program items.*

Program Information File (PIF): A file that provides Windows with details about how you want to run a *non-Windows application*—the name of the application's *executable file*, the amount of memory you want to allocate to it, and so on.

program item: An *icon* that can be used to start a program in Program Manager.

proportionally spaced font: A *font* in which some characters are wider than other characters. Proportionally spaced fonts produce a typeset appearance. See also *monospaced font.*

radio button: See *option button.*

RAM disk: A block of memory set up to behave as though it were a disk drive. A RAM disk provides extremely fast performance, but if power is interrupted, the contents of a RAM disk are lost. See also *RAMDRIVE.SYS.*

RAMDRIVE.SYS: A *device driver* that lets you set up a *RAM disk.*

raster font: A *font* in which characters are stored as *bitmaps.* Raster fonts are nonscalable and device-specific.

read-only attribute: One of four markers that MS-DOS can use to classify a disk file. Files with the read-only attribute can be read but not changed. (To save changes to a read-only file, either use File Manager to remove the read-only attribute or use the Save As command to give the file a new name.)

resolution: The number of dots per inch a printer or display can generate.

restore: To return an *application window* or *document window* to the size and position it had before it was *maximized* or *minimized.*

restore button: A double arrow that appears at the right side of a window's *title bar* when the window can be *restored.* Clicking the restore button restores the window.

sans serif font: A *font* in which the characters do not have finishing strokes. Arial is an example of a sans serif font.

saturation: One of three parameters used to specify a color (the others are *hue* and *luminosity*). Saturation defines the purity of a color; the lower the saturation, the more gray is mixed in.

scalable font: A *font* that can be generated in various sizes without distortion.

scroll bar: The bar at the bottom and right sides of a window that contains more information than can be displayed at once. *Click* the arrow at either end of the scroll bars, click in the scroll bar, or *drag* the box in the scroll bar to move the document within the window.

select: To mark a block of text or graphics for action by a command, such as Cut or Copy. Also, to place an X in a *check box* in a *dialog box.*

serif font: A *font* in which characters have finishing strokes. Times New Roman is an example of a serif font.

server: An application or document that can provide information automatically, via *DDE* or *OLE,* to a *client.*

shell: A program that makes it easier for you to interact with another program or (more commonly) an operating system. The Windows shell programs, Program Manager and File Manager, allow you to organize your program and application files and to start applications.

sizing buttons: The *maximize, minimize,* and *restore* buttons.

SmartDrive: The Windows *cache program.*

SMARTDRV.EXE: A *device driver* that creates Windows' *cache, SmartDrive.*

soft hyphen: A marker that indicates where a word processing program may hyphenate a word if the word is too long to fit at the end of a line. Also called a discretionary hyphen. Soft hyphens are not printed unless they are used at the end of a line.

source: The disk or directory from which you copy or move a file.

spool file: A temporary disk file used to hold data waiting to be printed.

standard mode: One of the two Windows operating modes. Windows runs in standard mode on systems with 80286, 80386, or 80486 microprocessors and at least 1 MB but less than 2 MB of memory. See also *386 enhanced mode.*

stop bits: Bits used to mark the beginnings and ends of characters in serial communications.

swap file: A file used to store information temporarily on disk when memory becomes full.

system attribute: One of four markers that MS-DOS can use to classify a disk file. Files with the system attribute are not ordinarily displayed in File Manager's *directory panes.* (You can use the View menu's By File Type command to make them appear, however.)

system disk: A floppy disk that you can use to boot MS-DOS.

SYSTEM.INI: A file used by Windows to store information about *device drivers* used by your system, whether you're attached to a network, the name of your default *shell,* how you want time to be divided between Windows and non-Windows applications, and other matters.

System menu: The *Control menu.*

target: The disk or directory to which you copy or move one or more files.

Task List: A Windows program that helps you switch or close programs, *tile* or *cascade* windows, or arrange *icons.* You can invoke Task List by *double-clicking* on the *desktop,* by pressing Ctrl-Esc, or by choosing the Switch To command on any *Control menu.*

temporary swap file: One of the two kinds of files used for *virtual memory* when Windows is running in *386 enhanced mode* (the other kind is a *permanent swap file*). A temporary swap file is not as fast as a permanent swap file, but it has the advantage of not using disk space when Windows is not running.

terminal emulation: The ability of a communications program, such as Terminal, to act like a particular terminal make and model by understanding and sending that terminal's commands.

text box: A *dialog box* element in which you enter words or numbers.

text file: A file that consists entirely of characters with ASCII values in the range 1 through 127.

tile: To make each window as large as it can be without overlapping its neighbor. See also *cascade.*

title bar: The bar at the top of an *application window* or *document window* that bears the window's name. You can *maximize* a window by *double-clicking* its title bar.

toggle: A command that acts like an on-off switch. Using a toggle command once activates a feature; using it a second time deactivates the feature.

tracking speed: A measurement of the responsiveness of your mouse. The higher the tracking speed, the farther Windows moves the *mouse pointer* in response to a given mouse movement. You can use Control Panel to adjust the tracking speed.

tree pane: One of the two directory views used by File Manager (the other is *directory pane*). The tree pane shows the subdirectory structure of the current disk.

TrueType: The *scalable font* technology built into Windows 3.1.

TSR: A *memory-resident program.* (The letters stand for Terminate and Stay Resident.)

virtual memory: See Appendix B.

volume label: A name used to identify a floppy disk or hard disk. You can use File Manager to assign volume labels.

wildcard: A character (usually in a filename or search specification) that stands for any single character or group of characters. For example, in MS-DOS filenames, a question mark is a wildcard that means any character; the asterisk is a wildcard that means any group of characters.

Windows application: A program designed specifically to take advantage of the Windows environment. A Windows application cannot be run without Windows.

WIN.INI: A file that records, among other things, most of the settings you specify with Control Panel. Windows reads WIN.INI each time you start Windows and sets up your system in accordance with its settings. Some *Windows applications* also record your preferences in WIN.INI.

work area: The area of an *application window* or *document window* where you enter data. Also known as *workspace.*

workspace: See *work area.*

XMS: The Extended Memory Specification, a set of conventions that allows programs to use *extended memory* more efficiently.

Index

Craig Stinson

Craig Stinson is a contributing editor of *PC Magazine* and *PC/Computing*. He edits the Spreadsheets column for *PC Magazine* and writes the Windows Help column for *PC/Computing*. An industry journalist since 1981, Stinson was formerly editor of *Softalk for the IBM Personal Computer*. Stinson is a coauthor of *Running Microsoft Excel*, Third Edition, and *Microsoft Excel 4 Companion*, both published by Microsoft Press. In addition to his numerous computer publications, he has written music reviews for publications such as *Billboard*, the *Boston Globe*, the *Christian Science Monitor*, and *Musical America*. He lives with his wife and children in Eugene, Oregon.

The manuscript for this book was prepared and submitted to Microsoft Press in electronic form. Text files were processed and formatted using Microsoft Word.

Principal typographer: Sandy Clements
Interior text designer: Darcie Furlan
Cover designer: Rebecca Geisler
Cover color separator: Color Service Inc.

Text composition by Electronic Word in ITC New Baskerville with display type in ITC Avant Garde Demi, using Ventura Publisher. Typeset output by Type Works using the Agfa Compugraphic 9600 laser imagesetter.

Printed on recycled paper stock.

Great Resources for Windows™ *3.1 Users*

WINDOWS™ 3.1 COMPANION

The Cobb Group: Lori L. Lorenz and R. Michael O'Mara with Russell Borland

"Covers the basics thoroughly...An excellent reference featuring dozens of live examples...Beautifully produced."

PC Magazine

This up-to-date resource thoroughly covers Windows version 3.1—everything from installing and starting Windows to using all its built-in applications and desktop accessories. Step-by-step tutorials, great examples, and expert advice for novice to advanced users.

550 pages, softcover $27.95 ($37.95 Canada)   Order Code WI31CO

CONCISE GUIDE TO MICROSOFT® WINDOWS™ 3.1

Kris Jamsa

Instant answers to your Windows 3.1 questions! Clear, concise information on all the key Microsoft Windows 3.1 features; covering everything from installation to customization. For beginning to intermediate users. Great complement to *Windows 3.1 Companion*.

192 pages, softcover $12.95 ($17.95 Canada)   Order Code COGWI

RUNNING WORD FOR WINDOWS™
Version 2
Russell Borland

This example-rich book is an outstanding reference for intermediate and advanced Microsoft Word for Windows users. Now completely updated, it highlights all the powerful new features of Word for Windows version 2. This book moves from a review of the basics to a full description of Word's power-packed features: styles, fields, macros, and templates. Throughout, special tips provide additional insight and suggest handy shortcuts. You'll discover the most effective—and easiest—ways to produce professional-looking documents. You won't find a more authoritative or comprehensive source of information than RUNNING WORD FOR WINDOWS.

592 pages, softcover $27.95 ($34.95 Canada)   Order Code RUWDWI

RUNNING MICROSOFT® EXCEL 4, 3rd ed.

The Cobb Group: Douglas Cobb and Judy Mynhier
with Craig Stinson, Mark Dodge, and Chris Kinata

RUNNING MICROSOFT EXCEL is packed with step-by-step instruction, scores of examples and tips, and dozens of illustrations. The easy-to-follow tutorial style will help you quickly learn both the basics and most advanced features of Microsoft Excel 4. Learn how to use Microsoft Excel with other programs, file linking and sharing with Lotus 1-2-3, and using Microsoft Excel with Windows.

896 pages, softcover $29.95 ($39.95 Canada)   Order Code RUEX4W